E   The Stresses of empire
188.5
.S77
1988

DATE DUE			

EARLY AMERICAN HISTORY

An eighteen volume series reproducing over three hundred of the most important articles on all aspects of the colonial experience

EDITED WITH INTRODUCTIONS BY
PETER CHARLES HOFFER
UNIVERSITY OF GEORGIA

A Garland Series

THE STRESSES OF EMPIRE

Selected Articles
on the British Empire
in the Eighteenth Century

EDITED WITH AN INTRODUCTION BY

PETER CHARLES HOFFER

Garland Publishing, Inc.
New York & London
1988

Library of Congress Cataloging-in-Publication Data

The Stresses of empire.

(Early American history)
1. United States—History—Colonial period, ca. 1600–1775.
2. Great Britain—Colonies—America—History—18th century.
I. Hoffer, Peter C.   II. Series.
EI88.5.S77   1988   973.2   88-4184
ISBN 0-8240-6243-4 (alk. paper)

The volumes in this series are printed on
acid-free, 250-year-life paper.

Printed in the United States of America

Contents

PREFACE

On the very eve of the War for Independence, most adult colonists, of whatever political persuasion, expected some resolution of the crisis short of permanent rupture. Was it not true that, but thirteen years before, the partnership of British and colonial forces had achieved final victory over the French and their Indian allies? Americans had then exulted in the knowledge that they were part of the greatest empire on earth. To be sure, the prolonged peace negotiations with the French bewildered and angered some colonial leaders, but none could doubt that the British Empire had become wealthy and secure by 1763. The articles in this volume probe the strength and weakness of that empire in the era before its sudden and violent collapse.

War itself was nothing new to the colonists. Great Britain was constantly involved in European dynastic rivalry and conflict, periodically dragging her American possessions into war. These imperial wars and their American consequences provide a first major theme of the articles in this volume. The French and Indian War was only the final act in a drama that began fifty years earlier. King William's war (the war of the League of Augsburg in Europe) was followed at regular intervals by two other major European wars, both of which spread to the New World. Here war was not fought by small, disciplined regiments of regular soldiers. Instead, colonial militias and levies battled French regulars, with Indians joining the combat as their diplomacy or advantage dictated. Unlike its predecessors, the Seven Years' War, to give this conflict one of its many other names, began in the wilderness of western Pennsylvania and spread east. It shifted Britain's attention from Europe to America, with consequences unanticipated in the colonies. British-Americans had not received such concerted attention from the mother country since the years surrounding the Glorious Revolution. The conduct of British officers and infantry sent to defend the colonies rankled and disgusted Americans. George Grenville's program to repay the cost of the war with new duties and taxes from the colonies caused even more dissent.

A second theme in these articles is the maturation of imperial trade. Scholars have now established price and volume estimates for all the major staples, even giving some of these schedules modern monetary equivalents. They have illustrated the firm attachment of American producers to a world market, and debated the rate of economic growth by region over time. Models of trade flow and growth based upon these data are now quite sophisticated, though by no means have any of the competing models established clear dominance. The "staple" model stresses the tie between investment of capital and changes in consumer demand. Other conceptualizations emphasize the development of institutions, fiscal practices, and networks among kin in overseas commerce. The increasing scope of the data that scholars have unearthed has even allowed them to employ some of the counter-factual methods of the econometricians, building hypothetical models for alternatives that did not occur.

The third theme in this scholarship is administrative. British imperial authorities made three concerted efforts to rein in colonial economic license before Grenville's ministry passed the Molasses and Stamp Acts. The first of these, in the 1700s, led nowhere, the second was subverted by corruptionist politics in England, and the third, during King George's war, bowed to the pressures of wartime priorities. These were, in the opinion of some historians, lost opportunities for enforcing the Navigation Acts. Grenville did stick to his guns, but, in the words of Jack Sosin, "by then it was too late."[1] James Henretta believes that the die was cast (and the game lost) when the duke of Newcastle, a veritable patronage machine, came to power as Secretary of State in 1730.[2] W.A. Speck thinks that the last clear chance for the English to assert their lawful supervision of colonial trade came and went during the French and Indian war.[3] These are no more than speculations, but each of them touches a vital moment in the history of the empire, and speculations like these are the stuff of thoughtful and original history.

Peter Charles Hoffer
University of Georgia

Notes

1. Jack Sosin, *English America and Imperial Inconstancy: The Rise of Provincial Autonomy, 1695–1715* (Lincoln, Nebr., 1985), 232–33.

2. James Henretta, *"Salutary Neglect": Colonial Administration Under the Duke of Newcastle* (Princeton, 1972), 104.

3. W.A. Speck, *"The International and Imperial Context,"* in Jack P. Greene and J.R. Pole, eds., *Colonial British America* (Baltimore, 1984), 401.

THE SOUTHERN FRONTIER IN QUEEN ANNE'S WAR

At the close of the seventeenth century South Carolina constituted the sole southern frontier of the English colonies in America, against the Spanish, the French, and several important tribes of Indians. Though but newly established and still among the weakest of the English plantations, this colony had already given proof of unusual enterprise. Neglected by the proprietors, unsupported by the crown, the colonists, of their own initiative, had pushed the first frontier of the province (the frontier of the Indian trade and Indian alliances) further into the wilderness than English traders elsewhere had ventured. From the first settlement in 1670 the Carolinians had been engaged in conflicts with their neighbors, the Spaniards of Florida.[1] Before the end of the century, they were in contact and keen rivalry with the French in the region of the Gulf and the lower Mississippi. The obscure struggles of Indian traders and their savage partizans on the farthest frontier of the English colonies made but small stir in a world absorbed in the momentous issue of the Spanish Succession. A few men only, in the outposts of the rival empires, understood that these incidents foreshadowed a contest for the richest prize of imperial ambition in America: the heart of the continent. It was on the southern frontier, in the course of Queen Anne's War, that the conflict was first clearly joined for the control of the valley of the Mississippi.

The success of the Carolinians among the southern Indians was due to a number of factors, physical, economic, political. In the first place, the position of South Carolina was more favorable to the development of the western trade than that of any other of the English colonies, with the possible exception of New York. The Appalachian range, so long a barrier to the expansion of Virginia and Maryland and Pennsylvania, was easily avoided by all but the Cherokee traders. Yet in the matter of location Carolina was less fortunate than Florida and Louisiana. Whereas the Spanish could reach the Lower Creek towns by the Apalachicola River, and the French, once Mobile was established, had direct water communication with the Alabama, Talapoosa, and Abihka, the Carolina traders had to convey their goods on the backs of Indian burdeners or on

1

[1] *Collections of the South Carolina Historical Society*, V. 169, 179, 187, 197–200.

pack-horses by an overland path which intersected nearly all the important rivers of southeastern America.[2] But even the possession of water-routes, and the ability which the Latins everywhere displayed in Indian diplomacy, were more than offset by another factor of crucial importance, the superiority of the English trade.

In nearly all the articles of the Indian trade the goods which the English offered were more highly esteemed by the Indians, for quality and price, than the corresponding products of their rivals. The fundamental reason for the success of the English in the tortuous politics of the wilderness was concisely expressed by the first Indian agent of South Carolina. In 1708 Thomas Nairne asserted that "the English trade for cloath always atracts and maintains the obedience and friendship of the Indians, they Effect them most who sell best cheap".[3]

The South Carolina trade, moreover, was actively fostered by the provincial government. Indeed, the leaders in the government and in the trade were for the most part identical. Charges of unfair and monopolistic practices were freely made against the great traders who controlled the council and the assembly. But the frontier interests of men like Joseph Blake (deputy governor, 1695–1700) and James Moore (governor, 1700–1702) had a consequence for the colony unrecognized by their critics.[4] At the end of the seventeenth century the Indian trade was weaving a web of alliances among tribes of Indians distant many hundred miles from Charles Town. Blake and his successor, active promoters of the trade, developed a conception of the destinies of the English in that quarter of America—an *imperial vision*—notably in advance of the parochial ideas of proprietors and provincials alike; in advance, too, of the notions of policy of the imperial government itself.

When Joseph Blake became deputy governor at the end of 1695, the Indian trade of South Carolina was just entering on a phase of more than local importance. A decade before this, in 1684, the revolt of the Yamasee against the Florida government and their emigration from the province of Guale to the borders of South Carolina had turned the scale against the Spaniards in the coastal

---

[2] *Mississippi Valley Historical Review*, III. 9 and note.

[3] Thomas Nairne [to the Secretary of State], July 10, 1708. Public Record Office, America and West Indies, vol. 620; now C. O. 5: 383. (Transcript, Historical Commission of South Carolina, Columbia, S. C.)

[4] Typical charges in W. J. Rivers, *Sketch of the History of South Carolina to . . . 1719* (1856), pp. 424, 455–456. Cf. also Hewat, *Historical Account of . . . South Carolina and Georgia* (1779) in B. R. Carroll, *Historical Collections of South Carolina* (1836), I. 134; and complaints by Edward Randolph against Blake in *Prince Society Publications, Randolph Papers*, VII. 554, 557.

region.[5] Already the expulsion of the Westo from the lower Savannah had cleared the way for trade expansion southwestward, among the inland tribes. Their route protected against flank attack from St. Augustine, the Charles Town traders made rapid progress among the populous Oconee, Ocheese (Kawita and Kasihta), and Ocmulgee Indians seated on the upper Oconee and above the forks of the Altamaha.[6] With her expanding Indian relations South Carolina became the centre of the traffic in Indian slaves, as well as in deer-skins, among the English colonies. When the early wars had exhausted the supply near the settlements the friendly Indians were encouraged to range farther afield, especially to the south, where slave-catching raids had the additional advantage of weakening the allies of the Spaniards. Timucuan Indians from the interior of Florida had long been bought from the Yamasee;[7] and now the inland Indians found ready sale for captured Apalachee, from the province of Apalachee, which fronted the Gulf between the Suwanee and Apalachicola rivers—the richest and, strategically, the most important of the outlying Spanish provinces. The raiders were supplied with arms, incited, and even led by the traders who lived among them; retaliatory expeditions were headed by Spanish officers.[8]

Thus on the eve of the War of the Spanish Succession the relations between the colonists of South Carolina and Florida, already disturbed by disputes over title of possession, buccaneering, and runaway slaves, were further embittered by the expansion of the South Carolina Indian system. By aggressive, belligerent methods even in time of peace the Carolina traders threatened the maintenance of Spanish authority everywhere beyond the protection of a few weak and isolated garrisons. Florida was endangered, and with Florida another colony which existed as yet only in the purposes of Iberville and the French ministers: Louisiana.

3

[5] Barcia, *Ensayo Chronologico para la Historia de la Florida* (Madrid, 1723), p. 287. Cf. also J. G. Shea, *Catholic Church in Colonial Days* (1886), p. 178.

[6] Later called by the English Creek, specifically, Lower Creek Indians. The name was derived by abbreviation, from Ocheese Creek Indians. Before 1715 the Kasihta and Kawita had their villages on Ocheese Creek, *i. e.*, the Ocmulgee River above the approximate site of Macon, Ga. For evidence of this derivation see *Mississippi Valley Historical Review*, V. 339. The Westo and their identity are discussed in *American Anthropologist*, n. s., XX. 331.

[7] Barcia, *loc. cit.*; *Coll. S. C. Hist. Soc.*, I. 93; Rivers, *Sketch*, pp. 410, 425.

[8] Archdale Papers, Library of Congress, pp. 19, 24, 41, 69, 97, 110, 116; W. E. Dunn, *Spanish and French Rivalry in the Gulf Region of the United States, 1678–1702*, in *University of Texas Bulletin*, no. 1705, p. 71; Shea, *Catholic Church in Colonial Days*, p. 459.

Throughout the last decade of the century the centre of the Carolina trade had remained at the forks of the Altamaha.[9] Several years before the century's close, however, the bolder traders had established their factories among the Alabama, Talapoosa, and Abihka, near the forks of the Alabama, and had laid in train an alliance with the Chickasaw, which, more than any other single factor, was destined to thwart the complete attainment of the French design in the lower Mississippi Valley. From the villages of the Choctaw, near the Tombigbee, and of the Acolapissa, at the mouth of the Pearl, to the country of the Arkansas, west of the great river, and even as far as the Illinois, the Chickasaw, now that they were supplied with arms by the English, who bought their captives as slaves, became the scourge of the defenseless western tribes.[10] The Chickasaw traders, of whom the chief were Thomas Welch and Anthony Dodsworth, sought also to extend their trade among the adjacent Indians. The most notable exploit in the early history of the western trade was the journey of Welch, in 1698, from Charles Town to the Quapaw village at the mouth of the Arkansas.[11] Within three decades from the planting of the colony —in a little more than fifteen years from the beginning of the western advance—the Carolinians had reached and even passed the Mississippi in their trading journeys.

This achievement, without parallel in the English colonies, and rivalled only by the feats of the Canadian *coureurs de bois,* had been watched with close interest by the South Carolina government. It might have passed unnoted outside of the province, however, but for the emergence, as an international issue, of the question of the Mississippi.

To England and the English colonies rumors were borne in 1698 of the French design to discover and settle the mouth of the Mississippi. Among the counter-measures proposed, the unsuc-

[9] Under Henry Woodward, Shaftesbury's agent in the Indian trade, the vanguard of the Carolinians had crossed the Chattahoochee (*ca.* 1684). This was the last instance of direct encouragement of inland exploration by the proprietors. With the passing of the proprietary monopoly of the trade with the distant Indians (undermined by the Westo war, 1681–1682), their interest in frontier policy ceased. Public Record Office, Colonial Entry Books, XX. (now C. O. 5: 286) 207 (transcript, Columbia, S. C.); Rivers, *Sketch,* p. 313; *Coll. S. C. Hist. Soc.,* I. 88; V. *passim.* Compare Dunn, *Spanish and French Rivalry,* p. 71.

[10] Margry, *Découvertes et Établissements des Français dans l'Amérique Septentrionale,* IV. 362, 372, 398, 516 *et seq.*

[11] Mitchell, *Map of North America* (1755), from an anon. map *ca.* 1720 (based on journals of Indian agents, etc.) of which a tracing exists in the collection of the South Carolina Historical Society, Charleston, S. C.

cessful attempt of Daniel Coxe, claimant of "Carolana" under the Heath patent, to plant an English colony to control the river, served only to hasten the French preparations.[12] Another project, put forward by Lord Bellomont of New York and Governor Nicholson of Virginia, had in view the promotion of trade with the trans-Appalachian Indians. Unfortunately Bellomont's scheme for a conference of colonial governors for co-operation in Indian affairs and western policy, which was sanctioned by the Board of Trade, also miscarried.[13] But as a result of the discussion it was becoming clearer that if the French were to be prevented from linking their settlements in Canada with the Gulf, trade with the distant Indians must be encouraged; and secondly, that the position of South Carolina gave that colony a unique advantage as a base for western expansion.[14]

5

The alarm occasioned in the northern colonies and in England by Iberville's enterprise was even keener in South Carolina, which had thereby become a frontier against the French as well as the Spanish and the Indians, and where the knowledge of a relatively easy communication with the Gulf and the lower Mississippi awakened fears of a speedy conquest by the French, or by the French and the Spaniards combined. The more timid settlers talked of removal to a safer region should the death of Charles II. unite the two crowns.[15] Not till the spring of 1700 was it definitely known by the report of the traders that the French were in possession of the coveted region.[16] In the meantime Blake, who had

---

[12] Margry, *Découvertes et Établissements*, IV. 58, 88, 361.

[13] Virginia Council Minutes, 1698–1700, Library of Congress, February 23, June 22, 1699; *Calendar of State Papers, Colonial Series, America and West Indies*, 1693–1696, p. 512; 1699, pp. 50, 320; 1700, p. 311 *et seq.*; *Documents relative to the Colonial History of the State of New York*, IV. 590, 632, 699–700; *Colonial Records of North Carolina*, I. 542; *Maryland Archives*, XXIII. 501.

[14] A vague appreciation of the imperial possibilities of the Carolina Indian system led the Board of Trade, in December, 1699, to summon a certain James Boyd, lately arrived in England, to advise them on " the expediency of promoting a new Trade with some Indians at the Back of Carolina". Boyd was able to inform their lordships that " the English Indian traders inhabiting there had made many Journeys through the Country westward to above 1000 or 1200 miles distance ". Board of Trade Journals (transcripts in the library of the Historical Society of Pennsylvania, Philadelphia), under dates December 8, 12, 1699.

[15] Board of Trade Papers, Proprieties, III. (now C. O. 5 : 1258) c: 22 (Pennsylvania transcripts). In November, 1698, when Iberville's fleet was not a month out of Brest, the Commons House formally requested Governor Blake to determine whether the French were settled on the Mississippi and, if they were, to consider the best way to remove them. Journals of the Commons House of Assembly of South Carolina, Columbia, S. C., under date November 16, 1698.

[16] *Cal. of State Papers, A. and W. I.*, 1700, pp. 326–327 ; 1701, p. 408.

warned an officer sent from St. Augustine that he intended to make good the English title to Pensacola Bay, occupied by the Spanish in November, 1698,[17] had also despatched a group of traders by way of the Cherokee country and the Tennessee River to lay claim to the Mississippi and to challenge the French control.[18] Confident that the influence which he had won among the southwestern tribes must prevail, he only awaited information from his agents before transmitting to the English government definite proposals for displacing the French. His death in 1700 interrupted these activities. As deputy governor and at the same time magnate of the Indian trade he had " ingeniously laid " the design for " the Enlargement of the Dominion of the Crown of England " in accordance with the inclusive terms of the proprietary charter.[19] It was left to his successor, James Moore, an adventurous explorer and trader, to formulate a scheme for the conquest of the region of the Gulf and the lower Mississippi.

By 1700 the extent and the character of the English interest among the western Indians were well understood by the French. Iberville, who had anticipated English opposition, but had not foreseen the direction of the attack, was impressed with the need of devising a comprehensive programme of resistance. In his first measures, however, he underrated the difficulties. A plan for the forcible expulsion of the English traders from among the Chickasaw soon proved impossible of execution.[20] The attempt of Iberville and the French ministry to persuade the Spaniards, now ruled by a Bourbon, that only the cession of Pensacola to France could check the advance of the Carolinians toward the mine-country, failed to overcome the jealous regard of government and people for the integrity of their colonial empire.[21] In default of Pensacola, Mobile was established, avowedly as a point of support for the Indians allied with the French and the Spanish.[22] The central object of Iberville's frontier policy was the promotion of a general peace among the southern Indians, based on friendship and trade with the French. Negotiations with the Chickasaw, begun by Tonti in 1700, were brought to a head only after two years. Meantime

17 Dunn, *Spanish and French Rivalry*, pp. 197–198.

18 *Miss. Valley Hist. Rev.*, III. 12, 13.

19 John Archdale, Description of Carolina (1707), in Carroll, *Collections*, II. 118–119.

20 Margry, *Découvertes et Établissements*, IV. 406, 418.

21 *Ibid.*, pp. 476, 484, 489–490, 543–575. *Cf.* also Dunn, *Spanish and French Rivalry*, pp. 206–215.

22 Margry, *Découvertes et Établissements*, IV. 578–579.

there had occurred a crucial event in the frontier history of Louisiana: the conclusion of an alliance with the Choctaw.[23] The traditional enmity between the Choctaw, the most numerous nation of southwestern Indians, and the Chickasaw, the most aggressive, which was the *raison d'être* of the alliance, proved in the event to be fatal to the success of Iberville's programme of pacification. In 1702, however, at a great council at Mobile, the Choctaw and the Chickasaw were reconciled, and were promised an ample trade from a factory to be planted in their midst. Shortly the truce was extended to include other tribes, notably the Illinois and the Alabama.[24]

Iberville's policy was not purely defensive. It looked beyond the immediate security of Louisiana to the expansion of the French interest among the Indians "au côté du Caroline", and to co-operation with the Spanish of Florida to strike at the flank of the English advance. A grandiose scheme for the rearrangement of the southern Indians, including the Cherokee, so as to expose the southern frontier of the English colonies, was distinctly impracticable. Something, however, was actually accomplished toward co-ordinating French and Spanish policy. In January, 1702, Iberville strongly advised that the Apalachee Indians be engaged to oppose by force the progress of the English and their allies. His counsel was accepted, and as an earnest of a more aggressive strategy, an expedition of several hundred Indians and Spaniards was prepared to go against the English Indians in August. But the latter had warning of the intended attack; headed by their traders they advanced to the Flint River and routed the invaders.[25]

More was involved in this frontier skirmish—the prelude to Queen Anne's War on the southern frontier—than in the familiar quarrels between the Carolinians and the Spanish of Florida. In effect it was the first blow struck by the English for the control of the Mississippi Valley. There was no doubt in the mind of Governor James Moore that the unity of policy which Iberville sought to attain was a fact to be reckoned with in the English programme.

In August, 1702, before the expected news of a declaration of war had reached Carolina, Governor Moore in an address to the Commons House of Assembly urged "the takeing of St. Augustin before it be strengthened with French forses". He added: "This

7

23 *Ibid.*, pp. 427, 429, 460; B. de La Harpe, *Journal Historique de l'Établissement des Français à la Louisiane* (Paris, 1831), p. 35, under date September 16, 1701.

24 La Harpe, *Journal Historique*, mars 1702, 12 mai 1702, pp. 71, 72; Margry, *Découvertes et Établissements*, IV. 507, 516–521, 531–532, 630.

25 Margry, *Découvertes et Établissements*, IV. 579, 594–595, 630; Carroll, *Collections*, II. 351. Anon. map *ca.* 1720 (*supra*, note 11) shows location of the battle.

wee believe will open to us an easie and plaine way to Remove the French (a no less dangerous Enemy in time of peace then warr) from their settlement on the south (*sic*) side of the Bay of Appalatia.''[26]   A hastily planned expedition was launched against St. Augustine in the fall. The town was soon reduced, but for lack of mortars the siege of the castle was prolonged until relief arrived from Havana.[27]   In spite of the burden of debt imposed upon the province by the unsuccessful campaign of 1702, tentative plans were laid for a second expedition in co-operation with Her Majesty's naval forces. In a letter to Admiral Whetstone of January 28, 1703, the governor and assembly outlined the larger objects of their strategy.

8

If it Pleaseth God to Give us Success, it is a Matter of that Great Consequence that if to that Wee ad the conquest of a small Spanish Town called Pancicola, and a new french Collony. . . . Both, Sea Port Towns . . . It will make her Majestie Absolute and Soveraigne Lady of all the Maine as farr as the River Mischisipi, which if effected the Collony of Carolina will be of the Greatest Vallue to the Crown of England of any of her Majesties Plantations on the Maine except Virginia by ading a Great Revenue to the Crown, for one halfe of all the Canadian Trade for furrs and Skinns must necessarily come this way, besides a vast Trade of furrs and Skinns—extended as far as the above mentioned River, Mischisipi, which is now interrupted by those Two little Towns.[28]

Five months later Colonel Robert Quary, a colonial customs official with pronounced imperial ideas, whose former residence in South Carolina had familiarized him with the problems of the southern frontier, wrote from New York to the Board of Trade emphasizing in similar fashion the relation of the Florida campaign to the larger question of continental dominion.[29]

[26] Commons House Journals, August 20, 1702.

[27] For a narrative see Rivers, *Sketch*, p. 197 *et seq.* Condemned by the enemies of Moore in South Carolina as a free-booting raid (John Ash, *The Present State of Affairs in Carolina* [1706?], pamphlet in Force collection, Library of Congress; repr. Salley, *Narratives of Early Carolina*, p. 272), and as a slave-taking expedition (Colleton County Representation, in Rivers, *Sketch*, p. 456), and by the historians of Spanish Florida as a " mark of English provincial hatred against the Church of God " (*vide* Shea, *Catholic Church in Col. Days*, pp. 459–461), the St. Augustine expedition of 1702 has not been placed in its true setting as one of the first stages in the intercolonial contest for the control of the region of the Gulf and the Mississippi.

[28] Commons House Jour., January 28, 1703.

[29] The reduction of Florida would, he believed, " put a stop to the French designs who are endeavouring from Canada, to secure the Inland parts of the whole Maine . . . by our securing the Southern Parts, we shall prevent them, and break all their measures by securing the Indians to the Interest of England, which will be easily effected, since they must depend upon us for the supply of Indian Trade." *Docs. rel. to the Col. Hist. of N. Y.*, IV. 1048.

Quary and Moore saw farther into the future of the intercolonial conflict than most of their contemporaries. Moore had
been discredited by the St. Augustine fiasco; he was succeeded by
a capable but unimaginative soldier, without the keen interest of
the recent governors in frontier policy. At the beginning of his
government, however, Sir Nathaniel Johnson gave his sanction to a
blow at the Spanish interest which reaped a larger measure of success than any other military enterprise of the war, and which was
definitely directed against Louisiana as well as Florida: the Apalachee expedition of 1704.

In 1702 and 1703 the progress which the French were making
among the Alabama and Talapoosa, and more especially the potential danger to the "Coweta" (Kawita) and Yamasee, revealed by
the abortive Spanish-Apalachee attack of 1702, awakened anxiety
among the Carolinians for the stability of their Indian system. A
general movement northward of the tribes which composed the
bulwark of the province seemed imminent. Measures to protect
these Indians and to confirm them in the places in which they lived
repeatedly engaged the attention of the government. It was at
length determined, at the solicitation of the assembly, to despatch
a force of a thousand friendly Indians and fifty whites under the
recent governor, James Moore, to assist the Kawita by attacking the
Spanish frontier province of Apalache.[30] On January 14, 1704,
Moore successfully stormed the first and strongest fort, at Ayubale.
The invaders then captured one post after another until the rich
province with its flourishing missions was almost completely ravaged
and subdued. Besides many Indians killed in battle, or carried
away as slaves, three hundred men and a thousand women and children who had submitted were persuaded to remove to the neighbor-
hood of Savannah Town to strengthen the immediate frontier of
South Carolina. By this energetic proceeding Moore destroyed the
chief weapon upon which the Spanish and French had relied for
offensive action against Carolina, before it could be made really
effective. "Before this Expedition", Moore informed the proprietors, "we were more afraid of the Spaniards of Apalatchee and
their Indians in Conjunction with the French of Mississippi, and
their Indians doing us Harm by Land, than of any Forces of the
Enemy by Sea. This has wholly disabled them from attempting
anything against Us by Land".[31]

9

---

[30] Commons House Jour., January 14, 1702; January 15, 16, 19, 20; February
3; September 2, 3, 6, 7, 15, 17, 1703.

[31] "Extracts of Colo. Moore's Letter to the Lords Proprietors, 16 April 1704",
in Transcripts of Correspondence with Spanish Authorities, America, British

The immediate consequence of the new security against inland assault was an increased activity of the Carolinians on the Louisiana frontier.   Already the Charles Town traders, with the aid of Moore's government, had undermined the weakest support of Iberville's structure of alliances, the friendly understanding with the Alabama Indians.   It had early been recognized by the English that the amity of the tribes seated at the forks of the Alabama was essential to the western expansion of their trade ; and between 1701 and 1703 efforts had been put forth to counteract the advantage enjoyed by the French in their control of the water-routes.   An effect had soon been produced.   In May, 1703, the French traders had been waylaid and murdered by the Alabama.[32]   The hostilities thus begun continued nine years.   Punitive expeditions from Mobile accomplished little ; somewhat more effective were the attacks of the French Indians spurred on by liberal offers of reward for scalps and captives.[33]   Meanwhile the Alabama war greatly facilitated the work of the South Carolina traders, who, on the farthest frontier of the English colonies, advanced hand in hand their own profit and the political interests of their province.

From 1703 to 1715 the French policy was of necessity largely defensive.   That this policy was successful in its main object, though not in detail—that the new establishment was enabled to survive the assaults of the Carolinians and their allies—was due primarily to the adroit Indian management of Iberville's brother and successor, Bienville.   Through French youths whom he sent to live among the Indians behind Mobile, Bienville kept in touch with the rapidly shifting currents of Indian politics.   By flattery, by "caresses", he made good in part the meagreness of French presents and the insufficiency of the French trade.[34]   Yet from time to time Bienville's

Colonies, Library of Congress, VI. 888 *et seq.* ; Moore to Sir Nathaniel Johnson, of same date, *ibid.*, p. 892, also printed in *Boston News-Letter*, April 24–May 1, 1704 (*Historical Digest of the Provincial Press, Massachusetts series*, I. 64–66). *Cf.* also Robert Quary to Board of Trade, May 30, 1704, in *Cal. of State Pap., A. and W. I.*, 1704–1705, p. 145.   Compare with the account, based on Spanish sources, in Shea, *Catholic Church in Col. Days*, pp. 461–463.

[32] Commons House Jour., August 15, 29, 1701 ; January 14, 20, 1702 ; February 3, and April 17, 1703 ; La Harpe, *Journal Historique*, 3, 24 mai 1703, pp. 77, 79.

[33] La Harpe, *Journal Historique*, 22 décembre 1703, 18 novembre 1704, 21 janvier 1706, 21 février 1706, novembre 1707, pp. 82, 86, 95, 96, 103, 104.   Pénicaut, Relation, in Margry, *Découvertes et Établissements*, V. 429–432, 435, 483.

[34] For an appreciation of Bienville's ability as an Indian diplomat see Mémoire de Duclos, 25 octobre 1713, in Archives Nationales, Colonies, C13 A 3, p. 265 *et seq.*   References here and throughout are to Louisiana transcripts, Library of Congress.   *Cf.* also Gravier [to Pontchartrain] [1706], Arch. Nat., Col., C13 A 1, p. 575.

skill was severely tested. The poverty of the colony played directly into the hands of its enemies. Funds set aside for Indian presents and trade had to be used for the maintenance of the garrisons. The building of the post promised to the Chickasaw in 1702, and impatiently demanded by the Indians, was postponed. In this juncture the English, by cultivating the Chickasaw seated among the upper Creeks, and by liberal presents to their kinsmen, were imperilling the central object of the French policy, the pacification of the southwestern tribes. In 1705 hostilities occurred between the Chickasaw and the Choctaw, and in 1706 the patched-up truce was definitely broken.[35] Though the French for a number of years retained a party among the Chickasaw, the English re-established their control over the majority of the nation. The Chickasaw and their neighbors the Yazoo were added to the Talapoosa, the Alabama, and the other tribes which the English had been using with disastrous effect in their assaults upon the allies of the French. In the autumn of 1705, for instance, the Choctaw had been raided by three or four thousand Carolina Indians, headed by several Englishmen, their villages and fields ravaged, and many prisoners carried away. Among the weaker tribes a veritable reign of terror was now instituted. The Tohome and Mobilians north of Mobile were exposed to constant attack. In 1706 the Taensa and Tunica were compelled to remove nearer the mouth of the Mississippi.[36] A climax in the English offensive was reached in 1707–1708 when Pensacola town was burned, and an elaborate intrigue was set in motion for the destruction of Mobile and Louisiana.

The reduction of the Florida Indians after the Apalachee expedition had been even more thorough than the harrying of the allies of the French. The remnants of the Apalachee, with the Tawasa and the Chatta, were forced by the Creeks to flee to the protection of Mobile. In peninsular Florida only the walls of St. Augustine furnished security against the attacks of the English and their Indians.[37] These now made so bold as to press their slave-catching raids as far into the interior as the "broken land" of the Ever-

[35] Arch. Nat., Col., C[13] A 1, pp. 387–396, 523, 575; A 2, p. 574; La Harpe, *Journal Historique*, 8 octobre 1704, 1 février 1705, 10 avril 1705, 9 décembre 1705, 5 mars 1706, pp. 85, 89, 91, 96; Commons House Jour., February 3, 1703.

[36] Arch. Nat., Col., C[13] A 1, p. 509; A 2, pp. 95, 396, 407. La Harpe, *Journal Historique*, janvier 1706, 25 août 1706, 20 octobre 1706, pp. 95, 97–98, 100–101; Pénicaut, Relation, in Margry, *Découvertes et Établissements*, V. 483.

[37] La Harpe, *Journal Historique*, 22 juillet 1704, p. 84; Pénicaut, Relation, in Margry, *Découvertes et Établissements*, V. 457, 460, 486. [Nairne?], *Letter from South Carolina* (London, 1710), p. 33; Mitchell, *Map of North America* (1755): "Timooquas destroy'd by the Carolinians in 1706".

glades.[38] Close to the Louisiana frontier the isolated outpost of Pensacola invited attack. In the summer of 1707 Pensacola town was destroyed in a surprise assault by a body of Talapoosa under English leaders, and the fort itself just escaped capture. In November Pensacola was again invested, but the siege was raised when Bienville, with characteristic promptness, headed a party of French and Indians for its relief.[39]

In 1707 the Carolinians were aiming at a more difficult prize than Pensacola, and one more essential to their ultimate object—at Mobile, the key to the control of the eastern Gulf region and the lower Mississippi. The programme adopted by the assembly was conceived by Thomas Welch, the veteran Chickasaw trader, and by Thomas Nairne, the first official Indian agent of the province.[40] In the autumn of 1707 both Nairne and Welch urged that an attempt be made to win over the French Indians, particularly the Choctaw, as a preliminary to an attack on Mobile.[41] In the assembly the proposal found support as the most practicable method to remove the French, an object regarded as " of absolute necessity ", especially since the Spanish-French sea-attack on Charles Town in 1706. Plans for an expedition to fall upon the French from the Talapoosa were made contingent upon the success of Nairne and Welch in seducing the western Indians.[42] In the spring Nairne " ventured his life and made a peace with the Choctaws "; while Welch summoned a council at the Yazoo of the chief river tribes—Arkansas, Tourima, Taensa, Natchez, and Koroa—with similar results. Unfortunately for the larger English design, their further proposals for

[38] Moll, *New Map of the North Parts of America* (1720) shows the route of " an Expedition in Florida Neck, by Thirty-three Iamesee Indians Accompany'd by Capt. T. Nairn " which may have reached Lake Okechobee. *Cf.* also Nairne, *doc. cit. supra*, note 3.

[39] Arch. Nat., Col., C13 A 2, pp. 95–99; La Harpe, *Journal Historique,* 25 août 1707, 16; 24 novembre 1707, pp. 103–104.

[40] When, after long agitation, an act was finally passed, in 1707, to regulate the abuses of the Indian trade (*Statutes at Large of South Carolina*, ed. Cooper, II. 309), the agent chosen by the assembly to control the traders and to negotiate with the Indians was a gentleman from Colleton County, on the southern border of the province, whose frontier interests, stimulated by service in the Florida campaigns, and by long experience among the Yamasee, qualified him, in peculiar degree, to continue the work of Blake and Moore. He was a leader of the popular party in the assembly in the controversy with the governor over the appointment of the public receiver (1707), and in the parallel struggle for a regulation of the Indian trade under exclusive control of the assembly through its commissioners; probably the author of the Indian act of 1707. Commons House Jour., 1702–1707 *passim.*

[41] Commons House Jour., October 23, 28, November 1, 22, 1707.

[42] *Ibid.,* November 8, 20, 1707. Nairne, *doc. cit.*

(1) assistance or neutrality in an attack on Mobile, and (2) the removal of the tribes which formed the bulwark of the French colony to the Tennessee river, in order to divert the fur-trade of the upper Mississippi to Carolina, were rejected. This partial failure of the English diplomacy (a failure which precluded an assault on Mobile) was mainly due to the energy and adroitness of Bienville, who had taken prompt measures to counteract the influence on the western Indians of English presents and arguments.[43]

After this defeat Nairne set to work to create the necessary condition for the success of future efforts to extend "the English American empire" in the southwest—the education of the English colonial authorities in the strategy of the southern frontier. Hitherto the home government was not only without a policy for the southern frontier, but without the data upon which to construct a policy. In 1708, in a notable memorial which he accompanied by a map of the country from Virginia to the mouth of the Mississippi,[44] Nairne urged that in the expected treaty of peace due weight be given to the western claims of Carolina, based upon her ancient trade with the Indians behind Mobile. The advantages to be expected from planting a new English colony in the south or southwest he discussed in the spacious tone of a frontiersman who had "had a personall view of most of those parts". His most practical counsel was to the effect that the French design in the west could be checked "only by trading and other management"; and "that this province being a frontier, both against the French and Span'd, ought not to be Neglected".

It was not until a destructive Indian war had imperilled the results of three decades of expansion, that Nairne's arguments, repeated by others, won the ear of the home government. In the meantime Nairne, a dissenter, whose administration of the Indian act had brought him into conflict with Sir Nathaniel Johnson, had been disgraced and driven from office by the governor and the Church party.[45] For several years thereafter the frontier policy of the provincial government lacked the aggressive and imaginative qualities which Nairne, like Blake and Moore before him, had imparted to it. Under the combined strain of maladroit management,

13

[43] Nairne, *doc. cit.*; Arch. Nat., Col., C¹³ A 2, p. 168 *et seq.*, 177, 328–329, 341–348; P. de Charlevoix, *Histoire et Description Générale de la Nouvelle France* (Paris, 1744), IV. 41–42.

[44] Nairne, *doc. cit.*; Crisp, *Map of South Carolina* [1711?], Library of Congress, has an inset based upon Nairne's 1708 map.

[45] Commons House Jour., November, December, 1708 *et passim.* Cf. also *Coll. S. C. Hist. Soc.*, I. 202.

the licentious conduct of the traders, and the skillful diplomacy of
Bienville, the South Carolina Indian system was beginning to show
ominous signs of weakness. The first break occurred in 1712, when
the French succeeded in making peace with the Alabama Indians.[46]
But the Carolinians, alarmed by the "aparant danger . . . from the
conjunction of . . . the Choctaws and Chickisaws",[47] had already
resumed their western offensive. Although the province was engaged at the time in helping to suppress the troublesome Tuscarora
rising in North Carolina, energy remained for an effective prosecution of the Indian trade and for a vigorous renewal of the partizan
warfare which was the characteristic method of the Carolinian
advance. With the reopening of the Choctaw-Chickasaw feud in
1711, the assembly equipped an expedition of thirteen hundred
Creek Indians, under Captain Theophilus Hastings, which marched
through the Choctaw country, burning, killing, taking prisoners.
A smaller force of Chickasaw, under Welch, joined this assault on
their old enemies, now the main support of the French colony.[48]
The year was one of achievement for the frontier forces of Carolina. John Barnwell, reporting the success of his North Carolina
expedition, in February, 1712, congratulated Governor Craven on
the "hon'r and Glory of virtuous South Carolina whose armies are
the same winter gathering Laurells from the Cape Florida and
from the Bay of Spiritta Sancta even to the Borders of Virginia".[49]

The hope voiced by Nairne in 1708 that in the terms of peace
"the English American empire" in the southwest might "not be
unreasonably Crampt up" was not disappointed in 1713. To be
sure, the southern frontier was not specifically mentioned in the
treaties of Utrecht; but the lack of defined boundaries made it possible for the English colonists to continue to assert their old inclusive claims, based on the charter and on the Indian trade. The
French, at all events, found the Carolinians quite as uncomfortable
neighbors in peace as in war. In vain La Mothe Cadillac invited
Governor Craven to co-operate in establishing a general peace
among the southern Indians, English and French alike; to withdraw his traders from the nations which had traded first with the
French; and to comply with the spirit of the peace by preventing

[46] Arch. Nat., Col., C13 A 2, p. 576; La Harpe, *Journal Historique,* mars 1712,
p. 110; Indian Commissioners' Journals (MSS., Columbia, S. C.), July 9, 1712.
Nairne charged that the mismanagement of his successor was "the true cause of
the Albamas deserting to Mobile". *Ibid.,* August 18, 1713.

[47] Commons House Jour., June 21, 1711.

[48] *Ibid.,* June 21, 22, 1711; May 24, 1712.

[49] *South Carolina Historical and Genealogical Magazine,* IX. 36.

those traders from instigating slave-catching raids among the French allies.[50] After 1713 there was no longer question of an attack on Mobile, but in the field of Indian politics and in partizan warfare the two years ending in 1715 marked the climax of the first English effort to displace the French in the Mississippi Valley.

Nairne had been restored to the principal Indian agency in 1712, and had promptly won the praise of the Indian commissioners for "capacity and diligence" displayed in negotiations with the western Indians. In 1713 he sent goods among the Choctaw, seeking to renew the relations he had established in 1707 with this all-important tribe.[51] It was another than Nairne, however, who was made active director of the new enterprise for the conversion of all the southern Indians to the English trade and alliance. This semi-official Indian diplomat was a certain Price Hughes, Esq., "an English Gent., who had a particular fancy of rambling among the Indians"—such was the character given him by Spotswood of Virginia. By testimony of Cadillac, "il etoit ingénieur, et géographe"; and, moreover, "homme d'esprit".[52] In 1713 and 1714–1715 he was encouraged by the provincial government to undertake highly important missions among the western tribes. His commission from Governor Craven set forth the sweeping claims of Blake and Moore and Nairne to the Mississippi, and to the country westward as far as the Spanish settlements. As a result of his efforts, in co-operation with the traders, new factories were established; a firmer league was formed with the Chickasaw; and even the Choctaw (with the exception of two loyal villages which fled to Mobile) were persuaded to desert the French alliance. Of the Mississippi River Indians, the Yazoo had long inclined toward the English; and now the Natchez as well admitted Carolina traders to their villages, and joined in raids on the weaker tribes down-stream. While the Cherokee were endeavoring to convert the Illinois to the English trade, Hughes and the Carolinians on the Mississippi were intriguing with the French *voyageurs* to the same purpose. Had Hughes succeeded in his further measures, there was a real prospect that the highway of trade and communication between Canada and Louisiana would be closed. The French authorities were informed that this enterprising "mylord Anglais" planned to visit the tribes of the Red River, and then to descend to the mouth of the

15

[50] Arch. Nat., Col., C¹³ A 3, pp. 489–492, 530.

[51] Indian Comm. Jour., June 10, 1712, July 17, 1713; Commons House Jour., November 27, 1712, December 18, 1713.

[52] *Virginia Historical Society Collections, Spotswood Letters* (1882), II. 331; Arch. Nat., Col., C¹³ A 4, pp. 521–522.

Mississippi, hoping to win, by presents and trade (the potent instruments of English expansion), the friendship of the Huma, the Bayogoula, the Chawasha, and the Acolapissa.[53]

At precisely that juncture, in 1715, when the Carolina Indian system had reached its farthest extension, the ambitious structure of alliances suddenly crumbled; and in the crash which followed the province itself narrowly escaped destruction. The arrest of Hughes at Manchac by the French, his release, and his murder in the woods between Pensacola and the upper Creek country,[54] occurred simultaneously with the outbreak of the Yamasee-Creek rising—one of the most dangerous Indian attacks sustained by any of the English colonies. The Carolinians naturally saw a connection between the collapse of their western project (precipitated by the watchful activity of Bienville) and the greater calamity which spread massacre and destruction from the plantations on the Stono and the Santee to the trading factories among the distant Chickasaw; they believed that the French and the Spaniards were the instigators of the Indian war.[55] In reality the disaster was largely, if not solely, due to the long accumulating evils of an ill-regulated Indian trade.[56] But the Spanish and the French were not slow to take advantage of their neighbors' extremity. When, after two anxious years, the attacks on the settlements had been suppressed, the wavering Cherokee secured in their allegiance, communication reopened with the loyal Chickasaw, and an uncertain peace concluded with the Creeks, the situation on the southern frontier had been seriously altered in a sense unfavorable to English ambitions.

---

[53] Indian Comm. Jour., August 19, November 18, 30, 1713; Commons House Jour., June 4, 7, 8, 12, December 16, 1714; Arch. Nat., Col., C13 A 3, pp. 491–492, 518–522, 827–828; A 4, pp. 237, 522; Bibl. Nat., MSS. Fr., Nouv. Acquis., vol. 9301, f. 300–300 vo.; La Harpe, *Journal Historique*, avril 1714, 1715, pp. 115, 117 *passim*; Richebourg, Mémoire, in B. F. French, *Historical Collections of Louisiana*, III. 241; Pénicaut, Relation, in Margry, *Découvertes et Établissements*, V. 507, 519; *Wisconsin Historical Collections*, XVI. 303, 318–319; anon. map *ca.* 1720, *supra*, note 11.

[54] Arch. Nat., Col., C13 A 3, pp. 827–832; Arch. Nat., Marine, B1, vol. IX., pp. 271–272.

[55] Bd. of Trade Jour., July 16, 1715; Bd. of Trade Pap., Proprieties, X. (now C. O. 5: 1265), Q: 72, Q: 95, Q: 97.

[56] The Indian Comm. Jour. were filled with complaints of the conduct of the traders in abusing and cheating the Indians. Trading without license, enslaving free Indians, sale of rum, sale of goods on credit, were practices which the commissioners and agents sought vainly to reform, and which contributed to the revolt. *Cf.* preamble to Indian act of March 20, 1719, in *Stat. at Large of S. C.*, II. 91; "History of the Dividing Line", *Writings of Col. William Byrd* (New York, 1901), ed. J. S. Bassett, p. 239; Bd. of Trade Pap., Proprieties, X. (C. O. 5: 1265), Q: 51.

With the desertion of the Yamasee to Florida, and the removal of the lower Creeks from the upper waters of the Altamaha to the Chattahoochee, the Spaniards, from negligible rivals, had become formidable contenders for the alliance of the Creek Indians. The French, moreover, had recovered their control of the Mississippi River tribes, and by planting Alabama Fort (Fort Toulouse) at the forks of the Alabama River, had secured the most valuable strategic position in the southern Indian country.

In one important respect, however, the position of South Carolina as the southern frontier of the English colonies was markedly improved as a result of the Indian war. The English colonial authorities had at length been forced to recognize the existence of an imperial problem in that quarter of America with which the proprietary government had been unable to cope. By slow degrees, as control of the province passed to the crown, the point of view developed by Blake and Moore and Nairne, and now set forth by the Carolina agents—that South Carolina was "a Barrier and might be made a Bulwark to all his Majesties Colonys on the South West part of the Continent"[57]—was impressed upon the Board of Trade and the Privy Council. The first concrete result of outstanding importance—the culmination of a series of efforts to strengthen the southern frontier against the French as well as the Spanish—was the establishment of the march colony of Georgia.

By 1733 it had become axiomatic that the crux of the intercolonial contest in America was the control of the Mississippi Valley, a theorem first demonstrated on the southern frontier in Queen Anne's War.

VERNER W. CRANE

[57] Boone and Berrisford, "Memorial to the Board of Trade on the importance of securing Carolina" (read June 23, 1716). Bd. of Trade Pap., Proprieties, X. (C. O. 5: 1265), Q: 76.

17

American versus Continental Warfare, 1739-63

18

WHEN England went to war with Spain in 1739, all Europe was at peace except the emperor and the Turks. The English ministers had no temptation at first to turn the conflict with Spain into a general European war. They believed their own armies and fleets were a match for the enemy ; and if they too eagerly applied to the Dutch for help, that was in part a precaution against an inconvenient mediation, or an antidote to the unpopularity which would attend the overthrow of the American equilibrium by one Power alone. They began the war without knowing whether they would find other allies, or where. This was even more true in 1755, when England was equally uncertain of foreign help, yet entered cheerfully upon a struggle, this time with the greater, not the lesser of the Bourbon Powers. In fact, the middle of the eighteenth century was the period of the English offensive, in which pessimists were prepared, and optimists even anxious, for a single combat with France and Spain.

Not everybody found this dangerous position congenial. The diplomatic isolation of England was one of the strongest reasons alleged by the Walpoles and Henry Pelham for trying to make up the quarrel with Spain ; and when a remarkable mortality among the crowned heads of Eastern Europe opened new prospects and uncertainties in the autumn of 1740, the English ministers began to look for allies as quickly as they could. This opportunity happened at the same time that the intervention of France in behalf of Spain became much more likely ; and whatever Newcastle may have thought of that danger at a distance, his first motion, upon its approach, was a nervous scurry for allies. In this way the great debate began over the relation of England to the continent of Europe on the one hand, and on the other, to the colonies and dependencies beyond the seas.[1]

[1] A great deal of the material of this article is covered by Admiral Richmond's *History of the Navy in the War of 1739-48*, Sir Richard Lodge's *Studies in Eighteenth Century Diplomacy*, Sir Julian Corbett's *England in the Seven Years' War*, Dr. von Ruville's and Professor Basil Williams' lives of Chatham, and M. Waddington's *Louis XV et le Renversement des Alliances* and *Histoire de la Guerre de Sept Ans*.

The question was posed in two forms. What were the objects for which a war was worth fighting ? What was the best way to fight a war with France and Spain ? Three alternative policies were possible : a Continental policy, a Hanover policy, and a maritime and American policy. Both the first and the last admit of further distinctions still. A Continental policy might assert an unqualified devotion to the balance of power, or it might aim only at protecting certain countries whose interests were thought to be specially connected with our own. On the other side, the zealots for America were likewise divided between conquests in North America and conquests in the West Indies. With all this choice of methods and objects, there was only one great and inevitable enemy France, or at most the combined House of Bourbon.

19

Historians sometimes treat the preoccupation with the balance of power as an essentially Whig principle, and the preference for colonial aims as characteristic of Toryism. Whatever foundation this view may have in the history of Queen Anne's reign, it has little relevance to that of George II. There were indeed some Tories who stolidly adhered to the doctrine that we should only fight at sea and for commercial or colonial objects. They continued to resist the Austrian subsidy treaty in 1741, when most of the Opposition Whigs assented to it in order to make their court to the king.[1] Beckford, one of the loudest declaimers in this sense, called himself a Tory at first, and Pitt's popularity with the Tories may have been increased by his identification with the American policy ; but Bolingbroke (who should presumably be called a Tory in 1743, though a slippery one) admitted that England might sometimes be concerned in upholding the balance of power. 'Our true interests require ', he told Marchmont, ' that we should take few engagements on the Continent, and never those of making a land war, unless the conjuncture be such, that nothing less than the weight of Britain can prevent the scales from being quite overturned. This was the case, surely, when we armed in the Netherlands, and when we marched into Germany.'[2] There were Whigs like Joseph Yorke who could applaud Newcastle's insistence on the Continental war as ' recalling our wandering thoughts to the true principles of the Revolution '; but Pitt and Temple, Bedford and Halifax were also Whigs, yet they were all zealots for America. In fact, there is a complete confusion of Whigs and Tories on this point, which illustrates the general uselessness of those superannuated labels.

The doctrine of the balance of power was inherited from the

[1] Chesterfield to Marchmont, 24 April 1741, *Marchmont Papers*, ii. 249.
[2] *Ibid.* ii. 314.

days of William III and Marlborough, when it met a genuine need and could easily be realized in practice. It had descended, with a great deal of paltry rhetoric about the ' common cause ' and the ' ambitious House of Bourbon , to be used as a cant term by secretaries of state, who did not inquire too closely whether it retained any sense or utility. It was not, however, devoid of either, although the reiteration of it is wearisome in Newcastle's dispatches. France still desired to be the arbiter of Europe,[1] though she pursued the aim with patience and finesse, instead of the cruder and bolder methods of Louis XIV. She was no longer equal to her former reputation in war, nor did her cunning in negotiation achieve any very useful results between the days of Fleury and those of Choiseul ; but she still had some ostensible claim to be considered the first nation in Europe, and so far the balance of power may have been the right one for her nearest rival.

Almost all Englishmen assumed that France was the nation against whom the balance of power was invariably to be maintained. For some time after the Peace of Utrecht, the Whig ministers had tried to establish the system in a more universal and speculative form ; its object, they said, was to control and weaken the strongest state in Europe, whatever that state might be. In the name of this doctrine they justified their understanding with France and their abandonment of the Austrian alliance, for Austria, rather than France, was then to be considered as the greatest and therefore the most dangerous Power in Europe. The renewed competition of French commerce and the successes of Cardinal Fleury were later held to discredit this view, and when the Spanish war broke out, Walpole's enemies attacked him with a great display of historical detail for strengthening our inevitable enemy and weakening our natural ally. The great topics were the Treaty of Hanover in 1725 and the neutrality of England in the war of the Polish Succession. Had we ranged ourselves on the side of Charles VI at those two crises, we might have obliged Spain to abandon the right of search. At any rate we should have had a grateful and vigorous ally instead of having to face France and Spain without one useful friend in the world. So the Opposition argued, and the reasoning with which the Walpoles tried to prove the inexpediency of war at the present

[1] The instructions which Bussy, as a senior clerk in the French Foreign Office, drew up in 1740 for his own use as minister in England, represent the jealousy of England against France as one of prestige rather than interests, and refer to ' the ambition of England, all the more irritated at seeing France the sole arbiter of the universe, because she cannot conceal from herself that her own imprudence has excluded her from any share in that honour ' (Affaires Étrangères, Mém. et Doc. Angleterre, 40, fo. 85). This piece of professional vanity was justified at the moment of writing, for Fleury then had Europe at his feet ; a year or two later it was out of date.

juncture was interpreted as the conclusive proof of their past mistakes. In this light the death of Charles VI in the autumn of 1740 was to be considered a blessing in disguise. He owed us no goodwill, and was not likely to have done anything to help us had he lived. When his inheritance came to be disputed, there must be at least one party to which we could attach ourselves if we needed allies, and if we believed that they were worth the trouble we must take on their behalf.[1]

The practical difficulty of keeping the balance even was greater than either the ministry or the Opposition believed. It had much increased since the wars of the Spanish Succession. Then the foundation of all such calculations had been the rivalry of Habsburg against Bourbon; but this traditional policy had lost some of its recommendations in the strange diplomatic convolutions of the last twenty-five years. Not only was Charles VI an exacting ally, whom we had sometimes had occasion to offend; but the Habsburgs had not lately been reckoned a fair counterweight to the Bourbons, and could still less be so, now that a Bourbon possessed the throne of Spain.

Writers on the balance of power sometimes confused and sometimes distinguished two ways of preserving it. We might either support the strongest single state against France, or try to unite all against her. In the first case it was not so easy as it had once been to choose our ally, in the second it was infinitely more difficult to effect the combination. Statesmen and pamphleteers made the mistake of thinking that another Grand Alliance could be formed against France, as in King William's reign. When Newcastle heard that Fleury had sent his fleet to the West Indies to protect the Spanish colonies against us, he suggested at once that ' some kind of concert might be set on foot with the Dutch, the emperor, the czarina, the king of Prussia, the king of Poland, the landgrave of Hesse, &c., to form a kind of grand alliance to oppose the ambitious views of the House of Bourbon '.[2] He would at all times have had great difficulty in collecting such an omnium gatherum, but as the emperor was not yet dead, he can hardly be blamed because he did not foresee the inevitable conflict between Austria and Prussia over Silesia. Yet he should have known better than to repeat the mistake so often. In 1748 he would have welcomed a Prussian alliance.

21

---

[1] *Parliamentary History,* ii. 635 and 1067 (Carteret), 645 and 1087 (Newcastle), 1121 (Hardwicke), 1270 (Pulteney), 1308 (Sandys), 1337 (Stephen Fox).

[2] Newcastle to Harrington, 6 Sept. 1740, Brit. Mus. Add. MS. 32695, fo. 7. Newcastle's passion for attempting to square the circle is perhaps explained by his timid maxim ' that he that is not for us is against us ', a principle which seems to have inspired his domestic politics as well, and to account for his pursuit of unanimity, as vain in the house of commons as in the concert of Europe.

but as a supplement to that with Austria, not a substitute for it.[1] It was not to be had upon such terms.

Seven years later he made an astonishing blunder of the same kind. He concluded a treaty with Russia, in order to deter Frederick II from attacking Hanover. This and other measures having produced overtures from Frederick, Newcastle made a treaty with him too, hoping that Russia would make no objection, as if she had no ends of her own to serve by her arrangement with us, beyond the subsidy she was to receive. He was then very indignant when both Russia and Austria renounced our alliance as soon as Prussia showed signs of acceding to it. (It is true this was not an act of sudden impulse, nor prompted by hostility to Prussia alone, but Newcastle ought to have reckoned on a continuance of the Austro-Prussian antagonism.) Finally —and this was the crowning mistake of a long career of diplomatic ineptitude—it was Newcastle who induced Bute to make the fatal overture to Austria in January 1762, which did as much as anything else to make Frederick II an intractable and untrustworthy associate.[2] Newcastle believed the rest of the world would be as much concerned and frightened by the Bourbon Family Compact as he was himself, and that Austria would at once come round from her French alliance and fall into the arms of England.

This sort of conduct might be called a Continental policy, but it was in truth the most barbarous insularity. It assumed that the other Powers of Europe had no occupation in life but to fear and resist the House of Bourbon, and would sacrifice any private aims for this. Newcastle may have been right in thinking that such resistance was the supreme and general concern of all Europe, just as the younger Pitt may have been right in believing that it was everybody's duty to oppose Napoleon. Newcastle may have seen the interests of other countries better than they could see them for themselves; but he did not understand that, while this general concern of Europe happened to correspond with our private interest—almost the only interest of any kind which we had on the Continent—the same fortunate coincidence could not be expected in other countries. What was the House of Bourbon to Poland or Sweden or Prussia? Certainly a very powerful agent for good or evil, but not the

[1] Sir Richard Lodge, *Studies in Eighteenth Century Diplomacy*, p. 360, n.

[2] Compare the first and second drafts of Bute's dispatch to Yorke of 12 Jan. 1762, Add. MS. 32933, fos. 82, 221; Newcastle to Bute, 7 Jan., fo. 84; to Yorke, 8 Jan., fos. 112–16. These overtures to Austria do not wholly justify Frederick's disingenuous behaviour to England. He did not hear of them until the beginning of April 1762, by which time he was far advanced in a secret and disloyal negotiation with Russia, of which the English ministry would have disapproved the terms if it had known them. Bute's and Newcastle's blunder was therefore his excuse rather than his reason. (*Politische Correspondenz Friedrich's des Grossen*, vol. xxi, nos. 13590, 13594.)

immediate and inevitable enemy to the public welfare. The self-centred diplomacy of England was too slow to see the growth, especially in Germany and Italy, of local conflicts as necessary and important to those who were engaged in them as our struggle with France was to us. It therefore made the mistake of thinking that it had only to raise the cry of 'the liberties of Europe in danger' to obtain the harmonious support of Powers which could never remain long or sincerely on the same side of any question.

Newcastle was not the most intelligent, though he was far the most experienced foreign secretary of his generation. The same unenlightenment is to be found among pamphleteers and parliamentary orators. They could not get the Grand Alliance out of their heads, and ignored the incompatibilities of foreign states, however fundamental. Frederick II, in their opinion, was merely shortsighted, and Maria Theresa merely obstinate, in continuing to quarrel over Silesia when they ought to have been making common cause against France. Both Walpole and Carteret were criticized severely for their inability or omission to reconcile Austria with Prussia and Bavaria, and later ministers were condemned in the same way for policies which perpetuated, by trying to exploit, the rivalries of those countries.[1]

Perhaps the argument was never put more intelligently than by Israel Mauduit in his famous *Considerations on the Present German War*, published in 1760. He assumed that there was only one way to fight France in Europe : a revival of the Grand Alliance. England could not profitably be connected with the Continent unless the Continent were connected with itself. This was particularly true of Germany, which united might be a match for France, but was no more than a battlefield, and an inconvenient one for us, when divided. Mauduit saw the conflict between Austria and Prussia as a German civil war, which we only aggravated and prolonged by taking sides in it ; our part should have been that of mediation, that peace might be restored as soon as possible and both the rivals induced to direct their arms against France.[2] The only fault of Mauduit's theory was that it was too speculative. There was no such thing as Germany at that time ; indeed, in this sense there was no such thing as Europe ; for this reason all the attempts to form a sacred league against France were bound to fail.

23

---

[1] *Parl. Hist.* xii. 255 (Carteret), 348 (Henry Pelham), 925 (Bance), 961 (Waller), 979 (Quarendon) ; xiii. 156 (Pitt), 175 (Winnington), 192 (Lyttelton), 260 (Dodington), 384 (George Grenville), 409 (Murray) ; *A Compleat View of the Present Politicks of Great Britain, in a Letter from a German Nobleman to his Friend in Vienna* (1743), p. 34 ; *An Englishman's Answer to a German Nobleman* (1743), p. 17 ; *The Case of the Hanover Forces in the Pay of Great Britain* (1743), p. 48.

[2] *Op. cit.* pp. 2–17.

The policy which Mauduit attacked may have been illogical, but it was the only one possible. The most practicable way of maintaining the balance of power was not by combination, but by supporting the strongest nation that could be found to resist France. Nearly everybody believed this to be Austria ; that was the ' good old system ' to which Newcastle was attached, as an alternative to his dreams of a Grand Alliance. Most speakers and writers treated Austria as the natural ally, a fact which helps to explain the sentimental cult of Maria Theresa in the early years of her reign. When her bravery developed into an exacting though pardonable obstinacy—when, in fact, she refused to make the sacrifices required by our schemes of a Grand Alliance—Carteret's patronage of her began to be looked upon as romantic knight-errantry ; but here the English public was the victim of its own confusion of thought. If the league of all Europe against France was the object, certainly Maria Theresa's firm resistance to Prussia was inconvenient and perhaps even selfish ; but if we were to support the strongest power available, it was absurd to invite her to weaken herself.[1] Circumstances forced the English government into an uneasy combination of these policies ; it refused to abandon Austria, but pressed her to part with territories, first in order to bribe her allies and then in order to put an end to the war by contenting her enemies. Friendship does not flourish upon such terms, and the breach between England and Austria was prepared long before 1756, in spite of Newcastle's blind tenacity to the ' good old system.' The alliance was unnatural, or at least no more natural than any other, when Austria began to withdraw from western politics and to canton herself in Germany and Italy.

The Prussian alliance, which then succeeded the Austrian, might be in some respects a better one for England. Prussia was a nearer neighbour to Hanover, to whom she could do either good or harm ; indeed, the opponents of the Continental war represented the help we gave to Frederick II as a tribute paid to induce him to keep his hands off Hanover.[2] In view of the way in which the diplomatic revolution came about, the accusation has some justice. Some English ministers, notably the Walpoles, had already begun to prefer Prussia to Austria by 1740, but the alliance was never popular until it was made. Though the ' Protestant hero ' then became twice as great a favourite as the gallant queen of Hungary ever had been, some of the older politicians, especially Newcastle and Granville, kept

[1] This point is made in *An Englishman's Answer to a German Nobleman, loc. cit.*

[2] *Considerations on the Present German War*, p. 38. In fact, when we began to quarrel with Frederick in 1762, Newcastle suggested that perhaps he would seize Hanover in revenge (Newcastle to Legge, 18 Feb. 1762, Add. MS. 32934, fo. 411).

in their hearts a secret attachment to the 'good old system ';
their futile return to their old flame had deplorable results in
the last year of the war.

Not everybody believed that the balance of power was a
legitimate object of English policy. Temple declaimed against
' the phantom of keeping your power on the Continent ', and
Pitt said in 1755, ' We have suffered ourselves to be deceived by
names and sound , the balance of power, the liberty of Europe,
a common cause and many more such expressions, without any
other meaning than to exhaust our wealth, consume the profits
of our trade, and load our posterity with intolerable burdens '.[1]
According to the politicians of this school, the balance of power
had nothing to do with us, so long as we had a superior navy to
guard us from invasion. We were a great commercial nation,
uninterested in conquest ; an expensive Continental policy
could only load our trade with taxes which would disable it from
competing with its nearest rivals.[2] Others would admit that
the balance of power was worth a certain price, but a very low
one. If we were to be the sole paymasters of the alliance against
France, the expense would be intolerable ; it would be less so if
the Dutch would share it with us. This was one of the reasons
why we usually tried to involve the Dutch in our general wars
against France, and why those wars became more onerous and
unpopular when they ceased to take part in them.[3]

Again, the relation of England with her allies, and the argument for interference in Continental politics, must depend on the
way in which the alliance was formed. There was a great difference between entering into a Continental war as principals and
as auxiliaries. For a war which we provoked in the defence of
our own interests, we should have to pay more heavily than for
one in which we conferred a favour by taking part. The government usually argued that we must set up our standard on the
Continent in order that the oppressed enemies of France might
rally to it ; that we must act first, to encourage others.[4] The
Opposition distinguished applying to the other Powers of Europe
from being applied to by them. If we first appealed to them in
the name of the balance of power, they would exploit our necessity ; we should commit ourselves to paying them to look after

25

[1] *Parl. Hist.* xv. 357 (Beckford), 530 (Temple) ; Almon's *Anecdotes of the Earl of
Chatham*, i. 279 (6th edn.).
[2] *Parl. Hist.* xii. 336 (Pulteney), 1161 (Lonsdale).
[3] *Ibid.* 913 (John Philips), 950 (St. Aubyn) ; xiii. 384 (debate on Grenville's
motion), 1052 (Powlett). The Dutch are defended against the aspersion of back-
wardness in *A Letter from a Member of the States-General in Holland to a Member of
Parliament in England* (London, 1743).
[4] *Parl. Hist.* xii. 14ₚ (Cholmondeley), 174 (Walpole), 614 (Winnington), 942 (Yonge) ;
xiii. 178 (Winnington).

their own interests. If they sued to us for help, we could limit our obligations and our expense.[1] Some orators went farther, and suggested with perverse flippancy that we should be justified in provoking quarrels on the Continent when it suited our interest.[2] The English government was far from acting upon such cynical principles, but continued its inept effort to glue the whole of Europe together by subsidies and cant into a coalition against France.

The adversaries of the Continental war founded their argument on a further assumption. The balance of power, they said, could very well look after itself. We were not the only nation to be afraid of France, and when the others came to see their true interests, they would be just as anxious for a Grand Alliance as we were. Instead of interfering in their politics or pressing them for help, we should stand aside and let the course of events bring them to their senses. In this spirit Lee and Vernon argued that we ought not to have stopped the war in 1748 on account of the distress of the Dutch, because if the French had pursued their conquests in Holland any farther, they would have made enemies within the Germanic body, and so the balance would have righted itself.[3] Temple used the same argument in 1755, when he hinted that Hanover could and would be defended against French aggression by the affronted solidarity of the Empire. Mauduit and other writers of this school suggested that, if we left France to make herself thoroughly odious in Germany, we should the sooner be able to raise up a league against her.[4]

They assumed two things. First, that France could never use enough force to overcome the repugnance of Europe to her domination, that the more she exerted herself the stronger the reaction would be. In the second place, they flattered themselves that everybody was afraid of France and nobody had any reason for jealousy or dislike of England.[5] That was because they thought only in terms of territory and political independence ; we desired no possessions on the Continent, therefore we could not be dangerous to any state. They reckoned without the commercial jealousy which France did her best to exploit. If trade is riches and riches are power, then we were the strongest nation in the world. Since our own jingo pamphleteers boasted of it it is no wonder that the French propagandists made the

[1] *Parl. Hist.* xii. 928 (Bance), 1034 (Pitt) ; xiii. 159 (Pitt), 425 (Waller) ; xiv. 159 (Velters Cornwall), 175 (Samuel Martin), 197 (Beckford).
[2] *Ibid.* xv, 345 (Potter), 356 (Beckford), 370 (Egmont).
[3] *Ibid.* xiv. 339 (Lee), 602 (Vernon).
[4] Mauduit, *op. cit.* p. 12 ; the *Monitor* of 6 Sept. and 8 Nov. 1755 ; *Parl. Hist.* xiv. 163 (Velters Cornwall).
[5] The *Monitor* of 22 Nov. 1755.

most of it.[1] The excesses of our privateers, and the official encroachments of our navy upon the rights of neutrals, sharpened this feeling into something like hatred, especially among those maritime peoples whom we least wished to see subject to French influence. It was therefore idle to imagine that Europe, left to itself, would always resist France and court England.

The advocates of Continental measures were not quite content with declaiming about the liberties of Europe, or with assuming that France must be fought wherever we could encounter her. They tried to meet the Opposition on its own ground. They denied that a commercial country like England could be indifferent to the fate of Europe. France was admittedly our rival in trade, and we could only keep our customers by safeguarding their political independence. What if one sole monarch of Europe should force all the nations bordering on the sea to shut their ports to English trade ? This hint of a ' Continental system ' was thrown out by Hardwicke as early as 1738, and was later developed into a stock argument by government pamphleteers.[2] Frenchmen saw the same point ; Silhouette recommended it to the attention of his superiors in 1739, and Choiseul began to execute the scheme in 1762 when he tried to make Portugal exclude English shipping from her ports.[3] Both Pitt and Newcastle saw the danger that France might treat other states in the same way, and shut the whole of Europe against us from Genoa to the Elbe.[4] What would be the value of prizes or American conquests if their produce could not be re-exported abroad ? They would glut the home market and ruin the English producers ; England in fact would ' starve by satiety ' as Napoleon later intended.[5]

The mercantilist assumptions of the age strengthened this argument. If prosperity could only be achieved by a favourable balance of trade, foreign exports were necessary. If England and her overseas possessions became a closed system exchanging goods only within itself, it could not grow any richer.[6] The colonial and maritime party made a feeble attempt to repel this reasoning by pretending that we had an unfavourable balance of trade with those parts of Europe from which France could

27

[1] *Britons Awake, and Look About You, or Ruin the Inevitable Consequence of a Land War, whether Successful or not* (1743), p. 13 ; *Le Politique Danois* (Copenhagen, 1756), pp. 19–52.

[2] *Parl. Hist.* x. 1156 (Hardwicke); xii. 1173 (Hardwicke); xiv. 167 (Fox), 184 (West) ; *The Conduct of the Ministry Impartially Examined* (1760), p. 38.

[3] Silhouette to Amelot, 26 Nov. n.s. 1739, Aff. Étr., Angleterre, 405, fo. 292.

[4] Newcastle to Hardwicke, 15 Nov. 1761, Add. MSS. 32931, fo. 47 ; to Yorke, 8 Jan. 1762, 32933, fo. 113 ; Horace Walpole. *Memoirs of the Reign of George III* (1845), i. 164.

[5] *A Compleat View of the Present Politicks of Great Britain*, p. 65.

[6] *The Important Question Discussed* (1746), pp. 4–6, 13.

exclude us in this way. They were thinking chiefly of Germany, 'from whose Bourne, like that of Death in Shakespeare, no British Guinea ever returned '.[1] That was not true. The trade statistics of the day may not prove very much as to the value of the imports and exports, but they were the only ones that contemporaries had, nor can they be mistaken beyond a certain degree. The figures given by Whitworth appear to show that our exports to Holland never exceeded our imports thence by less than three to one, and that our exports to Germany were worth, on an average, half as much again as our imports. What is more, our exports to Germany usually went up when a German war was at its height.[2] Adam Smith afterwards attributed this to the war itself. Contemporaries offered the same explanation, though in a somewhat crude form ; they suggested that it was due to the enrolment of manufacturers into the French army, which reduced the industrial power of our rivals. Some of them used this as an argument for the Continental war.[3]

The universal domination of Europe by France might have a yet more fatal consequence. Perhaps the English navy was equal to those of France and Spain, though by no means everybody

28

[1] *A Second Letter from Wiltshire to the Monitor, on the Vindication of his Constitutional Principles* (London, 1759), p. 12.

[2] The following abstract is taken from Whitworth's *State of the Trade of Great Britain* (1776). Whitworth's figures were based on the reports laid before Parliament. They are useless as a guide to the value, but are generally held to reflect accurately the rise and fall of the quantity of goods imported and exported in this period :

		Exports to Germany,	*to Holland.*
1731–40 average (peace)	. .	£1,111,174	£1,867,142
1741–8 (war)	. . .	1,519,478	2,390,669
1749–55 (peace)	. . .	1,345,212	1,978,351
1756–62 (war)	. . .	1,616,537	1,764,480

The effect of the figures given for Holland is perplexing ; they do not rise in the second war, except at the very end : from which we might infer that it was a war with Spain which caused the exports of Holland to go up, and that the increase represents goods shipped to Spain by way of Holland. But this impression is contradicted by the fact that the rise does not take place in the first war until 1743, when a war with France was also expected. If therefore it was caused by the cessation of direct trade between England and Spain, we must assume that between 1741 and 1743 France, not Holland, was the intermediary. That is possible, but there may be something in the correspondence between the Dutch and German figures. In Germany, too, it is 1743 which marks the beginning of the great increase ; and again in the Seven Years' war the exports do not rise to great heights until the last two years. The normal trade of Holland with England consisted largely in distributing English goods to Germany and the North. so any alteration in the figures is likely to be due to events in that part of the world.

[3] *Parl. Hist.* xiii. 128 (Carteret), 316 (Bathurst). The author of the plan for carrying on the war, printed in Almon's *Anecdotes of the Earl of Chatham*, i. 300, says that ' in England, the manufactures, more especially the woollen, sell at higher rates when at war with France, than in times of peace ', and Kinnoull found in 1759 that the Yorkshire woollen manufactures were doing so well during the war that they might be inclined to captious criticism of the terms of peace (Kinnoull to Newcastle, 28 July, 1759, Add. MS. 32893, fo. 331).

admitted this ; Admiral Norris, for example, did not.[1] It
could not be a match for those of the lesser Powers as well,
Holland, Denmark, Portugal, and perhaps Sweden. If France
held undisputed control of Europe by land, she would be able
to make herself equal to us at sea by this method.[2] The failure
of Choiseul's Family Compact discovered a weakness in the
argument. If France meant to press into her service the navies
of the smaller Powers, she must do so before her own was ruined ;
that of Spain was of little help to her in 1762, because her own
had ceased to exist. But the reason why the colonial and maritime party in England proposed to abstain from interference on
the Continent, was that they might destroy the French navy
first of all. It would, therefore, be a race between the French
domination of the land and the English domination of the sea.
The calculation of the colonial party in England assumed that
the second must happen at least as soon as the first.

29

The amateur strategists of England had to take one thing
more into account. England or Ireland might be invaded.
This was a favourite plan of the French government, but the
English colonial and naval party denied that it could be executed ;
so long as we were superior at sea to France and Spain, it was
logically impossib e.[3] The advocates of Continental measures
replied that, if France dominated all Europe, we should not long
remain superior to the fleet which she could bring together ;
moreover, command of the sea is always uncertain, especially in
the Channel, where the same wind would in some circumstances
blow the French forces towards our coasts while it held our own
fleet in port. There might be no genuine instances of this, for
the Armada was dispersed by a storm, King William III was
not properly resisted, and Monmouth had landed almost like
a smuggler without fleet or army ; but it could still happen. A
momentary loss of command or lapse of vigilance would give the
enemy his chance ; perhaps his flat-bottomed boats might cross
the strait under cover of a single night.[4]

This was not a great danger, considered in the light of strategy
alone. Our fleet could never be blown off its station long enough
to let a great invasion through ; and what harm could a small
one do ? Here politics entered into the question. If Englishmen had been united and loyal, ten thousand Frenchmen landed
in England could have done nothing but get themselves taken
prisoners ; but there was disaffection and Jacobitism in Scotland

---

[1] Norris' diary, 22 Sept. 1740, Add. MS. 28133, fo. 60.
[2] Newcastle, notes for a speech, Add. MS. 32996, fos. 315 *seqq.* ; *Parl. Hist.* xiv.
686 (Henry Pelham) ; xv. 629 (Chesterfield).
[3] *Ibid.* xiii. 502 (Strange) ; *The Present Ruinous Land-War Proved to be a H——r
War*, p. 18.
[4] *Parl. Hist.* xi. 1027 (Hardwicke), 1028 (Abingdon).

and the south-west, however the Opposition leaders might pooh-pooh it.[1] Walpole was really afraid of it, and the panic of 1745 justified him. There was, therefore, some colour for the opinion that though a great invasion could not take place and a small one could not succeed by itself, it was the duty of the government to see that nothing of the sort was even tried.[2]

After the collapse of Jacobitism, this might have ceased to be true, but another argument took its place. English ministers as well as French were impressed by the delicate and fragile structure of our credit and finance. A small invasion might bring it to the ground by a Stock Exchange scare, and paralyse the whole machine. Even Pitt admitted this. ' Paper credit ', he said, ' may be invaded in Kent ' ; he described ' the consternation that would spread through the City, when the noble, artificial, yet vulnerable fabric of public credit should crumble in their hands.' This fine piece of mischievous rhetoric, with its ' striking and masterly picture of a French invasion reaching London ',[3] probably conduced as much as anything else to the panic which inspired Newcastle to so many mistakes.

Panic was the real danger, and the real remedy a tonic for the nerves. The militia was such a tonic. Its value in the field might be doubtful, but it reassured the propertied classes of England by making them proud of themselves, and alone accounts for the vast difference between the invasion scares of 1756 and 1759.[4] The militia had always been popular with the Opposition leaders. They represented it as a safeguard of British liberty which would make the unpopular standing army and the policy of the balance of power alike unnecessary. Nevertheless the ministers of the old school continued to believe that the best way to stop France from invading us was to raise up trouble for her in Europe.

The advocates of Continental measures made little impression on the public rage for a maritime war. This can hardly be accounted for but by prejudice and rant. The appeal to the demonstrable necessity of European trade ought to have had some weight ; but public opinion suffered from a curious blindness on this subject. Many orators and pamphleteers seemed to think we could live by American trade alone. As Hervey complained in the house of lords, the Opposition talked as if ' there is not a shilling comes to us by our trade with any quarter of the world but with America '.[5] Bedford spoke of it in 1739

[1] *Parl. Hist.* xii. 614 (Winnington), 621 (Carew).
[2] *Ibid.* xi. 650 (Newcastle), 944 (Pulteney) ; xii. 911 (Yonge).
[3] Walpole, *Memoirs of George II* (1846), ii. 87.
[4] A difference which Pitt belittled out of consideration for his colleagues, but cannot have failed to have seen (West, House of Commons report, 13 Nov. 1759, Add. MS. 32898, fo. 223).
[5] *Parl. Hist.* x. 785.

as 'almost the only profitable trade which this nation enjoys, unrivalled by others', a curious opinion from the man who thought in 1762 that we were in danger of over-colonizing. Even Hardwicke, who had no motive for exaggerating in this respect, once said that the North American colonies alone 'constitute one-half, at least, of the trade of this Kingdom'.[1] That was nonsense. In 1760, when the exports to the colonies reached an unprecedented figure, they were still hardly more than a quarter of the whole export trade ; the colonial imports bore a somewhat higher proportion, but even when the West Indian figures were included, they did not approach a half.[2]

It is difficult to see why the colonial trade was valued so much beyond its real importance. The chief ostensible reason was, that it was the only one for which we need not depend on the good graces of foreign governments ; the only one which, in a mercantilist age, we could not lose to foreigners. Particular colonies were prized for particular merits, military or economic : the West Indies for the re-exports of their produce which had once swelled the favourable balance of trade ; the northern colonies for their large population able to bear arms in American expeditions ; the fisheries for the training of seamen. Colonies were also a profitable and perhaps a safe field for the investment of capital. All this barely explains why the colonial trade should have been regarded as the one certain salvation of the country in spite of its insignificant proportion to the whole overseas commerce. This exaggeration led the nation to sacrifice other trades to its security in the war of Jenkins' Ear. Not only was the interruption of the trade to Old Spain—so far as it really was interrupted—borne for this sake, but the losses of English shipping in the war seem to have fallen very severely on the European trades in general.[3]

31

[1] *Parl. Hist.* x. 1040 ; Hardwicke to Joseph Yorke, 5 Jan. 1758, Add. MS. 35357, fo. 223.

[2] Whitworth's figures. Malvezin gives in his *Histoire du Commerce de Bordeaux* (iii. 322–3) some interesting statistics which bear on the proportion of the colonial trades to other foreign trades in France. I do not know from what authority he took them, nor whether they include overland trade in 'Europe' ; but they show the comparative insignificance of the colonies. Even if the East India trade is included, the trade of the French dependencies does not seem to have exceeded a third of the total imports or a fifth of the total exports in any of the periods for which he gives averages, before 1763–76.

[3] The figures given by the *Gentleman's Magazine* (xi. 689, xiii. 23) are bad, but I know of none better :

In 1739	9 ships were taken in the American trades, 33 in others.					
In 1740	34	„	„	„	„	85 „
In 1741	108	„	„	„	„	63 „
In 1742	75	„	„	„	„	67 „

These figures are probably too low for the shipping of the American colonies, from which full and reliable information was not so likely to be had as from Europe ; but for some time, while Vernon was in the West Indies, the losses there were very slight.

England had other reasons for concerning herself with the Continent, besides the fetish of the balance of power. There were certain parts of Europe in whose security we were supposed to have a special economic or strategic interest. These were Portugal, the Netherlands, and, some said, Hanover. Portugal was valued chiefly as the European terminus of the considerable trade which we carried on with Brazil, and through its dependency of Nova Colonia, with Buenos Ayres and Chile. Since this trade brought in gold, it was particularly valuable during a German war which was supposed to cause an export of bullion to the Continent.[1] For this reason one of the favourite schemes of France for putting military or diplomatic pressure on us was a threat to Portugal. It was not executed during the war of 1739. In the next war it could not be done by France alone ; but when Spain took her part in 1762, one of the most important points of Choiseul's strategy was the invasion of Portugal. He also intended an expedition against Brazil, which might have the same effect upon the trade and revenues of England that an attack on the Spanish West Indies had on France : to dry up the sources of our wealth. This last scheme was never executed, because it was only designed a few weeks before the preliminaries of peace were signed.

Portugal only appeared upon the scene in the last year ; but the problem of the Low Countries was a chronic one. From the days of Edward III to the German invasion of Belgium, the Low Countries have always been of the first importance to the military and naval security of England, and for a long time they also harboured her chief commercial rivals in North-Western Europe. It has always been a maxim of her policy to prevent the nation of whom she is most afraid from possessing them ; it was particularly so at this period, when their defence was supposed to be ensured against France by the Austrian alliance and the Dutch barrier fortresses. The sovereignty of most of Belgium was meant to bind Austria closer to England, but had

It should also be remembered that the average size and value of American shipping was small; only the ships which traded from Europe to America would be worth as much as those in the European trades. A deputation which professed to represent the merchants of London, but consisted almost entirely of West Indians, told the Admiralty in April 1747 that 1212 English ships had been lost in the French war, of which 800 were in the plantation trades (Adm. 3/57, minute of 14 April). Only 311 prizes, worth 11,128,676 livres, or about £500,000, were brought into Martinique, which was the chief port for privateering in the French colonies (Archives Nationales, Colonies, C 8, B 21). Not many prizes can have been taken into the other colonies, but as the ships bound to and from the colonies were oftenest taken in the Channel, 800 is not an incredible figure. Yet the proportion of two ships lost in the plantation trades for every one in all others differs very materially from the figures of the *Gentleman's Magazine*, and is not in itself very probable.

[1] Hardwicke to Newcastle, 1 April 1762, Add. MS. 32936, fo. 261.

rather the reverse effect.[1] Both England and Holland had their
commercial difficulties with the Austrian Netherlands, and the
political relations which arose out of the Barrier Treaty were
not much more satisfactory. The gratitude of Austria was very
much attenuated when she ceased to be interested in Western
Europe. She showed this by her secret treaty with France in
1757, when she promised to give up Ostend and Nieuport to
Louis XV if he would help her to recover possession of Silesia.
Even while the gratuitous interference of France in German
affairs kept Maria Theresa loyal to our alliance, she brought
difficulties on us by her inability to defend the Netherlands
against the French armies, so that we had to ransom them for
her by restoring Cape Breton at the Treaty of Aix-la-Chapelle.

33

The Dutch, too, were at least as much a liability as an asset.
Perhaps the English ministry had not realized their financial and
military weakness, and their political timidity, when it spent all
its efforts to drag them into the war of the Austrian Succession.
Even then, there were people in England who doubted the
wisdom of it ; the participation of the Dutch would draw on
them an invasion from France, and the war would become a land
war in the most dangerous part of Europe.[2] This caution was
lost on the ministers, especially the Pelhams, who overthrew
Carteret in 1744 because they would not carry on the Continental
war unless the Dutch joined in it.[3] Fortunately, they could not
execute their plan quickly, because it took years to persuade
the Dutch to any active measure ; meanwhile the French carried
the war into Flanders and reduced the barrier fortresses. The
Opposition made this an excuse for coming to terms with the
Pelhams. They might not have approved the way in which the
war had been begun, but since it was now being waged for the
Dutch barrier they could justify themselves to their constituents
as fighting for a real English interest :[4] a significant incident,
which shows how popular was the distinction between general
and local interference on the Continent.

[1] Chesterfield prophesied that it would do no good ; see his letter to Newcastle,
6 Dec. 1745 (Dobree's edition, no. 896).

[2] Hop to Fagel, 25 Oct. 1740, State Papers, 107/46. Long afterwards, Pitt blamed
Carteret's efforts to force the Dutch to enter the war, and Halifax said in 1755 that
he hoped the government would not press them to take any step which would involve
them in a land war, for then we should have to contribute more to their defence than
they could possibly do to ours (*Parl. Hist.* xv. 638).

[3] See the document of 1 Nov. 1744, printed by P. C. Yorke, *Life of Lord Chancellor
Hardwicke*, i. 333.

[4] *Parl. Hist.* xiii. 1055 (Pitt), 1056 (Barrington), 1250 (the abstract of the 'new
courtiers'' argument). The Dutch barrier fortresses were not situated in Dutch
territory, but in the Austrian Netherlands. Hence it came about that the French
reduced them two or three years before they began to threaten the frontiers of the Dutch
Republic itself.

This might be a political success for the Pelhams, but it was a military disaster. The war went from bad to worse in Flanders, and the crowning misfortune was the co-operation of the Dutch, which came about gradually in 1747 and gave the French army an excuse for invading them. It was their bankruptcy and their military failure which forced Newcastle to put an end to the war at once.[1] So far from bringing us any strength, the Dutch alliance nearly proved our Achilles' heel. The English government ought to have known it long before ; indeed, Chesterfield, who had been ambassador at The Hague, did know it, and thought a permanent neutrality of the Austrian Netherlands the best thing that could happen.[2]

34   Many people thought that this fiasco had furnished a conclusive argument against any dependence on Continental allies ; but it did not even cure Newcastle of his passion for the Dutch. There was a moment when he desired in good faith the succour of six thousand men which we required of the States-General in the spring of 1756, though the ministry as a whole had ulterior motives and would have been embarrassed if the demand had been complied with.[3] Not only did Newcastle continue to hope intermittently that the Dutch would take an active part·in the Seven Years' war ; the English Government, the English minister at The Hague, and the English party in Holland did their best to promote, with inept and hide-bound devotion to tradition, an increase of the Dutch army which was not only likely but designed to embroil the States-General with France. How much wiser was Pitt when he said he would rather feed the war in Germany than have it carried into Flanders.[4] When Pitt's influence was removed, Bute and Newcastle tried in 1762 to revive the phantom of Dutch participation. It was all of a piece with Bute's plan of a Continental war contracted to the defence of our immediate interests in Europe ; but for Newcastle it was a consequence of the Family Compact, and of his belief that all the powers of Europe could be united against the House of Bourbon because the House of Bourbon would at once dictate with theatrical haughtiness to all the Powers of Europe.[5]

[1] Lodge, *Studies in Eighteenth Century Diplomacy*, c. vii.

[2] Chesterfield to Newcastle, 24 Oct. and 6 Dec. 1745, 20 March 1746, Dobree's edition, nos. 881, 896, 923 ; to Trevor, 20 May 1746, no. 934 ; to Dayrolles, 17 July and 2 Oct. 1747, nos. 1304, 1408 ; *An Apology for a Late Resignation* (1748), pp. 5 seqq.

[3] Newcastle to Yorke, 10 Feb. 1756, Add. MS. 32862, fo. 430 ; Walpole, *Memoirs of George II*, ii. 184.

[4] Walpole, *op. cit.* iii. 18.

[5] The suggestion that the States-General should be roused by jealousy of the Family Compact to resist the House of Bourbon is in the first draft of Bute's dispatch of 12 Jan. 1762 to Yorke (Add. MS. 32933, fo. 82). It was, therefore, probably his own   Newcastle's contribution was the fatal hint of treating Austria in the same

The most vexed question of all was Hanover, with which England had no connexion but their common sovereign. I have distinguished Hanover politics from true Continental politics, because they sometimes had different effects. In the early days of the war of the Austrian Succession, the Opposition tried to prove that the measures which were meant to be taken for the defence of Maria Theresa were warped by the sinister influence of Hanover. The most conspicuous example is the convention of neutrality in 1741, which certainly rendered Hanover itself useless to Maria Theresa.[1] George II was afterwards accused of withdrawing for the defence of Hanover the troops which were to have been sent to Austria ; of precipitating a war in Flanders for the sake of an excuse to hire Hanover troops ; of advising Maria Theresa, against her real interest, to continue the struggle against Frederick, in order that he might have an excuse for acquiring Prussian territory for Hanover.[2] Some of these accusations were true, others tortuous and absurd.

35

The difference between the Hanover and Continental policies was apparently more obvious than ever at the opening of the Seven Years' war. The hope of a grand alliance against France had entirely vanished, because we found we could expect no help from Maria Theresa or the Dutch Republic. Newcastle had, therefore, to abandon Continental measures for the time being, and declare for a purely naval and colonial war.[3] Nevertheless, as the king's minister he was forced to provide something for the defence of Hanover. He therefore encouraged George II to conclude and renew subsidy treaties for its protection. He thought it unfair that he should be attacked for incurring a Continental war when he had taken particular pains to avoid it, and justified what he had done as a mere Hanover policy.[4] The justification was worse than the offence. There might be

way, and the idea that the commercial jealousy of the Dutch could be excited against the clauses in the Compact which dealt with exclusive privileges in trade (Newcastle to Yorke, 8 Jan., Add. MS. 32933, fo. 113). Newcastle had noticed in November that Bute was especially struck by the question, what would become of Holland if we abandoned the Continent (Newcastle to Hardwicke, 15 Nov. 1761, Add. MS. 32931, fo. 47).

[1] *Parl. Hist.* xii. 255 (Carteret), 269 (Argyll), 285 (Bathurst); see Professor Vaucher's account of the Neutrality, *op. cit.* pp. 394–407.

[2] *Parl. Hist.* xii. 870 (Barnard), 925 (Bance), 956 (Waller), 997 (Quarendon) ; xiii. 157 (Pitt), 193 (Lyttelton) ; *A Vindication of a late Pamphlet, intitled, The Case of the Hanover Troops* (1743), p. 51 ; *A Letter from a Member of the States-General in Holland to a Member of Parliament in England* (1743), passim ; *The Present Ruinous Land-War Proved to be a H——r War* (1745), pp. 32 seqq.

[3] Newcastle to Holdernesse, 2, 11 and 18 July 1755, Add. MS. 32856, fo. 448, 32857, fos. 1, 183 ; Holdernesse to Newcastle, 30 July, Add. MS. 32857, fo. 446 ; Newcastle to W. Bentinck, 16 Oct., Add. MS. 32860, fo. 64 ; Bentinck's reply, 31 Oct. fo. 256.

[4] Newcastle to Hardwicke, 3 Sept., Add. MS. 32858, fo. 413 ; to Hartington, 20 Sept., Add. MS. 32859, fo. 160 ; his notes for a speech, ? Nov. 1755, Add. MS. 32996, fos. 315 seqq.

something to be said, as Pitt afterwards admitted, for a scheme which united against France some of the greater Powers of Europe ; there was no excuse for amassing a heterogeneous German force for the protection of Hanover.

Moreover, this particular way of distinguishing Hanover and Continental measures was unreal. The ambitions of the electorate might traverse the proper conduct of a Continental scheme, but Hanover could not be defended without involving Germany in the war. This was an aggravation of Newcastle's crime in the eyes of his enemies, but in the end it saved his policy from failure. He came to terms with Prussia in order that she might keep her own hands off Hanover and discourage France from entering the Empire to attack it. This stroke cost him, it is true, the tepid and useless friendship of Maria Theresa, also that of Russia ; but it gave England a better ally, with whose help an impracticable defence of Hanover was turned into a glorious Continental war.

No doubt there was a great deal of factious noise in the perpetual clamour against Hanover. Perhaps the majority of English people had not actively desired the accession of George I ; and the Whig schisms in the reign of Walpole had created a new Opposition which was willing to strike at the minister through the king. All the ministers of George II—Walpole, Carteret, and even Newcastle—depended on his favour much more than constitutional historians have usually admitted. They were sometimes forced to purchase their influence by improper compliances with his passion for his electorate, and thus to give frequent occasions to the criticism of unreconciled enemies and dissident friends of the dynasty. The former could only express their animosity against the king, and the latter could best create embarrassments for the ministers, by harping on the sinister influence of Hanover upon English policy.

There were also genuine reasons why the connexion of England with Hanover was a misfortune for both parties to it. The Act of Settlement laid it down that England should undertake no war for Hanoverian objects ; but it did not provide for the case of an attack made upon Hanover by the enemies of England for no other reason than the identity of king and elector. Yet this was what happened in 1741 and 1756. There might be some colour for it the first time, for it was the king of England's interference in German politics that provoked Maillebois' invasion ; but in the Seven Years' war, France proposed to attack Hanover solely in order to avenge herself for England's aggressions at sea and in America. It was easy to say that the elector of Hanover ought not to pay for the king of England ; [1] but

<hr/>

[1] The expression used by George II (Bussy to Amelot, 6 Sept. 1741, in Flassan, *Diplomatie Française*, 2nd edition, 1811, v. 134).

what was the elector of Hanover to do ? If he concluded a neutrality for his German dominions, as he did in 1741, he incurred great unpopularity among his English subjects and was accused of betraying their allies on the Continent. Yet he could not defend himself against the whole power of France, with his own soldiers or those he could hire out of his electoral revenues ; and if he used the money and diplomacy of England for these purposes, he involved her in the Continental measures which it might be her interest to avoid.

The disadvantage to England was even greater. Either she must allow herself to be drawn into that full system of Continental alliances which some believed to be the inevitable consequence of any step taken for the protection of Hanover, or she must try to defend it by herself. That was almost as difficult, expensive, and elaborate a task as a general war on the Continent, for Hanover had no natural frontiers.[1] Thus whatever form the defence of Hanover might take, it must deprive England of all the military and diplomatic advantages of an island. This was particularly resented as a grievance in 1755, when we were beginning a war with France which had nothing whatever to do with the Continent, and was not meant to be fought there. If England was to be reduced to terms, or involved in a general European war, on such an occasion as this, by the pressure of France upon Hanover, there would never be a time, so long as the connexion of the kingdom and the electorate subsisted, when we could pursue unhampered our real interests in a maritime and colonial war.[2]

Pitt, Temple, and Bedford proposed to cut the knot by abandoning Hanover to its fate during the war, and procuring compensation for it at a peace. Perhaps they would purchase its recovery by restoring to France some colonial conquests ; perhaps they would give it a money indemnity out of the revenues of England.[3] Shrewder observers foresaw that the reluctance to sacrifice English interests to Hanover would only be postponed, not overcome by this method ; the statesmen who would not defend Hanover at England's expense, would hardly give

37

[1] Holdernesse believed that 'defending Hanover only will be attended with very great difficulty and perhaps with as much expense as a more extended and more useful plan ' (Holdernesse to Newcastle, 30 July, 1755, Add. MS. 32857, fo. 446), and Pitt dismissed the idea of doing so as laughable. The military weakness of Hanover was one of the stock themes of the Opposition (Walpole, *Memoirs of George II*, ii. 60).

[2] *Britons Awake, and Look About You*, p. 46 ; *Parl. Hist.* xv. 533 (Temple's protest), 640 (Halifax) ; Walpole, *op. cit.* ii. 51 (Dodington). Even the defenders of Newcastle's policy had to admit that Hanover ' took off from our insularity '.

[3] *Parl. Hist.* xv. 530 (Temple) ; Hardwicke to Newcastle, 9 Aug. 1755, Add. MS. 32858, fo. 76 ; Potter to Temple, 5 Oct. 1755, *Grenville Papers* (ed. W. J. Smith), i. 146 ; see Dodington's plan of ' leaving Hanover in deposit ', in his letter to Bute of 16 Jan. 1761 (Adolphus, *History of England*, i. 548).

up the colonial acquisitions on which they had set their hearts, in order to buy back the hated electorate. This prophecy was right ; for Pitt, who in 1755 would compensate Hanover but would not defend it, declared in 1761 that he would defend it but would never hear of compensation for it if it were lost or damaged.[1] Newcastle was always afraid of the political dilemma with which the government would have to deal, if Hanover should be conquered ; but the French never had very much hold on it at any time after 1758. There was, therefore, no question of ransoming it. George II, however, wanted more ; he expected some territorial compensation for such inconvenience as Hanover had suffered in the war. That both Pitt and Newcastle vowed he never should have ; but this ambition had the effect of attaching him to the party which would rather continue to conquer the French colonies than make peace. He appears to have seen that he would never get anything for Hanover until England could afford to be generous. He was probably mistaken in thinking that she would in any circumstances make a present to Hanover ; but his illusion had the effect of ranging him, for a time, on the side of Pitt against Newcastle.[2] In the end, this difficulty proved unimportant. At the beginning of George III's reign, Hanover ceased to have any influence on English policy. The king and his confidants ostentatiously proclaimed their indifference to it, and had it been in danger during the last year of the war they might have indecently sacrificed it to their popularity.

The antithesis of America and the Continent was not only expressed in discussion of the legitimate objects of war ; it came out also in a similar controversy over the strategy. For example, nobody could dispute that the origin and motive of the Seven Years' war was commercial and colonial rivalry ; but that did not conclude the question, how it was to be conducted, and whether a diversion on the Continent was good or bad policy. The parties to the debate were the same as in the other, but the arguments were different.

The upholders of the American war began with the truism that the military and naval efforts of the country should be directed to their real object, instead of pursuing it by the roundabout way of a war elsewhere.[3] The war had been begun in North

[1] *A Full and Candid Answer to a Pamphlet entitled, Considerations upon the Present German War* (1761), p. 33 ; Newcastle's memorandum of 10 April 1761, Add. MS. 32921, fo. 381.

[2] Newcastle to Hardwicke, 17 Sept. and 19 Oct. 1758, Add. MSS. 32884, fos. 33, 436 ; Hardwicke to Newcastle, 22 Oct., 32885, fo. 38 ; Devonshire to Newcastle, 10 July 1759, 32892, fo. 500 ; Newcastle to Stone, 1 Aug., 32893, fo. 406 ; to Hardwicke, 31 Aug. and 19 Sept., 32895, fos. 83, 490 ; 31 Oct., 32897, fos. 513–15 ; 16 Nov., 32898, fo. 285.

[3] Walpole, *Memoirs of George II*, ii. 56 (Pitt) ; the *Monitor*, 6 Dec. 1755.

America, and its real design, so far as the Government could be
said to have one, was to drive the French from certain disputed
territories there and in the West Indies. Indeed, public opinion,
which was more conscious and explicit on this subject than the
ministers who conducted the war in its first stages, intended
nothing less than the expulsion of the French from all North
America. What more natural than to concentrate the attack
there ? Indeed, how else could the object be achieved ? If the
German war was a diversion, as some of its supporters claimed,
it was a diversion chosen and started by France to distract us
from the objects in which we were interested and the kind of
warfare in which we were at home.[1] So far as the war had a
diffused secondary object, it was the destruction of French
trade ; this, too, could only succeed if it was pursued directly.

A Continental war could only be undertaken by the dis-
trusted and despised army, unpopular outside the circles of the
Court ; a maritime and colonial war was to be preferred because
we were in our element and the French were out of theirs.[2] So
at least the argument went ; but there was some doubt of its
truth. By no means all the English successes of the Seven
Years' war were achieved in America ; by no means all the
failures in Europe. Even an American war could not be fought
by sailors alone. The long series of military defeats in its earlier
years proved that regular soldiers were not at all at home in the
backwoods ; nor were the efforts of the colonists proportionate
to a population twenty times as large as that of Canada. The
English navy was more numerous than the French, and far more
money was spent on it ; but it is doubtful if it had much other
advantage. If the commanders of French squadrons—d'Antin,
Bompar, Du Gué Lambert, and Blénac—lacked enterprise and
moral courage, one could find English parallels such as Lee and
Cornelius Mitchell ; and was there ever a more celebrated case
than that of Byng ? The French captains showed as much address
and gallantry as the English, in the presence of equal or superior
forces. Newcastle was reduced to despair by the punctual and
neatly concerted movements by which, so long as Machault was
in charge of the Marine, inferior French squadrons got out of port,
crossed the Atlantic, joined and reinforced each other, relieved
and protected their colonies, and slipped home without interruption. It was a type of war for which Newcastle was unfit,
and he had not made a fair trial of it ; but he had a little justification when he complained that our boasted superiority at sea
did not offer any certain means of bringing the enemy to instant

39

[1] *Considerations on the Present German War*, pp. 2, 32, 116.
[2] *Parl. Hist.* xii. 913 (John Philips) ; xiii. 233 (Waller) ; xiv. 601 (Vernon) ; xv.
355 (Beckford).

submission or preventing him from transferring his superiority on land from Europe to America.[1]

The advocates of a Continental war argued that nothing but neglect of her army for her navy could prevent France from becoming equal to us at sea, as she had been in King William's war. Complete freedom from all danger on the Continent would enable her to do so in a few years.[2] This was to assume that military and naval power were interchangeable at will. However, there was at least this much truth in the suggestion : the starvation of the French navy for the sake of the army was one of the greatest causes of our naval victories.

40

In the spring of 1760 a crisis arose which illustrates the competition between army and navy for the resources of France. Berryer, minister of Marine, wanted to relieve Martinique from the danger of an English attack. He had already demanded in December 1759 an appropriation of 40 million livres for this and other services, but though his projects had been approved, they had not been executed for want of the money. If the English had attempted the island in the winter campaigning season, it had nothing but its own resources to defend it. The budget of the Marine had now been reduced to 30 millions, out of which 21 had to be deducted for the ordinary expenses of the colonies, for stores sent to Canada, for old debts, and for some articles which had nothing to do with the Marine. That left only 9 million livres, or half a million sterling, for the ordinary expenses of the navy. This was a very small sum compared with the £3,640,000 voted for the English sea service in the same year (and that did not include the payment on the navy debt and the ' Ordinary of the navy ', which amounted to nearly a million and a quarter more). Berryer laid the deplorable case before his fellow-ministers. Martinique was one of the most important colonies ; it was the military and commercial capital of the Windward Islands, and its fall would be a serious blow to the prestige of France. There could be no two opinions about the necessity of saving it ; but how could that be done ?

The ordinary peace-time budget of the Marine had been so inadequate between 1748 and 1755 that it did not enable the Marine to pay off the debt of 30 millions contracted in the preceding war, which therefore still subsisted. The necessary supplies could not be bought for readiness at the outbreak of the

---

[1] Newcastle to Hardwicke, 4 Oct. 1755, Add. MS. 32859, fo. 361. Newcastle even seems to have been frightened by the ' immense ' French fleet (see his letters to Hardwicke, 28 Dec. 1755, Add. MS. 32861, fo. 487, and to Devonshire, 2 Jan. 1756, Add. MS. 32862, fo. 6). See also the speeches of his supporters, *Parl. Hist.* xv. 340 (Conway), 362 (Horace Walpole).

[2] *Ibid.* xii. 909 (Yonge), 974 (Horace Walpole) ; xiii. 409 (Murray) ; xv. 362 (Horace Walpole), 369 (Egmont).

Seven Years' war, with the result that heavier expenses had to be incurred after it began. Nothing was ever ready in time, or up to the standard necessary for success. Stores were bought too cheap, insufficient labour employed at the arsenals, new constructions prevented, old ones suspended, repairs badly done ; the marines reduced, departments closed, officials turned off, pensions denied. Some said the Marine should try to pay for current operations and let the old debts look after themselves ; but this was impossible, for arrears of pay could not be kept up indefinitely. Berryer finished this jeremiad with some general remarks :

> We must not flatter ourselves that a navy which has been long neglected and in the greatest disorder can resist, with very inadequate resources, one which has been manned, armed and supplied long beforehand, and has besides 150 million livres a year spent on it to keep it in commission ; and since the occasion offers, I will add that we do not go the right way about it. We make plans, and only then do we fit out the fleets ; it seems to me that, on the contrary, we ought to have the fleet ready and then make the plans. Besides, we ought to be sure of our ways and means before we get the fleets ready at all. To explain more precisely, I believe that France will never succeed in making war with advantage, or even on an equality, against a maritime power such as England, unless the French navy is in commission all the year round like the English ; without that, all plans and expeditions are liable to fail. The reason is obvious ; for when the French navy wants to make an expedition it is forced to let the world know it four or five months in advance ; the English soon hear of it, and are in a condition to prevent it by blockading the ports, and in fact to frustrate any measures that may be taken, while in the period for which the French fleet is out of commission, the English fleets, convoys and coasting trade sail safely by without being molested.[1]

41

This lamentable deduction of the consequences of insolvency is perhaps exaggerated, for Berryer was aware of his own insufficiency and made the worst of his task. His paper was communicated to three soldiers—Belleisle, Soubise, d'Etrées—and to Puysieulx, the minister of finance. Only Puysieulx was wholly in favour of the expedition to Martinique, and offered to provide the necessary 12 million livres by cutting the expenses of other departments. He said

> I do not know of any real enemies of France except the English. Because they are fortunate and have got the upper hand of us, are we to abandon everything to them ? Is it not humiliating to think that the loss of Martinique will transfer to them a trade worth 70 million livres, or two-thirds of the interest of their national debt ?

The three soldiers acknowledged the importance of Martinique, and wished something might be done to save it ; Soubise con-

---

[1] Office *mémoire* of 3 March 1760 ; *Mémoire* of Berryer for the *Conseil du Roy*, 6 March 1760, Archives Nationales, Colonies, C 8, B 10

curred half-heartedly with Puysieulx, but Belleisle and d'Etrées were prepared to content themselves with some half-measure. One of them suggested equipping some vessels at Brest for six months, in the hope that they might be able to cruise in the Channel for the protection of the coasts and trade, or even that their existence might intimidate the English into keeping a large force at home. Failing that, something might be done with the famous flat-bottomed boats, which had terrified Newcastle out of his senses the year before but were now powerless, since the calamitous defeat of the French navy at Quiberon, to effect a really formidable invasion. Belleisle, the minister of war, pointed out that his departmental estimate for this year had originally been 190 million livres. He had reduced it to 145 millions, by retarding certain payments, and the Contrôleur Général had slashed it down again to 120 millions. Farther he would not go, and if the Marine could not relieve Martinique without encroaching upon the finances of the army, it must content itself with something less. The expedition did not sail.[1]

This controversy would have delighted and justified the English advocates of a Continental war ; for it was obvious that the decrepitude of the French navy was chiefly caused by want of money. Want of spirit too, perhaps ; for when Choiseul succeeded the doleful and frugal Berryer, the naval affairs of France took a brisker turn, in spite of the difficulties to which Berryer called attention.[2] Yet even Choiseul could not raise the Marine at once from the debility to which years of starvation had reduced it. Besides, the suspension of payments on the French government's bills of exchange from the Colonies gave the Continental politicians of England an argument against their adversaries. When the latter asserted that the Continental diversion made no real impression on France, the former replied that she had already defaulted.[3]

England was never reduced to such an alternative between her army and her navy ; but the land and sea wars competed for her resources as they did for those of France. A maritime war was believed to be cheaper to us than any other. It could be pursued for many years without straining public credit. The financial dangers of a Continental war were demonstrated by the

[1] Replies of d'Etrées, 16 March 1760 ; of Puysieulx, 17 March ; of Soubise, 22 March ; of Belleisle, 26 March (ibid.).

[2] Choiseul succeeded in sending Blénac off to the West Indies, but could not get d'Aubigny out of Rochefort to follow him. Ternay took St. John's, Newfoundland, but it was soon recaptured. Choiseul's schemes for 1762 are to be found in the Plan de campagne par mer pour l'Année 1762, Archives Nat., Marine, B 4, 104, and in his dispatch to Ossun of 5 April 1762 (Aff. Étr., Espagne, 536).

[3] A Full and Candid Answer to a Pamphlet entitled, Considerations upon the Present German War (1761), p. 11 ; The Conduct of the Ministry Impartially Examined (1760), p. 44.

crisis of 1748, when the subscribers to the loan had the greatest
difficulty in paying their instalments and might never have
succeeded in completing them if peace had not intervened.[1]
This would have realized a danger which the Opposition always
prophesied, namely that we should spend so much on an in-
conclusive effort upon the Continent as to disable ourselves from
carrying on our own war at sea.[2]   Various amateurish calculations
were made, which showed that, while the respective costs of
keeping up an English and a French warship were roughly the
same, an English soldier in Germany was twice as expensive as
a French one.   This belief that we got better value for money in
a naval war was heightened by the hard bargaining, not to say
exorbitance, of our subsidized allies, among them the king himself as elector of Hanover.   It created the legend of 'the German Gulph, which cries "give, give", and is never satisfied '.[3]
Another considerable argument was the drain of bullion for the
upkeep of armies in Germany.   A naval war spent money at home,
and even brought some into the country by prizes ; our expenditure in our own colonies only increased their power of purchasing
English goods.[4]

Mercantile considerations like these appealed no doubt to a
nation of shopkeepers ; but the adversaries of the Continental
war were on still stronger ground when they asserted, like Legge,
that ' no nation can afford a greater quantity of war of any species,
than it is able to pay for, and that if we add greatly to our expenses at one end of the scale and are not able to abate at the
other, we shall soon be bankrupt '.[5]   The politicians who conducted
the Seven Years' war were haunted by the fear of a necessary
option to be made between its two branches, and this financial
danger enabled each party in the ministerial coalition to denounce
the expensiveness of measures which it disliked for other reasons.

It was impossible to come to any agreement about the financial aspect of the struggle between England and France.   There
was none as to the premises, which were founded upon ignorance
and guesswork on both sides.   The question was, which country
had the greater resources, and how would they be affected by

43

---

[1] This was used as an argument to justify the peace in 1748 (*Parl. Hist.* xv. 331
(Murray)), but was later turned by Temple and others against the Continental policy
(*Parl. Hist.* xv. 621).   In fact, the movements of the stocks were striking.   The
3 per cents. fell from 86¾ in April 1747, when there was a hope of a peace, to 74 in
March 1748, just before the conferences began ; by the end of April they had risen
to 86¼ and in June, after the preliminaries were signed, to 92¼.
[2] *Parl. Hist.* xiii. 425 (Waller), 503 (Strange) ; Legge to Newcastle, 15 Feb. 1762,
Add. MS. 32934, fo. 351.   Grenville took the same view (Hardwicke to Newcastle,
April 14, Add. MS. 32937, fo. 103).
[3] Bolingbroke to Marchmont, 9 June 1741, *Marchmont Papers*, ii. 258.
[4] *Britons Awake, and Look About You*, p. 58 ; *Parl. Hist.* xii. 924 (Bance).
[5] Legge to Newcastle, 4 Sept. 1758, Add. MS. 32883, fo. 276.

the war ? If either could afford to outlast the other, its interest
would be to engage in a contest of expense. As Choiseul put it,
the longest purse must win ; but each nation imagined itself to
possess it, so that Count Viry, who managed the peace treaty of
1762, remarked that the war would soon come to an end if each
side would give up the vain hope of ruining the other financially.[1]
Some Frenchmen were obsessed by the precariousness of the
English credit system, and recommended a Continental war as
the shortest way to overload and destroy it.[2] This reasoning
was accepted by many Englishmen, who therefore urged the
necessity of avoiding such a war ; but some were of another
opinion, and justified the Continental war on the ground that
it would exhaust the resources of France first.[3]

44

    Again, there was some doubt how far a purely maritime war
would affect the two nations. Most Englishmen were agreed
that it would be fatal to France, by destroying her shipping and
her trade, and drying up her sources of revenue so that she could
no longer support her campaigns in Europe. There were Frenchmen who took the same view. It was true that, as England
had much more shipping than France, her losses would be absolutely greater ; but while English shipping might be reduced,
that of France would be annihilated.[4] This argument, however,
was contradicted by others who thought the absolute losses more
important as they would conduce to bankruptcy and shrinkage
of revenue.[5] Besides, would French trade be destroyed because
French shipping was so ? This turned on the rights which England was prepared to accord to neutrals, and their courage in
claiming them.[6]

    There was another thing to be considered ; the mercantilists
were always afraid that a temporary diversion of trade might
become a permanent loss. One must, therefore, take into account

[1] Stanley to Pitt, 12 June 1761, in Thackeray, *op. cit.* i. 525 ; Viry to Solar (private),
27 March 1762, Aff. Étr., Angleterre, 443.

[2] Silhouette to Amelot, 24 Dec. 1739, Aff. Étr., Angleterre, 405, fo. 368 ; Bussy
to Amelot, 17 May 1741, 412, fo. 50.

[3] Yorke expressed both these opinions within little more than a year. (Yorke to
Newcastle, 18 June 1756, Add. MSS. 32865, fo. 344 ; 15 July 1757, 32872, fo. 91 ;
Walpole, *Memoirs of George III*, i. 164.)

[4] On this matter, Silhouette and Bussy took different sides in the letters quoted
above ; Silhouette attached more importance to the relative losses of English and
French shipping, and Bussy to the absolute losses of the latter. D'Argenson reported
in 1739 that the French and Spanish navies were thought equal to a defensive war
against England during which the French privateers could ' soon cause the insurance
on English ships to rise to 50 per cent., which is the thermometer of a maritime war ',
always provided the rest of Europe was not inspired by jealousy of the House of
Bourbon to arm against it (*Diary*, ed. Rathery, ii. 307).

[5] Bunge to Höpken (intercept), 31 Jan. 1756, giving the supposed views of the
French Court, Add. MS. 32862, fo. 301 ; *Parl. Hist.* x. 1192 (Hervey).

[6] This point was taken into consideration in the debate of 14 November 1754
(*Parl. Hist.* xv. 333 *seqq.* ; speeches of Beckford, Horace Walpole, and Egmont).

not only the damage to the trade of each country during the
war but the situation after it.   Much of the English commerce
and navigation was ordinarily carried on for other peoples, or
supplied them with goods which our rivals would be glad to
offer them.   That of France and still more of Spain, on the other
hand, was more confined to their own coasts and dominions, or
consisted in the export of goods which could not equally well be
obtained elsewhere.   The latter must revive at a peace, and could
be reserved once more for native merchants and shipowners,
even if it had to be thrown open to neutrals in war-time.   The
former, once lost, was gone for ever.[1]   Lastly, there were points
which escaped most people's notice.   All the foreign trade of
England was overseas trade ;   that was not true of France.
Moreover, France was a self-contained country whose foreign
trade played a smaller part in her whole economy than did that
of England.

There was so little material for a solid judgement of these
problems that both sides of the question were supported in
both countries.   Each had its advocates and opponents of
Continental war ;   but the diplomatic conjunctures of Europe
tempted both to engage in it.   To trace the process by which
the maritime wars of 1739 and 1755 became general all over
Europe would be beside the point here.   Both England and
France came to lay more and more stress on the Continental side
of the action.

In spite of the fanatics for America, we had allies in both
these wars, and the fact raised a new set of debates.   What
kind of help should we give them ?   The maritime party maintained that we could do them more good by activity in our
proper sphere than by meddling in theirs.   If we destroyed French
trade and seized the French colonies, we should hamstring France
so that she could not afford to play the tyrant in Europe.[2]   This
indirect salvation never satisfied our allies ;   they demanded
something in hand.   Then the question arose, whether men or
subsidies ?   Even if we set forth armies on the Continent, the
territories of our allies were sometimes invaded ;   must we then
make peace ?   Here again the maritime party was ready with
an answer.   Let us sacrifice our allies for the time being.   To
defend them in their own countries would be expensive and
useless.   We must therefore leave them ' in deposit '.   Our
strength and money would be better spent in amassing cheap
conquests outside Europe.   The superfluity of these would be
enough to ransom our allies at the peace, and perhaps to procure

45

---

[1] *Parl. Hist*, xi. 944 (Pulteney), xii. 253 (Talbot).

[2] *Ibid.* xiv. 163 (Velters Cornwall), 198 (Beckford) ; the *Monitor* of 8 and 15
Nov. 1755.

them a compensation for their sufferings. In this spirit Pitt proposed to leave Hanover ' in deposit '. Nivernois found in 1762 that nobody in England would mind if Lisbon fell ; instead of redeeming Portugal with Cuba, we should leave it in the possession of Spain for a year, while we conquered Mexico. Then we should buy the freedom of Portugal by restoring Mexico, and keep Cuba as pure gain. To the allies thus left in pawn, this must have appeared to be the most heartless commercialism that ever called itself strategy ; no doubt the maritime party in England thought it merely good business.[1]

These questions gavé rise to more than pamphlet contro-versies ; there was a real struggle over them in the cabinet from the beginning of the Spanish war. Even before the troubles on the Continent began, Walpole was questioning the wisdom of sending all our forces to the West Indies, because he was afraid of an invasion. Newcastle overrode him, and remained passion-ately keen to promote the American expedition, even after that venture had been frustrated and rendered ridiculous at Cartagena. Slowly, however, the interest of the ministry and even the public was beginning to turn from American expeditions to the contest over the Austrian succession. Hardwicke told Newcastle that ' It looked last year as if the old world was to be fought for in the new ; but now the tables are turned, and I fear that now America must be fought for in Europe. Whatever success we may have in the former, I doubt it will always finally follow the fate of the latter.' Even then Newcastle was for hurrying out reinforcements to Vernon and making another attempt in the West Indies ;[2] but he soon acquiesced in Hardwicke's reasoning. When the Continent was quiet, English statesmen could make good resolutions to have nothing to do with it ; but they could not keep them when a disturbance arose and allies went begging.

When Carteret succeeded Walpole, the change was complete. He might profess to be the slave of the English merchants,[3] but that was a piece of popular affectation which never sat worse on anybody's shoulders than on his. He was a typical Continental statesman, who only liked and understood the highly artificial ousiness of juggling electors, grand dukes, and empress-queens into uneasy and astonishing alliances. The political associates over whose shoulders he had just climbed into power naturally

46

---

[1] Viry to Solar, 10 July 1762, Aff. Étr., Angleterre, 446 ; Nivernois to Comte de Choiseul, 15 Sept., vol. 447. Frederick II suggested in February 1762 that the king of Portugal had better retire to Brazil, so that Spain would gain very little and England lose very little by the conquest of his country (*Politische Correspondenz*, vol. xxi, no. 13468).

[2] Hardwicke to Newcastle, 17 Aug. 1741, Add. MSS. 32697, fo. 426 ; Newcastle to Harrington, 20 June, 4 July, fos. 215, 310 ; to Hardwicke, 15 Aug., 35407, fo. 68.

[3] Bussy to Ameloti 17 May, n.s. 1742, Aff. Étr., Angleterre, 414, fo. 431.

reminded him of the cry of ' Take and hold ' ; yet though Carteret repelled the charge of neglecting the Spanish war for the German, he satisfied the public not by American adventures, but by a strong reinforcement in the Mediterranean which blocked up the Spanish forces in Italy.[1]

No more was heard of America in Carteret's time. The Pelhams hardly gave it another thought, until the capture of Louisbourg. This seems to have inspired Bedford, the first lord of the Admiralty, with a passion for North America ; he planned an expedition to Quebec for 1746. Newcastle conspired to prevent it. He believed it would determine the Dutch (who were not yet technically at war) to make a separate peace.

47

1st, as the Dutch will think it a proof that we are not disposed to peace, but are resolved to continue the war, and that in a manner, that will not promise a speedy end of it. 2dly, that by sending our troops to America, we disable ourselves still more from sending any to their assistance, and 3rdly that if we make these conquests, we shall be disposed to keep them, which will be in a degree as disagreeable to them as to France herself.[2]

It may have been Newcastle who was responsible for some of the delays which prevented the forces from sailing until it was too late in the year to go to America at all ; Bedford seems to have suspected something of the sort.[3] Next year Newcastle had got over his fear of the effect upon our allies, to whom he thought to justify the enterprise as a severe blow to the French trade and finances.[4] Besides, he was no longer so anxious for peace, and having convinced himself that the conquest of Canada was strongly desired by the public, he had to fear criticism from an even more dangerous quarter than the allies if he gave up the attempt. He believed that the popularity of the government and the war depended on it, and would be injured by its abandonment. That was enough for Newcastle ; he and Bedford stood out for the expedition against the rest of their colleagues, and were only frustrated by the professional opinion of Admiral Warren.[5]

[1] Bussy to Amelot, 29 March, n.s 1742, Aff. Étr., Angleterre, 409, fo. 274 ; 28 June, n.s. 415, fo. 62 ; *Parl. Hist.* xii. 1083 (Carteret), 1109 (Hervey), 1141 (Chesterfield), 1154 (Newcastle).

[2] Newcastle to Hardwicke, 2 April 1746, Add. MSS. 35408, fo. 220 ; 21 May, 32707, fo 230.

[3] This may be an exaggerated deduction from a peppery letter written by Bedford to Newcastle's secretary, 10 Nov. 1746 (*Bedford Correspondence*, i. 182). Pitt speaks of Bedford as the only supporter of the Canada expedition in the ministry ; he might know, being secretary-at-war, but he was not in the effective cabinet (*ibid.* p. 131).

[4] Draft declaration of (?) January 1747, Add. MS. 35409, fo. 16.

[5] Newcastle to Sandwich, 23 Dec. 1746, Add. MSS. 32806, fo. 298 ; 31 Jan. 1746-7, 32807, fo. 43. In this correspondence with Sandwich, Newcastle doubtless overrated the fervour of his concurrence with Bedford, for Sandwich was Bedford's disciple and confidant.

Newcastle's record in the war of 1739 thus offers no ground for condemning him outright as a slavish devotee of Continental politics. In 1755 he was converted once again to the American and naval war. That, indeed, was only because, as the duke of Cumberland quite truly said, ' he could get nobody to take his money ', or, as he put it himself, the weakness of the Dutch and the bad behaviour of Maria Theresa left him no choice .but to give up Continental politics for the time being.[1] It was, therefore, no true conversion, and Newcastle went back upon it as soon as he saw a chance of forming a system on the Continent.[2]

During the Seven Years' war Newcastle did not constantly obstruct Pitt's American projects. He and his party in the coalition bickered with Pitt about the kind of help which should be sent to Germany, and disliked the descents upon the coast of France. That was only contrasting one kind of Continental war with another, for the descents were chiefly important to Pitt because they diverted French troops from Germany.[3] Newcastle never tried to stop the conquest of the French colonies ; he sometimes proposed it himself, or believed himself to have done so. It is easy to be misled into a one-sided view of Newcastle's policy by his constant whinings and whisperings for Continental operations during the coalition ministry. He only meant to correct Pitt's inclination to neglect that side of the war. He was not responsible for the conduct of the whole war, but only for seeing that Pitt conducted it. He would not have exclaimed so vehemently on behalf of his favourite measures if he had not believed them to be slighted by his partner. Pitt. insisted on an ostensible preference for the American war, as Newcastle did for the German. Symbolical action was immensely important to both of them ; each was always looking out for an opportunity to establish his doctrine by implication from a trifle, or to repel an attempt of the other to strengthen his own in the same way.

There was nevertheless a real difference between Newcastle

---

[1] Dodington's *Diary*, 22 July 1755, p. 346 (1784 ed.) ; Newcastle to W. Bentinck, 16 Oct. 1755, Add. MS. 32860, fo. 64.

[2] In January 1756 Newcastle was already less convinced of the impossibility of a Continental war, partly because of the Prussian alliance, and partly for the curious reason that France appeared to desire a purely maritime war against us ; he argued that if it was to her interest it could not be to ours (Newcastle to Devonshire, 2 Jan. 1756, Add. MS. 32862, fo. 6). Newcastle expressed a strong preference for a Continental plan after his experiences of 1756 ; see his letters to Yorke, 11 June 1756 and 19 Aug. 1757, Add. MSS. 32865, fo. 261, 32873, fo. 174 ; to Anson, 7 July 1758, 32881, fo. 189. But though he sometimes disparaged the naval war, he usually took care to refer to the German operations as a diversion.

[3] Hardwicke seems to have misunderstood when he imagined that the chief object of these expeditions was to destroy ships and dockyards (Hardwicke to Newcastle, 9 Oct. 1757, Add. MSS. 32874, fo. 489 ; Newcastle to Hardwicke, 14 May 1761, 32923, fo. 68).

and Pitt, but it has been obscured by the imaginary distinctions
which Pitt and his admirers drew in order to justify his conversion to the German war.. In fact that conversion was natural
enough. Responsibility sobered the declamatory patriot until
he saw the necessity of what he had denounced. He found
himself in charge of a war in which England had already got, as
much by blunder as design, an important ally in Germany.
Measures were already taken for an army of observation. Pitt
could hardly have retreated abruptly from these preparations
already made ; he wisely made the best of them, and invented
a new doctrine to excuse them. If, he said, we were to have
Continental allies at all, we should rather connect ourselves with
some great Power like Prussia, than compile a nondescript force
of mercenaries from all the small principalities of Germany.[1]
This was good sense, but it was hardly the language he had talked
two years ago, when he merely denounced the treaties as likely
to lead us into a new Continental war.

49

   Five years afterwards, he was probably thinking of the same
thing when he said, in a famous speech, ' As Germany had
formerly been managed, it had been a millstone round our necks ;
as managed now, about that of France '.[2] That might be true,
but he did not deserve all the credit of it, for he had not made
the Prussian alliance. If he was thinking of distinctions in the
strategy of the war, there again they were less important than
they looked. Newcastle's treaties were designed, perhaps ineptly,
for the same purpose as Pitt's ' containing operations ' : to keep
Europe quiet while we pursued our proper aims in America.[3] At
one time and another, Pitt prevented Newcastle from making
concessions to Germany ; but he afterwards made most of them
himself. Indeed he seems to have admitted the unimportance
of the difference between himself and Newcastle, when he said
of his colleague that ' he borrowed their majority to carry out
their own plan '. His hero-worshippers have thought it necessary
to ignore this admission and to claim the merit of consistency
where inconsistency would have been more meritorious still.
Pitt was a great man ; not necessarily a good or a clever man,
still less a consistent man. His greatness consisted in learning
the lesson, not in having nothing to learn.

   If there was a difference between Pitt and Newcastle, it consisted in Pitt's efficiency and driving force, and still more in the
fact that he had a purpose where Newcastle had none. If Newcastle, like Pitt had meant to drive the French out of North

---

[1] Compare Pitt's language of 1755 (Hardwicke to Newcastle, 9 Aug. 1755, Add.
MS. 32858, fo. 76) with that of 1757 (Walpole, *Memoirs of George II*, iii. 17–18).
[2] Walpole, *Memoirs of George III*, i. 106.
[3] Newcastle to Holdernesse, 9 May 1755, Add. MS. 32854, fo. 460.

America, he would have been inexcusable if he had not carried on the war in the way that Pitt did ; but he meant nothing of the kind.   He had drifted into the war he hardly knew how ; he wished to put general pressure on France in order to make her give up her pretensions and practices on the North American frontier.   As his object was not North America but peace, it is no wonder the war was, for him, a general war with France, not a war for North America.

Everything helped to reconcile Pitt to the German war. His colleagues in the coalition put few intentional difficulties in the way of his American schemes.   As long as Pitt could have no excuse, and give none to others, for complaining that America was neglected, he could afford to feed the war in Germany with the overplus of our strength.   After the essential objects of the war had been achieved in America, Pitt could see as well as Newcastle that France must be prevented from redeeming them by important conquests in Germany.   That was Choiseul's calculation and, after 1759, his only hope ; [1] therefore, until we could make peace, we must defend the front in Germany and prevent him from making an impression on it.   Indeed we must do more : a defensive campaign was not enough.   Positive victories were needed which would both cause Choiseul to lose heart, and clear the French troops out of such territories of our allies as they still held. [2]

In another way, though with a worse grace, Pitt's colleagues satisfied the requirements of his strategy.   He had been impressed by the need of a militia at home, and had overcome the political objections of Hardwicke and Newcastle.   Having done so, he could afford to lavish soldiers on Germany as well as America, and to disperse his fleets to all the quarters of the world.

The connexion between Germany and the militia is pretty clearly shown by the compromise of 1760 ; Pitt consented to send more soldiers to the Continent if Newcastle and Hardwicke would procure the passage of his cousin's bill for continuing the militia. [3]

[1] Choiseul to Bussy, 19 June 1761, Aff. Étr., Angleterre, 443 ; Stanley to Pitt, 12 June 1761, printed in Thackeray, *History of William Pitt*, i. 525–6 ; Choiseul to Ossun, 17 April and 16. May 1762, Aff. Étr., Espagne, 536.   Choiseul still treated the German war as a thing of secondary importance in 1759 ; he told Bernstorff that a detachment of the army would ruin the elector of Hanover's possessions for several generations, but the main effort of France would be an invasion of England ; a few months later he said that as the German war was useless as a diversion from America and did no good to the allies, and as France did not want any conquests in that part of the world, he was willing to bring it to an end when England would (Choiseul to Bernstorff, 29 July and 23 Sept. 1759, *En Brevvexling mellem Grev J. H. E. Bernstorff og Hertugen af Choiseul, 1758–66* (Copenhagen, 1871), pp. 46–74).

[2] Newcastle to Bedford, 15 Jan. 1760, Add. MSS. 32901, fo. 276 ; to Devonshire, 8 April, 32904, fo. 259 ; to Pitt, 1 June, 32906, fo. 408 ; to Hardwicke, 21 July, 32908, fo. 399 ; to Hardwicke, 13 Sept. 32911, fo. 269.

[3] Barrington to Newcastle, 18 April 1760, Add. MS. 32904, fo. 424.

Pitt had a still stronger justification for revising his opinion on the Continental war ; he was not merely converted from America to Europe, but combined them. Having conducted the war during four years, he had come to understand the connexion between all its parts. He saw that a diversion in Germany kept busy French troops and money that would otherwise be employed in Flanders, Portugal, America, or an invasion. He understood the necessity of a financial strain which he believed we could bear and France could not. He insisted on the totality of the war.[1]

Newcastle came to believe in this principle almost as much as Pitt, but he never went quite so far. Pitt was not only willing to carry on a war with Spain as well as France ; he was anxious to provoke it. Newcastle would not give up the German war for a Spanish one, dared not give up the Spanish war for the German, and therefore had to proclaim, like Pitt, the necessity of supporting them both ; but if he could have avoided this additional war with Spain he would have done so. However, though their reasons and their spirit were very different, Pitt and Newcastle agreed in defending the policy of the whole war against the new party which had arisen for contracting it.

51

After the 'wonderful year' of 1759, the chief purpose of the war was achieved by the virtual expulsion of the French from North America. A reaction began to arise against the continuance of the effort. France could not yet be forced to terms which would satisfy our allies as well as ourselves ; but while statesmen could see the necessity of keeping up the war until then, public opinion, less able to understand the policy of altruism, began to call a halt.[2] The financial burden was great, and the elasticity of our resources difficult to guess. Both Pitt and Newcastle scented the possibility of opposition, and each met it in his characteristic way, Pitt by vehemently denouncing the Treasury for frauds and overcharges in the German commissariat, Newcastle by tentative economies, whose insignificance he was the first to admit, in the disposition of our forces in America. At this point George II died, and a new actor

[1] Walpole, *Memoirs of George III*, i. 97, 163–5. The language of Pitt's admirers, Beckford and Charles Townshend, was very much the same.

[2] Many pamphlets were published in this sense, but none of them made such an impression as Mauduit's *Considerations on the Present German War*. It is so much superior to the common run of eighteenth-century pamphlets, that contemporaries naturally ascribed it to some very exalted author. Why anybody should have chosen Lord Hardwicke for that honour is more than I can understand. Admittedly he was the best strategist in the cabinet, but neither the style nor the ideas are his. Moreover, Newcastle wrote to Joseph Yorke that an *answer* to Mauduit (of which they both approved) was thought to have come 'from a *great Hand*', and Yorke replied that he believed it too. Newcastle's underlining is often mysterious, and deserves a special study by itself ; but I think it possible that the '*great hand*' may have been Yorke's father, Lord Hardwicke.

appeared upon the scene, resolved to take the principal part but undetermined how to play it.

·Lord Bute's chief aim was popularity, not for himself but for his master.　In the earliest months of the new reign, he was casting about for the most certain means of obtaining it.　Public opinion was in a moment of transition.　The cries of patriotism were still loud, but the complaints against the German war were increasing.　Nobody could tell whether the fall of Pitt would provoke a revolution or a sigh of relief; but in most people's opinion the former was the more likely.　Bute wanted to end the war, but to do so gloriously, and he had to steer between the parties of war and peace, adhering now to one, now to the other, perhaps without any more cunning calculation than a desire to play the safest cards.　Already at the New Year of 1761 he had his eye on the possibility of withdrawing from the German war and carrying on more vigorously the popular part of it, expeditions to the West Indies and so forth.　His friends advised him to do this as his own act, that he and the king might have the merit of it.　He feared that the ministry might pre-empt this acceptable line of policy, and seems to have been relieved when he found that Pitt was ' madder than ever ', and had no intention of giving up the Continent.　Yet he was not entirely determined, and Dodington thought him disposed to carry on the whole war, or to see difficulties in the way of contracting it.[1]　Bute saw his opportunity a few months later in the approach of a war with Spain.　Before it was declared—even before Pitt had resigned on account of his colleagues' refusal to declare it—Bute had foreseen that this option between the Spanish and the German wars would force the resignation of a minister who insisted on carrying on both.[2]　In the end, Pitt left the ministry for a different reason; nor does Bute seem to have been glad of his departure.[3]　Bute now had his hand on the engine which would remove Newcastle, the Spanish war or the German war, but not both.[4]　It would

[1] Dodington's *Diary*, 2, 9 and 16 Jan. 1761, pp. 422, 426–7, 430–1 ; Dodington to Bute, 16 Jan. 1761, in Adolphus, *History of England*, i. 547.

[2] Bute told Newcastle that, if we had a Spanish war, we should have to give up our operations in Germany, and Pitt would probably resign on that account (Newcastle to Hardwicke, 26 Sept. 1761, Add. MS. 32928, fo. 363).　Hardwicke did not think Pitt would or should do anything of the kind, for he still believed that Pitt and Temple would agree with Bute in giving up the German war, if an option had to be made. Pitt's public-spirited declarations against doing so must therefore have surprised Newcastle and Hardwicke after his resignation.　Bute had taken Pitt's measure better than they had, perhaps because he was not obsessed, as they were, by Pitt's past record on this subject.

[3] Bute to Dodington, 8 Oct. 1761, printed by Adolphus, *op. cit.* i. 548.

[4] This edifying dialogue took place one day between them.　Bute told Newcastle that the popular opinion was ' That we had worked Mr. Pitt out, and were now following his extravagant measures (meaning the Continent measures), and that we had better have Mr. Pitt again '.　Newcastle replied that people really said ' That Mr. Pitt went out because we would not declare war against Spain ; and as soon as he was

hardly be just to accuse Bute of involving himself in the Spanish war at the end of 1761 on purpose to force this alternative upon his colleagues. He and Egremont did, indeed, provoke it by a diplomatic *brusquerie* worthy of Pitt himself, but they did so because they were afraid to yield anything which Pitt would not have yielded.

There is no need to describe again the process by which Bute edged out Newcastle and shuffled out of the Prussian alliance. He advanced slowly. In November 1761 he was angry with Shelburne for making a speech against the German war, because he was afraid his friend would appear to be flying a kite for him ; but on 10 January he spoke in the cabinet for giving it up.[1] The new prospect which was opened by the accession of Peter III of Russia made him waver ; for though he let it be understood that he was resolved to abandon the Continental war, he opposed Bedford's motion for that purpose in the house of lords, only, it is true, by the previous question.[2] It soon appeared, however, that Peter III was going to increase the embarrassment between England and Prussia by his wild-cat schemes in the Baltic, and Bute determined to deprive Frederick of the subsidy which we had paid him since 1756.[3] He went no farther ; he did not abandon the German, as distinct from the Prussian war. In fact, 1762 was one of the most successful campaigns of the English army under Prince Ferdinand ; but the controversy over the Prussian subsidy was enough to bring on the quarrel of Bute and Newcastle.

At first it was George Grenville who forced the pace. Newcastle wanted peace, and believed that the best way to get it was to carry on the war on all fronts, Continental as well as American. Grenville wanted not peace but conquest and dignity ; he therefore advocated a kind of war which could be carried on for ever. Newcastle thought him ripe for giving up the German war in November 1761, though he defended it in the house of commons as an unwelcome moral obligation.[4] (This point of view explains

53

out, we did the same thing ; and that being the case, Mr. Pitt would carry on his own measures better than anybody ' (Newcastle to Devonshire, 13 April 1762, Add. MS. 32937, fo. 88).

[1] Fox to Shelburne, 12 Nov. 1761, 8 Jan. 1762, in Fitzmaurice's *Life of Shelburne*, i. 100, 103 ; Newcastle to Hardwicke, 10 Jan. 1762, Add. MS. 32933, fo. 179 (but a fortnight later Newcastle thought the king and Bute were still undecided ; Newcastle to Yorke, 26 Jan., 32934, fo. 13).

[2] *Parl. Hist.* xv. 1217 (Bedford), 1218 (Bute), 1220 (Protest) ; according to Fox, George III was very angry with those who spoke on Bedford's side against Bute (Memoir, in *Life and Letters of Lady Sarah Lennox*, i. 60).

[3] Newcastle to Devonshire, 13 April 1762, Add. MSS. 32937, fo. 85 ; Hardwicke to Newcastle, 14 April, fo. 103 ; Yorke to Newcastle, 16 April, fo. 141 ; Newcastle to Rockingham, 4 May, 32938, fo. 50 ; Bute to Mitchell, 26 May, 1762, printed in Bisset's *Memoirs and Papers of Sir Andrew Mitchell*, ii. 294–302.

[4] Newcastle to Hardwicke, 9 Nov. 1761, Add. MSS. 32930, fo. 374 ; to Yorke, 16 Nov., 32931, fo. 60 ; West, house of commons reports, 9 Dec. 1761, 32932, fo. 74. See also the correspondence of Newcastle and Legge upon this subject, Add. MS. 32934, fos. 351 and 410.

the efforts of the ministry to prove Frederick in the wrong ; only so could his moral claim be repudiated.) George Grenville represents a more definite kind of policy than Bute. While Bute shuffled confusedly between war and peace, Grenville always knew what he wanted. He was for limiting the war to the sea, the colonies, and such European countries as Portugal, where England had a special economic interest. In these fields, he was ready to fight Spain as well as France. This was the Opposition cry of 1755, revived as the policy of the government. It was now Pitt who claimed that America had been conquered in Germany, and Grenville who denied, with a show of pedestrian reason, that we owed Wolfe's victory or Hawke's to anything but English valour.[1] George Grenville stole the suit of clothes which Pitt had deliberately discarded as too small for him. In the end he wore it alone ; for Bute, having turned out the war minister and the peace minister, did not mean to suffer the dictation of his new colleague whose programme was the limited war, and turned back to his original policy of peace at almost any price. In the spring of 1762, however, Bute took Grenville's part against Newcastle. It is a degrading story, for the silly old man deprived himself, by shameful half-surrenders, of all the merit of his final stand for his principles. He had already abandoned Frederick before he fell, and the German war for which he sacrificed his place was a thing without substance or outline. The events of that year proved that it was not impossible to fight a German campaign without co-operating with Frederick ; but Newcastle had no clear idea how to do it.[2]

Perhaps these quarrels between the isolationists and the interventionists have little relevance for our own time ; but they illustrate the dilemma which English foreign policy has often had to deal with in the last two centuries. There is a third light in which they could be considered. England has often had to decide how much of her colonial conquests she would restore to her enemies in order to procure for her allies the recovery of their lost territories or the satisfaction of their legitimate ambitions. It was of no use to conclude a war of intervention by an isolationist peace, as Lord Bute did in 1762. But that is another story, which has often been told.   RICHARD PARES.

[1] West, report of, 9 Dec. 1761, Add. MS. 32932, fo. 74.

[2] For example, his chief objection to depriving Frederick II of his subsidy was a fear that it would look like abandoning the German war, which he was resolved to continue ; he thus distinguished between the two and thought one was possible without the other (see his letter to Hardwicke, 25 Feb. 1762, Add. MS. 32935, fo. 74). Hardwicke kept him true to his ally for a time ; but when Newcastle resigned, it was not because the ministry had decided not to pay the subsidy, but rather because he insisted on an additional vote of credit in order to show the world that we should continue to carry on the *German* war (Newcastle to Mansfield, 2 May 1762, Add. MS. 32938, fo. 18 ; tc Yorke, 14 May, fo. 239).

55

Mr. LEONARD W. LABAREE read a paper entitled:

The Royal Governors
of New England

BY the terms of the charter of 1629 the freemen of the Massachusetts Bay Company were authorized to choose annually their governor, deputy-governor, and assistants. Few of the powers derived
from the charter were more highly prized by the Puritans, for few were
more fundamental to the complete maintenance of their ideas of Church
and State than the naming of their own chief officers of government.
Jealously did they guard this vital privilege. The very report of the appointment of a governor-general by the Crown in 1634 was enough to

lead to the strengthening of the military defenses of the Bay Colony. But for fifty years more the annual elections continued without successful interference.

It is not surprising, therefore, that when the charter was finally vacated and Massachusetts found herself ruled by governors not of her own choosing, the conservative Puritans showed resentment and looked with utmost suspicion upon governors who took office by virtue of the king's commission instead of the mandate of God's elect. In time, as the more militant Puritans passed from the scene and others became somewhat reconciled to the inevitable, the hostility to the royal governors underwent a change in character, if not in strength. The rise of new economic problems led to a division of sentiment within the province, with the conservative, propertied, and mercantile interests arrayed against the underprivileged and the rural classes. Since the governors almost always sided with the conservatives, they drew upon themselves the hatred of the economic radicals, who, quite correctly, recognized in the king's representatives the most powerful opponents of inflation and ready help for debtors. Finally, the general rise of colonial discontent, especially at the new British policies adopted after 1763, led to a further shift in the basis of hostility to the royal governors. The political radicals, or patriots, came rightly enough to look upon them as the leaders of the prerogative party, as the standard-bearers of toryism and repression, and hated them for what they represented. At all times, therefore, from the destruction of the first charter to the outbreak of the Revolution, there were strong and articulate groups ready to attack the royal governor of the moment, to denounce him as mercenary and incompetent, and to leave upon the pages of later sympathetic historians a reflection of their own hostility.

In the course of the past forty years or so, historians have come to take a more objective view of the men and events of that earlier age than was taken in the days when Bancroft and Palfrey set the tone for all writers on New England history. Scholars have studied the documents afresh; new materials, not available to the older writers, have found their way into print; while competent and sympathetic biographies of several of these royal governors have appeared.[1] It is now possible to resurvey these officers

[1] The more recent biographical studies of New England governors include: Mrs. Napier Higgins, *The Bernards of Abington and Nether Winchendon*, vols. I and II constituting a biography of Sir Francis Bernard; Everett Kimball, *The Public Life of Joseph Dudley*; James K. Hosmer, *The Life of Thomas Hutchinson, Royal Governor of the Province of Massachusetts Bay*; Viola F. Barnes, "The Rise of William Phips" and "Phippius Maximus," *New England Quarterly*, I. 271–294, 532–553; C. A. W. Pownall, *Thomas Pownall M.P., F.R.S., Governor of Massachusetts Bay, Author of the Letters of Junius*; George A. Wood, *William Shirley, Governor of Massachusetts, 1741–1756, A History*; Lawrence S. Mayo, *John Wentworth, Governor of New Hampshire, 1767–1775*. A good short account

as a group, estimating their careers and their personalities, both in comparison with the governors of other royal colonies and in relation to the New England stage on which they played their parts. Since New Hampshire, the only other royal province in New England, was under the jurisdiction of Massachusetts during much of the seventeenth century, and for the first forty years of the eighteenth had the same governors as her larger neighbor, it may be well to include the chief executives of that province in the analysis.

Sir Edmund Andros, as head of the Dominion of New England,[1] was the first of fifteen men to assume office as royal governor in New England. For a few years after the collapse of the Dominion the two provinces had separate executives—Sir William Phips in Massachusetts[2] and Samuel Allen in New Hampshire.[3] From 1697 until 1741 there was a personal union of the two provinces, with separate legislatures, but with common governors in the persons of the Earl of Bellomont,[4] Joseph Dudley,[5] Samuel Shute,[6] William Burnet,[7] and Jonathan Belcher.[8] Then came a separation. While Massachusetts was entrusted successively to the care of five men—William Shirley,[9] Thomas Pownall,[10] Sir Francis Bernard,[11]

57

of Jonathan Belcher is in Clifford K. Shipton, Sibley's Harvard Graduates, IV. 434–449. In addition, the Dictionary of American Biography contains sketches of all the New England royal governors except Samuel Allen: Jonathan Belcher, Sir Francis Bernard, William Burnet, Joseph Dudley, Thomas Gage, William Shirley, and Samuel Shute, by James Truslow Adams; Sir Edmund Andros and Sir William Phips, by Viola F. Barnes; the Earl of Bellomont, by Charles W. Spencer; Thomas Hutchinson, by Carl Becker; Thomas Pownall, by Leonard W. Labaree; Benning Wentworth, by Isabel M. S. Whittier; and John Wentworth, by Wayne E. Stevens. For biographical data not otherwise credited in subsequent footnotes, I have usually relied upon the above works.

[1] Assumed office, December 20, 1686; arrested and deprived of authority by the insurgents, April 18, 1689.

[2] Assumed office, May 16, 1692; departed for England, December 4, 1694; died in London, February 18, 1695.

[3] Appointed in 1692, but active governor only from September 15, 1698, until superseded on July 31, 1699.

[4] Appointed in 1697; assumed office in Massachusetts, May 26, 1699; in New Hampshire, July 31, 1699; died in office, March 5, 1701.

[5] Assumed office in Massachusetts, June 11, 1702; in New Hampshire, July 13, 1702; commissions not renewed in 1715.

[6] Assumed office in Massachusetts, October 5, 1716; in New Hampshire, October 17, 1716; left for England, January 1, 1723; commissions not renewed in 1727.

[7] Assumed office in Massachusetts, September 17, 1728; in New Hampshire, October 2, 1728; died in office, September 7, 1729.

[8] Assumed office in Massachusetts, August 10, 1730; in New Hampshire, August 25, 1730; superseded, August 14, 1741.

[9] Assumed office, August 14, 1741; sailed for England upon recall, September 15, 1756.

[10] Assumed office, August 3, 1757; sailed for England upon recall, June 3, 1760.

[11] Assumed office, August 2, 1760; sailed for England, August 1, 1769.

Thomas Hutchinson,[1] and Thomas Gage[2]—New Hampshire had only two governors—Benning Wentworth[3] and his nephew John.[4] These are the men with whom we have to deal.

When we compare these New England executives with the English royal governors elsewhere during the same period, certain differences appear. The first and most striking fact is the large proportion of natives chosen to rule the New England provinces. Among all the colonies hardly more than one in eight or ten of the governors was born in America; but six of the fifteen in New England were born in the provinces which they later administered. Phips, Dudley, Belcher, Hutchinson, and the two Wentworths were all New Englanders,[5] descendants of first-generation settlers, and steeped in the New England tradition. No other royal province among those that revolted in 1775 could boast a native son as its full governor, though one in New York came from Jamaica,[6] and three in New Jersey were born in other continental colonies.[7] It would seem as if the home authorities, conscious of New England's pride in her own stock, had sought to conciliate this section by appointing her own sons to rule over her. And, as if to take additional precautions in the management of this difficult region, the Crown selected the remaining governors as far as possible from men who had previously resided in the colonies and were familiar with colonial problems. Of the nine governors born outside New England, only three—Allen, Bellomont, and Shute—were practically complete strangers to America when they assumed office.[8] Andros, Bur-

[1] Assumed office as acting governor, August 1, 1769, and as governor, March 4, 1771; superseded, May 17, 1774.

[2] Assumed office, May 17, 1774; sailed for England during siege of Boston, October 10, 1775.

[3] Assumed office, December 13, 1741; superseded, June 13, 1767.

[4] Assumed office, June 13, 1767; fled to Boston, August 23, 1775.

[5] The places and dates of birth of these men were as follows: Phips: Woolwich, Maine, February 2, 1650/1; Dudley: Roxbury, Massachusetts, September 23, 1647; Belcher: Cambridge, January 8, 1681/2; Hutchinson: Boston, September 9, 1711; Benning Wentworth: Portsmouth, New Hampshire, July 24, 1696; John Wentworth: Portsmouth, August 9, 1737.

[6] Sir Henry Moore, Bart. (governor of New York, 1765–1769), was born at Vere, Jamaica, February 7, 1712/3.

[7] Lewis Morris (governor, 1738–1746), born at "Bronck's Land," New York, October 15, 1671; Jonathan Belcher (governor, 1747–1757), born at Cambridge, January 8, 1681/2; William Franklin (governor, 1763–1775), born, probably in Philadelphia, in 1731.

[8] Allen, though never in America before his assumption of the governorship, had a considerable stake in New Hampshire, since he had bought the proprietary claims to the province from the heirs of John Mason.

net, and Bernard had previously been governors of other colonies;[1] Shirley had lived ten years in Boston;[2] Pownall had been a free-lance observer and general handy man to colonial officials for four eventful years;[3] and Gage had spent long years as a soldier in American campaigns and as commander-in-chief of the British forces.[4] This was a record of colonial experience such as the governors of no other province could boast. One may question, perhaps, whether it was of any practical benefit to a colony to be ruled by men who knew America at first hand, but the home officials, by selecting four fifths of its governors from this class, gave New England, above all sections, the benefit of the doubt.

The New England governors generally came from less exalted ranks of society than did many of their contemporaries in other provinces. Although peers and sons of peers were fairly common elsewhere, only two governors in New England belonged to noble families. Bellomont, son of an Irish baron and himself raised to an earldom in the Irish peerage, was something of a courtier as well as a politician in the British Isles, having been treasurer and receiver-general to Queen Mary as well as governor of County Leitrim in Ireland.[5] Massachusetts and New Hampshire were flattered by the appointment of this noble lord, and the assembly at Boston gave him twice the salary they had paid his predecessor.[6] General Gage, the other high-born governor, was the younger son of a viscount. But by his time Massachusetts was no longer interested in the families of the British peerage. The absence of enthusiasm at his inauguration bore eloquent

59

testimony to the changed conditions since Bellomont was first received.[1]
Most of the other Englishmen who ruled these provinces belonged to the
upper middle class or to the country gentry. Andros was the son of a
Guernsey gentleman and was himself a knight; Bernard and Pownall were
members of old county families; Burnet was the son of the famous Bishop
of Salisbury; Allen and Shirley, and probably Shute, came from London
merchant stock.[2] Among the New Englanders, all but Phips belonged to
the colonial aristocracy, proud of their ancestry and local prominence, but
hardly to be considered the social equals of the leading English families.
Phips was the only truly self-made man in the entire lot. Of a poor family
from down-east Maine, he rose by an adventurous spirit, cleverness, and
good luck to ultimate knighthood. Yet neither he nor the people over
whom he ruled ever quite forgot his humble beginnings. New England's
governors, then, were men of moderate position in the world. The salaries
and the society there were not such as to attract the more giddy or impecu-
nious sons of England's aristocracy, nor would the staid Puritans have
wished them. Massachusetts had no governors like the Duke of Albemarle,
bon vivant and crony of James II, who sailed off to his government of
Jamaica in 1687 in his own private yacht, taking with him in his escort of
frigates five hundred tons of household goods and one hundred servants.[3]
Everyone realized that the New England sun would have shone but
bleakly upon such exotic branches of England's great family trees.

The governors of Massachusetts and New Hampshire were comparatively well educated. While about one quarter of the chief executives of all
the provinces matriculated at colleges or universities, New England's proportion was two thirds. Eight of the fifteen actually took their bachelor's
degree at Oxford, Cambridge, or Harvard.[4] All but Phips among the

[1] Instead of being met upon arrival at Boston by the General Court, leading officials,
and citizens, and escorted through the streets to an immediate induction, Gage found,
when he reached Boston, May 14, 1774, that a town meeting was in progress, called to
consider the news of the Port Bill. "The late Governor Hutchinson, The Cheif Justice,
the Commissioners of the Customs, and the Consignies, were either at the Castle, or dispersed in the Country, not daring to reside in Boston. I Went to Mr Hutchinson and
remained with him at Castle William till Preparations were made for My Reception in
Boston, where My Commission Was read and Published in the usual Forms on the
17th Inst." Gage to Dartmouth, May 19, 1774, Carter, *Gage Correspondence*, I. 355. Cf.
the account of the enthusiastic reception of Belcher in 1730 as given in the *Boston News-
Letter*, August 6–13 (reprinted in large part in Sibley, IV. 439–440).

[2] The ancestries of most of these men are conveniently summarized in their biographical
sketches in the *Dictionary of American Biography*.

[3] Colonial Office Papers 138: 5, pp. 245–246, 250, 254–255; *Calendar of Treasury Books*,
1685–1689, pp. 1258, 1463; Estelle F. Ward, *Christopher Monck, Duke of Albemarle*, pp.
273–278.

[4] The list, with the years of receiving the bachelor's degree, is as follows: Oxford: Bernard, 1733 (Joseph Foster, *Alumni Oxonienses*, I. 100); Cambridge: Shirley, 1714 (J. and

native sons could boast of Harvard degrees, though a supercilious don of an English university might think the boast an empty one. Still, the schooling given there was the best that the colonies had to offer at the time. The list of college graduates among the governors might be longer if Shute had not left Cambridge after matriculation to read law in the Middle Temple,[1] and if Burnet had not been removed from the same university by his father, the bishop, for idleness and disobedience.[2] But Burnet also read law in the Middle Temple, studied at the University of Leyden, and was later granted an M.A. at Cambridge.[3] As a fellow of the Royal Society he contributed papers to its *Philosophical Transactions* on such varied subjects as the mountains of Switzerland, an eclipse of a satellite of Jupiter, and a set of "Siamese twins" from Hungary.[4] He also published an essay on Scriptural prophecy,[5] and consequently perhaps ought to be included among the intellectual aristocracy. Three others are noteworthy for their literary achievements. Bernard was a versifier of sorts and gained some notice when he edited the Latin odes of his stepfather, Anthony Alsop.[6] Pownall not only put his justly famous *Administration of the Colonies* through six editions,[7] but also wrote extensively upon economics, topography, archaeology, and philosophy.[8] His philosophical work, indeed, deserves a closer examination than it has yet received from recent students of that subject. And lastly, but perhaps most noteworthy of all, Thomas Hutchinson devoted his spare

61

J. A. Venn, *Alumni Cantabrigienses*, IV. 67); Pownall, 1744 (*id.*, III. 389); Harvard: Dudley, 1665 (Sibley, II. 166–188); Belcher, 1699 (*id.*, IV. 434–449); Benning Wentworth, 1715 (*Harvard University Quinquennial Catalogue*, 1636–1930, p. 175); Hutchinson, 1727 (*id.*, p. 178); John Wentworth, 1755 (*id.*, p. 186).

[1] Shute was admitted at the Middle Temple, November 23, 1683. Venn, *Alumni Cantabrigienses*, IV. 72.

[2] T. E. S. Clarke and H. C. Foxcroft, *A Life of Gilbert Burnet*, pp. 426–428; H. C. Foxcroft, *A Supplement to Burnet's History of My Own Time*, pp. 511–512 (autobiographical extract).

[3] Venn, *Alumni Cantabrigienses*, I. 261.

[4] Burnet's papers in the *Philosophical Transactions* have the following titles: "On the Icy Mountains in Switzerland" (XXVI. 316); "Observations on the eclipse of the first satellite of Jupiter, in 1723, made at New York" (XXXIII. 162); "Account of a double-bodied child" (L. 315).

[5] *An Essay on Scripture-Prophecy, Wherein it is Endeavored to Explain the Three Periods Contain'd in the XII Chapter of the Prophet Daniel. With some Arguments to make it Probable, that the First of the Periods did Expire in the Year* 1715. [New York], 1724. This remarkable treatise demonstrates that the Kingdom of God was due to arrive in the year 1790. The Yale University Library copy was presented by the author to Samuel Johnson, the first Anglican minister in Connecticut, and later the first president of King's College (Columbia).

[6] *Aedis Christi Olim Alumni Odarum. Libri Duo.* London, 1752.

[7] London, 1764, 1765, 1766, 1768, 1774, 1777.

[8] Bibliographies of Pownall's writings are in the *Dictionary of National Biography*, and C. A. W. Pownall, *Thomas Pownall*, appendix, pp. 3–6.

moments for many years to that historical work for which we are all so much
indebted to him.[1] Clearly, Massachusetts, which prided itself on its high
level of education and intellectual activity, had a higher average of educated and literary governors than any other royal province.

On the other hand, the governors of these two strategically important
provinces were for the most part deficient in military training or experience. While half the governors generally were men of military or naval
rank, only three of the fifteen in Massachusetts and New Hampshire were
professional soldiers. Andros had been a major,[2] Shute a brevet-colonel,[3]
and Gage a lieutenant-general[4] before assuming civil office. Dudley, it is
true, won the rank of colonel during King Philip's War, but, if questioned in a candid moment, would probably himself have admitted that the
title should be construed only in a Kentuckian sense. Shirley also became
a major-general and commander-in-chief during his administration, but
he had had no military experience before coming to America, and perhaps
the less said about his real generalship the better.[5] On the whole, the governors of New England were an unmilitary set, enthusiastic organizers
when army expeditions were on foot, but devoid of that inner knowledge
and understanding of military problems which usually come only from
long years in camp and field. The appointment in 1774 of the one important soldier of the lot, Thomas Gage, was a compliment to the bellicose
spirit of Massachusetts, but a compliment which the inhabitants would
readily have done without.

Any attempt at exact comparison between the New England governors
and those of other royal provinces as to motive in seeking office, person-
ality, and general ability must inevitably result in failure. These things do
not lend themselves to ready measurement, especially at a distance of several generations. Men must be considered individually against the background of their own time and environment. Only thus can sound conclusions be drawn.

We must lay aside any notion that these men were actuated by higher
motives in seeking office than those that led others in England or the colonies to ask for political appointments. Whatever may be the ideals of

[1] *History of the Colony of Massachusetts Bay*, 1628–1691 (Boston, 1764); *History of the Province of Massachusetts Bay*, 1691–1750 (Boston, 1767); *History of the Province of Massachusetts Bay*, 1749–1774 (London, 1828).
[2] Charles Dalton, *English Army Lists and Commission Registers*, 1661–1714, I. 37, 75, 115, 119, 168–169.
[3] *Id.*, v, part ii, pp. 16–17; Dalton, *George the First's Army*, 1714–1727, I. 105.
[4] Promoted in 1770. War Office, *Army Lists*, 1772, pp. 2, 76.
[5] For a recent appraisal of Shirley as a military leader see Stanley M. Pargellis, *Lord Loudoun in North America*, especially pp. 134–135.

public service today, we are dealing with the eighteenth century, not the twentieth, and as historians we must be realists. In those days men sought political preferment primarily for the prestige, the power, the opportunities for advancement, and the money they might win thereby. Among these fifteen only one—Thomas Hutchinson—stands out as not definitely coveting the appointment as governor. Shortly before the Stamp Act tumults he was accused of being an engrosser of public offices, and there may have been some justice in the charge, for he was at that time lieutenant-governor, president of the council, chief justice, and judge of probate.[1] But the sacking of his house by the mob, the hostility of the Boston populace and its leaders, and, above all, the cares and responsibilities of the lieutenant-governorship after Bernard's departure seem to have cured him of the desire for higher office for its own sake. There is a certain ring of sincerity in the repeated statement in his letters to England that he hoped that someone else would be appointed to the burdensome governorship.[2] But when his commission came, he did not refuse it. He could have been under no illusions as to the difficulty and thanklessness of the task before him, and, as far as we can judge, he accepted the promotion, in part at least, in the hope of leading back to the path of loyal obedience the province which he so dearly loved.

63

No such thoughts of service above self are apparent in the efforts of the other native sons to win the highest office of their community. To Phips the governorship was the pinnacle of ambition. To return to the Massachusetts which had known his lowly youth, rich with the spoils of his treasure hunt, sponsored by no less a leader of the old régime than Increase Mather, knighted, and now royal governor—what more could the former ship's carpenter ask? To Joseph Dudley, also, the return as governor held out the prospect of personal triumph and vindication. Upon no other official, not even Andros himself, had the Puritans so heaped their reproaches and their wrath in the days of the Dominion as upon the pro-English son of their own former governor, Thomas Dudley. But when, after years of scheming,[3] the son returned, holding as governor the one office that would

[1] J. K. Hosmer, *Thomas Hutchinson*, pp. 66–68.

[2] For example, he wrote Hillsborough, March 27, 1770: "I shall faithfully endeavor to support such person [as might be appointed governor] according to the best of my abilities, and I think it not improbable that I may be capable of doing his Majesty greater service in the Province, even in a private station, than at present." *Id.*, p. 188. To Richard Jackson he wrote in the same month: "I find my constitution is not strong enough to bear so great a burden [as the governorship], and I hope the next vessel will bring us news of a person of weight and importance appointed to the government." *Id.*, p. 189.

[3] Dudley's efforts to win the governorship are fully described in Kimball, *Joseph Dudley*, chap. iv.

compensate him for the harsh treatment he had received, it must be said to his credit that he showed no vindictive spirit, but set himself to the task of providing for the public welfare as he understood it.

While Phips's and Dudley's very human motives in seeking appointment may arouse some measure of sympathy, the same cannot be said for Jonathan Belcher. Above all others he was an opportunist, seeking first of all his own political and financial advancement. A leader of the provincial group opposed to Governor Burnet, he was sent to England by the assembly to contest the royal demand that they provide the governor a permanent instead of an annual salary. Suddenly word came that Burnet was dead. Belcher, quick to see his chance, besought his own appointment to the vacancy on the ground that he alone could persuade the assembly to grant the required permanent salary.[1] And, to complete the estimate of his disinterestedness, it must be recalled that when as governor he failed completely to accomplish this result, he almost tearfully begged permission to accept the proffered annual grants on the ground that in any case "to take the people's money must be a punishment to them."[2]

Fortunately for New England no other governor was so frankly a time-server. Others were undoubtedly just as interested as Belcher in enhancing their own prestige and fortunes. But to most of the native-born governors, and notably to the Wentworths in New Hampshire, the office was but a logical step upwards for members of leading local families long prominent in the political and economic life of the community.[3] That most of them were really men of second-rate abilities is not to be denied—though Hutchinson is again a shining exception. But their mediocrity is only an-

64

[1] Hutchinson, *History of Massachusetts Bay*, II. 367; Sibley, IV. 438–439. In 1745, however, Belcher wrote to Newcastle: "I never sought the government of New England, but it was offered me." British Museum, Additional MSS. 32,704 (Newcastle Papers, XIX), fol. 547. Although he repeated this assertion in the following year (Add. MSS. 32,706, Newcastle Papers, XXI, fol. 292), the independent evidence runs overwhelmingly to the contrary.

[2] Belcher to the Board of Trade, June 12, 1731. *Acts and Resolves*, II. 633–634. Further light on Belcher's zeal for office-holding is shed by the letters and memorials with which he and his friends bombarded the British ministers in 1745 and 1746, pleading that the South Carolina governorship be given him after his removal from Massachusetts. Add. MSS. 32,704, fol. 547; 32,706, fols. 235, 292–293, 314–315.

[3] In a typical letter to Newcastle in support of Benning Wentworth's candidacy, Joseph Windham Ashe wrote, November 23, 1739: "I therefore would humbly recommend to Your Grace Benning Wentworth, Esq. one of His Majesty's council in the said Province of New Hampshire (Now in London) to be made Governor of His Majesty's said Province. I shall only mention to Your Grace that he was eldest son of the late Lieutenant Governor Wentworth of the said Province and to his capacity and integrity there can be no objection. He has been a very great sufferer by the Crown of Spain, but as to any pretensions he may have to hope for Your Grace's favour on this account, I must beg leave to refer Your Grace to Mr. Keene who designs to wait on Your Grace in his behalf so soon as his health will permit him to come abroad." Add. MSS. 32,692, fol. 475.

other illustration of what has long been recognized—that the second and third generations in New England produced few men who compared in stature with the first-generation settlers.

In time, hostility to the governors appeared largely because of the conservatism of their political and economic policies. They represented the Crown, and in their efforts to uphold the prerogative they came inevitably into conflict with the representatives of the popular point of view. Their natural allies were the wealthy merchants and landed aristocrats, whose economic interests were often directly opposed to those of the plebeian artisans and frontier farmers. The economic contests of the period were usually indistinguishable from the political struggles. In these engagements the governors were almost always found fighting on the side of the wealthier battalions. A notable exception was Pownall, who, for reasons partly political and partly temperamental, cultivated the popular party. In a courtly age he alienated the aristocrats of Boston by the carelessness of his dress and the informality and gaiety of his manner.[1] Hutchinson, then chief justice and lieutenant-governor, was disgusted, but John Adams, writing years later, called Pownall "the most constitutional and national governor in my opinion, who ever represented the crown in this province."[2] Several of the governors brought the popular leaders raging like hornets about their ears because of their conservative views on currency questions. Dudley and Belcher especially earned the undying hatred of the inflationists by their successful opposition to schemes for establishing land banks.[3] Hutchinson, too, gained his first political laurels when, as Speaker of the House of Representatives, he brought about, almost single-handed, the restoration of the Massachusetts currency to a specie basis.[4] In these days of loose and ill-digested talk of inflation and "baloney dollars," it is particularly easy to understand why disputes over currency and similar problems should have produced so much bitter feeling between men who sincerely believed that their opponents' policies would lead straight to economic ruin.

In fact, a broad survey of all these governors and their administrations leads definitely to the conclusion that the times in which they lived rather than the characters and capacities of the men themselves are chiefly responsible for the unsympathetic treatment which they have usually re-

65

[1] William Tudor, *Life of James Otis of Massachusetts*, p. 44; C. A. W. Pownall, *Thomas Pownall*, pp. 90–91.
[2] Charles F. Adams, editor, *Works of John Adams*, x. 243.
[3] Hutchinson, *History of Massachusetts Bay*, II. 206–208, 392–399; Kimball, *Joseph Dudley*, pp. 157–174; James T. Adams, *Revolutionary New England*, pp. 93–96, 154–160.
[4] Hutchinson, *History of Massachusetts Bay*, II. 435–440; Hosmer, *Hutchinson*, pp. 26–35.

ceived from historians. Few of them were first-class statesmen, though they might stand comparison with the governors elected in some of our States today. And, except for their lack of military knowledge, their background and experience put them, as a group, distinctly above the average of royal governors of their age. But from the nature of their office and the problems of their times they became storm centers for the economic and political conflicts of the most independent and articulate section of the colonial world. Even the best of them could hardly hope to emerge from the tenure of their trying office with reputations unscathed. Historically, the course of events was against them, for they represented a losing cause. The royal authority which they personified was finally driven from the land, and the popular factions which they opposed evolved into the successful party of a revolution. To the victors went the historical spoils. But now, with the passing of many years, whether we study the royal governors individually or as a group, we can see more clearly that they did not deserve all the abuse which has been heaped upon their memories.

66

THE ENGLISH BACKGROUND OF AMERICAN ISOLATIONISM IN THE EIGHTEENTH CENTURY

By Felix Gilbert*

When the colonists began their opposition to the encroachments of the British government, the legal justification of their resistance was their conception of the rights of Englishmen. Before the War of Independence Americans had lived in the intellectual and cultural atmosphere of England; they were the proud heirs of the great English tradition of freedom, handed on in an unbroken succession from the days of Magna Carta; they had taken from English political experience the principle of "no taxation without representation". When drafting their new Constitution, they intended merely to improve the old English version by divesting it of those features which had made possible the lapse of the British government into despotism.

This English tradition formed no contrast to the spirit of Enlightenment philosophy which dominated all Europe and also the minds of the colonists in the eighteenth century. Europe's enlightened "philosophes" took Montesquieu and Blackstone as their teachers and thereby accepted the British constitution as the ideal constitution per se or they admitted at least that it contained the basic principles of an ideal political organization. The English tradition could easily be fused, therefore, with those general ideas about the nature of man and about the "Rights of Man" which eighteenth century philosophy had developed. Beneath the philosophical and generalizing language of the Enlightenment in which the constitutions of the new world were couched the English tradition remained clearly perceptible.

Similarly, the roots of the guiding principles of early American foreign policy exhibit the English influence. A public discussion of foreign affairs formed an intrinsic element of English political life in the eighteenth century. Certainly England was not ruled by the will of the people or by public opinion in the eighteenth century; political power rested sol-

---

*This essay is an adaptation of part of an extended study by Dr. Gilbert on the European background of American foreign policy, which will be published in the near future.

Dr. Gilbert has been a member of the Institute for Advanced Study, Princeton, New Jersey, since 1939. He is a Ph.D. of the University of Berlin, and was formerly assistant to the editors of the German diplomatic documents on the origins of the war of 1914. A student of political ideas and international affairs, he was co-editor with E. M. Earle and Gordon Craig of *Makers of Modern Strategy*, (Princeton, 1943).

idly in the hands of a small clique of Whig aristocrats. But whereas on the European continent absolutism stifled public political discussion, and foreign affairs especially were considered as an arcᵢnum—managed and understood by the monarch and a few nobles alone; in England the Whigs, as the heirs and beneficiaries of the "Glorious Revolution" and bound to its traditions, had an interest in airing political issues in Parliament and in gaining the support of public opinion. Debates in Parliament were secret then; but speeches of parliamentary leaders were frequently published anonymously, and all political problems of significance were extensively discussed in numerous pamphlets. Thus throughout the years from the Peace of Utrecht to the American Revolution a steady trickle of pamphlets concerned with the issues of British foreign policy appeared and developed into a spate in times of war and political crisis.

Thus English political life certainly could provide patterns of thought from which the colonists could draw their lessons in forming their system of foreign policy. It is difficult, however, to determine the precise nature of the influence exerted by this English discussion on the ideas of the colonists concerning foreign affairs. The English discussion on foreign affairs showed no consensus of opinion; on the contrary, divergent and contradictory counsels were given for the conduct of British diplomacy. This lack of clarity may be explained by the fact that the period between the Peace of Utrecht and the Seven Years War was one of profound change: England left the steady course which she had pursued previous to the eighteenth century, and embarked on new waters. The practical tasks which confronted British diplomacy in the eighteenth century must be clearly grasped in order to understand the issues which stimulated the English public debate on foreign affairs and the lessons which it could teach the colonists.

During the eighteenth century, the European state system underwent a complete transformation in accordance with which England's role in European power politics changed decisively.[1] Since the beginning of the sixteenth century, when the contest for the possession of Italy had covered Europe with a network of antagonisms and alliances, European di-

---

[1] Recent works of fundamental importance, covering the English history of the period, are Basil Williams, *The Whig Supremacy 1714-1760* (Oxford 1939) and W. L. Dorn, *Competition for Empire 1740-1763* (New York 1940); Dorn's and Williams' work contain extensive bibliographical guides; A. M. Wilson, *French Foreign Policy . . . of Cardinal Fleury 1726-43* (Cambridge 1936) also has an excellent bibliography.

plomacy had been dominated by the rivalry of two great dynasties, the houses Bourbon and Hapsburg. The center of action had been mainly in central and southern Europe. England had been more a spectator than a participant in this conflict; she was interested only in the prevention of the danger which the continental supremacy of one power and the establishment of a universal monarchy might present to her security and independence. The war of the Spanish succession was the last great struggle between the houses of Bourbon and Hapsburg. Then Louis XIV's bid for European hegemony had been checked by the Great Coalition, led by Austria and England. After this war a new situation arose. The statesmen, influenced by the doctrines of mercantilism, which stressed the importance of economic centralization and foreign trade, became increasingly aware of the connection between economic and political power. Economic advantages became the openly acknowledged motive of political struggles between nations. The influence of commercial and colonial interests made itself increasingly felt in diplomatic decisions. International conflicts no longer grew out of struggles for territorial expansion and continental hegemony but out of the desire for trading privileges and colonial possessions. Consequently the political center of gravity shifted from southern and central Europe to the Atlantic seaboard, and the importance of England in the European state system was enhanced. The significance of the Franco-Austrian hostility paled in comparison with the importance of the Anglo-French "competition for empire". The leadership in the fight against France devolved upon England.

69

Other events accentuated the emergence of a new political constellation. Austria, excluded from direct access to the ocean and to the new sources of wealth, tried to replace this relative loss of strength by embarking on a new policy; she turned to the southeast, building an empire in the Danube valley and in the Balkans, and was drawn into the new orbit of Eastern European politics. It is the century of the appearance of Russia in the politics of Europe and of the rise of Prussia which, by its territorial expansion, bridged the formerly separated eastern and western half of Europe. Europe began to be formed into a connected whole; the foundations were laid of a concert of European power, extending from Petersburg to London and Madrid.

The gradual disappearance of the continental conflicts between France and Austria, the vehemence of the Anglo-French colonial rivalry, and the incorporation of Russia and Prussia into the European system were events that made the eighteenth century a landmark in the history of European diplomacy. It was the great achievement of the elder Pitt that he perceived this rise of a new political constellation in Europe and firmly adapted England's foreign policy to the new situation. He saw that the old Anglo-French rivalry had changed its objects. In planning the course of English foreign policy, he placed commercial and colonial aims above all others. Oceans and colonies needed to be the main scene of action. England's relations to the European continent became of secondary importance and had to be subordinated to these new aims. The main task of British continental diplomacy was to restrict France to the Continent and to keep her from employing her forces overseas. With Austria gradually losing interest in western Europe, Prussia was to take Austria's place as England's ally in checking France.

Thus, at the beginning of the Seven Years War, Pitt reorganized English foreign policy in accordance with the new economic interests and political aliginments. Yet before this decisive and lasting turn in British history was reached, statesmen and public alike, dimly aware of the changing conditions, groped in search of a popular foreign policy. One ·indication of the prevailing uncertainty is to be found in the frequent shifting of alliances and sudden diplomatic revolutions. Zigzag diplomacy was characteristic of the first three decades of the eighteenth century. England entered this period in alliance with Austria; in 1717 she moved over to the side of France, but in 1730 she returned to the Austrian entente after she had gone through a series of negotiations, treaties, and alliances with nearly all the European powers.

Significantly, the attitude towards foreign policy of the two parties contesting for power in England also underwent a revolution. In the seventeenth century, the Whigs and Tories had been the representatives of opposite systems not only in regard to domestic affairs but also in regard to foreign policy. As King George I once said[2], the "old Tory notion" which had developed during the seventeenth century was "that England can subsist by itself, whatever becomes of the rest of Europe"; and he added that this notion had been "justly exploded by the Whigs ever since the revolution". The Whigs represented the opposite point of view, claiming that England's safety was dependent on the maintenance of a balance of power on the European continent. England, therefore, should take an active interest in the diplomatic movements of the continent.

---

[2] Townshend Manuscripts, *Historical Manuscripts Commission Eleventh Report*, Appendix, pt. IV (London 1887), p. 103.

Yet just when, after the accession of the Hanoverian dynasty, the Whigs had come to power, the foundations of European diplomacy began to shift, and the Whigs themselves became doubtful of the wisdom of rigid adherence to their old principles. They split into various groups, recommending various courses of action. The differences of opinion which once had formed the dividing line between Whigs and Tories now became sources of discord within the Whig party itself. It was said of Robert Walpole, the first Whig Prime Minister, that he adopted the foreign policy of the Tories for the Whig party. He proclaimed: "My politics are to keep free from all engagements as long as we possibly can,"[3] and once he emphasized in the House of Commons: "This nation is a trading nation and the prosperity of the trade is what ought to be principally in the eyes of every gentleman of the House".[4] His main goal, therefore, was the preservation of peace, because peace was the presupposition of a flourishing trade. Walpole always used England's influence on the continent to remove possible causes of friction and to compose conflicts. He saw the foremost interest of British foreign policy "not in the maintenance of the balance of power, but in the tranquility of Europe,"[5] and thereby he clearly deviated from the traditional "meddling" policy of the Whigs. In contrast to Walpole, his successor, Carteret, who guided English foreign policy in the war of the Pragmatic Sanction, returned to the "old system"[6] of the Whigs. He considered it his task to "jumble" the heads of princes, to depose kings and establish emperors. Under the pretense of the maintenance of the "balance of power," he gave free rein to his inclination to pile up alliances and accumulate treaties. It was the great realist Pitt who ended this wavering between divergent lines of policy and placed English foreign policy on a new basis. He united the opposing systems, taking from each what seemed useful. He acknowledged England's interest in the affairs of the continent, but he subordinated it to the strengthening of England as a maritime and trading power.

This fluid diplomatic situation formed the background for the arguments of the pamphleteers who were discussing the issues of foreign policy.[7] The battle of the pamphlets started along the

---

[3] Walpole to Townshend 1723, quoted in Coxe, *Memoirs of the Life and Administration of Sir Robert Walpole* (edition of 1816), II, 408.

[4] House of Commons, Debate of March 8, 1739.

[5] Bathurst in House of Lords, February 13, 1741.

[6] Cf. R. Lodge, "English neutrality in the War of Polish succession," *Transactions of the Royal Historical Society*, Fourth Series, XIV (1931), 143.

[7] As far as I can see, the pamphlet literature of the period has never been systematically analyzed. W. T. Laprade's *Public Opinion and Politics*

traditional lines of the seventeenth century struggle between Whigs and Tories. There were those who stood for England's interest in the preservation of the balance of power, and there were others who emphasized the advantages of England's insular position, characterizing the attitude of their opponents as "Quixotism" and an attempt to "revive the Ages of Knight Errantry."[8]

In the course of the eighteenth century, however, the fundamental controversy—"interest in maintenance of balance of power on the continent" versus the advantages of insular position—was enriched through the introduction of economic and constitutional considerations. It was said by those who stressed England's indifference to the affairs of the continent that trade was England's main interest and that trade flourished best in peace. "A trading nation should avoid war if possible."[9] Constitutional considerations were brought into the discussion as a result of the accession of the Hanoverian dynasty to the English throne. Was the participation in the strifes of Europe really beneficial to the English people or did it serve merely the interest of the Hanoverian dynasty and enhance the glory of its continental dominion? The Act of Settlement had explicitly established the provision that "in case the Crown and Imperial dignity of the Realm shall thereafter come to any person not being a native of this Kingdom of England, this nation shall not be obliged to engage in any war for the defense of any dominions or territories, which do not belong to the crown of England, without the consent of Parliament." The desire to demonstrate to the crown the limits of its influence and to prevent any undue extension of its power stimulated the discussion of this question.

Nearly all contributions to the public discussion on foreign affairs can be reduced to one of these arguments or to a combina-

---

in Eighteenth Century England deals only with the first quarter of the century and is merely a factual reproduction of the content of newspapers and magazines.   A. M. Wilson's book on *Foreign Policy . . . of Cardinal Fleury* discusses a few single pamphlets of special importance. B. Williams's (on p. 67) and B. Turnstall's (on p. 282) *Pitt* biographies refer to the effect of Mauduit's "Considerations"; R. Pares's article, "American versus Continental Warfare 1739-63", *English Historical Review*, LI (1936), 429-465 is of fundamental importance. It covers the military aspects of the public controversy comprehensively and brilliantly.

My analysis of the battle of the pamphlets is based on a collection of English pamphlets in the Cornell University Library; this collection was brought together by an Englishman, James Hustler of Acklam, at the beginning of the last century and was bought for Cornell when his library was dissolved. In addition, I used pamphlets of the New York Public Library and of the Huntington Library in San Marino.

[8] *Considerations offered upon the approaching peace . . . .*, London 1720.
[9] *The Treaty of Seville, and the measures that have been taken for the last four years, impartially considered*, 1730.

tion of them. Bolingbroke's "Patriot King,"[10] a comprehensive political program which contained a systemtic survey of the guiding principles of English foreign policy, neatly balanced and summarized all these arguments: "Great Britain is an island, and, while nations on the continent are at immense charge in maintaining their barriers, and perpetually on their guard, and frequently embroiled, to extend or strengthen them, Great Britain may, if her governors please, accumulate wealth in maintaining hers; make herself secure from invasions, and be ready to invade others where her own immediate interest, or the general interest of Europe requires it . . . I said the general interest of Europe; because it seems to me that this, alone, should call our commerce off from an almost entire application to their domestic and proper business . . . as we cannot be easily nor suddenly attacked, and as we ought not to aim at any acquisition of territory on the continent, it may be our interest to watch the secret workings of the several councils abroad; to advise and warn; to abet and oppose; but it never can be our true interest easily and officiously to enter into action, much less into engagements that imply action and expense. Other nations, like the *velites* or light-armed troops, stand foremost in the field, and skirmish perpetually. When a great war begins, we ought to look on the powers of the continent, to whom we incline, like the two first lines, the *principes* and *hastati* of the Roman army; and on ourselves like the *triarii,* that are not to charge with these legions on every occasion, but to be ready for the conflict whenever the fortune of the day, be it sooner or later, calls us to it, and the sum of things, or the general interest, makes it necessary. This is the post of advantage and honour, which our singular situation among the powers of Europe determines us, or should determine us to take, in all disputes that happen on the continent . . . by a continual attention to improve her natural, that is her maritime strength, by collecting all her forces within herself, and reserving them to be laid out on great occasions, such as regard her immediate interests and her honour, or such as are truly important to the general system of power in Europe; she may be the arbitrater of differences, the guardian of liberty, and the preserver of that balance, which has been so much talked of, and is so little understood . . . ."

73

Although the debate of the pamphleteers on English foreign policy revolved around a few identical fundamental arguments, it developed in different stages, clearly distinguishable from each other. In the first half of the century the discussion is entirely dominated by the Hanoverian argument. The popular preoccupa-

---

[10] Bolingbroke, *Works,* IV, 310-312.

tion with this question, whether or not the Hanoverian continental commitments deflected English foreign policy from the proper course, may be deduced from the outspoken titles of some of the pamphlets which asked: Was "the interest of Great Britain steadily pursued," or was "the interest of Hanover steadily pursued"?[11] This controversy became particularly heated when, after Walpole's fall, Carteret imposed on England an extremely active role in the war of the Pragmatic Sanction. Pitt, then still a young man, and lacking the balanced judgment on foreign affairs which he achieved in later years, spoke bitter words in the House of Commons:[12] "This great, this powerful, this formidable kingdom, is considered only as a province to a despicable electorate," words that were echoed frequently in the pamphlets of the period. The most trenchant formulation can be found in a pamphlet ascribed to Chesterfield:[13] "The whole strength of the British empire was to be steer'd by the Hanover rudder." Chesterfield, who had had a rich diplomatic experience, was convinced that Carteret, with his numerous treaties of subsidies and alliances, had exceeded the limits of a sound British foreign policy; yet he did not take the extreme stand that England had no interest in the continent at all or that the balance of power was a mere chimera. He tried to devise a definitive rule for England's relation with the continent. "We might lay it down as an invariable Maxim, never to enter into a Land-War, never, but when the Dutch Barrier was in Danger."

A few strategically minded pamphleteers looked upon the problem from a more comprehensive point of view. They asked:[14] "Whether it might be more conducive to the true interest of this nation to rely wholly upon that situation which disjoins it from the rest of the world, to encrease its naval force, and to give its great application to the marine without concerning itself with the intrigues of the neighbouring states; or once more to cover Flanders with our troops, to negotiate, to fight, and to expend our treasure, in restraining the overgrown power of France, and in preserving the balance of Europe?"

On the whole, however, the public preferred to look at the alternatives of British diplomacy from a simple but more in-

---

[11] *The Interest of Great Britain steadily pursued, in answer to a pamphlet entitled The Case of the Hanover Forces*, London 1743. H. Walpole is considered to be the author of this pamphlet. It was answered by a pamphlet ascribed to Chesterfield: *The Interest of Hanover Steadily Pursued*, London, 1743.
[12] December 10, 1742.
[13] *The case of the Hanover forces in the pay of Great Britain impartially and freely examined . . . .* London 1743.
[14] *The Interest of Hanover steadily pursued . . . .* London 1743.

triguing angle—the question whether their foreign policy served the British people or the Hanoverian dynasty.

The basis of the discussion shifted when, in the fifties, England became again a participant in a great European war. It was an entirely changed situation, in which the debate on foreign affairs was then renewed. One pamphleteer states frankly[15] that he has been "no friend to Continental Measures in general" and that he was especially opposed to "such continental measures as engaged us during the three last Wars, as Principals," but the continental measures now adopted are "necessary both with regard to our Honour and Our Interest."

Now no one dared to charge Pitt, who steered England through the Seven Years War, with un-English and Hanoverian sympathies. Factions and constitutional bickering had disappeared from the debate, and the discussion centered much more objectively around the true alternatives of British foreign policy. A pamphleteer,[16] at the beginning of the war point by point enumerated the arguments which could be made in favour of the alternative propositions. He explained first the reasons why England should keep aloof from the continent: "(1) Great Britain, being an Island, is secure from an Invasion, and having no designs of making conquests, and no interests of her own to pursue on the continent, has no need of foreign Assistance. (2) The strength of Great Britain lies in her Fleets: these should be her principal, her only care. And if we carry on the War wholly by Sea, and have nothing to do with the Continent, we shall have everything to hope and nothing to fear." Similarly, he listed the arguments in favour of England's intervention in the affairs of the continent.

This pamphlet showed the widened scope of the controversy. The purposes as well as the means of English foreign policy were scrutinized. Did England's interest lie mainly on the continent or mainly in colonial expansion; was it possible to limit military efforts to naval warfare, or was it necessary to enter the continental battlefields with a standing army?

As long as the French were contesting the English expansion over the American continent, Pitt, without much obstruction by the clamorous, yet unconvincing and inefficient opposition, could pursue his dual policy of colonial aggrandizement on the one hand and of the Prussian alliance on the other. Yet the opposition had a much better case when, after

75

---

[15] *The Important Question discussed, or a serious and impartial Enquiry into the Interest of England with regard to the Continent.*

[16] *The Important Question concerning Invasions, a Sea War, Raising the Militia and paying Subsidies for foreign Troops,* London 1755.

the defeat of the French in Canada, Pitt stuck to the Prussian alliance and a continuation of the war.[17] At this moment the most famous of all English pamphlets of the eighteenth century appeared: Mauduit's "Considerations on the present German War." It has been said of this pamphlet that it caused Pitt's downfall. Its amazing success was due no less to the brilliancy of its reasoning than to its timeliness.

Mauduit did more than marshal the outworn arguments; he tried to discover the reality behind the concepts used in the controversy; his pamphlet culminated in an analysis of the term "continental connections." He showed that this term had a different meaning when applied to the war of the Spanish Succession than when used to describe England's policy towards the continent in his own time. In the war of the Spanish Succession, the whole continent had been united against France. England had been only one member of a large coalition; in his time, England was allied only to a few secondary powers like Prussia, Hanover, and Brunswick.

The present alliances served much more limited objectives than the participation in the Great Coalition. No longer did issues like the freedom of Protestantism or the prevention of a Universal Monarchy necessitate England's interference in continental politics. Even subsidies were no longer necessary; on the contrary they were even detrimental to the English interests, for they kept alive disunity among the German states. Without British interference one power would get the upper hand in Germany and establish unity. A united Germany would form then a perfect counterweight against France. Thus, if England stayed out of the continent, she could ultimately benefit by the creation of a balance of power, the perennial panacea of British diplomacy. There was a mixture of falsehood and truth in Mauduit's reasoning. In his time, a united Germany was an Utopia; he also failed to see that even a disunited Germany neutralized an important part of the French forces. But he judged correctly when assuming that the aims of the British and their allies in the War of the Spanish Succession were fundamentally different from those which Pitt pursued when he allied England with Prussia in the Seven Years War. None had shown more convincingly than Mauduit that continental connections did not always have a beneficial effect on the strength of the English position.

This battle of the pamphleteers about the English continental interests and the advantages of an insular position was, in a sense, a continuation of the old Whig and Tory strife

---

[17] *A Letter addressed to two great men . . . .* London 1760.

over foreign policy, despite the many new elements which entered the discussion in the course of the eighteenth century.
Yet the discussion of the eighteenth century made the English public for the first time fully aware of the implications of
the old Tory position, which recommended seclusion from continental quarrels, and thus this whole idea seemed quite new
to them. As one of the pamphlets[18] said, the idea of keeping
away from continental wars "never entered into any Man's
Heart till of late years." What, asked the Dutch diplomat,
Count Bentinck, with astonishment, in 1745,[19] would the English statesmen of the last century, should they be alive, think,
"if they had heard an English nobleman say that it signify as
little who is Emperor, as who is Lord Mayor of London?"

77

   In his letters to the Netherlands, Bentinck also mentions
that he had heard in London drawing rooms a new term used
to characterize this policy of keeping away from the continent:
"des principes isolés." The great popularity of this view in
eighteenth century England was well known also on the continent. A French handbook on European politics explicitly
referred to the new English trend "a rompre ce qu'elle appelle
Continental connections, ou liaisons avec le continent."[20] As
we have seen, in this controversy over the issue of "continental connections" the alternatives had been a colonial and maritime expansion or a European policy with continental wars.
Yet there was even a third group; they were thorough pacifists who declared that the insular position of England made a
complete abandonment of all power politics entirely possible.
Their motto could be found in a pamphlet[21] ascribed to Lord
Hervey: "From a warlike Genius, and an Enterprizing Minister, Good Lord deliver us." England was in no need of bellicose statesmanship; for[22] "Nature has separated us from the
continent . . . and as no man ought to endeavour to separate
whom God Almighty has joined, so no man ought to endeavour to join what God Almighty has separated." This
group claimed that its view served the trading interests better
than any other. Some of these pamphleteers willingly ad-

---

[18] *The Important Questions concerning Invasions,* London 1755.
   [19] *Briefwisseling en Aantee Keningen von William Bentinck, Heer von
Rhoon* . . . . uitgegeren door C. Gerretson en F. Geyl: Deel I (Utrecht
1934); Letters to the Countess of Portland, August 10 and September 7,
1745, p. 131 and 139.
   [20] Peysonnel, *Situation Politique de la France et ses Rapports Actuels
avec toutes les Puissances de l'Europe,* (Neuchatel 1789) p. 71.
   [21] *Miscellaneous Thoughts on the present Posture of our foreign and
domestic Affairs,* London 1742.
   [22] The Earl of Pomfret in the House of Lords, December 10, 1755.

mitted that England had a strong interest in intercourse with
other powers because of her commerce:[23] "Treaties of commerce are Bonds that we ought to contract with our neighbours," yet as to the nature of such bonds the same author
stated that "a trading nation ought not to concern itself with
particular nations, or Schemes of Government in distant countries
... her interest requires that she should live if possible in
constant Harmony with all Nations, that she may better enjoy
the Effects of their friendship in the benefits resulting from
their Commerce." Another writer[24] assumed that Britain
could be sure of being left in peace because of other nations'
interest in continuing trade with Britain. Still another pamphleteer[25] stated that all treaties of Great Britain with the various
powers of Europe "have not produced any advantage to us."
Therefore he drew up a general rule: "A Prince or State ought
to avoid all Treaties, except such as tend towards promoting
Commerce or Manufactures . . . All other Alliances may be
looked upon as Encumbrances." The pamphlets of this pacifist group represented the most radical position in the discussion on the aims and means of English foreign policy during
the eighteenth century.

Although it may lie somewhat outside the range of this
study, it seems impossible to leave the discussion of the "battle of pamphlets" without touching upon the question as to
their practical impact and influence on the conduct of English
foreign policy. Probably the mighty Whig families were not
swayed one way or another by the arguments of the scribblers.
Reared on their country estates and drawing their strength
from their ruling position in their counties, with the self-assur-
ance of a class traditionally accustomed to wield power, they
relied more on their instinct than on technical knowledge,
more on an imperturbable confidence in their ability to handle
emergencies as they arose than on any capacity to prevent
them by foresight. Yet they had come to power as the protag-
onists of Parliament and people against the crown, and, even
under the Hanoverian dynasty which they themselves had
established, the contest between crown and parliament was
a living issue. Thus they needed to keep contact with public
opinion and to make sure of its continued support. The special emphasis on the dangers of the Hanoverian influence in

---

[23] *A modest Enquiry into the Present State of Foreign Affairs,* London
1742.
[24] *A detection of the Views of those who would, in the present crisis,
engage an incumber'd Trading Nation, as Principals, in a ruinous expensive
Land-War,* London 1746.
[25] *Political Maxims,* by Phil. Anglus.   London 1744.

English foreign policy might be partly explained by the particular effectiveness of this argument in arousing the distrust of the public against the court. The stress on the trading interests of England may be linked with the special position of the merchants in English political life. They were a small, yet an independent and influential group, which could make its voice heard and, if necessary, turn the scales of a decision at a critical moment. Thus all the concrete issues of eighteenth century England's domestic and foreign policy are involved in this debate on the corollaries of England's peculiar geographical situation, her special interests in trade, and the question whether it was possible to keep England free from "continental connections."

79

Bostonians subscribing to the austere *News Letter* or the equally bleak *Evening Post,* the more fortunate Philadelphians enjoying the lighter and more entertaining fare of Franklin's *Pennsylvania Gazette,* the Virginians with their *Virginia Gazette* of Williamsburg, or Charlestonians imbibing the refinements of Southern civilization by reading the highly literary *South Carolina Gazette*—all found foreign news predominating in their newspapers.[26] The newspapers reported not so much the events of their own town or region or news from other colonies, as the "latest intelligences" from distant Europe. When the dispatches from Europe were late, publication of the papers was sometimes deferred until the arrival of the next boat. European news not only dealt with events in the mother country, with parliament and court, but also with affairs from Warsaw and Madrid, from Paris and Vienna. Editors kept a continuous record of European events, sometimes even withholding more recent news from publication in favor of older dispatches that had been delayed. In short, the colonists did not lack factual knowledge of the political situation in Europe.

However, the information that a reader could glean from his newspaper was limited. Newspapers were licensed by the government and were in constant danger of suppression in case of undue criticism; editorial comment was hardly known. Were the colonists able to penetrate beyond factual statements? Were they informed about the preceding deliberations and discussions? More specifically, was the debate then taking place in England on foreign policy, and its issues known to the colonists?

One way of learning about the English trends of thought was a sojourn in England. During the critical period of the Seven

---

[26] Cf. F. L. Mott, *American Journalism* (New York 1941), particularly pp. 48-49.

Years War, Franklin stayed in England and participated in the debate on the question of continuing the war after the French defeat in Canada.   In two pamphlets he revealed himself as a follower of Pitt.   His main purpose was to call attention to the great value of Canada in order to prevent the exchange of Canada for Guadeloupe.[27]   At the same time, however, he attacked those pamphleteers who demanded immediate peace.   Notes which he jotted down some years later[28] show that he had become well acquainted with the arguments of the debate.   He spoke disparagingly of the "whims about the balance of power," of the "English European quarrels" and of the "continual connexions in which [the colonies] are separately unconcerned."   Franklin was, of course, an unusually acute observer and no other American had a better opportunity to gain intimate knowledge of the English political scene than he; but lesser men with lesser opportunities often brought home considerable knowledge of the questions that were agitating Parliament and the coffee houses.   Indeed, the number of those who had been educated in the mother country or who had visited it and therefore had some contact with English politics should not be underestimated.

Certainly the intellectual life of the colonies was not cut off from English thought.   Important intellectual developments and productions of England had their repercussions in the colonies. John Adams's *Autobiography* reveals the impression which the reading of Bolingbroke made on him.[29]   From this source we learn —not without amusement in view of Adams's future revolutionary career—the great satisfaction he felt with George III's first speech to Parliament which proved him worthy of the title of a "Patriot King."[30]   Bolingbroke's views on English foreign policy, therefore, were known to Adams.

The fame of Israel Mauduit's "Considerations on the present German War" had also spread across the ocean.   Jasper Mauduit, the brother of Israel, seems to have owed his election as Agent of Massachusetts to the fact that he was mistaken for this famous kinsman.   Even more important in informing the colonies of the main issues of the English debate on foreign affairs was the *Political Disquisitions,* by James Burgh.   This book was regarded

27 *The Interest of Great Britain Considered with Regard to her Colonies and the Acquisitions of Canada and Guadeloupe;* also *Of the Means of Disposing the Enemie to Peace,* cf. C. vanDoren, *Benjamin Franklin* (New York 1941), pp. 288 *et seq.*
28 B. Franklin, *Works,* ed. Bigelow, IV, 308 *et seq.*
39 J. Adams to James Burgh, December 28, 1774, *Works,* IX, 351.
30 J. Adams, *Works,* II, 141.

as the "bible" of the Whigs.[31] Burgh emphasized that the people
were the "fountain of all authority and government." He demanded a more adequate representation of the people in Parliament and attacked the influence of the court and the parliamentary
corruption; he also denounced a standing army and spoke in favor
of a militia. In short, all tenets of British eighteenth century
progressivism were set forth in the book, including a program of
foreign policy. Burgh was a pacifist who considered war "the
peculiar disgrace of human nature,"[32] and who thought it wiser
"to keep clear of quarrels among other states."[33] Since the times
of Queen Anne, England unfortunately had "attached herself
to continental schemes."[34] There was no reason "to intangle
ourselves with the disputes between the powers of the continent";[35]
"continental connections" had only "ruinous effects."[36]

Small wonder that Burgh's ideas found an enthusiastic reception in the colonies, for his radical Whiggism was the political credo
of the American revolutionaries. Moreover, Burgh was a great
champion of the American cause; he devoted a special chapter to
proving that Parliament had no right to tax the colonies. He was
eager to befriend the leaders of the colonies, taking great pride in
his intimacy with Franklin[37] and sending his work to John Adams
"as a small token of respect for his Patriotic Virtue."[38] Adams
reciprocated by promising "to make the Disquisitions more Known
and attended to in several parts of America."[39] Adams seems to
have been successful. Burgh's book was frequently quoted in
newspapers; the list of subscribers to its first American edition
in 1775 contained many leading names of the colonists such as
Washington, Jefferson, Bowdoin, Hancock, and others. Moreover, there is ample evidence that the *Disquisitions* was carefully
read in its entirety by many Americans and achieved for a time
at least the position of a minor classic in this country. More than
a decade after publication, the authors of Publius's essays on
the new Constitution considered Burgh's book one of the few
worthy'of direct quotation in *The Federalist*.[40] Jefferson, in 1814,
included it in a reading list for a friend as one of the half-dozen

81

[31] Cf. the article on Burgh in *The English Dictionary of National Biography.*
[32] Burgh, *Political Disquisitions*, Philadelphia 1775, II, 341.
[33] Burgh, *Ibid.*, III, 288.
[34] Burgh, *Ibid.*, II, 388.
[35] Burgh, *Ibid.*, I, xxii.
[36] Burgh, *Ibid.*, I, xxii.
[37] Burgh, *Ibid.*, II, 276.
[38] Inscription in the dedication copy of Burgh's work in the Adams
Library in Boston.
[39] J. Adams to James Burgh, December 28, 1774, *Works*, IX, 351.
[40] *Federalist* 58.

books essential to an understanding of "Modern Politics" and rated it as comparable to Locke, Sidney, Montesquieu, Priestley and *The Federalist*.[41] The popularity of Burgh's book in the colonies is an indication that at least the fundamental outlines of the debate on the advantages and disadvantages of "continental connections" were known in America at the time of the first Continental Congress.

It is unnecessary to scrutinize still further the exact channels through which the colonists became acquainted with the British controversy over foreign policy. For by one stroke the English controversy on foreign policy and continental connections was transferred to the colonies, on the eve of independence, by Thomas Paine in his famous pamphlet *Common Sense*.

At first glance, it may seem surprising to connect Paine's words with the political controversy which had developed in England, for they seem the hurried product of an emergency situation, peculiar to the colonies, written to press a few timely political demands like that of declaring independence. A closer study, however, will show that these practical political recommendations form only a part of a very skillfully organized whole. The pamphlet contains two parts. In the first section, a few general considerations on the difference between society and government and on the purposes of government led Paine to a thesis which in the age of Montesquieu and Blackstone must have sounded extremely revolutionary. He maintained that the English constitution was not perfect, that on the contrary, it was a most unsatisfactory instrument of government. In justification of this unusual statement he argued that a "simple thing" is better than a "complex thing"[42]; the mixed nature of the English constitution with its monarchial, aristocratic and republican elements, and its complicated system of checks and balances was proof of its imperfection. He implemented this criticism by a detailed discussion of the faults of any monarchial constitution and the first section ended with the statement that monarchy can never be an ideal system of government. This first part was mainly critical in character, yet through this negative attitude it reveals what Paine considered the ideal form of government to be—a republic, in which all power emanates from the people.

In the second part, Paine plunged rather suddenly into the discussion of the "state of American affairs"[43] and advised a constructive program for a policy of the new world. Yet there is a

---

[41] H. S. Randall, *Life of Thomas Jefferson*, (New York, 1858), I, 55.
[42] *The Life and Works of Thomas Paine*, Patriots' Edition, (New York 1925), II, 102.
[43] "Thoughts on the Present State of American Affairs", Paine, *Ibid.*, p. 122.

significant connection between the first and the second sections:
the constructive program of the second part is the logical sequence
of Paine's criticism of the European monarchies in the first part.
Because the English constitution was faulty, and because Europe
was unable to achieve a perfect constitution, it was the duty of
America to break with Europe, to make use of her unique opportunities, and to realize the ideal republic. Paine proclaimed
that now the propitious moment for the separation from the old
world had come, that America had all the means necessary to
achieve independence. Just because Europe had failed it was
America's responsibility to fulfill her own political tasks. This
grandiose plea culminated in the brief outline of the future constitution of America.   *83*

If we analyze the various threads out of which the fabric of
Common Sense is woven, the fibre of American political and social
conditions seems to predominate. Unquestionably, Paine tried to
enliven his work with local coloring. He illustrated the danger
of being tied to England's "rotten constitution" by a reference to
the severe moral customs of New England according to which
"a man who is attached to a prostitute is unfitted to choose or
judge a wife."[44] The familiar theme in eighteenth century political
literature of the emergence of society and government from the
state of nature reads like a new story as told by Paine in the light
of American frontier conditions. When, in describing the origins
of government, he wrote about the "convenient tree under the
branches of which the whole colony may assemble to deliberate on
public matters"[45] and which will serve as the first state house, we
are reminded of the first representative assembly in America con-
vening on wooded Jamestown Island, and of the Pilgrims taking
their first steps towards an organization of social life in their new
home.

Still more strongly *Common Sense* bears the imprint of the
extremely critical situation in Philadelphia during the last months
of the year 1775, when Paine was writing his pamphlet.[46] Gal-
loway, Duane, Dickinson, the early leaders of the opposition movement, were beginning to cede their place to the Adamses and the
Lees, the radicals from Massachusetts and Virginia. Discord
among the leaders of the opposition had been long concealed. Each
faction had pursued its own line of action while avoiding all funda-

---

[44] Paine, *Works*, II, 107.
[45] Paine, *Ibid.*, p. 100.
[46] A few remarks on the connection between the program of action of the
radicals and Paine's pamphlet can be found in P. Davidson, *Propaganda
and the American Revolution 1763-1783* (Chapel Hill, 1941). Otherwise,
this question has hardly been discussed.

mental. issues such as that of independence which would of necessity have led to a rupture between them. At the end of the summer of 1775, however, circumstances 'had become such that a continuation of this policy of evasion was no longer possible. The position of the moderates became weakened by the English government's unfavorable reception of the colonists' attempts at reconciliation. The commercial situation made it impossible to postpone any longer definite decisions. After the non-exportation agreement became effective in September 1775, it was clear that this complete suspension of exports could not last beyond the winter. Either the whole measure would have to be abandoned—and such a step clearly would have meant the beginning of a capitulation to England—or American ports had to be opened to the ships of other powers, a measure that would have meant a definite break with England, since the claim of the mother country to exclusive trade with its colonies was the cornerstone of the whole colonial-mercantile system of the eighteenth century. In the fall session of the Continental Congress, a most important debate was concerned with the problem of the "opening of the ports." No decision was reached. The moderates did not want to alienate England permanently, and some of the radicals believed that America should try to continue to live on her own resources. Similarly, the issues of naval armament and of confederation remained undecided. In other important respects, however, the radicals gained the upper hand. The Congress vigorously applied itself to the organization of the army. It recommended the adoption of constitutions to the various colonies and established a committee of secret correspondence for the purposé of exploring the attitude of foreign powers. Still, in spite of these measures, the radicals were not satisfied. The letters of John Adams show their disappointment in the failure of their program to find complete acceptance.

This was the state of affairs when Paine composed *Common Sense*. The practical demands of this pamphlet suggest that he knew well what happened behind the closed doors of the Continental Congress. All the arguments of the radicals in the fall and winter of 1775 were summarized in Paine's pamphlet. He spoke disparagingly of continuing petitions to the king, advocated the building of an American navy,[47] urged the immediate formation of a confederation,[48] stressed the importance of foreign assistance and advised opening the ports. The culmination of Paine's treatise, the first public call for independence, was only the logical

[47] Paine, *Works*, II, 154 *et seq.*
[48] Paine, *Ibid.*, pp. 144 *et seq.*

corollary of these postulates. It was as though Paine had been asked by the radicals to set their program before the public.

So much for the American background of *Common Sense.* As we have seen, Paine's pamphlet argued that the foundation of an independent America was necessary not only for reasons of political expediency but as the fulfillment of a duty to mankind. The demands for an independent America were embedded in a general social philosophy which can clearly be traced to trends of political thought, which were current in England whence Paine had come to the colonies only twelve months before.[49]

When discoursing on the defects of the monarchies, Paine re-tells a well known biblical story; Samuel announced to the Jews that they had provoked the ire of God by begging for a king, and he forewarned them of the sufferings they would have to bear under a monarchy. This chapter of the Bible is famous in the history of political thought.[50] A stumbling block to the political theorists of the Middle Ages who believed in the monarchy as the ideal form of government, it was popular with all thinkers of republican convictions. Milton used it extensively in his *Defensio pro populo Anglicano;* so too, did Algernon Sidney in his *Discourses on Government.*[51] By alluding to the same story, Paine reveals himself a true follower of the great republican tradition in English political thought.

At the same time, Paine's ideas were intimately related to contemporary English political thought. He seems to have been an attentive-reader of Hume's political essays. What Paine states about the origin of government and particularly about the different ways of acquiring monarchies corresponds exactly to Hume's explanations in the essays "Of the original contract" and "Of the origin of government." Furthermore, Paine's distinguishing between republican and monarchial elements in the English constitution and his evaluation of their relative importance are an obvious elaboration of a question which Hume had raised in his essay "Whether the British Government inclines more to absolute monarchy, or to a Republic?"

---

[49] Despite the many biographies written on Paine, no study on the development of his "mind" has been made, although it is easy to reconstruct the evolving pattern of his ideas.

[50] P. Kirn, "Saul in der Staatslehre," in *Staat und Personlichkeit,* E. Branderburg zum 60. Geburtstag dargebracht (Leipsig 1928), pp. 28-47.

[51] Algernon Sidney, *Discourses on Government,* Vol. II, Chapter III, Section III; "Samuel did not describe to the Israelites the glory of a tree Monarchy; but the evils the people should suffer, that he might divert them from desiring a king."

But of all the works which influenced Paine, Priestley's *Essay on the First Principles of Government* was the most important. Their fundamental political ideas were identical; both claimed that the people should enjoy as much liberty as possible and should have complete political power. Priestley had not openly attacked the monarchial system of government, yet he had expressed some doubts about the wisdom of the principle of heredity by saying that "in its original principles" every government was an "equal republic."[52] He had broached the idea on which Paine's criticism of the English constitution was based—that a "simple thing" is better than a "complex thing."[53] This notion was by no means familiar to the eighteenth century. Usually, the eighteenth century conceived life in terms of an artificial mechanism, thus the more complicated machine appeared as the more perfect one. Consequently, involved mechanical concepts such as "balance of power" and "mixed government" were favorite principles of political thought. Yet the greatest similarity between Paine and Priestley is to be found in their descriptions of the emergence of a representative government.[54] Paine's passages are nothing but a paraphrase of Priestley's words; whoever reads the respective sections of the two books side by side will be inclined to assume that Paine wrote *Common Sense* with Priestley's pamphlet on his desk.

The prevalence of the English element in Paine's ideas on constitutional questions makes it seem natural that he also followed English trends of thought in his ideas on foreign policy. The group of Utilitarian philosophers, to which Priestley belonged, whose philosophical and political outlook,[55] Paine shared, had very definite ideas on foreign affairs; they were pacifists and therefore bitter enemies of England's involvement in continental quarrels. An analysis of Paine's

---

[52] J. Priestley, *An Essay on the First Principles of Government and on the nature of political, civil, and religious liberty.* (London 1771), p. 40.

[53] Priestley, *Ibid.*, p. 19: "The more complex any machine is, and the more nicely it is fitted to answer the purpose, the more liable it is to disorder."

[54] Cf. Priestley, *Ibid.*, pp. 6-7 and Paine, *Life and Works*, pp. 98-101.

[55] The development of radical Whiggism into utilitarianism, in which Paine takes part, needs further elucidation; for instance, there is no satisfactory study on Priestley. The fundamental work remains E. Halévy, *The growth of philosophic Radicalism*, translated by M. Morris (London 1934); L. Whitney, *Primitivism and the Idea of Progress* (Baltimore 1934) is very suggestive, and H. V. S. Ogden's article, "The decline of Lockian Political Theory", *American Historical Review*, XLVI (1940), 21-44 is good in describing the negative side of this development, namely the loss of prestige of the theory of natural rights.

ideas on foreign policy will show that, also in his views on
foreign policy, he followed their pattern of thought, and had
evidently been much impressed with the arguments directed
against England's involvement in continental quarrels.

Since the main purpose of Paine's pamphlets was to point
out the advantages of an immediate declaration of independence, it was from this angle that he viewed the question of
foreign affairs.   He held the opinion that a declaration of independence would procure the immediate assistance of France
and Spain, while as long as the bonds between England and
the colonies were not formally severed, France and Spain
would never dare to help the colonies; they would fear a possible betrayal by a compromise between mother country and
colonies, not to mention that their help would be a striking
violation of international law.   Paine claimed, however, that
independence would have advantages lasting far beyond the
present emergency.[56]   It would secure peace for America:
"France and Spain never were, nor perhaps ever will be, our
enemies as Americans, but as our being subjects of Great Britain."   There is not "a single advantage that this continent can
reap by being connected with Great Britain."   On the contrary, America's "Plan is commerce, and that, well attended to,
will secure us the peace and friendship of all Europe; because
it is the interest of all Europe to have America a free port."
These arguments were summarized in the famous sentence:
"Any submission to or dependence on Great Britain tends directly to involve this continent in European wars and quarrels
. . . As Europe is our market for trade, we ought to form no
partial connexion with any part of it.   It is the true interest
of America to steer clear of European contentions."

Thus Paine's program of foreign policy is obvious: he advocated not only separation from England, but renunciation of
all political alliances; America should become a free port to
serve the commercial interests of all nations.   The arguments
on which this program was based are America's peculiar geographical position and her trading interest which protected
her from attacks, because all states were interested in maintaining trade with America.   The similarity of this program
to the ideas of the English radicals who had attacked England's "continental connections" and had emphasized the
peculiarity of the English geographical situation and her special interests as a trading nation is striking.   Paine himself
mentions in *Common Sense* the "miseries of Hanover"[57] there-

87

[56] Paine, *Works,* II, 129-131; also p. 126.
[57] Paine, *Ibid.,* p. 126.

by showing that the English parallel was uppermost in his mind. There can be no doubt then that Paine in his program on foreign policy merely applied to America the ideas and concepts of the English controversy on the merits of "continental connections."

It is well known that the success of *Common Sense* was sensational. The propaganda of the radicals quickly made it known all over the country[58]; more than 120,000 copies were reputedly sold in less than three months. Now the movement for independence became a powerful political force. Before the publication of *Common Sense*, hardly anyone had dared to voice "this dreadful, this daring sound"[59] of the word independence; after the success of *Common Sense*, it was continuously discussed in homes and in meetings, in letters and newspapers.

Paine's indubitable merit consisted in that, through him, the thoughts of others came to life; by the brilliancy of his style, they were transformed into a political weapon. Moreover, the most unique and effective feature of *Common Sense* is the fact that it combines the practical with the ideal, political advantage with moral duty. Thus he represented independence "not merely as a striking practical gesture but as the fulfillment of America's moral obligation to the world."[60] The same must be said about Paine's program of foreign policy in general. If Paine's proposals were adopted, foreign trade would flourish, foreign aid would be secured, but more than that: these measures would lead to a better and more peaceful world.

However, the strongest reason for the lasting influence which Paine's ideas on foreign policy exerted was that they filled an absolute gap. Faced by the necessity of a declaration of independence, it became essential to lay out the system of foreign policy which the new republic should follow; but the position of America in the constellation of the political powers of the world had as yet not attracted the attention of the colonists.[61] Thus they turned eagerly to the ideas which just at the moment of need were developed in *Common Sense*, and from now on every utterance on foreign policy seems to start from Paine's words and to echo his thoughts. It is in the brilliant synthesis of *Common Sense* that one must look for the

---

[58] Cf. P. Davidson, *Propaganda and the American Revolution*, p. 215.

[59] Force, *American Archives*, 4th series, III, 1013, "To the people of Pennsylvania, Oct. 11, 1775."

[60] Crane Brinton in his article on Paine in *D. A. B.*, XIV, 159-166.

[61] The approach of the colonists to foreign policy is discussed in the first chapter of my book.

immediate background of both the Federalist Foreign Policy crystallized in Washington's *Farewell Address* and the "republican tack" upon which Jefferson set the ship of state in 1801.   And back of Paine's ideas and principles, adapted though they were to the American situation, lay more than fifty years of hot, confused debate as to the correct foreign relations for England to follow in a world in which suddenly the horizons of power policy had shifted and widened.

89

JOHN HANCOCK: NOTORIOUS SMUGGLER OR NEAR VICTIM OF BRITISH REVENUE RACKETEERS?

By O. M. DICKERSON

Most recent histories of the Revolutionary period represent John Hancock as a smuggler. In some accounts this is only an impression that is left;[1] in others it is stated as a fact.[2] One writer even vividly describes Hancock openly running his wine ashore in defiance of the customs officials in typical western movie gunman style.[3] What are the ascertainable facts?

I

The evidence upon which the smuggling charges are based is either the sloop *Liberty* affair or the information of Thomas Kirk, a tidesman in the employ of the customs service.

The *Liberty*, owned by Hancock and used by him as a common carrier, arrived in Boston from Madeira on May 9, 1768, and was entered at the customhouse the next day with a cargo

[1] George Elliott Howard, *Preliminaries of the Revolution, 1763-1775* (New York, 1906), 193; Sidney George Fisher, *The Struggle for American Independence* (2 vols., Philadelphia, 1908), I, 127; Arthur Meier Schlesinger, *The Colonial Merchants and the American Revolution, 1763-1776* (New York, 1918), 103-104; John Fiske, *The American Revolution* (2 vols., Boston, 1891), I, 51-3; Evarts Boutell Greene, *The Foundations of American Nationality* (New York, 1922), 419.

[2] Claude H. Van Tyne, *The Causes of the War of Independence* (Boston, 1922), 122, 283; James Truslow Adams, *The March of Democracy* (2 vols., New York, 1932-1933), I, 93; *ibid.*, *Revolutionary New England, 1691-1776* (Boston, 1923), 353-4; Ralph Volney Harlow, *Samuel Adams: Promoter of the American Revolution* (New York, 1923), 121-2; Mellen Chamberlain, "The Revolution Impending," in Justin Winsor (ed.), *Narrative and Critical History of America* (8 vols., Boston, 1889), VI, 43.

[3] John Hyde Preston, *Revolution 1776* (New York, 1933), 3-4. In this fanciful story the officers of the *Romney* watch the *Liberty* enter port, summon the customs officers, help search the *Liberty*, find the wine, announce the seizure of the vessel. Hancock arrives, orders them off his vessel, goes personally into Boston, raises the mob, drives the customs officers from the deck of the *Liberty*, and chases the customs officers out of Boston. All on June 9, 1768. It is a thrilling account without a single fact stated correctly.

of twenty-five casks of wine. The regular duties were paid.[4] For
the next month the *Liberty* lay at Hancock's wharf apparently
preparing for a voyage to London. A new cargo of 200 barrels
of whale oil and 20 barrels of tar, both of American origin, had
been placed on board. On June 10, one month after the *Liberty*
had been regularly entered, late in the afternoon, Hutchinson
says about seven o'clock "or near sunset,"[5] representatives of
the Boston customhouse, acting under a direct written order
from the Board of Customs Commissioners, searched the *Liberty*, found the new cargo on board, forcibly seized the vessel
and had her towed out into the harbor and anchored under the
guns of the *Romney*, a British warship.

91

On June 22, the following suit was filed: "Joseph Harrison,
Esq. *vs.* Sloop Liberty. 20 barrels of tar 200 barrels of oil."[6]
Claimants were cited to appear on July 7, the case was continued to July 18, and finally on August 1, 1768, ship and cargo
were ordered confiscated.[7] Is this seizure and confiscation proof
that the *Liberty* was concerned with the illegal landing of wine
the night of May 9 when she entered Boston harbor?

Not at all. No reference of any kind to wine is made in the
charge. It is a suit against the *Liberty* and a new cargo of tar
and oil. A writ of assistance was used in making the search.
Surely they were not searching the *Liberty* on June 10 for wine
that allegedly had been unloaded illegally a month earlier. Even
Lieutenant-Governor Hutchinson admits that the seizure was

[4] This is the statement of the Board of Customs Commissioners in its official report of the seizure made to the Treasury Board in England on June 15, 1768.
Treasury Papers I, Bundle 465 (Public Record Office, London). In future these will
be cited as Treasury Papers. Ben Hallowell, Comptroller of the Customs in Boston,
who accompanied the Collector, Joseph Harrison, when the *Liberty* was seized, made
a similar statement when examined by the Treasury Board in London. Reprints are
available in the excellent article by George G. Wolkins, "The Seizure of John Hancock's Sloop 'Liberty'," Massachusetts Historical Society, *Proceedings*, Oct., 1921-
June, 1922 (Boston, 1923), LV, 239-84.

[5] Thomas Hutchinson, *The History of the Colony and Province of Massachusetts-
Bay* (3 vols., Cambridge, Mass., 1936), III, 137. Writs of Assistance could not be
used legally after sunset. There was much contemporary discussion of the exact time.
Patriots insisted it was after sunset. The whole procedure was very close to the
edge of the law.

[6] Vice Admiralty Court Records (Office of the Clerk of the Supreme Judicial
Court, Boston, Mass.).

[7] *Idem.*

"for want of a permit," [8] *i.e.*, a formal permit to load, which the law provided should be given after bond had been filed.[9]

This seizure and later confiscation were clearly made under clause XIX of the Navigation Act of 1660 and clause XXIII of the Sugar Act of 1764. The first of these covered enumerated goods only, providing that bond must be given to land such goods at another British port.[10] The second covered non-enumerated goods and provided that *before* any such goods were placed on board, bond must be given that any foreign molasses that might be on board should be landed at another British port. Even if a vessel had no molasses on board and was not planning to load any, the bond had to be given.[11] The penalty in each case for not giving bond *before* cargo was placed on board was forfeiture of ship, furniture, equipment, and all cargo.

Under the Navigation Act compliance had been easy because it called for a general bond covering a specific class of goods without any listing of particular packages. Under clause XXIX of the Sugar Act, complete lists of all cargo items had to be supplied at the time bond was given. A general bond would no longer suffice.

The universal practice in America had been to load both enumerated and non-enumerated articles as they became available and when the ship was loaded, proceed to the nearest customhouse and furnish the various bonds, cockets, certificates, and other papers necessary for a proper clearance. This was

[8] Hutchinson, III, 137.

[9] The account on this point is confusing to investigators, limited to the use of material available in Boston, because Governor Bernard in his correspondence did not reveal to the authorities at home the exact facts concerning the seizure and always referred to it in such a way as to give the impression that the real reason for the seizure was the alleged running of a part of the cargo of wine ashore the night of May 9. He was under so much criticism at home because of his avariciousness that he did not care to have authorities in London know he was a party to seizing a merchant's vessel on such technical grounds as were used in this case. See Edward Channing and Archibald C. Coolidge (eds.), *The Barrington Bernard Correspondence and Illustrative Matter, 1760-1800* (Cambridge, Mass., 1912).

[10] 12 Car. II, C. 18. Text in *Statutes of the Realm*, I, 246-50.

[11] 4 Geo. III, C. 15. Text in Pickering, *Statutes at Large*, XXVI, 33-52. Extracts of both the above statutes, including the full text of the clauses referred to may be found in William Macdonald (ed.), *Select Charters* . . . (New York, 1899), 110-115, 272-81.

called giving bond at the time of clearance. The fact that most non-enumerated goods had to be loaded at points remote from the nearest customhouse made the regular practice the only practicable method of carrying on trade.

The law, however, was specific. The 200 barrels of oil and the 20 barrels of tar found on board the *Liberty* while lying at Hancock's wharf constituted a direct violation of clause XXIII of the Sugar Act since bond had not been given prior to loading. Doubtless every other ship in Boston Harbor that was preparing for a voyage could have been seized on a similar charge, but no other ship was disturbed. The Customs Commissioners were trying to get Hancock and were determined to harass him as much as possible.

The revenue laws also recognized informers and provided that the proceeds of all forfeitures for violations within the colonies were to be divided: one-third to the governor, one-third to the informer, and one-third to the Crown. If the *Liberty* had been seized immediately after May 10 on the charge of unloading uncustomed goods, the officials would have had only the value of an empty ship to divide. By waiting until June 10 they got the ship with new provisions, 200 barrels of oil and 20 barrels of tar, which gave about twice as much to divide. In addition they had a case against the *Liberty* impossible of successful defense. The presence of the goods on board was full proof of the violation of the letter of the law and insured condemnation.

A riot followed the seizure of the *Liberty* and started a chain of events closely linked with the Revolution. The spontaneous rising on June 10 was not of men interested in protecting a wealthy wine smuggler, nor was it the work of a carefully organized and drilled mob. Hancock's employees and the others about the wharf knew on what grounds the *Liberty* and her cargo were being taken. It was the first instance in Boston of a seizure on such technical grounds and the only seizure known to have been made at that port on such a charge. The crowd also knew how the proceeds of seizures were divided.

The riot was undesired by the Boston leaders and unfortunate; but it was such a plain case of public plunder — not for any violations of the law affecting either the revenue or the

93

course of trade — but obviously for the personal profit of the
governor and the customs officers — that the crowd reacted as
would western cowboys when rustlers came boldly in daylight
to steal their employer's herds.

Thus the *Liberty* seizure and confiscation supplies no evidence
that Hancock was a smuggler; but is the plainest evidence that,
for following the regular commercial practice which was a technical departure from the letter of the law, he had valuable
property taken by Governor Bernard and the customs officers
and appropriated to their own personal use. The admiralty record shows that Bernard received his third on November 9, 1768.
We do not know just how the customs officials divided their
third.

94

II

Many writers depend upon an information signed by Thomas
Kirk, a tidesman, for proof of Hancock's smuggling activities,
but do not indicate that they have examined the trustworthiness
of the document or the use made of it.[12] Tidesmen were not
considered a very reputable group of workers. We know very
little of Thomas Kirk. His name is not included in the list of
regularly employed tidesmen and he seems to have been a super-
numerary picked up for the occasion, possibly for a reason. His
regular pay would have been four shillings for a day and a night
on duty. If he had been a regular full-time employee he might
have earned from £20 to £25 a year.[13]

Kirk and a companion were placed on board the *Liberty* when
she docked late on May 9. The next day he and his companion
were carefully examined and questioned by the Customs Commissioners. Both swore that nothing irregular had happened

[12] W. T. Baxter, *The House of Hancock: Business in Boston, 1724-1775* (Cambridge, Mass., 1945), 264-7, admits Kirk was a liar and that the Attorney-General
of England considered his evidence flimsy, but accepts Kirk's unsupported statement as true.

[13] From time to time the Customs Commissioners transmitted to the Treasury
Board in London lists of employees at the various ports with their regular compensation. The sums given are those paid in Boston in 1768. On April 10, 1768,
Joseph Harrison, Collector at Boston, made a very long and detailed report of the
port of Boston, the customs service there, conditions of trade, lists of officers, how
long they had served, their compensation, etc. Treasury Papers I, Bundle 465.

during the night and that the cargo had not been disturbed. That was on May 10, 1768.[14]

One month later, on June 9, Kirk signed an information which is very different from his regular report. This information recites that while he was on board the *Liberty*, a Captain Marshall with several men, none of whom he knew, came on board about nine o'clock. A proposition was made concerning the unloading of some wine. When Kirk refused the proposition he was forced below deck and confined for about three hours. During that time he heard noises like heavy walking and sounds like the ship's tackle being used to hoist out goods. He was then released and threatened with dire consequences if he revealed what happened.[15] When questioned, his companion denied any knowledge of such occurrences, but admitted he might have been asleep. Kirk asserted his companion was drunk and had gone home to bed.[16] Captain Marshall had died during the month and could not be called for questioning.[17]

Kirk states nothing of his own knowledge. He only heard noises. He mentions no noticeable changes on deck the next morning, nor does he mention any ascertainable disturbance of the ship's cargo. No member of the regular crew or any other employee of Hancock is mentioned. Apparently he and his companion reported to none of Hancock's representatives when they went on board. Are we to believe that Hancock permitted all of his employees to leave a newly-arrived ship with valuable cargo on board and turn it over with unlocked doors and hatches to the tender mercies of tidesmen, particularly recently-appointed supernumeraries? So far as the Kirk statement shows, he simply invaded the *Liberty* without reporting his presence to any one, without seeing or being seen by the owner of the vessel or any of his employees.

Surely some of the crew or other of Hancock's men were on board all night. After his experience with the *Lydia* (to be dis-

95

[14] Report of the Customs Commissioners to the Treasury Board, June 15, 1768, *Ibid.*; Wolkins includes much of this report in his article.
[15] Wolkins prints a copy of Kirk's statement which seems to be an accurate transcript, taken from Treasury Papers I, Bundle 465.
[16] Letter of Board of Customs Commissioners, June 15, 1768, *ibid.*
[17] Abram English Brown, *John Hancock, His Book* (Boston, 1898), 156.

cussed later) a few weeks earlier, Hancock cannot be presumed to have trusted tidesmen aboard any ship without several dependable men to watch their actions. Especially would he be expected to be suspicious of the actions of tidesmen who were not regular employees. With all the talk that was circulating in Boston and the known personal hostility of the Commissioners, it must be presumed that Hancock kept the *Liberty* and all his other ships carefully guarded by his own trusty employees.

The Treasury Papers in London contain many reports by customs officers of difficulties and opposition encountered by them. None of these reports is so lacking in specific facts and details as this sworn statement of Kirk. On the contrary they invariably name persons, actions, incidents, describe individuals, and otherwise give evidence that could be used in court.

96

This information is an amazing document. The signer is a self-confessed perjurer. If his statement on May 10 was true this one must be false. If this is true his earlier sworn statement is false. In either case he is a self-confessed liar. There are no possible witnesses indicated. He rules out his companion — says he was home drunk. Both were apparently sober when placed on board and were sober when they reported the next morning. Captain Marshall, the accused, was dead and could not be called to testify. Kirk recognized none of Marshall's alleged companions. He does not even identify them by size, build, dress, actions, language, or in any other way. It seems strange that he would not be able to describe some of the men who came aboard thus irregularly, connived with him, then assaulted him and forced him below deck. Men who attempt to unload a ship in the dark have to know their business. It seems incredible that a tidesman in a town as small as Boston in 1768 would not know by sight some of a group of men used for the speedy unloading of a boat.

In addition Kirk was himself personally interested in the outcome of his testimony, which in any fair court would bar him as a witness. Legally he was entitled to one-third of all sums that could be secured as a result of his evidence. His portion alone might run from ten to more than a hundred times his annual earnings as a tidesman, depending upon whether one considers the value of the *Liberty* and her oil or the far larger sums which the customs officials attempted to extort from Hancock by the later suits.

Clearly no ordinary tidesman could have concocted so clever a statement. The document itself does not pretend to be the work of Kirk. His sole connection with it is that he signed it before Hallowell and a justice of the peace. No action for libel or indictment for perjury against Kirk could be sustained, because no living person's name was mentioned and no positive assertions were made concerning any violations of law. Only a clever lawyer skilled in handling trade and revenue cases and directly interested in the use that could be made of such a document could have drawn it. David Lisle, the newly-arrived Solicitor for the Board of Customs Commissioners, was such an individual. The information was referred to him and upon his legal advice the seizure of the *Liberty* was made. Presumably he himself concocted the statement and Kirk was induced to sign it for a consideration. Kirk's name does not reappear in the many pages of official correspondence dealing with this case. We must assume that he had served his purpose and had received his pay. Even John Adams, Hancock's attorney, does not indicate that he knew of Kirk.

The Kirk information was signed on June 9. For the next four months and more it was passed around to the Board's legal staff. A copy was even sent to England for a report by Attorney General De Grey who pointed out the flimsiness of the document and advised that a case could be based upon it only if the court would believe Kirk.[18]

97

---

[18] Attorney General De Grey's opinion bears date of July 25, 1768. The original in his own peculiar handwriting, written on the last pages of the report of the Commissioners of Customs, is in Treasury Papers I, Bundle 465. The main part of this is reprinted in Wolkins, 273-6. The close of De Grey's opinion states that action against the persons engaged in any alleged unloading of the *Liberty* on May 9 might also be taken, but such suit would be dependent upon the proof of the fact of such unloading in a case against the *Liberty*. There was no such proof, since the action against the *Liberty* was clearly on a different charge. The Customs Commissioners obviously did not await De Grey's opinion for the suit against the *Liberty* because that case was closed on August 1, long before De Grey's opinion could have been received.

III

Did the *Liberty* have on board more wine than Hancock entered at the customhouse on May 10, 1768? We do not know positively. Hancock's letter books show that he actually ordered eleven pipes and four quarter casks of wine from his agent in Madeira. Of these, five pipes were for his own use, four pipes and four quarter casks were for sale to public houses, two pipes were for Harrison Gray, the colonial treasurer. In addition two pipes had been ordered by Jonathan and John Amory to be shipped as freight.[19] This makes a known total of thirteen pipes and four quarter casks of which four pipes were for well-known Boston Tories.[20] A pipe is a definite measure of quantity; casks are not. The "25 casks" entered at the Boston Custom House on May 10, 1768, seem to account for all of the wine ordered by Hancock.

There is a possibility that additional wine was accepted for shipment by the Master, Captain Barnard, before sailing from Madeira. Such a possibility rests upon conjecture only; there is no record to substantiate it. Hancock did not order it and it does not show on the invoice of Hancock's Madeira agent. At no point in the prosecution of Hancock was it charged that he was the owner of the alleged wine. Common report in Boston before and after the arrival of the *Liberty* was that she carried more wine than was entered. Common gossip is not evidence.

IV

Was Hancock the near victim of British revenue racketeers? If so who were the racketeers and what personal gains were they seeking? Hancock was one of the outstanding political leaders in Boston. His position rested upon great personal popularity, especially with the lower and middle classes of the city, his inherited wealth, and a vigorous expansion of his shipping and mercantile business. He held no appointive office and sought none. He could only be reached by attacking his wealth and his

[19] Brown, 149-150, 162; Baxter, 263.

[20] Harrison Gray and John Amory are listed among the Loyalists who left Boston about the time of its capture by the Americans. E. Alfred Jones, *The Loyalists of Massachusetts* (London, 1930), 151, 266.

business and undermining his business reputation. The attack
upon Hancock has many of the same personalities and purposes
back of it as the attack upon the political liberties of Massachusetts, involving the bringing of soldiers to Boston. They
went on at the same time and were led by the same men.

At the head of the officials in the plot must be placed Governor Bernard, whose motives were personal and financial. His
political motives have been adequately discussed elsewhere. His
personal financial interest was in making money out of the customs service of which he was the official head in his own colony
and from which he received one-third of the value of all seizures.
If Hancock's fortune could be successfully attacked through
seizures and vexatious suits under obscure provisions of the
trade and revenue laws he would get one-third of what was
taken. At the same time the career of a politically-powerful
American leader could be checked.

Lieutenant-Governor Hutchinson's activity threads through
the story in serpentine obscurity. Apparently his political interests were similar to those of Bernard, but his private interests were largely those of promoting the interests of his family
— elimination of an active trade competitor for some, the undermining and removal of men who stood in the way of official promotion for others.

Ben Hallowell, Comptroller of the Port of Boston, David
Lisle, Solicitor of the Board of Customs Commissioners, and
some members of that board were apparently actuated by hopes
of personal gain from the suits against Hancock (they were also
entitled to one-third of all that they could get an Admiralty
court to confiscate), or by personal pique because of Hancock's
social and official manifestations of disrespect.

Governor Bernard more than any other person in Massachusetts advised the Ministry to apply harsh terms to America.
He was grasping and avaricious and, according to Temple, who
was in a position to know, had operated some of the custom-
houses in his province for his own personal profit.[21] He did not

[21] The fullest evidence on this is in the various reports made by John Temple,
Surveyor General of Customs, from 1760 until the creation of the Board of Customs
Commissioners of which he was a member. Some of these may be consulted in *The
Bowdoin and Temple Papers*, Massachusetts Historical Society, *Collections*, Sixth

like Hancock, because he was not one of the "well affected toward government." Hancock obviously disliked Bernard as an official who was secretly seeking to destroy the liberties of the colony.

Bernard had two direct clashes with Hancock in the latter part of 1767 and early part of 1768. The governor arranged a reception and a public parade to welcome the Customs Commissioners when they arrived in Boston and directed Hancock, who was in command of the local cadet company, to have his company act as a guard of honor for the governor in the parade. Hancock flatly refused to participate in any official welcome to the Commissioners. Bernard and the Board were deeply incensed at Hancock for this open insult and began laying plans to humble him.[22]

The second clash came soon after the *Liberty* docked. It had been customary for the governor to hold a public dinner for all royal officials on the annual election day. The governor announced that such a dinner would be held as usual on May 25, 1768. Hancock, suspecting that the governor intended to include the Commissioners among his guests, wrote him that he and his company of cadets would not participate if the Commissioners were included as guests. Bernard premptorily ordered Hancock and his company to attend him as usual. Hancock refused to obey the order and threatened to resign his commission; his men supported him and even threatened to withdraw from the organization rather than obey the order. The town supported Hancock and the cadets and voted not to permit the governor to use their drill hall — Fanueil Hall — for the banquet if

100

Series (Boston, 1897), IX, 27-41. Many others are in Temple's communications to the customs officers in England. Bernard even boasted of his power to secure "indulgences" from the customs officials. *Barrington Bernard Correspondence* . . . , 163. The official report of the famous Captain Daniel Malcolm episode states that he first went to the customs officials and asked for the "usual indulgence." When this was refused he said he would then "take his own measures." Board of Customs Commissioners to the Treasury Board in London, March 28, 1768, Treasury Papers I, Bundle 465. There are enough reported incidents of this kind to indicate the strong probability that the worst statements regarding Bernard's collusive operation of the customs are true.

[22] Memorial of the Commissioners of Customs to Treasury Board in London, May 12, 1768, Treasury Papers I, Bundle 465.

the Commissioners were among his guests.²³ These events could not be kept from the public and were the talk of the town in the weeks immediately preceding the seizure of the *Liberty*. Many people believed that the governor would attempt to punish Hancock in any way he could.

The Commissioners had both an official and a personal animus against Hancock. The reasons for their personal animus have already been indicated — Hancock's public snub at the time they were welcomed by the governor and his more recent insult. The public animus was that Hancock was not "one of the well disposed"²⁴ but on the other hand was open in his denunciation of the legality of the revenue laws and his political agitation for their repeal. This animus of the Commissioners is reflected clearly in their letters to the Treasury Board in England. Not once in these letters do they charge that Hancock was engaged in illicit trade, but he is pictured as dangerous because of his hostility to the ministerial policy. It is further shown in the singling out of Hancock for special attack by the Boston *Chronicle*, whose owner, John Mein, was in the pay of the Commissioners.²⁵

101

²³ This is not local gossip, but is from an official "Memorial" to the Treasury Board in England, dated May 12, 1768, *ibid.* A fuller extract is given to show the real animus against Hancock:

We cannot omit mentioning to your Lordships that Mr. Hancock before named is one of the Leaders of the disaffected in this Town, that early in the Winter he declared in the General Assembly that he would not suffer our officers to go even on board of any of his London Ships, and now he carries his opposition to Government to an even higher pitch.

²⁴ This expression appears frequently in the official correspondence as applied to Americans who were opposed to the taxation policy.

²⁵ These attacks ran through a considerable part of 1769 and portray Hancock as a violator of his own non-importation agreements. Week after week Mein printed the agreement in one column, and in adjoining columns printed the sworn manifests of cargo of vessels owned by Hancock and other merchants taken from the custom-house records. Hancock's reputation as well as those of other prominent merchants in Boston was injured, especially in other colonies. The *Chronicle* seemed to carry undeniable proof that the Boston merchants were violating their own non-importation agreement. Mein was driven out of business in Boston and fled to England. In the Treasury Papers is a letter from him to the Ministry describing the service he had rendered in Boston and asking for a pension. His request was apparently granted because his name is in Lord North's list of pensioners as receiving £200 per year from 1770. *Correspondence of King George the Third* (6 vols., London, 1928), V, 468.

David Lisle was a newcomer from the customs service in Britain, sent by the Ministry as Solicitor to the Board of Customs Commissioners. He frankly admits that he hoped to make money out of his position and states that he had been led to believe that the expected pickings would amount to two or three times his salary of £100 per year.[26] He reveals that he dined with Bernard the day he arrived in Boston and at once become a keen partisan in the feud of the governor and the Board with Hancock.[27] His previous experience and legal training (he had served for several years prosecuting fraud in the Scottish customs) equipped him as no other customs official in America to make maximum use of the technical clauses of the trade and revenue acts for vexatious suits against Hancock and his fortune.

Besides these more prominent individuals, there were the lawyers and admiralty officers who would profit from the prosecution of Hancock through fees and other payments for their professional services. Those known to be employed were Jonathan Sewall, Robert Auchmuty, and Samuel Fitch. There may have been others. There is no evidence that Tories as a group in any way were parties to or approved the attack upon Hancock.

Late in 1768 Hancock had also made himself obnoxious to the recently arrived military force that had been sent to Boston. He was one of the Selectmen and had taken every legal step to deny the soldiers quarters in the town. In addition he joined with others to file formal criminal charges against one of the captains of the 59th Regiment, John Willson, for attempting to incite a Negro insurrection in Boston.[28] Three days later Han-

102

[26] Letters of the Board of Commissioners to Treasury Board, February 10, 1769, and David Lisle to Customs Commissioners, February 16, 1769, Treasury Papers I, Bundle 471.

[27] After referring to the widespread popular opposition to the new revenue laws he continues "one of their number in the Assembly has had the assurance to declare that if the Board is not removed before Christmas he would undertake to send them all away himself: I should doubt the Fact and not believe any one would dare to make use of such insolent menaces, had I not my information from the best Authority. . . . The Governor's guard revolted Thursday and chose their own officers. I dined with him the day I landed." Lisle to Secretary of Treasury Board, May 14, 1768, Treasury Papers I, Bundle 465.

[28] This accusation is printed in full as one of the items of the "Journal of the

530 THE MISSISSIPPI VALLEY HISTORICAL REVIEW

cock was himself under arrest to answer a new suit instituted
against him in connection with the *Liberty*.

V

Aside from the bonding clauses of the Sugar Act the other
clauses in the revenue acts most possible to use against Hancock
were those providing penalties for landing goods without paying the duties and for resisting customs officers. The first effort
to use these clauses against Hancock was connected with his
ship *Lydia* from London which docked late in the afternoon of
April 9, 1768. Two tidesmen as usual were placed on board. One
of these was Owen Richards, a notorious Tory and informer.²⁹
Instead of remaining on deck they attempted to go below. Hancock came on board, inquired their business, examined their
commissions, found them defective, asked if they were trying to
search his vessel, and demanded to know if they had a writ of
assistance. They admitted they had no writ, and said they were
merely trying to keep warm and insisted that they had no intention of searching the vessel. Hancock said they could search
it if they wished but they could not tarry below. He then gave
positive orders to his men not to allow the tidesmen below deck
without proper authority and later that night, when they persisted in their efforts to go below, had them picked up and
placed forcibly on deck.³⁰
The Board attempted to make this episode the basis for suits
against Hancock for interfering with and assaulting customs officers in the discharge of their duties. Jonathan Sewall, Attorney
General for Massachusetts and himself a Tory, ruled that they
had no case.³¹ His opinion deserves a place in all accounts of the

Times'' for October 31, 1768, and very widely circulated in American and British
newspapers. O. M. Dickerson (comp.), *Boston Under Military Rule [1768-1769]*, as
revealed in a Journal of the Times (Boston, 1936), 16. It is obviously part of the
basis for the charge in the Declaration of Independence about stirring up Negro
insurrections. Capt. Willson was later indicted, his trial postponed, and finally ordered out of the jurisdiction of the Massachusetts courts, *Ibid.*, 84, 91-2, 105.

²⁹ In 1770 he made himself so obnoxious that he was publicly mobbed. He was
pensioned by the Crown after the Revolution, Jones, 243.

³⁰ A detailed account of this episode, with the sworn testimony of Richards, is
in a formal report of the incident by the Board of Customs Commissioners, dated
May 12, 1768, Treasury Papers I, Bundle 465.

³¹ *Ibid.* In delivering this opinion Sewall showed the fearless independence and

development of constitutional government in this country. It was extremely displeasing to the Commissioners of Customs who at once prepared a memorial to the Treasury Board in London, transmitted Sewall's opinion to be submitted to Attorney General De Grey of England, and asked for direct authority to compel Sewall as Attorney General to file the desired information against Hancock in the Supreme Court of Massachusetts.[32] So far as it is known this is the first and only effort to subject the Attorneys-General in America to mandatory process from their superiors in England. Had this move succeeded a unified system of executive law enforcement could have developed for the entire colonial empire. No similar incident has come to light.

104

The Commissioners next attempted to secure some kind of evidence when the *Liberty* docked. Disappointed in this, they waited for a seizure until cargo was on board. By so doing they secured additional gains for themselves and inflicted additional losses on Hancock.

The riot on the evening of June 10 served a double purpose. It furnished plausible grounds for demanding troops for the protection of the Commissioners and offered an opportunity to entangle Hancock with responsibility for the acts of the crowd. The seizure of the *Liberty* was so unusual, accompanied with such unnecessary violence, and created so much public irritation that the Board made a show of offering to return the vessel to Hancock's wharf, provided he gave bond for the delivery of ship and cargo if the case went against him when it came to trial. At first Hancock was disposed to accept this offer, but later it was revealed that the Board had insisted that he enter into a signed agreement to restrain the mob from any further interference with the activities of the customs officers.[33]

Hancock was too wary to fall into such a trap. A signed stipulation to restrain the mob from future interference would amount to an admission that he controlled its operations from the first

faithful regard for the law that has characterized many generations of American lawyers. Tory though he was, he adhered to the law as did so many other Tory judges when called upon to rule on Writs of Assistance.

[32] Memorial of Customs Commissioners to Treasury Board in London, May 12, 1768, Treasury Papers I, Bundle 465.

[33] There is a full account of these negotiations in the report by the Customs Commissioners to their superiors in London, June 14, 1768, *ibid.*

and might make him liable to a prosecution for the mob's action in assaulting and attempting to interfere with customs officers on June 10. The bond and written agreement could be used against him in a new legal action where they would amount to a confession of guilt and make effective defense very difficult. A conviction on that charge involved very heavy penalties. After going over the possibilities, Hancock decided neither to make verbal promises nor to sign papers and to permit the theft of the *Liberty* and his 200 barrels of oil and 20 barrels of tar without contest.[14]

Kirk's information is dated June 9, 1768. For the next six months a curious intrigue was in progress in Boston. Apparently it was an effort to combine the attack on Hancock's fortune with a movement to get rid of Sewall as Advocate-General and David Lisle as Solicitor of the Board of Commissioners. Governor Bernard, Lieutenant-Governor Hutchinson, and Robert Auchmuty, the acting judge of the Vice-Admiralty Court in Boston, were interested parties. The governor's interests appear to have been chiefly financial and political; *i.e.*, he wished to punish Hancock and he also ardently desired his third of the plunder. Hutchinson's interests were largely family; a crippling of Hancock's fortunes would reduce his business competition with Hutchinson's two sons; elimination of Lisle would give a lucrative position to Samuel Fitch, another kinsman; a part of whatever money was taken from Hancock would be within the family; and there may have been plans to promote some kinsman into Sewall's position. As for Auchmuty, he had been active in libel suits of all kinds brought by the Crown in connection with the customs and forest laws, he was an ardent supporter of Bernard, and he was an active candidate for one of the six new Vice-Admiralty judgeships carrying a fixed salary of £600 per year. To secure the latter he needed the support of Bernard and Hutchinson who were close to the all-powerful Hillsborough-North combination in England.

As already indicated the Commissioners filed an official complaint against Sewall immediately after his opinion in the case

105

[14] Both Collector Harrison and Ben Hallowell, Comptroller, state in their sworn reports that Hancock failed to make either verbal or written stipulations as a condition for releasing the *Liberty*. *Ibid.*

of the *Lydia*. This was followed up by other adverse comments in later communications. Information concerning these attacks may have reached Sewall from London where friends were urging him for the Vice-Admiralty judgeship at Halifax. Clerks in the Commissioners' office may have talked. Whatever the source of his information, he knew sometime in June that he was being attacked.

Sewall made the mistake of complaining to Governor Bernard, who at once passed on to the Commissioners that their attack on Sewall had leaked. The Commissioners at once denied the report and demanded of Sewall the source of his information, and the latter called for copies of communications concerning himself so he could judge whether his information was true or false. This the Commissioners refused to supply and also denied Sewall permission to see their communications to the Treasury Board in England. Bernard and Hutchinson then told the Commissioners that Sewall had received his information from David Lisle, the Solicitor, and Samuel Venner, the Secretary of the Board. These men were questioned by the Commissioners, and they frankly admitted that they had dined with Sewall, at his request, at his home in Cambridge, that certain questions had been asked and answered, but that they had betrayed no confidences. Renewed pressure upon Sewall elicited a renewed written refusal under any consequences to reveal information that had reached him confidentially. This letter closes with a very plain intimation that he intended to resign his position as Advocate-General.[15] Finally Bernard, Hutchinson, and

[15] Copies of Sewall's letters dated August 5, August 10, 1768, were transmitted to London by the Commissioners and are in Treasury Papers I, Bundle 471. In John Adams' "Diary" for 1768 there is a curious account of a surprise visit of Sewall to Adams with a long confidential talk in which Adams claims he was offered the position of Advocate-General in the Admiralty Court at Boston. This entry in the Diary was obviously written many years after the happening and is full of errors. He gives no dates nor does he identify the time of year. He is positive that Sewall called, that they had a long and confidential talk, that he was offered a job, and that it was pictured to him as "very lucrative." Adams says he declined it and urged Samuel Fitch for the place. He adds that Fitch never got the place — but Fitch actually was appointed in Sewall's place in November, 1769. (See Jones, 134-5.) He says Sewall claimed to be speaking for both Bernard and Hutchinson. Hutchinson claims Adams was only offered a position as justice of the peace. Obviously Adams was offered something as a part of the plot against Hancock. Possibly it was

Auchmuty were shown a part of the communications of May 12, 1768. Presumably they worked on Sewall who at last was permitted to see a part of the reports. Secretary Venner and Solicitor Lisle were made the goats of the incident; the former was suspended from office and a request sent to London for the latter's removal. Thus all the work Lisle had done in the case had achieved him nothing, and all his hopes for rich financial rewards from the pending suit vanished into thin air.

While this intrigue against Sewall was in progress, the suit against Hancock had made no headway. That suit could only be filed by the Advocate-General who was Jonathan Sewall himself. As already shown, he did not believe that a criminal prosecution could legally be instituted against Hancock by an "Information." The Common Law procedure required a grand jury indictment for criminal prosecutions followed by a trial by jury. In some way Sewall's scruples were overcome or he was whipped into line by joint pressure from Bernard, Hutchinson, Auchmuty, and the Board. Obviously there was a deal, the details of which can only be conjectured.

The records of the Commissioners show that on October 28, 1768, the clerk of the Board paid Sewall and Samuel Fitch "20 Johannes each" or a total of £72 sterling as "retainers fees for sundry causes depending for the Crown." The retainer fees are excessively high, since previous payments were about 5 per cent of the sums paid in this case. The next day, October 29, 1768, Sewall filed the long-delayed suit in Judge Auchmuty's court not only against Hancock but also against five other merchants, each personally for £9,000, or a total of £54,000 for allegedly aiding in unloading 100 pipes of wine valued at £30 each on the night of May 9, 1768, when the *Liberty* entered Boston.[36]

107

part of a plan to retain all able lawyers for the Crown so as to leave Hancock without capable attorneys to defend him. Sewall, Auchmuty, and Fitch are known to have been employed in the case — all friends of Adams. Charles Francis Adams (ed.), *The Works of John Adams* . . . (10 vols., Boston, 1850-1856), II, 210, 212; Hutchinson, III, 296.

[36] The amount of the suit is given as £9,000 in the "Journal of the Times" for November 3, 1768. Dickerson, 16, 18. General Gage, who was in Boston at the time, says he heard the matter discussed and says:

The People prosecuted are Messrs Hancock and Malcolm; accused of declaring publickly, that they would land their Goods, and would not pay the Dutys. That

The Sugar Act had a provision that any person in any way connected with or abetting the unloading, transporting, receiving, storing, or concealing uncustomed goods could be sued for triple the value of the goods allegedly landed. The Board determined to base its new suit upon these provisions, using the Kirk information as partial evidence. Much more would be needed, but money and official pressure upon employees might supply it.

108

This is the most unusual suit in the entire history of British revenue laws in America. The alleged events happened entirely upon land within the limits of the Province of Massachusetts Bay. It was a dragnet attempt to uncover evidence of a conspiracy to violate the revenue laws. Criminal conspiracy should have been tried in the regular courts of the province under the rules of the civil and criminal law with a jury to pass upon the evidence. Instead, the case was brought in the Vice-Admiralty court at Boston, without a jury, and under rules of evidence and procedure highly unusual if not openly illegal. It was an action against persons for what amounted to criminal acts, not against property, as was the suit against the *Liberty*. The marshal of the Admiralty Court arrested Hancock's person and placed him under excessive bail. This made the action essentially criminal and should have been begun by an indictment instead of an "Information" as was pointed out by Sewall in the case of the *Lydia*."

they did accordingly land their Goods, without paying the Dutys by Law Established, in Defiance of the Officers of the Customs. They were arrested during my Residence in Boston, Hancock, One of the most Opulent Men in this Country, I think for the Sum of £13000 and both after some time gave Bail. The Reason given why those Persons were not arrested before was, that the Prosecutors were affraid, and durst not attempt it . . . till they were protected by the Presence of the Troops; for both Mr Hancock and Malcolm were reported to have been Leaders or Abettors of the Mob. I confine myself to the general Heads of Accusation which I recollect to have heard; Some particular Circumstances relative to the Conduct of these persons were mentioned at the time, of which I have not sufficient Recollection to relate to your Lordship.

Gage to Hillsborough, New York, March 5, 1769, in Clarence Edwin Carter (ed.), *The Correspondence of General Thomas Gage with the Secretaries of State, 1763-1775* (2 vols., New Haven, Conn., 1931-1933), I, 220. A full copy of the charges against Hancock is in Josiah Quincy, *Massachusetts Reports* (8 vols., Boston, 1865), I, 459.

37 "This morning Mr. Arodi Thayer, Marshal of the Court of Admiralty for

In addition witnesses were examined by interrogatories; that is, a list of questions was made out in writing by the Advocate-General and the witness was required to answer them in writing. Witnesses were not put on the stand and compelled to give their testimony in open court in front of the accused where their entire-appearance, demeanor, and manner of answering became a part of their testimony. In no case was the attorney for the accused permitted to cross-question them in open court. Amendments to the Federal Constitution, VI, VII, and VIII are probably the result of the denial of such rights and the publicity given to the methods in this most spectacular prosecution in the pre-Revolutionary period.

109

Information concerning this second suit against Hancock and others was carefully kept from the Board's superiors in London. In none of the mass of reports and letters still preserved in the Treasury Papers in London is there any mention or report of the matter. Even Secretary of State Hillsborough apparently received his first information concerning these new suits from a letter from General Gage who was in Boston at the time the suits were filed and stated in his letter of November 3, 1768, that "some Prosecutions are commenced in the Court of Admiralty against two of the most popular Leaders. . . ." [38] This at once aroused Hillsborough's curiosity and on December 24, following, he asked Gage for full information concerning the "Grounds" for the new prosecutions.[39] Gage's reply of March

three provinces, with a hanger at his side, came to the house of John Hancock, Esq; to serve him with a precept for £9000 sterling, and having arrested his person, demanded bail for £3000 sterling. Mr. Hancock offered him divers estates to the value thereof, which were absolutely refused; he then made him an offer of £3000 in money, and afterwards of £9000, which were also refused; Mr. Thayer alledging that such were his directions. Mr. Hancock however having heard of the orders . . . prudently determined to give bail, as did five other gentlemen arrested for the same sum, and on the same account from the like prudent motives." "Journal of the Times," November 3, 1768, in Dickerson, 18. There is a copy of Auchmuty's order for the arrest of Hancock in Quincy, I, 458. The marshal obviously did what he was ordered to do. The others arrested at the same time as shown by the Admiralty Court Record in the office of the Clerk of the Supreme Judicial Court of Massachusetts were Daniel Malcolm, John Matchet, William Bower, and Lewis Gray. Nathanial Barnard was the sixth person, but the Admiralty Record shows no service was secured in his case.

[38] Carter, *Correspondence of General Thomas Gage*, I, 206.
[39] *Ibid.*, 220.

5, 1769, and the accounts of the trial in the newspapers appear to have been the only actual information supplied to the home government.

The Commissioners took personal charge of the prosecution and the securing of evidence. Hancock's office was entered and his desk rifled. His most confidential employees and his nearest relatives were secretly examined in the judge's chambers and subjected to third degree methods.[40] One tide waiter was dismissed and then offered his job back and a liberal reward if he would give the testimony desired.[41] The case was spun out for nearly five months, apparently to give time to examine every sailor that had ever worked on Hancock's vessels, or who might have been in Boston about the time the *Liberty* docked.

Warrants for summoning witnesses were handed to the Commissioners in blank to be filled in secretly, thus concealing the names of prospective witnesses, not only from Hancock's attorneys, but from the Advocate of the Board as well.[42] Money in large amounts was supplied by the Board to be used in securing evidence and tampering with witnesses.[43]

The testimony of one witness was so contrary to the truth that he was indicted for perjury by the local grand jury, but, before he could be brought to trial, the Board gave him a job on one of its revenue boats outside of the province and thus removed him from the jurisdiction of the Massachusetts court.[44]

The ordinary principles of the civil law as well as the common law were ignored in the taking of testimony. New witnesses and new evidence were introduced after Hancock's defense wit-

110 (margin)

[40] "Journal of the Times," January 2, February 11, 1769, in Dickerson, 43, 64.

[41] "Journal of the Times," February 18, 1769, *ibid.*, 66. Most of the statements in this widely-circulated contemporary account are supported by the brief entries in the Record of the Vice-Admiralty Court and by the account of John Adams who was attorney for Hancock and knew specifically what was done. *Works of John Adams*, II (Diary), 215-16. There is also full supporting evidence in Quincy, I, 459, taken from notes made by Adams.

[42] "Journal of the Times," January 5, 1769, in Dickerson, 45.

[43] It is impossible to determine accurately the full amounts expended in this prosecution, all diverted from the tax funds in the hands of the Customs Commissioners, because the latter attempted to conceal many items under other labels. The total of suspect items considerably exceeds £1,000.

[44] Joseph Muzzele or Maysel. Items in "Journal of the Times," for March 27 and April 22, 1769, in Dickerson, 84, 92.

nesses had testified. Other witnesses were called into the judge's
chambers, examined secretly, and subjected to typical third degree methods to extort information from them. It was not a trial
in ordinary court but persecution under conditions of Star
Chamber procedure.[43]

This is the only case in colonial history in which happenings
in the court were reported from day to day and supplied in a
news service to papers widely published in most of the colonies
and even in England.[44] The persecution of Hancock thus became known from one end of the Empire to the other. The case
stank with an odor that reached as far as London.   *111*

Hancock was prosecuted in what amounted to a criminal action without an indictment by a local grand jury. He was compelled to give evidence against himself through the seizure of
his papers, and the forced testimony of his most confidential
employees and his nearest relatives. As the court procedures
were not in accordance with usual legal processes, an attempt
was made to deprive him of valuable property without due process of law. He was denied trial by jury and was not permitted
to have witnesses against himself examined in open court in his
presence. He was required to furnish bail of £3,000, which was
manifestly excessive since he had large physical properties within the jurisdiction of the court and there was no possible reason to suspect he would attempt to flee the province. The proposed fine of £9,000 — three times the alleged value of the cargo
— was excessive even if the alleged offense had been committed.
Especially is this true where one-third of the proposed fine —
£3,000 — was to go into the personal pocket of the governor
who was a direct party to the suit, and an equal amount was
for the personal profit of those who concocted the evidence
against him. These were the very injustices that constitutional
provisions were designed to outlaw for the future.

As the prosecution was not only against Hancock but also

[43] *Ibid.,* 46, 67, 68.

[44] The full course of the trial can be followed in "Journal of the Times," a
day-to-day account prepared in Boston, first published in the *New York Journal,*
thence widely copied into colonial and English newspapers. This publication started
on September 28, 1768, and continued to August 1, 1769. It is the only service of
this kind during the Revolutionary period. See also Quincy, I, 463ff, for additional
items.

against five other residents of Boston, each for £9,000 sterling, Governor Bernard was seeking as his third of the plunder a total of £18,000 sterling — a sum larger than his regular total salary as governor for twelve years. Another £18,000 sterling was sought for distribution among a small number of fifty-to-one-hundred-pounds-a-year customs officers — a sum probably greater than their combined total salaries for twenty years. Such efforts to use official position for personal plunder are "racketeering," even according to the standards of the modern city underworld.

112   The extraordinary efforts of the Board, the unusual expenditures, the arbitrary procedure in the court seemed to indicate probable conviction regardless of the facts. But time was running against the conspirators. By March, 1769, it was obvious that Governor Bernard would be recalled. The Commissioners began to be blamed in England for stirring up much of the trouble in Boston. The Ministry was gravely embarrassed by the troubles growing out of sending troops to Boston. The Treasury Board bluntly informed the Customs Commissioners in Boston that they must mend their ways and try to win the respect and confidence of honest merchants.[47] They also became very inquisitive about how the Commissioners were expending the revenue funds in Boston. The men most interested in plundering Hancock were either out or on their way out. It was a bad case at best. Somebody decided it should be dropped.

Finally, March 25, 1769, Robert Auchmuty's permanent commission as judge of the Vice-Admiralty Court in Boston was read in open court, thus insuring him a permanent salary of £600 a year out of the colonial revenue — a very large income for officials at that time. On the same day Attorney-General Jonathan Sewall entered a motion formally withdrawing the suit.[48]

[47] Letter of Treasury Board in London to Commissioners of Customs, December 26, 1768, Treasury Papers I, Bundle 465.
[48] As these commissions were all issued at the same time, it is probable that the same convenance that brought Auchmuty's commission also brought Sewall's commission as judge of the Admiralty Court at Halifax. A report that these commissions had been approved was published in the "Journal of the Times" for November 29, 1768. See Dickerson, 28. The Vice-Admiralty Court Record shows the dropping of the suit on March 25, 1769, in the following words: "The Advocate General prays

VI

Such is the evidence. Hancock had established a reputation throughout the Empire for stubbornly standing up for his rights. No other American had been singled out for so much personal abuse and for such personal persecution as he had been. He stood his ground, kept his head, and insisted upon his legal rights. It was this reputation that made him President of the Second Continental Congress and first signer of the Declaration of Independence. The American people were placing their future in the hands of a tested patriot who had proved his worth by his sacrifices in the common cause, not a smuggler who used the popular agitation to make personal profits for himself.

113

leave to Retract this Information and says Our Sovereign Lord the King will prosecute no further hereon. Allowed.'' Such a termination of a suit barred any further legal action against the defendant. This action was reported in considerable detail in the ''Journal of the Times'' on March 26, 1769, Dickerson, 83-4.

TRENDS IN EIGHTEENTH-CENTURY SMUGGLING [1]

By W. A. COLE

ONE of the most serious, and certainly the most baffling, problems which confronts the student of eighteenth-century trade statistics is that of smuggling. It is well known that high tariffs and the complexity of their administration provided a constant stimulus to all kinds of evasion—fraudulent entries at the customs and the relanding of goods entered for re-export as well as direct import smuggling—until the incentive was at length removed by the triumph of free trade in the nineteenth century. But it has generally been held that although smuggling was certainly widespread, the problem of its precise extent, or even its probable order of magnitude, defies solution. If this view is accepted, it is difficult to escape the conclusion that, for the purpose of measuring the level and trends of eighteenth-century foreign trade, the official statistics—at any rate of imports and re-exports [2]—are virtually useless.[3] In this paper, therefore, I propose to try to make an estimate of the quantitative importance of smuggling which will help us to assess the possible margin of error involved in the use of the official statistics. Such an estimate is bound to be speculative and cannot be exact. But at least it should make possible an advance on the dubious practice of using the official figures as if the acknowledged deficiencies in the series did not exist.

I

At this stage, we cannot investigate in detail all branches of the illicit trade. Instead, we shall deal first with the traffic in one commodity, tea, and then consider what light the fluctuations in tea smuggling cast on the history of smuggling as a whole. The high value of tea in proportion to its bulk, coupled with a rate of duty which often doubled the legal price, made this particular traffic exceptionally profitable; and for a large part of the eighteenth century, tea was one of the staple goods of the 'free trader'.[4] In March, 1745/6, this clandestine trade was the subject of a special report by a Parliamentary

[1] This is the first of two articles on the growth of British foreign trade in the eighteenth century which have been prepared at the University of Cambridge Department of Applied Economics in connexion with an inquiry into the Economic Growth of the United Kingdom sponsored by the Committee on Economic Growth of the Social Science Research Council of the United States.

[2] Manufactured goods were exempt from duty for most of the century, so the figures for exports are not much affected by smuggling, although they are open to criticism on other grounds and the illegal export of raw wool continued until the outbreak of war with France in 1793. See G. N. Clark, *Guide to English Commercial Statistics, 1696–1782* (1938), pp. 15–16, 34–5; W. D. Cooper, 'Smuggling in Sussex', *Sussex Archaeological Collections*, X (1858), 91.

[3] Cf. G. D. Ramsay, 'The Smugglers' Trade: A Neglected Aspect of English Commercial Development', *Transactions of the Royal Historical Society*, 5th ser. II (1952), 157n.

[4] Most of the smuggled tea was imported direct by the smugglers from European markets, although some was landed from homeward-bound East India ships with the collusion of the Company's officers. It is also probable that when drawbacks were allowed on tea, a considerable part of the tea entered for re-export was illegally relanded. See W. Milburn, *Oriental Commerce* (1813), II, 536–7; 'First Report from the Committee appointed to enquire into the Illicit Practices used in Defrauding the Revenue', 24 December 1783, *H. of C. Reports*, XI (1782–99), 230.

Committee, and the question was again reviewed in the First Report of the Committee on Illicit Practices in December 1783.[1] On both occasions the committees considered estimates of the probable extent of the traffic in tea, and it is these which will form the starting point of our inquiry.

The best known of these estimates is the one supplied on the latter occasion by the deputy accountant of the East India Company. The accountant reckoned that from 1773–82 the annual exports of tea from China to Europe had averaged over 13 million pounds, and since 'The best information procurable, estimates the Annual Consumption of Tea by Foreigners in Europe' at under 5¼ million pounds, he argued that at least 7¾ million pounds must have been smuggled into Great Britain and her dependencies each year. This guess was supported by another, and supposedly independent estimate made by the Commissioners of Excise: on the basis of returns from the officers at the outports of the number of ships engaged in smuggling, their size, and the number of journeys they made each year they, too, reckoned that about seven million pounds of tea was smuggled into the country each year.[2] Another contemporary estimate, however, drawn up under the direction of William Pitt from sources similar to, if not identical with, those used by the Excise Commissioners, advanced the much more modest figure of three million pounds per annum.[3] Unfortunately, this estimate is undated, but it is clear from internal evidence that it relates to a period of three years after 1773, and the association with Pitt suggests that it was drawn up at about the same time as the Commissioners' return. It is difficult to see, therefore, how the three estimates could be reconciled, and one wonders whether the political influence of the East India Company helped to determine which figures finally appeared in the report of the Commons' Committee.

But whatever disagreements may have existed about the precise extent of smuggling, all parties were agreed that the problem was serious and could not be dealt with by repressive measures alone. Accordingly, in September 1784, the cumbersome tea duties of £55. 15s. 10d. per cent and 1s. 1⁴/₅d per pound were abolished and replaced by a window-tax and a duty on tea of 12½ per cent.[4] Following this reform, the sales of tea by the East India Company at once doubled, and soon trebled, while the imports of tea by the rival European companies showed a corresponding decline. By the 1790's Continental imports had fallen to about five million pounds per annum—a figure remarkably close to the estimate of European consumption which the East India Company's accountant had made ten years before.[5] At first sight, the increase in the English Company's sales seems no less significant: the accountant had reckoned that barely a third of the home demand had been met by these sales, and the threefold increase in legal consumption after the reduction of the duty apparently confirms his estimate.[6] But, as Professor Ashton points out, it should 'be remembered that the legal market for tea was controlled on the side of supply, and that the East India Company had a case to establish'.[7] Moreover, it is

115

[1] *H. of C. Journals*, XXV (1745–50), 101–10; *H. of C. Reports*, XI, 228–62.
[2] *H. of C. Reports*, XI, 231, 246–7.
[3] Printed in A. L. Cross, *Eighteenth Century Documents Relating to the Royal Forests, the Sheriffs and Smuggling* (New York, 1928), pp. 237–41.
[4] 24 Geo. III, c. 38.
[5] D. Macpherson, *Annals of Commerce* (1805), IV, 336–7.
[6] The accountant reckoned that apart from smuggled tea several million pounds of dyed leaves were fraudulently sold as tea each year, making the total illicit sales over 12 million pounds, compared with the Company sales of under 5¾ millions. See Macpherson, IV, 49n.
[7] T. S. Ashton, *An Economic History of England: The 18th Century* (1955), p. 165.

necessary to take into account the effect on prices of a drastic reduction of duty and the ending of a disastrous war. Clearly, therefore, before a convincing inference about smuggling can be drawn from the figures of legal consumption, we need to know much more about the character of consumer demand.

A similar reservation applies to the earlier estimates of smuggling given in the report of the Parliamentary Committee of 1745/6. On that occasion, the committee received evidence from excise officers, tea traders and ex-smugglers —some of whom claimed to know the quantity of tea being shipped to England from Continental ports—and here again the published account suggests fairly general agreement about the probable extent of the illicit traffic. A few months before the presentation of the report, at midsummer, 1745, the excise duty on tea of four shillings per pound had been replaced by duties of one shilling per pound and 25 per cent *ad valorem*.[1] It was estimated that in the three years immediately preceding this reform, smuggling had reached a peak of three million pounds a year—or more than three times the legal sales—while in the months which followed illegal imports had fallen and now stood at about one million pounds per annum.[2] The only direct evidence advanced in favour of the view that there had been such a substantial reduction of smuggling was the fact that legal sales had greatly increased. But since it was apparently assumed that the total home demand could be regarded as fixed at about three or four million pounds a year, no attempt was made to consider the effect of price changes on the consumption of tea.

II

None of the estimates discussed can, therefore, be accepted without further inquiry, but the consideration of them does suggest a method by which they may be checked. For if we can trace the effect of price changes on the demand for legally imported tea we should be in a much better position to judge how far the increase in consumption after 1745 and again after 1784 may reasonably be attributed to a decline in smuggling, and how far it was simply due to changes in the price of tea. Moreover—and perhaps more important—such an analysis should give us some indication of the trends in the illicit traffic during the intervening period, which at present is statistically blank. Fortunately the necessary material for this inquiry is available for most of the eighteenth century. From 1706 onwards, figures have survived of the quantity and sale value of all tea sold by the East India Company each year,[3] and from 1740 we also have statistics of the quantities retained for home consumption and the average sale price of each kind of tea.[4] In addition, the excise accounts preserved in the Customs Library record the quantities delivered out of the warehouse for home consumption in each excise year ending at midsummer as far back as 1724–5; and after midsummer, 1745, they give the sale value of tea for home consumption and the amount of excise duty.[5]

From this information, we have constructed an index of the wholesale price

116

[1] 28 Geo. II, c. 26.

[2] Evidence of Abraham Walter, *H. of C. Journals*, XXV, 104–5. Most other witnesses suggested figures of a similar magnitude.

[3] These are printed in R. Wissett, *A Compendium of East India Affairs* (1802), II (no pagination). See also, W. Milburn, *op. cit.* II, 534; J. Macgregor, *Commercial Statistics*, V (1850), 58. In Macgregor's table, the figures of sales are incorrectly described as the quantity imported.

[4] *Parl. Papers*, 1845 (191), XLVI, 593–7.

[5] I am greatly indebted to Dr S. J. Prais for his assistance and advice in carrying out the analysis which follows.

of tea including duty [1] from 1724 to 1829, which is given below in an appendix. Since we are interested in the price of tea for home consumption the index was based mainly on the excise statistics.[2] But for the first twenty years, it was necessary to use prices derived from the figures of all tea sold at the Company's sales, adjusted for differences in the years and the level of the two series.

If we wish to analyse the demand for tea over a long period, however, it is necessary to take into account the changes in population and the price of other consumer goods. For this reason, our analysis will be based on the 'real' prices of tea [3] and consumption per head of the population. Unfortunately, the available indices of the prices of consumer goods are difficult to use and much less reliable than the statistics of tea prices. Those constructed by Dr Gilboy [4] and Mrs Schumpeter [5] relate to harvest years, and are based to a large extent on contract prices, which were often insensitive to short-period fluctuations. Silberling's cost of living index,[6] on the other hand, which is not open to the latter objection, is for calendar years, and covers only a few years of the period of high duty before 1784. It therefore seemed best to use Mrs. Schumpeter's consumer goods' index, adjusted for the difference between harvest and excise years, for the whole of the period from 1724 to 1823, and to extend her series to 1829 on the basis of the Silberling index. This series was then used to deflate the tea index, and thus give us an index of the real prices of tea. As we have no population series for Great Britain as a whole in the eighteenth century, the figures of *per capita* consumption were calculated throughout on the basis of estimates of the population of England and Wales alone.[7] Finally, by taking five-yearly moving averages of both consumption per head and the index of real prices, some allowance was made for the defects in the figures for individual years.

117

III

The relationship between the real prices of tea and the average legal consumption per head in each of these five-yearly periods has been plotted on a

---

[1] It has sometimes been assumed that no duty was included in the price of tea sold at the East India Company's sales. This is true after 1784, but before that date the customs duty was paid by the company and was therefore included in the sale price. The excise duty, on the other hand, was paid by the buyer when the tea was cleared for home consumption and has to be added to the sale price to obtain the wholesale price inclusive of duty.

[2] The fuller information given in the excise statistics also makes it possible to calculate the price more accurately in years when the duty changed. Unfortunately, there are some gaps in the series. The data for the excise years 1785 and 1786 are incomplete as no excise duty was levied on tea from 15 September 1784 to 1 August 1785. The series ends at midsummer 1814, and a new series begins in January 1816. Thereafter, it is possible to give figures for calendar years. The figures of quantities sold are also incomplete for the excise years 1768–72, when the duty of one shilling per pound on black and singlo teas was temporarily suspended, but for this period I have used the quantities given by Macpherson (*op. cit.* IV, 336). Comparison of Macpherson's figures with those given in the excise records for other years reveals a few minor discrepancies, but they are not large enough to be significant.

[3] *I.e.* the prices of tea in relation to those of other consumer goods.

[4] E. W. Gilboy, 'The Cost of Living and Real Wages in Eighteenth Century England', *Rev. Econ. Stat.* XVIII (1936), 134–43.

[5] E. B. Schumpeter, 'English Prices and Public Finance, 1660–1822', *ibid.* XX (1938), 21–37.

[6] N. J. Silberling, 'British Prices and Business Cycles, 1779–1850', *ibid.* V (1923), 235.

[7] Until Census data becomes available in 1801, I have relied for this purpose on the decennial estimates given in John Brownlee's 'The History of the Birth and Death Rates in England and Wales', *Public Health*, XXIX (1916), 211–22, 228–38. It has been assumed that population changed at constant rates during the intervening years.

logarithmic scale in the accompanying diagram.[1] As we might expect, the arrangement of the points bears little resemblance to an orthodox demand curve except over relatively short periods of time: on the contrary, it suggests that the demand for legally imported tea was characterized by repeated and violent changes of level. To illustrate the behaviour of demand from year to year more clearly, the points have been linked up in chronological order within each of the periods specified. If we follow the sequence indicated by the arrows, we shall observe that at the beginning of our period, in the 1720's, labelled (a) in the diagram, the legal consumption of tea was rapidly increasing although the price of tea was almost stationary. In the early 'thirties, there was a sharp contraction in demand (b), and after a few years of comparative stability (c), there was a temporary increase in demand at the end of the decade (d). A much larger increase in 1745 was followed by another period of comparative stability (e), and a further upward movement during the Seven Years' War (f). Then, after 1763, legal demand dropped sharply (g), and, with the exception of the excise years 1768–72, remained at a low level until 1784 when there was again an enormous increase.

What explanations can we find for these sudden changes in the level of demand? How far can they be attributed to changes in the incentives to, and opportunities for, smuggling? From the data summarized in Table 1 it will be noted that most of them were associated with variations in the rate of duty. The two largest increases in demand followed the tariff reforms of 1745 and 1784,

Table 1. ESTIMATES OF THE REAL PRICE, CONSUMPTION PER HEAD, AND
RATES OF DUTY ON TEA

Excise Years ending at Midsummer	Average Real Price of Tea (1725 = 100)	Average Annual Consumption per Head (lbs)	Rate of Duty (Percentage of the Net Cost)
1726–30	95	.10	84
1731–35	89	.11	110
1736–40	80	.17	125
1741–45	78	.13	119
1746–50	67	.41	76
1751–55	60	.51	84
1756–60	58	.62	84
1761–65	60	.68	93
1765–67	53	.64	95
1768–72	38	1.00	65
1773–75	41	.76	101
1776–80	43	.68	103
1780–84	45	.66	110
1787–91	25	2.09	12.5
1791–95	23	2.24	12.5
1796–1800	22	2.54	29
1801–05	24	2.33	62
1806–10	29	2.07	95
1810–14	27	2.02	96
Calendar Years			
1816–20	28	1.89	97
1821–25	38	1.91	100
1825–29	34	2.00	100

[1] It has become conventional in economic diagrams to show the price level on the vertical axis. Since we are interested in the effect of price changes on the level of consumption, however, the procedure has been reversed here, so that an increase in demand at a given level of prices will appear as a movement upwards, rather than a movement to the right.

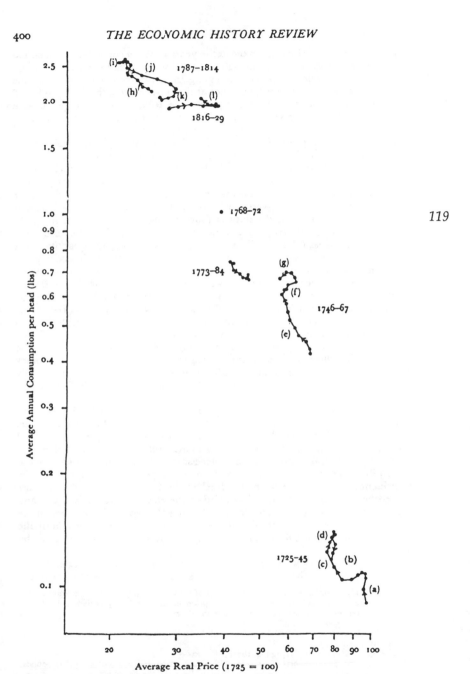

Fig. 1. *The Legal Demand for Tea, 1725–1829*

while the temporary increase in the excise years 1768–72 coincides with a period when the excise duty of one shilling per pound was suspended on all black and singlo teas in an effort to reduce smuggling.[1] For twenty years before 1745 the rates of duty were unchanged, but since at that time most of the duty was levied at a flat rate of four shillings per pound the total amount, expressed as a percentage of the net cost, was related inversely to fluctuations in the price of tea. It is significant that the fall in legal demand in the early 'thirties occurred at a time when tea prices were also falling sharply and when, in consequence, the rate of duty rose from 90 per cent in 1730 to 156 per cent in 1735.

This fits in with other evidence which suggests that smuggling increased in the 'thirties after a temporary fall in the late 'twenties. Before 1724 it was believed that large quantities of tea were being exported from England in order to claim the drawback and were afterwards illegally relanded.[2] Accordingly, at midsummer in that year, the duty of four shillings per pound was made an inland duty and transferred from the customs to the excise.[3] This measure seems to have been successful in checking one form of fraud, since the quantity of tea entered for re-export, which in the years 1719–23 had averaged 380,000 pounds, fell by more than 70 per cent.[4] But as the duties still amounted to 84 per cent of the net cost the incentive to evasion was as great as ever. In 1728, the Danish East India Company enlarged its stock and three years later a Swedish company was formed from the ruins of the old Ostend company. Both these companies were believed to exist mainly to supply the illegal British demand for duty-free East India goods, and in the early 'thirties the French and Dutch companies were also reported to be extending their activities.[5] It seems likely, therefore, that although the reform of 1724 may have resulted in a temporary increase in the revenue of the British government, in the long run its only effect was to extend the market of the East India Company's Continental rivals.[6]

In two cases the reasons for the change in demand are somewhat less obvious. It is possible that the increase in legal demand in the late 'thirties was in part due to the act of 1736 which offered an indemnity to all smugglers who turned King's evidence, provided they were not found guilty of subsequent offences.[7] Again, the outbreak of the Austrian Succession War in 1739 may have led to stock-piling by the 'fair' traders and to a temporary interruption of the Continental supplies on which the 'free' trade depended. But whatever the cause, the movement was short-lived and in the early 'forties the legal demand dropped to the level of the mid-'thirties. During the Seven Years' War, on the other hand, when a similar increase occurred, it was maintained until the return of peace, despite the fact that in 1759 the customs duty was increased by five per cent.[8]

Eighteenth-century wars were likely, of course, to affect the smugglers' trade in a variety of ways—indirectly through their effects on the legal trade of the

---

[1] 7 Geo. III, c. 56. In order to show the effect of these three major changes of duty on the demand more clearly, only the levels of consumption in the five-yearly periods immediately before and after the change have been marked in the diagram.

[2] Milburn, II, 536.

[3] 10 Geo. I, c. 10.

[4] See Milburn, II, 534.

[5] *Ibid.* 537; Macpherson, III, 143–4, 167–8, 183, 204–5.

[6] In 1721 European imports of tea from China had amounted to about 3,800,000 pounds, most of which was probably smuggled into Britain. By 1745 the figure was approaching nine millions. See Milburn, II, 536; *H. of C. Journals*, XXV, 103.

[7] 9 Geo. II, c. 35.

[8] 32 Geo. II, c. 10.

combatants, and directly because, on the one hand, duties were usually increased in war-time and, on the other, the danger of impressment greatly increased the hazards of the illicit traffic. Most of these wars had a temporarily adverse effect on Britain's legal import trade, but from 1756–63 imports rose fairly steadily by about 2.3 per cent each year.[1] Tea imports fluctuated considerably, but in 1760 the East India Company's ships brought home over nine million pounds, nearly twice the previous record. During this period, French colonial power was undermined, the French East India Company entered into a period of decline,[2] the British Navy dominated the seas and heavy fighting raged on the Continent of Europe. Such conditions must have made the smugglers' livelihood unusually precarious, and it is possible that the movement of prices was also against them. In England, the legal price of tea rose in the early years of the war, but fell again after 1760, and by 1763 was only eight per cent higher than in 1756. In Amsterdam, on the other hand, the price of black Bohea tea, the variety most favoured by the smugglers, rose by more than 70 per cent in the course of the war.[3] Hence, it is quite possible that the relatively high demand for legally imported tea in Britain at this time was at least partially due to the temporary scarcity and unusually high price of smuggled supplies.

121

IV

In general, then, it seems reasonable to associate the major shifts in demand before 1784 with fluctuations in smuggling. But before we consider the implications of this conclusion, something must be said about the influence of other factors. In this connexion the pattern of demand *after* 1784 is particularly suggestive. For eleven years after the passing of the Commutation Act the duty was much too low to make large-scale smuggling profitable, and we know that the long wars from 1793–1815 completed the ruin of the Continental companies which had been the main suppliers of the free traders.[4] Yet the demand for tea was still far from stable. Admittedly, in the period of low duty after 1784, labelled (h) in the diagram, consumption rose fairly steadily as the price fell, but at the end of the century, when the fall in prices was arrested and heavier duties were re-imposed, there seems to have been a further, though erratic, *increase* in consumption (i), and in the period of rising prices and duties which followed (j) consumption proved increasingly higher than at corresponding prices at the end of the eighteenth century. In the latter part of the Napoleonic War, when the duty had again risen to nearly 100 per cent of the net cost, the demand fell to the level of the late eighteenth century (k), but in the 1820's, despite continued high duties, it gradually moved to the right until it recovered the level of the early 1800's (l). It is possible that this 'dip' was due to the temporary revival of illicit trading. But what about the rest of the period after

---

[1] Based on figures extracted from P.R.O. Customs 3.

[2] Macpherson, III, 402; E. Levasseur, *Histoire du Commerce de la France*, I (1911), 474 *et seq.*

[3] N. W. Posthumus, *Inquiry into the History of Prices in Holland.* Vol. I, *Wholesale Prices at the Exchange of Amsterdam, 1609–1914* (Leiden, 1946). At Nantes, in France, the price of green tea apparently increased by only seven per cent during this period, although the series is unfortunately incomplete. The price of black tea is not given. See H. Hauser, *Recherches et Documents sur l'Histoire des Prix en France de 1500 à 1800* (Paris, 1936), pp. 487, 509.

[4] The Swedish East India Company survived until 1806, and was finally dissolved in 1813. Macgregor, V, 57; E. F. Heckscher, *An Economic History of Sweden* (Cambridge, Mass. 1954), pp. 195–6.

1800? How are we to account for such high sales in a time of rising prices and duties? [1]

The most probable explanation in this case is that consumers' habits had changed. At the beginning of the eighteenth century tea was a fashionable but expensive luxury enjoyed by comparatively few. By the end, according to the family budgets collected by Eden, it was in common use even in the households of the labouring poor, and the annual sales were sufficient to provide two-thirds of the population with a half pint of tea every day.[2] Initially, of course, this change was made possible by the steady fall in the real prices of tea. But it is also true that if the increased consumption were maintained over a long period we should expect it to become habitual: as a contemporary put it, though tea 'may be deemed an artificial necessary, it becomes a necessary that few would be disposed to relinquish'.[3] Indeed, we should expect that as more people began to drink tea and gradually acquired a taste for it, the demand would tend to increase. Thus, in a period of falling prices, consumption would rise both as a result of a movement along the demand curve and because of the effect of changing tastes on the level of demand. Or, to put the matter another way, the actual levels of consumption shewn in the diagram will represent points on a demand curve which is constantly moving upwards and to the right. While prices continue to fall, of course, the extent of this shift will be difficult to detect. But if prices begin to rise—as they did at the beginning of the nineteenth century—it will at once become apparent, since neither the consumption of individuals nor the number of consumers will be likely to revert to their former level.

These considerations cannot be overlooked if we are to assess the effect of smuggling on the legal demand before 1784. At that time there was no period of rising tea prices comparable to the first quarter of the nineteenth century. Nevertheless, the fall in prices was by no means continuous, and it is possible, for example, that the sudden increases in the demand for legally imported tea about 1739, and again during the Seven Years' War, were in part due to the effect of changing tastes on the level of consumption in years when prices were rising. Nor can we ignore the influence of changing tastes on the trend of consumption when prices were falling. If the change in tastes was continuous we should expect consumption to increase fairly smoothly so long as prices were also falling steadily. But if there were a sudden, violent fall in the price level such as occurred in 1745, 1767 and again in 1784 as a result of changes in the rate of duty, although there would be an immediate increase in sales, some time might elapse before consumers' tastes became adjusted to the new price situation.[4]

[1] It is possible, of course, that our estimates of the real price of tea during the Napoleonic Wars are less reliable than those for the eighteenth century, owing to the difficulty of measuring changes in the value of money during this period. The available price indices may well overstate the rise in prices during the wars, and if so our estimates of the real price of tea will be too low. This might account for the fall in demand in the latter part of the wars, when the real price of tea was apparently falling, although the market price remained exceptionally high until the return of peace. It would not, however, explain the difference between the level of demand in the early 1800's and the late eighteenth century.
[2] Sir F. M. Eden, *The State of the Poor* (1797); Wissett, II. Wissett reckoned that an ounce of tea gave an infusion of two quarts, and despite the change from China to Indian tea, the same is roughly true today. The branch manageress of a well known tea-shop tells me that she uses a pound of tea for 196 cups, or just over eight gallons.
[3] Henry Dundas, Viscount Melville, in a speech in March 1798, quoted by Wissett, II; Milburn, II, 535.
[4] This might explain why, when prices were temporarily reduced in the excise years 1768-72,

Similar difficulties arise if we consider the effect of changes in real incomes on the course of demand. If, for example, there was a secular rise in real incomes, consumption would tend to rise relatively rapidly when prices were falling, and to fall much more slowly when prices were rising. And if there was a sudden change in the price level which was not accompanied by a commensurate change in real incomes, there would be some alteration of the trend of demand quite apart from the possible effect of smuggling. It is unlikely that such considerations—and they could easily be multiplied—would completely invalidate inferences about smuggling drawn from the behaviour of consumer demand. For however great the long-term effects of changing tastes and real incomes, they would hardly account for fluctuations of the magnitude which occurred in this century.[1] But they do suggest that the reaction of consumers to price changes can give us only an approximate idea of the size of the problem with which we have to deal. Moreover, it should be remembered that our data will only indicate the effect on the legal demand of a given change in the legal price of tea. Since, however, smuggled tea sold for less than the legal market price, and the ratio between these prices was constantly changing, we cannot assume that changes in the legal demand accurately reflect the real extent of fluctuations in smuggling. For these reasons, we shall not attempt to make detailed quantitative estimates of changes in the volume of smuggling in the course of the century. Instead, we shall simply try to determine whether the major shifts in demand which followed the tariff reforms of 1745 and 1784 were large enough to substantiate the contemporary estimates of smuggling which were discussed earlier.

123

V

It will be convenient to deal first with the change in demand after the passing of the Commutation Act, since we can assume that in the years which followed large-scale smuggling of tea virtually ceased. After the act came into effect, the index of the real prices of tea dropped by eighteen points, from an average of 43 in 1773–83—the excise years to which the East India Company's estimate of smuggling most nearly relates—to 25 in the five-yearly periods *circa* 1789–90. Such a reduction in price might have been expected to produce an increase in consumption of roughly the same magnitude, i.e. from 0.7 to about 1.2 pounds per head of the population. This calculation is based, not simply on the somewhat erratic behaviour of legal demand in the American War period—when prices were rising—but on the long-term relationship between falling prices and

the demand was still relatively low compared with the level reached in the 1790's. Similarly, it would be unwise to base a judgment on the figures for the years immediately following the tariff reforms of 1745 and 1784 if we wish to assess the full effects of the change on the level of demand.

[1] Theoretically, it is possible to conceive of a situation in which the increase in legal consumption which took place in 1784 (when prices were reduced by about 40 per cent) might be explained without the assumption that there had been a considerable reduction in smuggling. If incomes were distributed very unequally the demand for tea might be elastic at very high prices and relatively inelastic as the price fell and the demand of the wealthy was satiated; then, if prices continued to fall, it would become elastic as tea came within reach of the poorer classes, and finally inelastic again as their demands were met. If the resulting 'dent' in the demand curve were large enough, and occurred at the right point, the increase in consumption after 1784 could be attributed to a movement *along* the curve. For these conditions to be satisfied, however, it would be necessary to assume, not only a wide gulf between the rich and poor, but also that tea was a luxury commodity in the 1770's. In fact, however, the latter supposition seems to be so much at variance with the contemporary evidence that it can be safely ignored.

the trend of consumption in the second half of the eighteenth century.[1] Yet, in fact, legal consumption rose to 2.1 pounds per head, which represents an increase in demand of 0.9 pounds or 75 per cent.

Now, according to the 1783 Report, smuggled goods sold for between half and two-thirds the legal price,[2] so it might be thought that the real price of legally imported tea after the Commutation Act was passed was about the same as smuggled tea before. Hence, if the whole of the increase in demand was due to a decline in smuggling, it could be argued that the illicit sales had averaged 0.9 pounds per head, or nearly seven million pounds each year. It should be noted, however, that the free traders usually found it more profitable to import the coarser varieties of tea, both because the excise duty weighed more heavily on cheap teas and because good quality tea required greater care in packing and transport.[3] And whereas the *average* price of tea fell by about 40 per cent as a result of the reduction of duty, the price of the cheapest black tea dropped 60 per cent. Moreover, it is possible that consumers would tend to buy more when they could obtain tea in the open market without the difficulties and risks involved in dealing with the free traders. It seems likely, therefore, that the total illicit sales before 1784 were a good deal less than seven million pounds. On the other hand, if we reverse the procedure outlined above and calculate the expected consumption in the period 1773–83 on the basis of the observed level of demand after 1784, we shall find that, at the legal prices then prevailing, the actual figure falls short of the expected by just under four million pounds a year. And since at that time smuggled tea could undoubtedly be bought for considerably less than the market price, it seems probable that the actual volume of contraband sales was greater than this difference implies.

We may conclude, then, that on the eve of the Commutation Act illegal sales of tea probably amounted to somewhere between four and six million pounds a year. If, as the East India Company's accountant asserted, large quantities of dyed leaves were being fraudulently sold as tea,[4] illegal imports of tea may well have been smaller than these figures suggest—unless the frauds continued on the same scale after the duty was reduced. Certainly, our calculations do not support the Company's view that the legal sales of tea accounted for barely a third of the total consumption. But at least we must admit that during the American War smuggling may have reached greater heights than Pitt's advisers feared, if not quite the level claimed by the East India Company.

It is more difficult to apply the same technique in analysing the consequences of the tariff reform of 1745. Before that date the legal demand for tea was much too unstable to permit accurate measurement of the effect of price changes on the level of consumption. All that can be said is that demand tended to be much more elastic than it was later in the century. In the twenty years before 1745 the increase in consumption was two or three times greater than the

[1] Between c. 1789 and c. 1793 a reduction of 7.6 per cent in the real price of tea was associated with an increase in consumption of 6.4 per cent. For 1749–53, on the other hand, the corresponding figures are 11.5 and 16.5 per cent. In the 'seventies, real prices were about midway between those obtaining in the early 'fifties and 'nineties. We might expect, therefore, that a small reduction in price in the 'seventies would have produced a slightly greater proportional increase in consumption, but that 'elasticity' would gradually fall below unity if the price continued to fall towards the level of the early 'nineties. It should be noted that in this, and the subsequent calculations, proportional changes have been measured as percentages of the upper values in the case of both quantity and price.
[2] H. of C. Reports, XI, 228.
[3] Cf. H. of C. Journals, XXV, 103.
[4] See above, p. 396n.

reduction in the real price, but by the early 'fifties the proportion had already fallen to about 1.4: 1. Hence the fall in prices following the act of 1745—which amounted to about 14 per cent—might have been expected to produce an increase in consumption of anything between 20 and 40 per cent. Even so, it is clear that the reduction in duty was accompanied by a substantial increase in demand. For on this basis the expected consumption after the act was passed would have been between .17 and .22 lbs per head, whereas the actual sales in the excise years 1747–51 averaged .43 lbs per head, which, with a population of about six millions, represents a difference of $1\frac{1}{4}$–$1\frac{1}{2}$ million pounds.

Since the price of smuggled tea was still slightly below the legal price of the cheapest black tea even after the act became law,[1] it seems reasonable to suppose that the decline in smuggling was at least as great as this increase in demand suggests. It seems equally clear, however, that the illicit trade in tea continued on a significant scale for some years after 1745. In the early 'sixties the legal sales of tea were about a million pounds greater than they had been a decade earlier, although the real price of tea was almost exactly the same at the two dates. Since this represents an increase in demand of nearly 40 per cent in one decade, it would clearly be unreasonable to attribute the change solely to the effect of changing tastes or real incomes. It seems, therefore, that between the early 'forties and the end of the Seven Years' War the average annual imports of tea by the free traders must have declined by about two million pounds. If this was so, it follows that the contemporary view that before 1745 about three million pounds of tea had been smuggled each year cannot have been a wild exaggeration. Whether it could have been a serious under-estimate, it is impossible to say on the evidence of the legal demand alone.[2] But it is difficult to believe that illegal imports of tea at that time could have reached the levels attained during the American War, if only because the total European imports were smaller.[3] Moreover, it is unlikely that the witnesses called by the Commons' Committee would have been guilty of minimising the extent of the problem. As we have already noted, several of them were smugglers, and most of them were traders, interested in demonstrating that high duties had meant extensive smuggling and that only a further reduction would ensure the elimination of the evil. In other words, like the East India Company nearly forty years later, they had a case to establish.

We may conclude, then, that contemporaries were not seriously misinformed about the probable magnitude of smuggling, although some of them had good reasons for erring on the high side in their estimates of the extent of the traffic. In the early 'forties, the tea legally sold by the East India Company almost certainly represented only a small fraction of the total consumption, and it seems likely that at least two million pounds, and probably more, was annually sold by the free traders. Thereafter, tea smuggling never assumed the same relative importance, and for a time it seems to have suffered an absolute decline. In the mid-'sixties, however, and still more during the American War, there was a renewed expansion of the illegal traffic, until by 1784 the smugglers'

[1] The retail price of the cheapest black tea in London was about five shillings a pound, while the price of smuggled tea was variously estimated as between four and five shillings. *H. of C. Journals*, XXV, 103–5.
[2] It would be possible, of course, to estimate the expected demand at the prices prevailing in the early 'forties, by a questionable process of extrapolation based on the observed level of demand at the end of the century, but since the bulk of the tea consumed in the earlier period must have been sold by the smugglers at considerably less than the market price, such a calculation would be virtually meaningless.
[3] See above pp. 396, 401n.

sales probably equalled, if they did not surpass, the quantities sold by the East India Company, and were almost certainly substantially greater in absolute terms than they had been forty years before.

VI

What light does this survey cast on the history of smuggling as a whole? Unfortunately, the scarcity of reliable price data would make it difficult to subject other branches of the contraband trade to the type of analysis attempted here. But the history of one other major commodity, tobacco, suggests that the apparent decline in tea smuggling in the middle of the eighteenth century may not have been exceptional. There is abundant evidence that in the early part of the century large quantities of tobacco were brought into Britain without payment of duty either by direct smuggling or by fraudulent entries at the customs.[1] At the beginning of the century, according to Davenant, the retained imports of tobacco averaged over 11 million pounds a year, whereas between 1730 and the mid-'forties they seem to have fluctuated between five and seven million pounds.[2] No doubt this fall was partly due to the apparent decline in the popularity of smoking in the eighteenth century.[3] But if so it is remarkable that by the early 'sixties net imports had climbed back to over 10.6 million pounds, or about 1.6 pounds per head—a figure which was not surpassed until the last decade of the nineteenth century.[4] Moreover, it has been pointed out that the total exports of tobacco from America after 1791 barely equalled the quantities which were officially recorded as passing through Britain in the period from 1761 to 1775.[5]

There are, indeed, grounds for the view that in the middle decades of the century there was a causal relationship between fluctuations in tea smuggling and movements in the illicit trade as a whole. Contemporaries believed that the profitability of smuggling other commodities depended to some extent on the possibility of running them with tea, and bulky goods, such as brandy, were often used as ballast in ships which were mainly employed in the lucrative traffic in tea. Thus, a witness before the Commons' Committee in 1745/6 argued that a reduction of the duty on tea, which was 'by far the most considerable Commodity that is run', would lead to a general decline in smuggling; and forty years later a similar view inspired the great reform of 1784.[6] This theory is supported by the available evidence of goods seized by the customs and excise officers. Such records tell us little or nothing about changes in the volume of smuggling, but they probably indicated fairly accurately variations in the importance of different commodities. Unfortunately, there are no figures of seizures available for the 'forties and 'fifties, and it is possible that after the reduction of tea duty in 1745 tea smuggling lost the pre-eminence which was claimed for it at that time. Nevertheless, the records which have survived show that in 1764-6 seizures of tea were not much smaller in value than those of all

---

[1] Cf. T. C. Barker, 'Smuggling in the Eighteenth Century: the Evidence of the Scottish Tobacco Trade', *Virginia Mag. Hist. and Biography*, LXII (1954), 387–99; Alfred Rive, 'A Short History of Tobacco Smuggling', *Economic History*, I (1929), 554–69.

[2] Alfred Rive, 'The Consumption of Tobacco since 1600', *Economic History*, I (1926), 61–2.

[3] *Ibid.* 63–4.

[4] See Macpherson, III, 583; Rive, 'The Consumption of Tobacco', *loc. cit.* pp. 72–3.

[5] L. A. Harper, *The English Navigation Laws: A Seventeenth-Century Experiment in Social Engineering* (New York, 1939), p. 262.

[6] *H. of C. Journals*, XXV, 108; *H. of C. Reports*, XI, 230, 286; Macpherson, IV, 49–50.

foreign spirits combined.[1] Nor did the relationship vary much in the next fifteen years despite fluctuations in the tea duty.[2] Admittedly, tea and foreign spirits did not exhaust the list of smuggled goods (though they probably accounted for about half), but the fuller records of seizures for 1769–73 and 1778–82 suggest that in the 'seventies, at any rate, there was little change in the importance of tea in the contraband trade as a whole. Although there were fluctuations in the seizures of other goods, tea seems to have represented about a quarter or a fifth of the total at both periods.[3]

After 1784, of course, the enterprising free trader tended to look elsewhere for easy profits, and although the virtual abolition of the tea duty probably contributed to a general decline in smuggling, there is no reason to suppose that it came to an end. Seizures of contraband goods, and armed clashes between the smugglers and the revenue officers continued well into the nineteenth century, but despite the reimposition of heavy tea duties, tea smuggling never regained its former importance. The official value of tea seized in 1822–4, for example, works out at a mere £1,900, compared with about £15,000 for tobacco, and £27,000 for brandy and gin.[4] Similarly, evidence of tea smuggling tells us relatively little about the fortunes of other branches of the illicit trade in the years before 1745. At the beginning of the century, tea was a newcomer to European commerce and can have played only a minor part in the smugglers' trade. An official return in May 1733, of the quantity of goods seized and condemned during the previous ten years, suggests that even at that time seizures of brandy were worth three times as much as those of tea.[5] Clearly, therefore, illegal imports of tea must have grown relatively rapidly to acquire the predominance which they apparently enjoyed by the 1740's.

Nevertheless, if fluctuations in tea smuggling provide us with an index, however crude, of the fortunes of the rest of the illicit traffic during the critical period from 1745–84, it should be possible to suggest the probable trends in smuggling during the century as a whole. We can probably assume that there was a general increase in smuggling in the years before 1745, even if in magnitude and phasing it did not correspond with the expansion of tea smuggling. The complaints of contemporaries and the repeated attempts to prevent smuggling by legislation both suggest that the problem became more serious as the tariffs grew more burdensome and complicated. We know that the 1740's were the heyday of armed bands of smugglers, such as the Hawkhurst gang, and it has been suggested that the organization of the contraband trade reached its full development only in the reign of George II 'when there was a systematic and permanent traffic in contraband, sympathized with by the bulk of the population of the maritime counties'.[6] Again it seems reasonable to accept the

127

---

[1] Figures of seizures in 1764–6, 1769–73 and 1778–82 are given in Appendix No. 4 of the 1783 Report. *H. of C. Reports*, XI, 240–3.

[2] At the official rates of valuation of imports, seizures of tea averaged about £11,000 in 1764–6, £12,000 in 1769–71 and £15,000 in 1778–82. The corresponding figures for foreign spirits work out at about £14,000 in 1764–6 and 1769–71, and £18,000 in 1778–82. At market prices tea would probably represent a smaller and fluctuating proportion of the total.

[3] This can only be a rough estimate, since the figures of seizures may not be complete and East India goods were not all valued at constant prices in the official trade statistics. It should be remembered, too, that tea was easier to conceal than many other smuggled commodities.

[4] Based on a return cited by Teignmouth and Harper, *The Smugglers* (1923), II, 222.

[5] 'The Report of the Committee appointed to inquire into the Frauds and Abuses in the Customs . . .' *H. of C. Reports*, I (1715–35), 610. It should be noted, however, that judging by the fuller returns preserved in P.R.O. T. 64/143–5, tea may already have taken second place by this time.

[6] Atton and Holland, *The King's Customs*, I (1908), 134.

view that smuggling was increasing in the 'seventies and that the decline in its importance may be dated from Pitt's reform of the customs in the 1780's.[1] But our evidence suggests that its growth had not been continuous: after reaching a peak in the 'thirties and 'forties, it apparently declined in the latter part of George II's reign before rising again to its fullest extent in the late 'seventies.

If this was so, it would appear that the legal and illegal branches of England's import trade tended to move in opposite directions in the eighteenth century. In the early part of the century, the legal trade was comparatively stagnant, and in the 'thirties and early 'forties there was a period of absolute decline. After 1745, on the other hand, legal imports rapidly increased, fell sharply during the American War, and then rose again at the end of the century. But it now seems likely that an allowance for smuggling would tend to damp down these fluctuations. We still cannot determine, of course, the precise extent of the margin of error involved in the use of the official statistics. But at least we can make a reasonable guess at the probable order of magnitude of the contraband trade. We have suggested that the illicit sales of tea averaged between four and six million pounds annually during the American War; and if, as the figures of seizures imply, illegal imports of tea represented about a quarter or a fifth of the total quantity of smuggled goods, valued at constant official prices, it seems possible that £2 or £3 million worth of goods may have been smuggled into Britain each year.[2] In the same period, total legal imports did not amount to much more than £12 millions per annum. Clearly, therefore, fluctuations in smuggling must have had a significant influence on the trends in legal trade. Admittedly, the estimate of smuggling might be reduced by about a third if, as the East India Company's accountant suggested, part of the illicit sales of tea were in fact accounted for by fraudulent substitutes made at home rather than by illegal imports of real tea. On the other hand, since smuggled goods represented a net addition to home consumption, estimates of their value should be compared with the values of officially retained imports. At present figures of net imports are not available, but we hope to meet this deficiency in a subsequent article on the official statistics of legal trade.

Department of Applied Economics, Cambridge

[1] Cf. A. L. Cross, *op. cit.* pp. 27–8.

[2] For what it is worth, it may be noted that a witness before the Commons' Committee in 1746, when the official rates of valuation probably still bore some relation to actual prices, reckoned that over £1 million was annually exported in specie to pay for smuggled goods, apart from illegal exports of raw wool. Another witness gave a figure of £200,000, apparently for tea alone. Before 1736, when the price of tea on the Continent was much higher, it was said that payments for tea were as high as £800,000. See *H. of C. Journals*, XXV, 102, 104.

APPENDIX

AN INDEX OF THE AVERAGE WHOLESALE PRICE OF TEA
FOR HOME CONSUMPTION, INCLUSIVE OF DUTY

$(1725 = 100)$

Year ending at Midsummer					
1725	100	1759	65	1794	31
1726	95	1760	66	1795	32
1727	106	1761	61	1796	33
1728	105	1762	63	1797	33
1729	98	1763	61	1798	36
1730	95	1764	62	1799	40
1731	95	1765	61	1800	39
1732	92	1766	59	1801	41
1733	88	1767	56	1802	41
1734	68	1768	43	1803	44
1735	67	1769	38	1804	45
1736	71	1770	38	1805	54
1737	74	1771	45	1806	56
1738	73	1772	46	1807	59
1739	78	1773	56	1808	60
1740	84	1774	50	1809	59
1741	80	1775	48	1810	63
1742	80	1776	49	1811	59
1743	85	1777	49	1812	61
1744	73	1778	50	1813	60
1745	74	1779	51	1814	63
1746	60	1780	55	Calendar Year	
1747	64	1781	53	1816	54
1748	72	1782	57	1817	54
1749	65	1783	57	1818	56
1750	65	1784	57	1819	53
1751	63	1785	—	1820	51
1752	57	1786	31	1821	53
1753	57	1787	32	1823	53
1754	55	1788	31	1824	53
1755	54	1789	33	1825	52
1756	57	1790	31	1826	48
1757	60	1791	32	1827	46
1758	60	1792	31	1828	44
		1793	31	1829	42

129

Speculations on the Colonial Wars

Howard H. Peckham [*]

ECCLESIASTES might have written, "Of making many memorials there is no end." Far from being neglectful of the past, we have been prolific with monuments, sculptures, markers, and plaques, especially in the East and in our capitals. Now we are on the threshold of a Civil War centennial that will fill the same function: to recall the past, but probably without interpreting it. From the earliest Fourth of July orators to the latest outdoor drama, we have gloried in our history as a kind of pageantry that did our ancestors proud. Yet the meaning of many events remains obscure.

Books may be monumental, too, creating images but not interpreting them. Detailed treatment of the four colonial wars is found in Francis Parkman's *France and England in North America,* but the emphasis throughout the seven volumes is on heroic men and military actions, a visualized sequence of personalized happenings that is fascinating to read. With occasional exceptions,[1] Parkman offers no summary of judgments about the century and a half of rivalry and battle and leaves the reader to draw his own conclusions. Partly because of this great work,[2] the struggle in North America between the two colonial powers still awaits a modern historian who will ask the pertinent questions and seek the

* Mr. Peckham is director of the William L. Clements Library and professor of history at The University of Michigan, Ann Arbor, Michigan. This article is a revision of an address delivered on the occasion of the annual meeting of the Associates of the John Carter Brown Library, April 14, 1960.

[1] See, for example, the preface to *Count Frontenac and New France under Louis XIV* (Boston, 1877), p. xiii, where Parkman spoke of a fate that New France's "own organic fault made inevitable," and *A Half-Century of Conflict* (Boston, 1892), p. iii, where he sought meaning in "the singularly contrasted characters and methods of the rival claimants to North America." Interested readers will find pertinent Otis A. Pease, *Parkman's History* (New Haven, 1953), chaps. 2, 3.

[2] Another deterrent is that as educators emphasize "recent history" and even "current history," pre-Revolutionary events sometimes seem to be receding into a limbo of a pseudomedieval period. Our country's history gets brutally telescoped: first there was Columbus' discovery, then the first settlements, and then the Revolution. In particular, the colonial wars are lost.

answers needed if we are to understand the significance of this part of our past.

Wars always epitomize civil policies, and a series of wars brings into focus opposing political philosophies and social cultures. Study of these colonial wars induces some reflections on the colonizing powers, on the eventual reversal of the positions of England and France in Europe, and on the incipient American nation. Eschewing in un-Parkmanlike method a review of the wars themselves, which ran from 1689 to 1760 with intervening truces, one may hazard some commentaries on the persistent issues and turns of events.

The tenuousness of legal claims to unoccupied lands based only on exploration stood revealed. France had her Cartier, and England her Cabots, but charters and grants written according to who saw what first were no more than vain boasts and paper challenges. Inevitably, perhaps, it was up to the Spanish, French, and English colonists themselves to make their own boundaries by the drift of their settlements, and along with ax and plow the musket was a recognized tool. Neither power would recognize a line that the other could not hold by force. Even the treaties had little effect on maintaining boundaries, and indeed they were usually not mentioned. The beckoning land had to be won—that is, reclaimed from the wilderness, wrested from the savage, and secured from the rival. International law was much too meager to invite appeals to reason or provide equitable decisions.

131

From this distance in time, the several wars appear to be an appalling tale of suffering and unnecessary death, a succession of convulsions that brought no peace until the fourth and final one. The ambitions of essentially little men could not be satisfied without the slaughter of children, the enslavement of women, and the torture of men in a vain attempt to settle a boundary that was finally eradicated. Early in the contest each side, although professing a desire for peace and knowing that strength was to be gathered only from peace, insisted on a peace that would permit expansion of trade and territory. Each country had developed a sense of mission, whether it was toward the fur trade, saving the souls of Indians, a new Zion, wider boundaries, or national prestige. It could not be fulfilled without possession of the interior continent. This was a contradictory or mutually exclusive ambition. One side had to conquer, even if it took two generations. This is our heritage, a challenge for us to do better with diplomacy.

The nagging question of why France lost is not simple to answer. Her ultimate defeat was no foregone conclusion in 1689. Throughout the seventeenth century France was the most powerful country in Europe and even in 1750 she had an army several times larger than England's. As late as 1757 she was winning the Seven Years' War. Yet in America she exhibited several weaknesses.

Canada and Louisiana together contained a very small population. When the wars began in 1689 New France contained not more than 13,000 whites, and by 1754 the number had increased to only 75,000. The English colonies in 1689 boasted of probably 200,000 white inhabitants, who multiplied to about 1,200,000 by 1754. The significance of this disproportion, however, is not so great as it first appears. In the early years most of the Canadian population was concentrated along the St. Lawrence River and in Acadia, and probably two-thirds of the population in 1754 was still located there. Similarly, her enemy's population should be counted as primarily the total inhabitants of New York and New England, or approximately 450,000. Further, lest these figures imply that France should have been easily defeated by England, let it be recalled that in Europe the situation was very much the reverse: England, Prussia, and their allies mustered a total population of twelve million while France and her allies counted an aggregate of more than one hundred million people.

The importance of the population disparity in America was further reduced by two factors favorable to the French. First, the proportion of men in the French population was higher than in the English colonies, because Canada and Louisiana were full of single men and married men without their families who had come to make a fortune. Secondly, this provincial population was under one government, or at most two, while the English by 1754 were under thirteen governments. The relative advantage in wartime was with the French, who were not only under a single system of authority but used to being commanded. Also, Canada tried to offset its manpower shortage by employing Indians, though they either failed her at critical moments or aroused overwhelming reaction by their barbaric cruelties.

In reality the small population was significant as a symptom of general internal weakness, rather than as a cause of weakness. In the period from 1689 to 1760 certain changes took place in the English colonies that were not paralleled in New France, and they were changes that developed strength. When the first English colonies were founded, England was

132

ruled by the King in Council, and there was no department or machinery for administering colonial affairs. In 1675 a standing committee of the Privy Council, called the Lords of Trade, was put in charge of them. After the Glorious Revolution of 1688, Parliament seated new rulers and asserted its constitutional supremacy over the monarchy; then the cabinet system of government, with executive ministers responsible to Parliament, began to develop. The colonies participated in this change in their own particular manner. Assuming that they occupied the same position relative to the Crown as Parliament did, the colonial assemblies proceeded to delimit the powers of royal governors in the same way and to assert increasing authority. They did not recognize any transfer of power over themselves from the Crown to Parliament. Hence, they continued their long struggle for increasing self-government, first against Crown officials and then against Parliament. The colonial wars placed the governors in need of money and compelled them to accede to assembly demands. This spirit of self-dependence was on every side encouraged by the immigration of non-English peoples, the growth of emotional religious sects against the established Anglican and Puritan formalism, the decay or denial of safeguards preserving social privilege, the evasion of restrictions on colonial trade, the increasing number of newspapers and schools, the vigorous expansion of settlement southward and westward, and so forth.

133

Nothing comparable happened in France or New France. Louis XIV, who occupied the throne from 1661 until after two of the colonial wars had been fought, was succeeded in 1715 by a great-grandson who inherited only his faults and ruled a nation that had been drained of riches and responsibility. Parlement had no actual governing power and was virtually ignored. No revolution curbed the monarch's powers. His rule extended across the sea in the persons of a governor in control of civil and military affairs and an intendant in charge of financial and judicial matters and who frequently served as a spy on the governor. In addition, the Catholic Church sent over a bishop, and these three officials chose five councilors to serve with them as a limited governing body. Just as there was no representative assembly, there were no competing sects.

In New France the fur traders and missionaries were not artisans or farmers, and hence developed no flourishing, large, and stable middle class. The French Huguenots, comparable in zeal and economic talents to the English Puritans—and more numerous—were barred from migration, as were aliens. Large grants of land—seigneuries—were made by the

Crown to prominent colonists, who rented plots to tenants, milled their grain for a fee, and served as their judges. Skilled artisans paid the seigneur for the privilege of working at their trades. New settlements were made by the granting of new seigneuries. There were no newspapers or political assemblies, and the church controlled the schools and hospitals. Whatever one may believe about national character under equal circumstances, it seems clear that as the eighteenth century progressed, the English colonists enjoyed opportunities to develop into more prosperous, informed, self-governing, articulate, classless home-builders than the overly regulated French.

134

The nature of settlement in Canada, as well as the harsh climate, did not make the province even remotely self-sufficient either in food supplies, clothing, or weapons. France had to export most of the necessities of life to her colonies just to prevent famine, and consequently the provincial army had no resources behind the lines. To prosecute a war, the sea lanes to France had to be kept open. Throughout the eighteenth century, however, Great Britain was increasing her navy and in the last war was able to defeat or bottle up its French counterpart. The stronger navy could also support troops in attacks on port cities, as was demonstrated at Louisbourg and Quebec.

All of these factors could not help but produce a difference in motivation, difficult as that is to measure. Parkman has been accused of prejudice in arrogating to the English several virtues he denied the French, but at least he emphasized that there was a difference in the outlook of the two nationalities in America. The prevailing attitude of most of the French in Canada and Louisiana was grounded on exploitation of the country. The inhabitants themselves, as well as the trading companies back home, were mercantile in outlook. The purpose of the colony was to make money for promoter and settler. In contrast, a large proportion of the English colonists were antimercantile, not in the sense of being indifferent to making money, but in primarily aiming to establish permanent homes under new governments. In time of war the French colonials fought for their king and church and then for their own safety; the English fought for their homes and their children's future and then for their king. Certainly they acted as if they had more at stake. Sometimes this motivation made a difference in persistence and daring; wars are won by the side that can hang on the longest.

I think this distinction is revealed at another level. For all the bickering between old country and new among the English, between regular and provincial officers and men, there prevailed an honesty of purpose, and the mistakes made by commanders were the errors of ignorance or incompetence. But in Canada some of the higher officials were playing a dishonest game against their own troops and people. After their return to France in 1761 the governor, the intendant, and forty other officers were thrown into the Bastille charged with flagrant corruption in the handling of supplies sent to Canada. Twenty-one of them were tried and all but eight were convicted of swindling the royal government. In contrast Sir Jeffery Amherst set an example of probity and fairness. The system of purchasing army commissions often resulted in officers of merit being passed over, and there was some political graft at home, but the military was more likely to be inept than corrupt.

135

There was always a third party, however: the Indian. Both European powers were invading a land on which he lived and hunted. Under international law, such as it was in the early seventeenth century, it could be argued that the continent was virtually uninhabited for two reasons: the Indians were neither civilized nor Christian and thus not entitled to belong to the recognized family of nations whose rights had some validity; secondly, scattered primitive tribes of small numbers did not appear to need a whole continent for sustenance, and if they did not need it, then they ought to share it. From these ingenious premises the Europeans easily persuaded themselves that they had a right to invade and a positive duty to carry the gospel to the heathen and by their own presence demonstrate what Christianity meant. The early English felt that surrendering land was an equitable price for the Indians to pay in return for receiving the gospel![1] I forbear to comment on the exhibition of brotherly love the whites offered, but the confrontation of a new race with a Stone Age culture having no concept of private property forced the Europeans to adopt a pattern of relationship that still provokes controversy.

Here, I think, the French come off somewhat better than the English. Their desire to proselyte the Indians was more intense, more widespread, and probably more persistent than that of the English. And although they encroached on an inhabited land and claimed jurisdiction over a larger area than the English, they managed to spot their settlements in a manner not entirely disagreeable to the Indians affected. Posts made up of traders,

[1] Fred M. Kimmey, "Christianity and Indian Lands," *Ethnohistory*, VII, No. 1 (1960), 45.

soldiers, and priests, each with little garden plots, were decidedly different from acre on acre of English farms from which the Indian was steadily excluded. In the one case, the foreigner brought to the Indian goods that raised his standard of living without disrupting his way of life; in the other, the benefit of the superior culture carried with it a tidal encroachment that destroyed the life it was supposed to enrich.

In face-to-face, daily contacts the French showed also a willingness to mingle and even intermarry, a camaraderie that prevented the proud savage from feeling too much inferior to the talented white man. By contrast, the British, who were not fundamentally as aristocratic in outlook as the French, found it impossible to conceal their distaste for their dusky neighbors and kept intercourse on a formal and commercial basis. The Indians were not long in sensing that the English simply did not like them. The Iroquois were proud enough not to care, either for the Frenchman's good fellowship or the Englishman's disdain; they were out to play the white man's game of exploiting others and they set themselves up as middlemen between the fur gatherers of the West and the fur buyers of the East. United, cynical, astonishingly perceptive, and practiced in a cruelty that was so useful in commercial relations, the Iroquois learned to play off the French against the English—and to hang on to their lands. For 175 years westward migration rolled past them and they did not budge. They didn't blunder until they sided with England in the American Revolution. Even so, they were not entirely displaced, for the Iroquois still hold land in central New York.

The last war—the French and Indian War—has been conceived of as a struggle on England's part to preserve the empire, not to enlarge it.[4] This was never William Pitt's view, and the long hostility of the English colonists toward the devilish combination of French Catholics and their savage minions was not to be satisfied with a repeated pushing back of such an enemy. They sought conquest, and a removal of the menace from the continent. Sir Jeffery Amherst was not concerned with preservation of the existing empire when he proudly won for his royal master a domain twelve times the size of England. The final victory elevated Britain to the greatest colonial power in the world, and the celebrated result appeared to justify the repeated efforts of four wars—wars *for* empire! That she lacked

[4] This argument is ably presented by Lawrence Henry Gipson, *The British Empire before the American Revolution*, VII (New York, 1954), 312-313.

the wisdom to rule such a vast empire was not apparent for another several years.

Over and above the military contest between France and England, we may see in these wars the Renaissance spirit making its final conquest of the feudal mind. France had clung too long to the outworn concepts of the Middle Ages. She represented a closed society under four authorities: monarch, church, aristocracy, and monopoly. She secured obedience and uniformity in New France at the expense of initiative and self-reliance. The dissatisfied at home could not escape by migration. The fur trade was awarded to companies that sent over employees. The Crown rewarded favorites and made sycophants; it dispatched troops and then gave them inducements to remain. The church sent priests and nuns. All these groups were overregulated by appointed officials, military officers, bishops, and company directors. Agricultural surpluses failed to accumulate, and even the fur trade never grew into big business because the English could offer better goods at lower prices. It could be entirely disrupted by an incursion of Iroquois across the St. Lawrence or Ottawa river routes of transportation. In Paris, Canada and Louisiana were regarded as parasites on the royal treasury. Time and again the whole idea of an overseas empire was questioned. Only a few individuals who broke from the feudal mold, like Champlain or La Salle, possessed the liberal faith or national patriotism to envision a French empire covering most of North America. Unfortunately, they never had a king with enough imagination to catch their vision, and the measures taken only exposed the ineptness of a quasi-medieval culture for expansion and variation. It was inelastic and so it cracked under pressure. New France (an actual misnomer) was truly an extension of the Old World, and therein lay its failing.[5]

By contrast, the English migrants put down roots in a New World and adapted themselves. It might be conceived that settlement of French and English on a common continent facing similar hardships would diminish the differences of the two peoples and ultimately produce common views and fellowship. Instead, the differences increased. The influence of New World geography was potent but it was not uniform and could not overcome all inheritance.

Since the French came primarily to exploit the land economically and the natives religiously, they settled in island clusters that formed no frontier

137

---

[5] This was the nub of Parkman's brief observation quoted in n. 1, above.

line. They could not or at least did not shake off control from home, and it tended to insulate them from their new environment. In contrast, New England was settled by persons in flight from their homeland, in disagreement with its religious and sometimes its political institutions, advanced as those were over French institutions. They came to establish new homes and new self-sustaining communities. They were also the happy victims of what Edmund Burke called "the beneficent negligence of government." In the eighteenth century they were joined by Scots and Germans with similar motives. Colonial assemblies spoke for colonial desires that verged away from English customs. As Ray Allen Billington has pointed out, the English colonists came from a background of a "well developed parliamentary theory that anticipated constitutional democracy, an emerging capitalistic philosophy fostered by a thriving commercial class, and a social structure sufficiently fluid to allow a greater degree of upward mobility than in autocratic nations."[6]

As the English moved inland more or less in a line, they were much more susceptible to the wonderful leavening effect of the frontier, as described by Frederick Jackson Turner. The democratizing influence, the nationalizing impact, the demands on resourcefulness, the experience in establishing governments, the rich rewards of individual work, the confidence in the future—all these factors infused Englishmen in America with much more ardor than Frenchmen and gave them strength. The Anglo-Saxon heritage, which, indeed, did differ from the French, was now distinctively shaped and colored by frontier experience, a subtle transformation of which only a few perceptive men were aware. The influence might have been fragmented and dissipated among the thirteen colonies had there been no international conflict to bring them together in repeated common effort. The required military exertion against the enemy forced intercolonial co-operation. With each war the English colonies found cooperation a little easier, and old fears and suspicions and jealousies somewhat allayed. They almost formed a confederation in 1754 to deal with intercolonial problems on which the British constitution was silent. They forged joint policies, uncovered common complaints, began to recognize the advantages of knocking down barriers, and experienced the joy of united strength.

[6] Ray Allen Billington, "American History," *The Case for Basic Education*, ed. James D. Koerner (Boston, 1959), p. 38.

Their greatest discovery by 1760 was not that with help from home they were strong enough at last to push France out of North America—a goal long sought and finally realized—but rather that they were a people distinct from their kinsmen in England. Cousins they might be, but Englishmen of the third and fourth generations born in America regarded the native Englishman with curiosity and even as a foreigner. This discovery was the issue of the colonial wars, the development accelerated by warfare. The difference was disquieting, like self-consciousness in adolescence, and it was politely ignored and even denied. But the notion was implanted that the connection between England and America was only the Crown. The foundation for separation and nationality was unwittingly laid in the long struggle for supremacy on this continent.

139

The Economic Growth of the Chesapeake and the European Market, 1697-1775

THE relative position of the Chesapeake in the economy of the thirteen colonies before the American Revolution is a matter of some ambiguity. On the one hand, we are traditionally taught to view Virginia and Maryland as somewhat backward compared to their northern neighbors, particularly in their lack of large towns and of those forms of a centralized market economy commonly based upon urban commercial centers. On the other hand, simple quantitative measurement[1] seems to indicate that they were among the most highly developed of the colonies. Virginia was the most populous of all, and even Maryland had more inhabitants than New York. If between them they were to account for about 30 per cent of the population of the thirteen colonies on the eve of the Revolution, they were even more strikingly to account for close to 50 per cent of colonial exports to England. If we add in oft-neglected Scotland as a recipient, then the Chesapeake's share of exports to Great Britain passes 60 per cent. If we had chosen to make our measurements as of a generation earlier, then the Chesapeake's share of colonial exports would have been even higher.

This seeming inconsistency cannot be resolved in the abstract; it must be understood in terms of the composition of trade. One commodity, tobacco, accounted for better than 90 per cent of the value of Chesapeake exports to Great Britain and for over 50 per cent of total colonial exports thither. The trade in this one commodity must therefore explain both the quantitative development of Virginia

---

[1] This paper contains the précis of an argument which will be developed in much greater detail in parts of a book on French-British-Chesapeake trade in the eighteenth century which the author expects to publish in 1966. Since very full documentation will be given there from French, British, and American archives, etc., footnotes will be kept to a minimum here. Unless otherwise indicated, all English tobacco statistics before 1772 are from Public Record Office, London (hereafter, PRO) Customs 2 and Customs 3; all Scottish tobacco statistics before 1772 from Customs 14; and British trade statistics from 1772 onwards from Customs 17. Summary data for Scotland were also taken from PRO B.T.6/185 folios 192, 204, etc., and from National Library of Scotland, Edinburgh, Ms. 60. General colonial trade and population data are from U.S. Bureau of the Census, *Historical Statistics of the United States, Colonial Times to 1957* (Washington, D.C., 1960) ch. Z. "England" is used throughout to include England and Wales only, "Great Britain" to include *England, Wales, and Scotland.*

and Maryland and the institutional character of their commercial life.

The long-term development of the Chesapeake tobacco trade can conveniently be divided into periods of a quarter or a third of a century each. During the first thirty years of settlement, between 1607 and 1637, the two colonies were established, a staple commodity found, and marketing arrangements worked out. At the end of this period, imports into England from Virginia and Maryland were in the vicinity of 1.5 million pounds a year. With the foundations thus securely set, the next thirty-odd years—the period of the most impressive growth—saw a tenfold increase in trade, English imports of tobacco from the Chesapeake reaching fifteen million pounds in 1668-1669.[2] In the last third of the seventeenth century, substantial growth continued, but at a much slower rate, only doubling to reach about 30 million pounds' weight in 1697-1699. In the first quarter of the eighteenth century, the deceleration continued, imports in 1722-1726 being scarcely more than those at the turn of the century, though Scotland had since joined the Union and the tobacco trade. In the second and third quarters of the eighteenth century, however, there was a marked resumption of growth reaching in round numbers about 50 million pounds' weight in 1738-1742, 70 million in 1752-1756, and 100 million in 1771-1775. This last was more than three times the level at the turn of the century or in the mid-1720's.

141

The general pattern is thus clear: after an initial period of experimentation, etc., very rapid growth between the 1630's and 1660's was followed by slower growth in the latter part of the seventeenth century and by complete stagnation in the first quarter of the eighteenth; then a resumption of growth occurred in the next fifty years that tripled Chesapeake exports. How, though, do we explain this long-term slowing down and then resumption of growth?

There is of course the familiar explanation based upon land use. The early period of most rapid growth was that in which new land was being opened up and fresh soil first cultivated. Soil exhaustion is thus made to account for the slowed rate of growth in the later seventeenth century and for stagnation in the first quarter of the eighteenth. The renewed growth of the middle decades of the eighteenth century can also be explained by the movement of settlement out of tidewater and onto new lands in the piedmont and

[2] Miscellaneous accounts of 1st Viscount Lonsdale: Muniments of the Earl of Lonsdale, Lowther, Westmoreland.

on the south side of James River. This may be a good description
of what happened, but it is not a complete explanation. It does
not explain the timing, nor does it explain why the piedmont settlers
devoted as much effort as they did after 1730 or 1740 to tobacco
rather than to wheat, which they also raised for export.

A second and more speculative explanation can be found in the
problem of the labor supply. The disturbed decades from about
1630 to about 1670, it can be argued, were particularly likely to induce emigration—including that to the Chesapeake. In the more
settled and prosperous England after 1670 or 1674, people had fewer
reasons to leave home. The Chesapeake and other colonies thus had
to look for additional population primarily to their own natural increase. Rapid economic growth resumed again in the mid-eighteenth
century only when an adequate supply of slave labor became available. This explanation, however, does not fit the data too well after
1700. It fails, for example, to explain the stagnation of the first quarter of the eighteenth century. It was precisely in the 1680's and
1690's that slaves were first introduced into the Chesapeake in large
numbers, yet we can observe no effects on production before the
late 1720's. There was of course a multiplication of the slave population of Virginia and Maryland between approximately 1730 and the
Revolution (threefold in the case of Maryland, more than sixfold in
the case of Virginia). Insofar as this increase was caused by the
increased importation of slaves, was it simply a cause and not also
an effect of the economic growth of the region? Why were the
merchants of London, Bristol, and Liverpool who trafficked in slaves
to Virginia and Maryland—all of them also tobacco merchants—so
much more inclined to send slaves thither after 1730 than they had
been between 1712 and 1730?

In this paper, we shall be concerned almost exclusively with a
third explanation, that of markets. We do not hold this to be a complete explanation of the pattern of economic growth in the Chesapeake, but merely an important and neglected one. Markets in common usage suggest prices, but it should be remembered that markets
can influence more than prices—they can influence the whole institutional structure of a trade. Prices by themselves are an inadequate explanation of what happened in the Chesapeake. The secular
trend of tobacco prices had been downward throughout the whole
of the seventeenth century, reflecting yet not seriously hampering
increased production. A good crop commonly lowered prices in the

142

Chesapeake; there is no evidence, however, that low prices one year ever caused reduced planting the next year. Relatively high prices between 1711 and 1725 were not inconsistent with stagnation in those same years. Except for a few abnormal years, prices of Chesapeake tobacco were generally low between 1726 and 1774, but no longer falling.[3] It was in these years of low but more stable prices that shipments from the Chesapeake tripled. These low prices can hardly have "stimulated" production in the Chesapeake, though they undoubtedly enabled the increased production of the area to find its markets. Where were these markets?

The most striking thing about the Chesapeake tobacco trade is that as early as 1669, when only fifteen million pounds of tobacco were being sent to England, eight million pounds, or over half, were being reexported from England.[4] Thus, almost from its cradle, the Chesapeake tobacco trade was dependent for its prosperity on remote markets about which it knew very little. Yet those remote markets absorbed ever increasing amounts of Chesapeake tobacco as the trade grew and grew. Of the 100 million pounds shipped annually to Great Britain in 1771-1775, roughly 85 per cent was reexported. In world competition, Chesapeake tobacco had the conventional advantages of price and quality. From the 1660's, it was noticeably cheaper than the competing quality tobaccos of the Spanish and Portuguese colonies. It was also a versatile commodity, shipped in dry leaf which could be made into any form of tobacco or snuff. Competing tobaccos were usually shipped manufactured or semimanufactured and were hence less versatile. Brazil roll tobacco, for example, was used in northern Europe exclusively as a chewing tobacco and suffered when that usage became unfashionable in the eighteenth century. The European tobaccos—particularly those of the Netherlands and Germany, but also those of Turkey and Russia, etc.—were on the other hand cheaper than those of the Chesapeake but were everywhere recognized as decidedly inferior. They were commonly mixed with Chesapeake tobacco in manufacture in proportions that varied with price fluctuations. In general, the popularity of snuff in the eighteenth century permitted the

143

---

[3] For Amsterdam prices, see Jacob M. Price, *The Tobacco Adventure to Russia . . . 1676-1722* (*Transactions of the American Philosophical Society*, n. s., LI, Part I (Philadelphia, 1961), 103. It is virtually impossible to compile a good, long-term series of London tobacco prices. It is hoped, though, that John M. Hemphill, II, will soon publish the Virginia price series on which he has been working for many years.
[4] As in note 2.

inferior tobaccos of northern Europe, thanks to mixing and scenting, to compete more effectively with American tobaccos than they had been able to do in the more honest seventeenth century when intrinsic quality was more readily revealed by smoking or chewing. Nevertheless, at least as early as 1740, the volume of tobacco shipped from the Chesapeake was equal to the combined volume of all the Spanish, Portuguese, Turkish, Russian, Dutch, and German tobacco that passed in international trade.

In the seventeenth century, the principal reexport markets for English colonial tobacco had been the Netherlands and Germany, and they remained important markets throughout the eighteenth century. English and later Scottish efforts to develop other markets were generally unsuccessful. In all the countries of the Christian Mediterranean, the tobacco trade was in the hands of a "stank" or monopoly farm (Spanish, *estanco*). The managers of these monopolies preferred either their own domestic or colonial tobaccos or foreign tobaccos cheaper than those of Virginia. In nothern Europe, farmed monopolies were somewhat less frequent, but strict protectionist policies prohibited or discriminated against imported tobaccos in favor of native products. Thus, even in Sweden and Finland, a domestic tobacco-growing industry was created in the eighteenth century—to the no great delight of tobacco takers there.

Amsterdam dominated the intra-European trade in tobacco in the seventeenth, and in the first quarter of the eighteenth, century. There, unlike the case in London, every important variety of tobacco grown in Europe or America could be readily procured. Amsterdam manufacturers mixed and manufactured the many varieties of leaf available and exported vast quantities of their output to Germany, Italy, and at first to the Baltic. The Dutch trade, however, changed significantly about 1725. By then most countries had their own manufactures and, insofar as they would take any foreign tobacco, would import only leaf. The Dutch trade about then became simpler, with native and imported tobaccos being exported in leaf unmanufactured. This qualitative change is associated with the shift in the main center of activity from Amsterdam, the processing center, to Rotterdam, purely a shipping center.

The Dutch market, although it took close to half the English tobacco exported in the seventeenth century and never less than a third of the whole in the eighteenth century, was a passive market as far as the trade in Britain was concerned. Tobacco was generally exported from Britain to Holland on British account. Tobacco merchants in London, Whitehaven, Glasgow, etc. received regular reports from Amsterdam and Rotterdam and when prices were attractive sent their tobacco thither, frequently whole shiploads at a time. This tobacco was consigned to merchants in Holland to be sold on commission for the British owners. It might wait months and months in Holland for the right sale, but loans could be obtained more cheaply on it there than in Britain. Since the trade was, however, meaningfully controlled from Britain, it is not evident that the Dutch market exerted any sort of institutional influence on that in Britain. Small British merchants could trade as easily to Holland as great ones.

145

The German market, though smaller, had been institutionally similar to the Dutch in the seventeenth century. However, the monopoly of exporting cloth to Germany, traditionally vested in the Merchant Adventurers or Hamburg Company, was abolished in 1689. This encouraged German firms in the eighteenth century to order their cloth direct from England and eventually to send over their own factors to make purchases there. There is evidence that such firms also bought tobacco in England on German account. Our evidence is thin, however; and the quantities and scale of purchases were not large enough to affect the structure of the British trade.

The only foreign market whose volume, whose scale of activity, and whose institutional structure were sufficiently weighty to affect the growth and organization of the British trade was a market entirely new to the eighteenth century—that in France. From virtually nothing in the 1680's, France after 1715 passed Germany to become the second most important market for British tobacco. Between 1730 and the British-French declaration of war in 1744, France surpassed Holland to become the first market for English exports. Though its share slipped in the wars of mid century, France remained a major market for British colonial tobacco down to the American Revolution.

This great role played by the French market requires some explanation, for we are conventionally taught to regard the years 1689-1815 as "the Second Hundred Years War," years in which Britain and France not merely fought seven major wars but in which their statesmen used every stratagem of which the legal or fiscal mind was capable to hurt the trade of the other: if English woolens were excluded from the French market, then French silks, linens, and wines had to be excluded from the English market. How many battles were fought over trading stations in India? Yet these same years saw the development of a major new British export to France in tobacco.

The explanation of this aberration is rather simple: the regulation of the tobacco trade in France was not governed at the test by conventional mercantilist ideas of national self-sufficiency or balance of trade, but rather by the fiscal needs of the French state.[5] From 1674 until 1791, the French tobacco trade was a state monopoly farmed out to private interests. The farmers of this monopoly found it increasingly convenient to buy Chesapeake tobacco. It was cheap and versatile, and French consumers liked it. In the end, the monopolists generally found that giving the consumer what he wanted was the surest way of discouraging him from dealing with smugglers. The tobacco which France had got from its colony of St. Domingue in the seventeenth century was relatively expensive, easily spoiled, and good only for chewing. The tobacco which came to it from Louisiana in the eighteenth century was a bit expensive and never arrived in quantities sufficient to develop a taste for it in France. Tobaccos from friendly Spain were much too expensive, and those from neutral Portugal were good only for chewing. It was not in the French monopolists' interest to encourage a familiarity in France with the tobaccos of the Low Countries and the Rhineland, for these could be too easily supplied by smuggling. For the same reason, the use of the tobaccos grown within France was confined to the area in which they were grown.[6] Hence the ultimate logic of buying from Britain.

[5] The most useful general accounts of the French tobacco monopoly are Jacques Bonneau, *Les législations françaises sur les tabacs sous l'ancien régime* (Paris: L. Larose and L. Tenin, 1910); and E. Gondolff, *Le tabac sous l'ancienne monarchie: la ferme royale, 1629-1791* (Vesoul: Ancienne Imprimerie Cival, 1914). There is a good chapter on this subject in George T. Matthews, *The Royal General Farms in Eighteenth Century France* (New York: Columbia University Press, 1958). All these accounts are highly institutional, neglecting both commercial and political-personal factors. For some indication of the complexity of the latter, cf. Jacob M. Price, "The French Farmers-general in the Chesapeake: the MacKercher-Huber Mission of 1737-1738," *William and Mary Quarterly*, 3d ser., XIV (1957), 125-53.

[6] The eastern provinces of French Flanders, Artois, Hainault, Cambrésis, Alsace, and Franche-Comté (all acquired in 1648 or later) were never within the monopoly's jurisdiction. Tobacco grown there was not imported into France proper in quantity by the monopoly except during wartime shortages. Before 1720, when tobacco cultivation was permitted in certain specified parishes in the southwest (within the modern departments of Lot-et-Garonne and Tarn-et-Garonne), such tobacco was rarely sold by the monopoly north of a line running roughly from La Rochelle to Lyons.

The tobacco monopoly was established in France in 1674 as a quite minor branch of the revenue at a time when tobacco consumption in France was still far less than that per capita in neighboring states. Local regulations against smoking were still being passed in Burgundy in the 1680's. The first farming company was not successful, and the monopoly was transferred in 1680 to the "United General Farms" which managed most other branches of French indirect taxation. In 1697 it was taken away from the united farms and given again to a special company in return for a higher price. In 1718, for a still higher price, the monopoly was taken away from this company and given to John Law's Mississippi company, subsequently the Company of the Indies. For a few months in 1720, at the height of Law's "System," the monopoly was abolished and the trade opened under a conventional import duty. To make this duty productive, the cultivation of tobacco within France was prohibited (except in the eastern frontier provinces from Flanders to Alsace which had always been outside the jurisdiction of the monopoly). Tobacco flowed in and was snapped up by new manufacturers and even more by businessmen buying any commodity as a hedge against the inflation brought on by Law's paper money. For a few months, the import duty was highly productive. Then a glut developed, imports and customs receipts fell off, and the accounts of the farm went into the red. With the fall of Law, the monopoly was restored and ultimately given back to the Company of the Indies. In 1730, primarily for fiscal reasons, it was transferred back to the united farms, where it remained until the French Revolution.

Fiscally, the crucial period in the monopoly's history was the two generations following the return of peace in 1713. With the new fashion and popularity of snuff-taking, tobacco consumption at last became a mass phenomenon in France. Consumption within the monopoly area increased around seven-fold between 1715 and 1775. State revenues from this source rose from 1.5 million *livres* annually in 1714 to 8 million in the 1730's and to 22 millions in the 1760's. This last figure was equal to about one million pounds sterling. Whereas the king of England had gained about twice as much revenue from tobacco as the king of France in 1700, by the 1760's, the king of France was getting about four times as much from that leaf as his Brittanic cousin.[7] Tobacco, from a trifling, had become a

147

---

[7] For English tobacco-tax yields, see Jacob M. Price, "The Tobacco Trade and the Treasury, 1685-1733" (unpublished Ph.D. thesis, Harvard University, 1954), 107-8.

major branch of French state revenues and the tobacco farm a power above effective criticism.

Regardless of the institutional or political character of the various changes in the tobacco farm between 1697 and 1730, they all meant one thing in practice: the purchase of more tobacco from Britain. The initial breakthrough had been made in the 1690's. Because of the war, imports from St. Domingue disappeared completely and those from Portugal became difficult and expensive. Fortunately for the monopolists, these losses were more than made up by the captures by French privateers of large numbers of English vessels with tobacco from the Chesapeake. So much was in fact captured that the monopoly was able to supply all its wants from the privateer owners at a price slightly under that prevailing on the London and Amsterdam markets. These losses ultimately proved a victory for Virginia, for the French consumers liked what they had to take and were never again won back to their old preferences for St. Domingue and Brazil tobaccos. During the peace interlude of 1697-1702, the monopoly for the first time began to import English tobaccos in significant quantities and continued to do so by surreptitious channels when in the next war the privateers did not capture enough to meet consumer demand. With the advent of peace in 1713, regular French imports of British tobacco resumed at double the rate of the peace interlude at the turn of the century. After Law's company took over the monopoly, such imports doubled again (although Law had ostensibly taken over the tobacco farm to develop Louisiana).

It was by no means certain that the high levels of tobacco imports from Britain realized in Law's time would be continued after his fall had it not been for two quite separate decisions reached in 1723. In that year, the French government decided to restore to normal operation the Indies Company which had been in official receivership since just after Law's fall. As principal compensation to the company for the hundreds of millions of state debt which had been absorbed into its capital structure during Law's "System," the government decided to regrant to the company the restored tobacco monopoly. The shareholders and directors who had seen the bulk of their nominal capital erased during the receivership were hungry for dividends and expected the tobacco monopoly to be administered in a way which would produce the maximum income for them. That same year, across the channel, the British government under Walpole decided that the stagnating tobacco trade needed relief.

This balm took the form of abolishing the last vestiges of retained duty on reexported tobacco, enabling the leaf to pass through the British entrepôt without any fiscal burden. This had the immediate effect of lowering the price of British tobacco in foreign markets by three eighths of a penny per pound and thus of eliminating the greater part of the price advantage which had been so stimulating to Dutch and German tobacco during the preceding generation. This revenue loss came to only about 37,500 pounds sterling in 1723 but was to be equivalent to 100,000 pounds by the 1760's, as the reexport trade expanded. The depressing effect of this cheaper Chesapeake tobacco upon Dutch tobacco cultivation was to be a long drawn-out story; the reaction in France was to be instantaneous: the Indies Company, although officially charged with the development of Louisiana, immediately started buying British tobacco in increasing quantities and by 1726 was, in a quite normal year, buying more British Chesapeake tobacco than had flowed into France in 1720, the frenetic year of speculation and open trade. When the even more businesslike United General Farms took over the monopoly in 1730, importations from Britain became even heavier, France becoming the largest reexport market for Chesapeake tobacco from 1730 until war came in 1744.

149

How does all this affect the growth and character of the British tobacco trade? At the superficial level, the connection with growth is obvious enough. In 1726-1727, following upon the permanent emergence of the French as large-scale buyers in 1723-1724, the British-American tobacco trade began its permanent rise from the trough of the first quarter of the century. Considering that any year's shipment from the Chesapeake to Britain was actually the previous year's crop, which in turn was based upon still earlier reports of market conditions, this is about as prompt a reaction as one could conceivably expect. That it was a reaction is not pure speculation, for there is surviving correspondence showing that Virginia and Maryland planters had become very much aware of French buying by the late 1720's.

The institutional influences are more difficult to explain. One must keep in mind the distinction between Holland as a passive market and France as an active market in comparing their abilities to influence trading conditions in Britain. The tobacco markets at Amsterdam and Rotterdam were classic open-commodity markets with many buyers and many sellers. British merchants, large and small, consigned tobacco there to be sold on their accounts according to their instructions. One cannot readily show any way in which a Dutch market so constituted influenced the geographical distribution or the institutional forms of the British tobacco trade. By contrast, in France the tobacco trade was a monopoly. The farm did all its buying through agents in foreign markets, originally in Lisbon and Amsterdam, later in various British ports. Wherever situated, the French agent exerted a monopsonistic pressure on his local tobacco market.

The British tobacco trade in the eighteenth century reveals three main lines of long-term development: (1) the consolidation of the trade into fewer and fewer hands; (2) the shift from commission trading to direct trading; and (3) the shift of the trade geographically from south to north. Each of these can be related to the pressure of the French monopsonistic buyer. Trading in tobacco had traditionally been on a hogshead-by-hogshead basis, each sold individually by quality. This method was ill suited to the needs of a French buyer who had to procure 10,000 to 20,000 hogsheads a year and more. He had to deal of necessity with the largest merchants, who could make bargains covering hundreds and thousands of hogsheads. The few big sellers, in turn, because they could supply the quantities needed, could demand concessions in price and terms which the small men could never extract. When the small men tried to form bargaining rings, they failed. Thus, as a countervailing force to the monopsonistic French buyer, there gradually emerged a few large houses in London, Whitehaven, and Glasgow in particular, who almost preempted the business of supplying the French. The French buyers would sit down with a half dozen or so of these big men in London or Glasgow and in an afternoon's negotiation would contract for France's supply for a year at a time. Tobacco that had not yet left Virginia would be sold at a flat price.

Not every merchant was free, however, to sell every hogshead. Back in the era of high European prices in the 1690's, most large and many of the better-off middling planters had acquired the habit of not selling their tobacco to merchants or supercargoes in the Chesapeake but of consigning it to a merchant in London, Bristol, or Liverpool to be sold on commission for their own account. They thus sought to realize some of the considerable wartime difference in prices between the Chesapeake and Europe. After the wars, consignment remained the normal way of trading for persons of a certain social and economic level who would have it understood that they grew premium-quality tobacco or had business in London which only a trusted factor could perform. The merchants in London, etc., who specialized in this commission business, though the leaders of the trade as late as the 1720's, were not able to sell in quantity to the French. The latter wanted to make bulk purchases at a flat price; the London commission merchant was obliged to sell each hogshead separately at a price shaved to the sixteenth of a penny per pound to reflect differences in quality. If two hogsheads were sold at the same price which the planter thought varied in quality, off he sent an indignant letter on the next boat to England. By the 1740's, as death, retirement, or bankruptcy took off many of the old commission merchants, a number of new large houses emerged in London, most of them of Scottish origin, which traded on their own account rather than on commission. These few new houses did most of the bulk supplying to the French. In the newly rising outports like Glasgow and Whitehaven there was virtually no commission business.

151

It was observable as early as the 1690's that at some of the remoter outports, like Whitehaven on the extreme northwest coast of England, tobacco might be regularly halfpenny a pound cheaper than at London. This reflected lower costs at Whitehaven and the quicker north-about-Ireland route from the Chesapeake; nevertheless, it did not then give Whitehaven, Lancaster, or Liverpool any marked advantages over London and the southwestern ports in this trade, for the southern ports were better situated for the domestic English market and for reexport to Holland and Germany. When the French entered the market in a big way, the situation changed. Differences were negligible in shipping costs to most French ports as between London and the northwest ports. A small foreign buyer might not find it worth his while to venture out of London; one who had to buy for all of France could afford some travel and postage expenses. At first, the French understandably bought only in London and Bristol. After the United General Farms took over the monopoly in 1730, this was changed, and regular buying arrangements were made at Whitehaven in Cumberland, and in Scotland. French purchases in Scotland became important in 1740; two years later, Glasgow became the most important tobacco port in the country after London. The biggest breakthrough for the northern ports came during the war of 1744-1748. Frightened by the approach of formal hostilities, the United General Farms, which usually kept their agents in Great Britain on commission, made a contract in 1744 by which their chief London agent agreed to supply them for the next six years, in war or peace, at an agreed price. To carry out this contract, the London agent had to use great political pressure to obtain special licenses from the British government to export tobacco to France in wartime. These licenses were granted in that (and the next) war on condition that no merchandise be returned on the vessels exporting the tobacco. More immediately at question, in order to cover himself in that risky contract, the London agent had himself to make advance contracts with British tobacco merchants who would agree to supply him at a fixed price. We do not know any of the details, but it was precisely during this contract and during the years of increasing French purchases in Scotland immediately preceding it that the Scottish ports emerged as a major factor in the tobacco trade. The Scottish trade, which had stagnated from the early 1720's till the late 1730's, quadrupled its volume between 1738-1740 and 1751-1754. All accounts agree that this phenomenal increase was based upon a tremendous expansion of credit on all sides. Nothing but the assurance of French sales could have supplied the basis for that credit expansion. French sales also enabled Glasgow merchants to turn their capital over more quickly, for tobacco sold to the French was commonly sold and paid for immediately on arrival in Scotland, while that exported to Holland could sit unsold in Rotterdam for a year and then be sold only on credit. (It might be remarked parenthetically that the chief French agent in Scotland was also a director of the Royal Bank of Scotland and not only handled the relations of the Glasgow tobacco merchants with that bank in the 1740's but from his French business also supplied that bank with a goodly share of its valued drafts on London.)

The French bought their tobacco in Glasgow primarily because it was cheaper than in England but also because the few large houses there were better organized than their English rivals to make the very large contracts the French required. Thus, as the Scottish share of the French market rose after 1740, the English declined. In the 1760's and 1770's, about three times as much tobacco was being shipped to France from Scotland as from England; the French monopoly was then taking about 40 per cent of Scotland's tobacco exports, but only 12 per cent of England's.

To get the tobacco they needed from the Chesapeake to fulfill their French contracts, the merchants of Glasgow ignored the great planters of tidewater and expanded their chains of stores in the interior to tap the supplies of the smaller farmer. Because the French preferred the cheaper tobaccos of the Potomac and James Rivers, the Scottish stores were concentrated mainly in those areas. When one rash manager placed a store on York River, where the best tobacco came from, his principal in Glasgow told him to move it to the James, because it was the French market they were interested in. By running a dozen or two stores under one or two general managers, the Scots saved enormously on salaries and managerial expenses.[8] By buying in advance of their shipping, they could turn their vessels around in the Chesapeake in weeks instead of months and save considerably on freight. Their ultimate success, however, was based on credit. The small planters of the back country came to the Scottish stores because they could get credit. The easiest way to clear that credit was to deliver tobacco. If a merchant wanted more tobacco, he had only to expand his credit to planters and the extra tobacco would flow in at the harvest. Thus, Scottish and other credit created its own tobacco supply much more effectively than did the price mechanism. And behind Scots credit was the French buyer; for, although the Scots sold almost as much of their tobacco to the Dutch as they did to the French, only the quick sales, the mass sales, and the advance sales to the French provided the basis for the bills of exchange on which credit was sustained within Scotland, hence ultimately in Virginia.

At this point, the statistically skeptical may well say, Isn't this being carried a bit far? What if the French bought twenty million or more pounds of tobacco in the years immediately preceding the American Revolution? The direct purchases of the French monopoly in Britain were only around 26 per cent of British reexports and only around 23 per cent of British imports from the Chesapeake. Is this enough to account for the effects described? I think most here will agree abstractly that in an open market a single buyer taking 25 per cent of a crop when all other buyers are small could seriously affect the market. However, we need not be so abstract. We must

---

[8] On the Scottish stores, see Jacob M. Price, "The Rise of Glasgow in the Chesapeake Tobacco Trade, 1707-1775," *William and Mary Quarterly*, 3d ser., XI (1954), 179-99; and J. H. Soltow, "Scottish Traders in Virginia, 1750-1775," *Economic History Review*, 2nd ser., XII (1959), 83-98.

rather consider the specific incidences of this single buyer in time and space. Chronologically, large-scale French buying became a permanent factor in the English market in the mid-1720's, anticipating by about two years the turning point when the Chesapeake-English tobacco trade came out of its 25-year stagnation and moved into a generation of very rapid growth. Similarly, French purchases in Scotland became important about the year 1740, on the eve of the greatest expansion of the Chesapeake-Scottish tobacco trade.

Geographically, we cannot expect the influence of the French 25 per cent to have been felt evenly throughout the Chesapeake. Although Maryland accounted for at least a third of the production in the Chesapeake, the French purchased no Maryland tobacco except that of the Potomac valley. This is the only part of Maryland in which we find thick clusters of Scottish stores. It is also the only part of Maryland in which the tobacco trade was expanding right down to the American Revolution. In Virginia, the influence of the French and hence of the Scots was confined primarily to the valleys of the Potomac and the James and to the area behind Petersburg. The last two were precisely the areas whose production increased the most in the eighteenth century. In 1713-1714, the York and Rappahannock customs districts accounted for 59 per cent of the tobacco shipped from Virginia; these were the districts unaffected by French demand, and their share of total shipments had fallen to 31 per cent sixty years later (1773-1774). The Potomac district had about held its own, while the shares of the Upper and Lower Districts of James River, most affected by French demand via the Scots, had risen from 22 per cent to 52 per cent of the total.[9] We cannot yet be precise, but it is evident that within the areas most affected by purchases for France, that market represented not the 25 per cent of production true for the Bay as a whole, but rather something in the vicinity of 50 per cent.

In summary, we can not understand the stagnation of the Chesapeake economy in the early eighteenth century and its impressive resumed growth after 1725 purely in terms of such local phenomena as labor supply and soil exhaustion. We must consider the European market, particularly the individual reexport markets to which the tobacco was sent from Britain. Of these, the French was the most

[9] Based upon the yields of the two shillings per hogshead export duty in Virginia. For 1713-14, see PRO T.1/175/18; for 1773-74, see PRO C.O.5/1352, pp. 79-82.

important because its opening up most exactly coincided with the resumption of growth in the trade and because its monopsonistic character exerted a powerful influence upon the institutional development of the trade in Great Britain. French buying policies gave an advantage to merchants trading on their own account as opposed to commission merchants, and they go far to explain the concentration of the trade in a relatively few hands by 1775 and the movement of the centers of trade from the south of England to the north and to Scotland. In the Chesapeake, the French market underpinned the chains of stores of London, and particularly of Glasgow, merchants. The advance credit offered by these stores brought forth the new and ever-rising supplies from the small settlers of the piedmont and of the south side of James River which made up the statistical phenomenon we have called the resumed economic growth of the Chesapeake.

155

JACOB M. PRICE, *University of Michigan*

The book in progress referred to in footnote 1 has since been published as *France and the Chesapeake: A History of the French Tobacco Monopoly, 1674-1791, and of its Relationship to the British and American Tobacco Trades*, 2 vols., Ann Arbor: University of Michigan Press, 1973, where full documentation can be found for most of the topics covered in this paper.

Background to the Grenville Program, 1757-1763

Thomas C. Barrow*

IN analyzing the fateful decision of the Grenville ministry to raise a revenue in the American colonies emphasis usually is placed on certain problems relating to imperial defense or finance. The Seven Years' War was expensive, and the English national debt grew rapidly. At the same time the difficulties encountered in the conduct of the war suggested the value of stationing permanent military forces in the American colonies. Both the problem of the debt and the establishment of adequate military forces cost money. Consequently the temptation exists to attribute the revenue measures of 1764 and 1765 primarily to a concern on the part of the English government with those two problems. However, there does exist a variety of evidence to indicate that in undertaking its program of imperial taxation and reorganization the Grenville ministry was motivated by something of more fundamental importance than a temporary concern over defense or finance.

George Grenville became head of the British administration in April 1763. On May 21 the Treasury Department, remarking that the American revenues amounted "in no degree to the Sum which might be expected from them," ordered the Commissioners of the Customs to examine the problem. On July 21 the Commissioners submitted to the Treasury their appraisal of the colonial situation. This report, with subsequent additions, provided the basis for the famous Treasury letter to the Privy Council in October, which in turn resulted the next year in passage of the Sugar Act.[1] Consequently there is a direct line of development traceable backwards from the Sugar Act to the Customs Com-

---

* Mr. Barrow is a member of the Department of History, University of Missouri.

[1] Treasury Lords to Customs Commissioners, May 21, 1763, Treasury Papers, Class 11, XXVI, 282, Public Record Office, London; Customs Commissioners to Treasury, July 21, 1763, T. 1/426, foll. 269-273; Treasury to Privy Council, Oct. 4, 1763, House of Lords Manuscripts 229, British Museum, London. On the specific chronology of events relating to passage of the Sugar Act, see Allen S. Johnson, "The Passage of the Sugar Act," *William and Mary Quarterly*, 3d Ser., XVI (1959), 507-514.

missioners' July report, which in this instance served as the source of
expert opinion required to formulate effective government action.

In their July report the Commissioners, noting the trifling revenue
collected in America, commented that the small returns obviously suggested the existence of great frauds. The expense of collection far out-
weighed the receipts, which probably would continue to be the case
until the high duties were lowered, with a consequent reduction in the
smuggling that pervaded the colonies. Some of the trouble arose from
the "collusive practices" of the colonial customs officers "who at this
distance from inspection, are too easily led off from their duty, to their
interest, in a Country, where the strict Observance of the former, is 157
rendered highly difficult and obnoxious." In justice to their officers the
Commissioners added that many of them had reported that a lowering of
the duties was essential. On the more general question of the over-all
situation in the colonies the Commissioners referred the Treasury Lords
to an earlier report they had submitted, that of May 10, 1759. When
the Treasury took up consideration of the July report they also located
the earlier communiqué and used both as the basis for their discussion.[2]
In this somewhat indirect manner the Commissioners' 1759 survey of the
colonial scene came to play an influential role in the decisions of the
Grenville ministry. The history of that document, and the views contained in it, are both enlightening.

The origin of the 1759 report actually can be traced back earlier
yet, to November 1757. In that month the Board of Trade received two
communications from America, from Governor Charles Hardy and
Lieutenant Governor James De Lancey, both of New York. De Lancey's
letter forwarded evidence of a "pernicious trade" between the American
colonists and the French islands in the Caribbean: "The Method they
take is to go to Monti Christo, a Spanish Port in Hispaniola, where
the Master and Mariners stay, and they get a Master and a Crew of
Spaniards to go with a Pass to Port Dauphin, or some other French
Port. . . . By this indirect Way his Majesty's Enemies are supplyed.
What Remedy to apply to this Evil may be difficult to say."

Enclosed in De Lancey's letter were depositions purporting to show
that during a seven-and-one-half month period fourteen ships from

[2] Customs to Treasury, July 21, 1763, T. 1/426, foll. 269-273; Treasury minutes of
July 22, 1763, T. 29/35, p. 125.

Boston and Rhode Island had visited Santo Domingo.³ Governor
Hardy added a few details and more evidence of the French island
trade in his letter, including papers showing that a ship from New
Jersey had used the Dutch island of St. Eustatius to carry on a trade
with the French.⁴

After examining these communications from New York, the Board
of Trade decided to launch a general investigation of illegal trade in
the American colonies. To provide the materials for such a survey the
secretary of the Board was instructed to comb the files and to present
to the Board any and all papers on that subject received over the
years from the colonies. The result was the accumulation of a major
collection of informed opinion on the operation of the colonial system, as
the secretary produced copies or extracts of twenty-six reports from the
colonies, ranging in date from 1739 to 1758. Occupied with problems
related more directly to the progress of the war, the Board delayed
consideration of the secretary's labors until November 1758, but in that
month it subjected the reports to close scrutiny. The consensus of the
reports, the Board discovered, was that illegal trade was an old,
established habit among the American colonists, that its existence had
created a potentially dangerous situation, and that the exact cure was
not easily discoverable.⁵

The first letter the secretary had selected was in its way typical of
the rest. It was from Lieutenant Governor George Clarke of New York
to the Board, dated December 15, 1739. Enclosed in the letter were
papers relating to a legal case concerning a seizure made by a customs
officer, which was then in progress but which Clarke expected would be
decided against the Crown, since it was a jury trial. Clarke commented
"that if some Method be not fallen upon whereby Illicit Trade may be
better prevented, I doubt it will be to little purpose to bring any
cause . . . to tryall by a Jury, and the Officers of the Customs will from
thence be discouraged from exerting themselves in . . . their Duty."⁶

³ De Lancey to Board of Trade, June 3, 1757, Colonial Office Papers, Class 5,
vol. 1068, foll. 5-7, Public Record Office.
⁴ Hardy to Board of Trade, June 14, 1757, *ibid.*, foll. 20-21.
⁵ *Journal of the Commissioners for Trade and Plantations from January 1754 to
December 1758* (London, 1933), 336-337, 423-424. A list of the 26 letters is included
in T. 1/392, foll. 45-46.
⁶ Clarke to Board of Trade, Dec. 15, 1739, C.O. 5/1059, fol. 131. The case was

The second communiqué laid before the Board was an extract from a letter written to the Treasury by Robert Auchmuty, judge of the vice-admiralty court in New England, dated December 30, 1742. After pointing out various unenforced provisions of the Navigation Acts, Auchmuty noted that the customs collector for Rhode Island "for many years . . . past has not resided there but farms out the same." The governor "being the Creature of the People and his Naval Officer . . . the same . . . both lyable to be removed at the next annual Election in case by an Unpopular Act they incur the Displeasure of the Free-men," obviously they do not enforce the trade laws "and in fact that Colony is virtually a free port." As a corrective Auchmuty suggested that tighter controls be placed on the naval officers and that officers of the navy operating in those waters be authorized to make seizures.[7]

159

The next report was from the popular governor of Massachusetts, William Shirley, dated February 26, 1742/3. Shirley wrote that he was concerned "because the Illicit Trade, which appears to have been carried on in this Province and some of the neighboring Colonies (within this last year more especially) is such as without the speedy Interposition of the Parliament to stop it, must be highly destructive . . . and finally weakening the Dependence which the British Northern Colonies ought to have upon their Mother Country." If allowed to continue, this illegal trade "will grow to so strong a Head that it will be no easy Matter wholly to subdue it." Shirley closed his letter with references to a case involving a ship seized for smuggling goods into Massachusetts from Holland.[8]

Accompanying Shirley's letter, and copied by the secretary of the Board of Trade as one of his specimens, was a report from William Bollan, advocate general of New England. Bollan's lengthy report is summarized effectively in his remark that "there has lately been carried on here a large Illicit Trade . . . by importing into this Province large Quantities of European goods of almost all sorts from divers parts of Europe." Ships, he claimed, came to Massachusetts directly from Holland, loaded with reels of yarn, paper, gunpowder, iron, and all

---

that of Archibald Kennedy *v.* the Sloop *Mary and Margaret.* Kennedy was the cus-toms collector for New York.

[7] Auchmuty to Treasury, Dec. 30, 1742, C.O. 5/883, Ee 90.
[8] Shirley to Board of Trade, Feb. 26, 1742/3, *ibid.,* Ee 86. The case concerned the brigantine *Hannah.*

kinds of clothing. He highlighted his remarks by adding, "I need only to acquaint you that I write this clad in a Superfine French Cloth, which I bought on purpose that I might wear about the Evidence of these Illegal Traders." Echoing Shirley, Bollan commented that "if Care be not soon taken to cure this growing Mischief . . . their proper Dependence on their Mother Country will . . . 'ere long be lost."[9]

Other later letters from Shirley, Bollan, and Auchmuty, telling much the same dreary story, were included in the Board of Trade's collection.[10] Less acceptable as evidence perhaps, for the planters had a personal stake in the problem, was the *Memorial of the Sugar Planters* to the Board of Trade, dated 1750, but it too dwelt at length on illegal trade in the colonies, observing generally that it was not hard to explain why the previous trade laws had been neglected when "it is considered that every Law must prove ineffectual, where the carrying it into execution depends upon those who are interested in the breach of it."[11]

That similar conditions existed in the Caribbean region was suggested by a letter, dated March 8, 1750/1, from Governor William Mathew of the Leeward Islands, who noted that there was an illicit trade carried on between the "Danes on St. Thomas . . . and their Correspondents at Bristol and in London" which involved passing foreign sugar products off as the growth of "our own Islands."[12]

A longer and more crucial report considered by the Board was that from Governor George Clinton of New York, dated October 4, 1752. Clinton, in his usual manner, was outspoken and vehement: "It is necessary . . . to inform your Lordships with the State of Trade in this Province, and of the entire disregard of the Laws of Trade." He complained that the merchant-dominated colonial government made enforcement of the trade laws impossible and added that "It is not easy to imagine to what an enormous hight this transgression of the Laws of Trade goes in North America." To his mind it was an open question as to whether it might not "be found that Holland and Hamburgh re-

^{margin} 160

[9] Bollan to Board of Trade, Feb. 26, 1742/3, *ibid.*, Ee 87. Bollan's letter is filled with technical discussions of various aspects of the Navigation Acts and the legal loopholes therein.
[10] Auchmuty to Board of Trade, Nov. 23, 1743, C.O. 5/884, Ff 12; Shirley to Board of Trade, Feb. 6, 1747/8, C.O. 5/886, Gg 3; Bollan to Board of Trade, Oct. 24, 1749, C.O. 323/12, foll. 260-262.
[11] "Memorial of the Sugar Planters, 1750," C.O. 323/12, foll. 253-255.
[12] Mathew to Board of Trade, Mar. 8, 1750/1, C.O. 323/13, foll. 103-104.

ceive more benefitt from the Trade of the Northern Colonies than Great Britain does, after the expence that Great Britain is at, when their support is deducted."[13]

The majority of the remaining letters chosen by the Board of Trade secretary related to the wartime trade between the Continental colonies and the French islands in the Caribbean and included communications from such diverse sources as Lieutenant Governor Francis Fauquier of Virginia and Governor Benning Wentworth of New Hampshire (who was the only correspondent to attempt to vindicate the colonists). Also in this collection were the two letters from Governor Hardy and Lieutenant Governor De Lancey of New York which had originally determined the Board of Trade to undertake its investigation.[14]

161

Enough has been said about the contents of these reports to indicate the nature of the information placed before the Board of Trade. Contrary to some interpretations of this period, which limit illicit trade primarily to violations of the Molasses Act,[15] these documents placed equal emphasis on illegal commerce with Europe, as in William Bollan's reference to his "Superfine French Cloth" and in Governor Clinton's comment that Holland and Hamburgh might have received more benefit from the colonial trade than had England. Taken together, these reports presented a description of a nearly total collapse of much of the imperial machinery in the American colonies. Isolated examples they may have been, but these reports give a fair indication of the type of information on the operation of the Colonial System to be found in

[13] Clinton to Board of Trade, Oct. 4, 1752, C.O. 5/1064, foll. 144-147.

[14] For the remaining letters see George Bellas to John Sharpe, Dec. 17, 1752, C.O. 323/13, fol. 179; Bollan to Board of Trade, Mar. 21, June 9, 1755, C.O. 5/887, Hh 48, Hh 51, Hh 52; Hardy to Board of Trade, May 10, June 19, Oct. 13, Dec. 28, 1756, C.O. 5/1067, foll. 95-96, 162-163, 197-198, 296; Governor Wentworth to Board of Trade, Jan. 16, 1757, C.O. 5/926, foll. 369-371; Hardy to Board of Trade, Mar. 11, 1757, C.O. 5/1067, foll. 392-394; De Lancey to Board of Trade, June 3, 1757, C.O. 5/1068, foll. 5-7; Hardy to Board of Trade, June 14 (incorrectly dated June 24), July 15, 1757, *ibid.*, foll. 20-27, 30-33; De Lancey to Board of Trade, July 30, 1757, *ibid.*, no folio number; Wentworth to Board of Trade, Nov. 13, 1757, C.O. 5/927, C 1; De Lancey to Board of Trade, Jan. 5, 1758, C.O. 5/1068, foll. 160-162; Lieutenant Governor Fauquier to Board of Trade, Sept. 23, 1758, C.O. 5/1329, foll. 82-85.

[15] For example, see Oliver M. Dickerson, *The Navigation Acts and the American Revolution* (Philadelphia, 1951), 82-87; also, George Louis Beer, *British Colonial Policy, 1754-1765* (New York, 1907), 124.

the possession of the Board. Collected and examined together they offered a disturbing picture.

After studying these papers the Board of Trade decided to consult the Commissioners of the Customs, since so many of the questions raised related to the revenue. Unfortunately for the Board of Trade, at this point its peculiar position in the English government created a problem. The Board was an advisory body, without executive powers of its own. Earlier, in the reign of Queen Anne, the Board had been prohibited from carrying on a direct correspondence with the Commissioners of the Customs.[16] Since that time the Commissioners occasionally had refused to co-operate with the Board "unless they are Commanded by the King in Council or the Lords of the Treasury."[17] Still, in view of the importance they attached to the subject, the members of the Board proceeded to forward to the Commissioners the twenty-six reports they had been considering. The Commissioners refused to communicate directly with the Board of Trade but finally did agree to consider the reports and to forward their opinion to the Treasury, which could do as it wished with the information.[18]

In their cover letter to the Commissioners on February 24, 1759, the Board of Trade explained that it had the workings of the Acts of Trade under consideration and that it seemed obvious that very great difficulties were being encountered in the colonies. The Board wanted to know if the Commissioners had received communications from their colonial officers concerning any "Doubts and Difficulties attending the Execution of the said Laws" and asked them to consider "what other measures it may be proper . . . to take."[19] By this time the Treasury too had become interested in the question of enforcement of the commercial laws in the colonies, and so added pressures were placed on the Commissioners to take a significant look at colonial affairs.[20] The result was the Commissioners' report of May 10, 1759.

[16] Dora Mae Clark, *The Rise of the British Treasury: Colonial Administration in the Eighteenth Century* (New Haven, 1960), 4. The prohibition, instituted by Sydney Godolphin, was the result of an effort to prevent the Board of Trade from encroaching on the preserves of other government agencies.

[17] Customs Commissioners to Board of Trade, Dec. 1, 9, 16, 1730; Dec. 17, 1731; July 11, 1737, T. 1/381, foll. 99-102.

[18] Customs Commissioners to Treasury, Mar. 6, 1759, T. 1/392, fol. 34.

[19] Board of Trade to Customs Commissioners, Feb. 24, 1759, *ibid.*, foll. 35-36.

[20] The Treasury, pressed by wartime expenses, was interested specifically in the

The irritation of the Commissioners over the fact that they were being forced to conform to the wishes of the Board of Trade is clearly evident in their reply: "We humbly presume, it cannot be intended that We should enter into a minute detail of the conduct of the Officers of the Customs in the Plantations for twenty years past. . . ." Instead, they suggested, the problems raised in the letters forwarded by the Board of Trade, as well as those uncovered through their own research, could be grouped under three categories:

1. The illicit Importation of Rum and Molasses from the French Islands into the British Northern Colonies.
2. The importation of goods from different parts of Europe (particularly Holland and Hamburgh) into North America, and the carrying Enumerated goods from thence to the said places, and others in Europe, contrary to Law, whereby all such Imports and Exports are restrained to Great Britain only.
3. The pernicious practice of supplying the French Colonies and plantations with provisions from his Majesty's Colonies, or from Ireland.

On the first point the Commissioners reported that "so long as the high Duty on Foreign Rum, Sugar, and Molasses imposed by the Act of the 6th of his present Majesty (and then intended, We apprehend, as a Prohibition) continues, the running of those goods . . . will be unavoidable." With the caution of good civil servants dealing with a sensitive political issue, they added that it was "difficult to foresee how far it may be expedient to attempt to remedy this Evil by an alteration of this Law, which was passed, at the request of the British Planters as an encouragement to their Trade."

As to the importation of European goods into the colonies the Commissioners observed that "the great extent of the Coast very much favors the running through, before the Masters make their Reports at the Customshouses." At present the only "cheque upon this practice" is a "strict Examination of their Clearances" which the customs officers

revenue. As early as 1757 the Treasury Lords had asked the Customs Commissioners to prepare a definitive statement of the revenue accounts, and in later communications they expressed concern over the problems of illegal trade and excessive fees taken by the colonial customs personnel. In November 1758, the Treasury Lords asked the Commissioners to investigate the problem further and to make suggestions for correcting the abuses. See Treasury minutes of Oct. 27, 1757, T. 29/32, p. 487; Treasury to Customs Commissioners, Jan. 18, 1758, T. 11/25, p. 329; same to same, Jan. 26, 1758, T. 1/382, fol. 3; same to same, Nov. 27, 1758, T. 11/25, p. 441.

have been instructed to perform. Concerning the exportation of enumerated goods to Europe the Commissioners noted that once a ship cleared a colonial port it was beyond the reach of the enforcement officers, and if it were "guilty of Frauds and deviation by carrying their goods to other Places in Europe" the only recourse of the customs officials was to put the bonds given for the "legal discharge of the Cargoes" in suit, which could be done if no certificate of such discharge were returned within eighteen months. But this procedure was ineffectual because "these prosecutions must be carried on in the ordinary course of proceeding in the Colonies, where it is apprehended, that Verdicts, upon points of this Nature, are not so impartial as in England."

The Commissioners were even more discouraging on the provision trade with the enemy islands: "In North America opportunities are so easy of supplying the French with provisions, and the distance from hence is so great, We dispair, by means of the Officers of the Revenue, of putting any effectual stop thereto" especially since the same trade is carried on "even from Ireland, where the Laws are so much less liable to abuse than under the proprietary government in North America."[21]

In this appraisal of the colonial scene there was nothing of a redeeming nature. The report itself was relatively brief, and couched in general terms, but it was uniform in its somber tone. Oliver M. Dickerson has described the trade and navigation system prior to 1764 as the "cement of empire," reporting concisely that it "worked."[22] Perhaps so, but an eighteenth-century administrator studying these documents might well adopt a more pessimistic attitude towards the machinery of empire. In fact, such an official, once confronted with this evidence, would have difficulty escaping the obvious conclusion that the colonial system never had worked as intended.

The Treasury Lords, after examining both the 1759 and 1763 reports from the Commissioners of the Customs, in October 1763 in turn forwarded to the Privy Council their famous letter, which opened with the well-known words that the revenue in America was "very small and inconsiderable, having in no degree increased with the Commerce of

---

[21] Customs Commissioners to Treasury, May 10, 1759, T. 1/392, foll. 38-39. Included with the report were various legal opinions on specific problems created by the Navigation Acts.

[22] Dickerson, *Navigation Acts*, xiv.

those Countries, and is not yet sufficient to defray a fourth part of the Expense necessary for collecting it." This statement lends support to the argument that revenue considerations were the prime motive behind the forthcoming alterations, but closer attention should be paid to the words that follow that passage in the Treasury letter: not only was the revenue impaired "through Neglect, Connivance and Fraud," but the commerce of the American colonies was "diverted from its natural Course and the Salutary Provisions of many wise Laws to secure it to the Mother Country . . . in a great measure Defeated." Echoing the warnings of William Shirley and William Bollan, the Treasury Lords added that the rapid growth of the colonies in territory and population made "the proper Regulation of their Trade of immediate Necessity, lest the continuance and extent of the dangerous Evils . . . may render all Attempts to remedy them hereafter infinitely more difficult, if not utterly impracticable."[23]

The wording of the Treasury letter, coupled with the reports of the Customs Commissioners and the results of the Board of Trade's investigation on which it was based, suggests that English dissatisfaction with the effectiveness of the colonial commercial restrictions has been underestimated as a motive behind the attempted imperial reorganization of 1764 and 1765. It was once said of George Grenville that he "lost America because he read the American despatches, which his predecessors had never done."[24] While this is an obvious oversimplification, there is a certain validity to its implication that the Grenville program originated in the files of the Board of Trade and the Customs Department, both of which contained report after report on the ineffectual operation of the colonial system. Under the circumstances there is no reason to discount the Treasury Lords' concern with the "dangerous Evils" existing in the colonies nor to disbelieve their insistence that "the proper Regulation of their Trade" was of "immediate Necessity." Certainly the evidence placed at their disposal by the Board of Trade and the Customs Commissioners warranted such pessimistic conclusions.

[23] Treasury to Privy Council, Oct. 4, 1763, House of Lords MSS. 229; same, printed in *Acts of the Privy Council of England. Colonial Series* (London, 1908——), IV, 569-572.

[24] Quoted in George Thomas Keppel, Sixth Earl of Albemarle, *Memoirs of the Marquis of Rockingham and his Contemporaries* (London, 1852), I, 249. The remark was reportedly made to Lord Essex by one of the under secretaries at the Board of Trade.

In a report forwarded to London shortly before the Grenville program was initiated, a colonial customs officer observed that the return of peace offered a splendid opportunity to achieve the proper "subordination" of the colonies: *"For which happy purpose never could a more favourable opportunity than the present I have offered, and if an effectual reformation be not introduced before those troops are withdrawn which could have been thrown in upon no less occasion without giving a general alarm, one may venture to pronounce it impossible afterwards."* In seconding recommendations for the reduction of the duties imposed by the Molasses Act, this same author commented that such a move, being popular in the colonies, would "effectually palliate any necessary severity in putting an effectual stop to future clandestine importations from Europe; the great object to be attended to, for which the prodigious expense this nation is now, gives so fair a pretence."[25]

It is questionable whether the Grenville ministry, following the advice of that particular colonial official, consciously used the problems of imperial defense and finance, which were in themselves legitimate issues, to screen their efforts to establish effective controls over colonial commerce. But it is true that the end of the war presented the English government with both an opportunity and an excuse for undertaking a general reorganization of the imperial machinery. And the evidence accumulated between 1757 and 1763 by the Board of Trade and the Customs Commissioners suggests that a prime factor in that attempted imperial reorganization was English discontent with the long-continued commercial independence of the American colonists.

Earlier, Bollan had advised that "if Care be not soon taken to cure this growing Mischief" the colonists' "proper Dependence on their Mother Country will . . . 'ere long be lost."[26] Such warnings, frequently repeated, eventually had their effect, and the English government too by 1763 was concerned to prevent that "growing Mischief" from further undermining the "proper Dependence" of the colonists. It was against this background that the Grenville ministry made its decision to raise a revenue in the colonies and inaugurated its reform program, which

[25] Mr. Comptroller Weare to the Earl of ———, in Massachusetts Historical Society, *Collections*, 1st Ser., I (Boston, 1806), 66-84.
[26] As above, n. 12.

was conceived not simply as a solution to problems of imperial defense
or finance but also as a means to achieve the final and effective subordination of the commercial interests of the Americans to the requirements of
the Mother Country.

167

A Quantitative Study of American Colonial Shipping: A Summary*

It is widely accepted that improvements in transportation were an important feature of Western development. However, in contrast to the research undertaken on transportation after 1775, very little study has been undertaken on the development of transportation before the Revolution. The main theme of this study is productivity change in ocean shipping on colonial routes, 1675-1775. The primary objectives are twofold: to estimate the change of productivity and to determine the sources of that change.[1]

Assuming a competitive industry, I have estimated productivity change by using freight rate indices for a number of commodity routes.[2] This provides a fairly direct measure of productivity change because the major input costs of seamen's wages and shipbuilding costs remain almost constant throughout the entire period. By piecing together rates from published and primary sources, seven series of freight rates have been constructed: wine, Cadiz to London (1640-1783); sugar, Barbados to London and Jamaica to London (1678-1717); tobacco, Chesapeake to London (1630-1775); oil, Boston to London (1700-1774); bullion, New York to London (1699-1789); and flour, New York to Jamaica (1699-1768).[3]

The data clearly indicate that substantial improvements were taking place in shipping during the colonial period. The decline in rates varies among routes, but the general trend is unquestionable. After correcting for changes in the units freighted (such as hogsheads of tobacco and sugar), the effective overall decline mirrors an uncompounded yearly increase in shipping productivity of approximately 1 per cent.

It should be mentioned that many problems of interpretation emerge in using freight rates, but an especially difficult problem is that of units shipped. Rates were generally expressed as a charge per ton, but the ton

* I am grateful to Professor D. C. North whose advice has helped nurture my dissertation. Financial support has been provided by the Ford Foundation.

[1] Some secondary purposes will not be reviewed here because of limited space. Briefly, they are a reexamination of trade patterns (especially the notion of triangular trades) in light of total tonnage movements, the derivation of ownership proportions by route, and an analysis of comparative advantage in shipping to explain the variation in ownership by route. To do this I have relied heavily on the manuscript sources of the Public Records Office, London, especially the Colonial Naval Lists and the Customs 16/1.

[2] A precise measure of productivity change would require a quantitative measure of output changes per units of input. However, such an ideal measure is not possible given the available data.

[3] The sources of these data are many. Though some of them are available in published form, I have relied primarily on manuscript sources available in the many historical societies, libraries, and archives on the East Coast and in England.

was made up of a particular number of hogsheads, barrels, or bundles, most of which changed in weight and size over the period. Consequently, a ton of one commodity did not necessarily equal a ton of another, and as these units changed over time even a ton of a particular good varied. For example, the freight charge on tobacco was on four hogsheads equaling one ton for the whole period, but hogsheads nearly doubled in weight because of tighter compression in packing and increases in the volume of the hogshead. Despite tighter compression, which is essentially productivity change in packing, the specific gravity of the packed tobacco remained well below that of water (and wine, the traditional ton unit) so that the charge, and shipping constraint, was on volume rather than weight. Using legal dimensions as a proxy for actual averages, the volume increase of approximately 70 per cent measures the productivity change in shipping, since the peacetime rate on tobacco remained unchanged for the hundred-year period preceding the Revolution.

169

The analysis of sources of productivity change is undertaken with the use of an explicit model portraying the cost determinants of shipping in a series of equations. Lack of data limits the complete analysis given by the model, but the following specific factors are examined: (1) ship size, (2) crew size, (3) seamen's wages, (4) armaments, (5) shipbuilding costs, (6) insurance costs, (7) sea time (speed), and (8) port times.[4] Of these eight factors, crew size, armaments, and port times declined precipitously, while moderate reductions occurred in insurance costs. In contrast, ship size, seamen's wages, shipbuilding costs, and ship speed remained stable over the period. These findings have led to some general conclusions.

First, labor and capital costs per voyage declined despite unchanging seamen's wages and ship construction costs. Declining crew sizes on colonial vessels created an increase in tons per man of approximately 50 per cent. Given the large percentage of total costs attributable to labor, this decline in crew size—on vessels which remained unchanged in average size overall—explains a major portion of the total cost decline. Also, armaments declined greatly between 1730 and 1775, which reduced capital costs and increased the stowage area. This decline in armaments and crew size was mainly the result of the reduction of uncertainties associated with pirates and privateering, and some of the reduction of crew size likely came from improvements in organization. Further evidence of the decline of risk and uncertainties is reflected in the decline in insurance rates during that period.

Second, although ship speed did not increase, port times fell substantially. Average port times for Jamaica, Barbados, Philadelphia, Maryland,

---

[4] Average ship size, crew size, armaments, sea time, and port time have been derived from the Naval Office Lists of American and Caribbean ports. These Lists are available at the Public Records Office, London, and the University of California at Berkeley in the care of Professor Lawrence A. Harper. I have not attempted to compute changes in load-factor over time, and the analysis assumes that utilization held constant.

Virginia, and Piscataqua tumbled greatly, resulting in significant economies in both labor and capital costs per voyage. Shorter port times increased the percentage of the year in which a ship was carrying goods
rather than standing idle or, in other words, allowed for more voyages
(and utilized ton/miles) over the life of a vessel. This decline in port
times resulted mainly from the growth of a market economy and improvements in commercial organization. The decline came more from
improvements in acquiring cargoes and making commercial transactions
than from changes in loading techniques. Also, as pirating, privateering,
and similar risks declined, the reduced need for convoys allowed vessels
to leave port immediately upon obtaining their desired lading.

170

Third, technological change, defined as a shift in the production function reflecting advances in knowledge, appears to have been a minor
factor. This conclusion is based on three accounts. First, the materials
used for ship construction and the source of power remained unchanged
over the period. The era of steam and iron came later. Second, it is true
that vessels became more complex in sail and rigging, and hull shapes
altered. However, if changes in the hull and rig which embodied the
latest techniques had important effects, one of their main effects would
have been to increase ship speed and to reduce voyage time. Nearly
500 voyage times (1686-1765) have been computed for the routes between New England, New York, and Barbados and Jamaica by using
the Naval Office Lists. There is no upward trend in speed, and vessels
sailing along these routes were not significantly faster on the eve of the
Revolution than they were one hundred years earlier. Third, it may be
argued that crew reductions might have been the result of technical
change. However, this assertion is refuted by the fact that by the early
seventeenth century the Dutch ship, the flute, possessed all the characteristics of manning and other input requirements found on the most
efficient and modern vessels 150 years later.

Finally, changes in average ship size in colonial trades were extremely
moderate and show no upward trend. Despite significant economies of
labor in terms of tons per man, large vessels were precluded from
efficient use in these waters because of high risks of underutilization
and longer-than-average port times.[5] Consequently, economies of scale,
as reflected in average ship size in *colonial waters*, also appear as a
minor factor.

In conclusion, the substantial increase in shipping productivity during the colonial period had favorable effects on the development and
growth of a trading Atlantic community. Falling costs of transportation
hastened specialization and division of labor according to the compara-

[5] Philadelphia port times show that large vessels were in port more than twice as
long on an average as small vessels. Port times for Philadelphia were derived from
an unpublished paper entitled "The Use of a Computer in Analyzing the Colonial
Trade of Philadelphia," given by Professor William I. Davisson at the 1965 Meetings
of the Western Economic Association. His data were gathered from the *Pennsylvania Gazette*.

tive advantages in production among regions of the Western world. The primary sources of changing productivity in shipping came from decreasing uncertainties and from improvements in market organization. Economies of scale (as reflected in average ship size) and technological change were not major factors. It was port times, not ship speed, that changed, allowing more trips per year. Also, as pirating and privateering decreased, armaments and manning requirements declined, and insurance rates fell as well.

GARY M. WALTON, *University of Washington*

J. ALAN ROGERS
Assistant Professor of History, University of California, Irvine

Colonial Opposition to the Quartering of Troops During the French and Indian War

NEARLY a century and a half of resistance to arbitrary military power was ignored when the Crown left the quartering of troops in America to the British army during the French and Indian War. Americans vigorously opposed the forced quartering of troops as a violation of the constitutional guarantee that the army should be subordinate to civil authority. Moreover, the colonists went beyond legalistic objections to the actions of the British army to a defense of the underlying principle articulated by that provision of the constitution. Specifically, they feared that if British military power were allowed to reign unchecked in America—as the Crown's new policy seemed to threaten—liberty itself would be destroyed.

Students of colonial history have not defined the issue as clearly as the colonists did. Historians of the French and Indian War who are interested in the problems faced by British leaders in its prosecution usually picture the colonists who spoke out against forced quartering as shortsighted obstructionists whose petty arguments undermined the war for empire. Those historians intent on tracing the development of political ideology have described the controversy over quartering simply as one more milestone on the colonists' march to democracy. Other historians have viewed the whole business as a power struggle masquerading as a constitutional debate. For instance, it is maintained that the Pennsylvania Assembly used the quartering issue to make gains in its contest for political supremacy with the governor. Another view is that the bitterness stirred up in the early years of the war was forgotten when General Jeffery Amherst assumed command in America. And finally, one student finds that the "'ideological' differences were overshadowed by the sure consequences of appearing laggard in the King's service." While this interpretation explains generally why the struggle over quartering was not more divisive than it was, it does not account for the widely held view that the British army's actions presented a real danger to American liberty.[1]

Since the revolutionary settlement of 1689, Parliament had enacted an annual Mutiny Act which among other things expressly prohibited quartering on private citizens against their will. In 1723, 1754, and 1756 certain provisions of the Mutiny Act were specifically stated by Parliament to be applicable in the colonies, but the sections on quartering were not extended to America until the war there had ended. During the war Americans were told only that they must follow the orders issued by the commanders-in-chief for quartering soldiers.

Early in 1755 General Edward Braddock acridly told the Pennsylvania Assembly that, as the assigning of quarters for the army was his province, he would "take due care to burthen those colonies the most, that show the least loyalty to his Majesty." Edward Shippen, a wealthy Pennsylvania merchant, wrote his son:

> The Assembly know not how to stomach this military address, but tis thought it will frighten them into some reasonable measures as it must be a vain thing to contend with a General at the head of an army, though he should act an arbitrary part; especially in all probability he will be supported in everything at home.[2]

The general did not live to carry out his threat. He and nearly half his men were killed in an ambush near the banks of the Monongahela River in July 1755.

Lord Loudoun, who arrived a year later to resume the military campaign in America, was well aware that the legal basis of his demands for quarters was ill-defined; but he was determined to get what he needed, by force if necessary. "As to quarters at Philadelphia and every other place," he instructed one of his senior officers in September 1756, "where I find it Necessary to have Troops, I have a Right to them, and must have them; I would have you go gently with the People at First, but [you] must not give up. . . ."[3]

In October Loudoun wrote Governor William Denny of Pennsylvania informing him that one battalion of royal troops was to be quartered in Philadelphia. Loudoun disingenuously added that he thought it unnecessary to spell out the army's needs because, as an ex-army officer, Denny was "so thoroughly acquainted with the Quartering in England in Time of Peace, and what Things are furnished in Quarters, for the Officers and Soldiers, and how much further Quartering extends in Time of War, and even must do so from the Nature of Things." In fact, neither Denny nor anyone else, including Loudoun, knew what effect war had on the provision of the Mutiny Act, because there had been no clear precedents for quartering in Great Britain in wartime since 1689.

Even the Privy Council's veto of a quartering act passed by the Pennsylvania Assembly in 1755 provided little positive help. The Council's negative opinion seemed to be provoked as much by its hostility to Pennsylvania's pacifist tendencies as by the idea that the rights of Englishmen in regard to quartering were not applicable in America. Thus, when the Assembly's new bill was sent to Governor Denny in December 1756 it contained the customary guarantee that citizens would not be forced to take soldiers into their homes. Denny refused to sign the bill, insisting that the Privy Council had rejected the first quartering act simply because it had included such a provision. When the bill was reconsidered by the Assembly on 8 December the objectionable passage was omitted, but so too was any reference to quartering in private homes. The new act outlined a procedure for lodging soldiers only in public houses.[4]

It was soon apparent, however, that there was a serious shortage of quarters. On 15 December Denny reported to the Council that despite his orders to city officials and the Assembly, "the King's Forces still remained in a most miserable Condition, neither the Assembly, Commissioners, nor Magistrates, having done anything to relieve them, tho' the Weather grew more pinching, and the small Pox was encreasing [sic] among the Soldiers to such a Degree that the whole Town would soon become a Hospital. . . ."[5]

Col. Henry Bouquet, the officer in command of British troops in Pennsylvania, had orders from Loudoun to take whatever quarters he needed by force and to march in as many more troops as necessary to carry out the orders. Bouquet was loath to use force, however. Instead, he asked Denny to issue a warrant to the sheriff authorizing him to quarter soldiers in private homes. The governor

deliberately left the warrant blank, so that Bouquet could have a free hand.[6]

The Pennsylvania Assembly was outraged; the legislators "did not think it possible your Honour could be prevailed with to issue Orders so diametrically opposite to an express Law passed by yourself but a few Days before. . . ." They insisted that Denny compel the city officials to reconsider their earlier estimate of the number of troops that could be quartered in public houses, but Denny's terse reply, delivered to the Assembly on 18 December, was "The King's Troops must be quartered."

For the first time in the colony's history, the Assembly met on a Sunday. A reply was drafted to the governor's demands, and carried to him "when the Streets were full of People going to their respective Places of Worship." The Assembly's reply reviewed the whole dispute and concluded by placing the blame for the present difficulties squarely on Denny and Loudoun. Neither had given the House specific information about exactly what should be provided, nor had they indicated how many troops were to be quartered. The Assembly's confusion was evident: "We thought we had by the late Law provided well for their Quartering in this Province; especially as we had exactly followed the Act of Parliament made for the same Purpose."[7] Although Denny found the message "a long Narrative filled with Abuses," he agreed to meet with a committee from the Assembly the following day in order that the dispute between them might be resolved.

Benjamin Franklin opened the conference by suggesting that soldiers might be quartered in public houses in the suburbs, or in the neighboring towns, but Denny answered bluntly that the commander in chief had demanded quarters in Philadelphia. If the people were unhappy about this arrangement, they should complain to Lord Loudoun. At this, the committee retorted that they "wished the Governor would consider himself somewhat more in his civil Capacity as Governor of the Province." He should protect the people, and, if a matter needed to be brought before Loudoun, the governor should present it. In other words, the committeemen wanted Denny to help them protect the constitutional rights of the people.

The committee then posed a question which came to the heart of the controversy. "What was to be understood," the legislators asked, "by Quartering being extended farther in Time of War, than in Time of Peace?" Denny said he did not know,

173

7   8

174

"unless it was Quartering on private Houses." That would be permissible, the committee said, if the people voluntarily offered quarters, but certainly no one should be forced to provide for soldiers. The governor replied that the general would decide if troops were to be forcibly quartered. One committeeman angrily reminded Denny what might happen if generals were allowed such power. A military officer "might say it was necessary to quarter the whole Army, not only in one City, but in one Square or one Street; and thereby harrass the Inhabitants excessively." At this point the governor broke in and declared he was interested only in facts.

This uproarious conference did much more than raise tempers. It served as concrete evidence to Pennsylvania's political leaders that Loudoun's demands for quarters were a clear threat to American liberty. Indeed, Franklin summed up this fear when he called Denny—who was nothing more than the general's go-between —"a meer Bashaw or worse." To Americans like Franklin, who were familiar with the writings of radical Whigs, there was no worse example of despotism than those Turkish bashaws whose armies allowed them to rule without the consent of the people.[8] The following day the Assembly invoked the spirit, if not the rhetoric, of Franklin's charge. When Denny told the legislators that the mayor of Philadelphia was certain there was not enough public housing to quarter Loudoun's soldiers, the Assembly insisted that the governor could do no more than enforce existing law. That was all any Englishman concerned with the preservation of liberty could do. Of this the House was confident. "We are contented," the Assemblymen declared, "that the King's Ministers should judge of these Proceedings and that the World should judge of the Decency of our last Message."

When Loudoun heard that his troops still had not been adequately housed in Philadelphia, he sent Denny a message on 22 December reiterating his demand that his soldiers be quartered. If Pennsylvania did not comply immediately, he intended to seize quarters; to "instantly march a Number sufficient for that purpose and find Quarters for the whole." With that sword dangling over their heads, Franklin and other provincial commissioners quickly agreed to rent additional housing and to make hospital space available for soldiers suffering from smallpox.[9]

The bitter, raucous quarrel between the Assembly and the governor and Lord Loudoun was more than just

another dispute between the legislature and the executive, or the Crown. It was more than a simple struggle for political power. It was a contest for political liberty which in this case had been clearly defined in England by Parliamentary statute and the charters of rights issued in 1628 and 1689. But during the winter of 1756 Pennsylvania's leaders learned that they did not have the same rights as other Englishmen. They saw that British bayonets, or the threat of them, would be used to dictate solutions and enforce measures which were resisted by local governments.[10]

Wherever the British army violated what the colonists believed to be the rights of Englishmen as to quartering, local political agencies reacted with hostility. The city officials of Albany also clashed sharply with the army during the latter half of 1756, for, although the New York Assembly had appropriated £1,000 to build barracks in Albany, nothing actually had been accomplished when the troops arrived. Without the barracks, troops would have to be quartered in private houses, for there were not nearly enough public houses in Albany to house two regiments. But the Assembly had not enacted legislation to cover this situation, and the mayor of Albany therefore refused to quarter Loudoun's troops. He told the general that he "understood the Law; that [Loudoun] had no right to Quarters or Storehouses, or anything else from them; and that [Albany] would give none." Loudoun promptly labeled the mayor "a fool" and thereafter communicated only with one of the mayor's staff, tersely informing him that as a military officer he "must Follow the Custom of Armies and help myself [to quarters]." When the mayor and his council remained adamant, Loudoun ordered his quartermasters to forcibly place soldiers into homes.[11]

Loudoun forced the residents of Albany to meet his demands, but he could not make them accept the arguments he used to justify his highhanded actions. In September 1756 the New York Assembly framed a bill which it hoped would protect homeowners from further forcible quartering. At first, Governor Charles Hardy demanded that the bill be amended to allow the military authorities more latitude, but after a month of debate Hardy swung over to the Assemblymen's position. He had become convinced, he told Loudoun in November, that it would be a great hardship for many families to have soldiers thrust into their homes. Loudoun was not sympathetic. He simply repeated his dogmatic contention that in wartime "no house has been exempt from Quartering the Troops the General thought Proper to have in any Place for carrying on the Service. . . ."[12]

Once again, therefore, in the winter of 1756, Loudoun threatened to send additional soldiers to Albany in order to compel the people there to house his troops. The mayor of that city told Loudoun that the people were opposed to such an illegal act; but, faced with British bayonets and political pressure from Lieutenant-Governor James de Lancey, the mayor's resistance collapsed. By the end of the day British soldiers were quartered in every house in Albany.[13]

Just as in Philadelphia, those who resisted forced quartering in Albany argued that a fundamental principle was at stake. Loudoun privately acknowledged the long-range implications of the conflict. Opposition to the army's tactics, he observed in a letter to the Duke of Cumberland, "seem not to come from the lower People, but from the leading People, who raise the dispute in order to have merit with the others, by defending their liberties, as they call them." In short, the clash between the British army and the people of Albany was not merely a petty local dispute but the thin edge of the wedge that was being driven between the colonies and the home country.

Governor Thomas Pownall of Massachusetts was one of the first English officials to grasp this fact. By the end of 1758 he had concluded that Loudoun's behavior was alienating the American people from the British Empire. He condemned Loudoun's aggressive methods as repulsive and unconstitutional; no military man had a right to interfere in civilian affairs, according to Pownall. A number of Massachusetts politicians, including Thomas Hutchinson and a substantial part of the lower house, were also disturbed by Loudoun's methods. A crisis did not arise until 1757, however, because Pownall's predecessor, Governor William Shirley, had convinced the Massachusetts legislature that in order to avoid trouble it should build barracks for British troops. Thus, by mid-1755 soldiers were safely quartered on an island in Boston harbor.

This amicable arrangement was upset in January 1757 when Loudoun told a legislative committee that during a war soldiers might very well be quartered in private homes as well as in barracks.[14] In speeches to the House, several committee members demanded an investigation into the army's right to seize quarters. Only a

clever move by Jeremiah Gridley, who belonged to the prerogative faction in the House, prevented a full debate on the matter. Gridley asked that a joint committee be formed to consider the problem, hoping that such a move would not only win time for those who supported the army but would also put the question in safer, more conservative hands.

For a while at least Gridley's maneuver seemed likely to be upset by Thomas Hutchinson. When the joint committee to discuss quartering met, Hutchinson read a prepared statement which asserted that only civil authorities had the right to determine what should be done to meet the army's needs. "With great warmth and Sputter," Hutchinson, according to Gridley's biased account, "began to catechise . . . about English rights." Gridley countered by pointing out that Loudoun had not demanded, but had asked the Massachusetts legislature to make quarters available. In this particular instance Gridley was correct, but Hutchinson must have known that Loudoun had threatened to seize quarters in Philadelphia and Albany when those governments refused to comply with his specific demands. Still, this was Massachusetts and so far Loudoun had abided by local law. Therefore, first Hutchinson and then the other members of the committee backed off from their hostile position and recommended that the House implement Loudoun's requests.

It soon became apparent how unimportant words were, for whether he "demanded" or "requested" the fact was that Loudoun held a powerful hand. Early in August he asked Pownall to quarter a regiment of soldiers. Realizing the significance of the situation, Pownall urged the House to pass a bill empowering Boston officials to assign quarters, thus maintaining local governmental control over the army. The governor warned the legislators that if this were not done the army would "plead necessity and provide for themselves." The threat worked: on 27 August the House appropriated money to build additional barracks for 1,000 men on Castle William. Although this was an expensive solution, it allowed the legislators to prohibit any quartering in Massachusetts' towns. Now, Pownall tried to convince Loudoun to play along. He pleaded with the general to work through local officials as the law stipulated, reminding him that this was constitutional procedure.

Everything went smoothly until two recruiting officers came to Pownall complaining that local officials had

175

refused them quarters in Boston. The governor promptly communicated with the city's selectmen. They were sympathetic, but they reminded the governor that Massachusetts law prohibited any quartering in public or private houses. As an immediate and temporary solution to the problem, Pownall suggested that the recruiters use the barracks on Castle William. At the same time, he sent Loudoun a detailed report outlining the steps he had taken and explaining Massachusetts' quartering law. The law was designed to safeguard "an Essential right of the Subject that no one could be quartered upon, unless by Law and there was no Law. . . . "[15]

Under almost any circumstances Loudoun would have been angered at this situation, and Pownall's letter reached the general at an especially bad time. He faced a frontier crisis in northern New York: French and Indians had overrun the colony's defense perimeter. According to Loudoun's view, therefore, the military situation was too serious to allow civilian authorities to obstruct military activities. There was no excuse for Massachusetts' disobedience, he stated in his letter to Pownall. He insisted that he had a right to quarters which superseded any provincial law, and he threatened to march three regiments into the city unless the recruiters were housed in Boston within 48 hours.

Loudoun's ultimatum arrived in Boston on the evening of 25 November. Early the next day, Pownall sent a brief message to the General Court, telling the legislators that the defense of the colonies depended upon compliance with his demand. The House remained in session well into the night and reconvened on Sunday in order to hammer out a bill which would, at once, satisfy their principles, their constituents, and Loudoun. On Monday afternoon the bill was presented to the governor for his signature. The act made it clear that the legislators believed a colonial law was the prerequisite to any quartering. Moreover, although it provided for quartering in public houses, the law allowed innkeepers to complain to a justice of the peace if they thought too many soldiers had been quartered upon them. In this way, the legislators preserved at least a modicum of the essential right of Englishmen to refuse to billet soldiers.

Neither the new law nor Pownall's explanation of his reasons for signing it pleased Loudoun. He renewed his threat to march troops into Boston and force the people to acknowledge his right to quarters wherever he chose them. Indeed, as he wrote Pownall on 6 December, the Massachusetts legislature had no business even debating the matter; the army's absolute right to quarters was "settled and regulated by an Act of the British Parliament, which no Act of theirs can infringe or diminish."

When Loudoun's latest condemnation of civil government became known, there was an outburst of public indignation. Pownall was accused of leading a military faction bent on subverting the Massachusetts constitution. "Were this Government [by] Elections as Rhode Island is," Pownall wrote to Loudoun, "I shou'd next year be turn'd out. . . . " Similarly, an Assembly committee reminded the general on 16 December that the "inhabitants of this Province are intitled [sic] to the Natural Rights of English born Subjects. . . . " The rest of the committee's report was more conciliatory, though it recommended that Massachusetts' law remain unchanged.

By the end of December Loudoun's temper had cooled and he accepted the Assembly's report as sufficient evidence of its acquiescence to his demands. In a letter to William Pitt on 4 February he boasted that, while the other colonies watched, he had settled the Massachusetts controversy in the army's favor. In fact, Massachusetts was the clear winner. Despite Loudoun's bluster, the quartering of troops was still dependent upon an act of the Massachusetts legislature, without which it was legally impossible to quarter troops anywhere other than in the barracks on Castle William. Thus, Massachusetts had effectually upheld the procedural political forms which allowed the colonists to continue to lay claim to the rights of Englishmen in regard to quartering.[16]

A quartering act for America was finally passed by Parliament on 3 May 1765. The act stipulated that soldiers were to be quartered in barracks; if there were not enough barrack space, they were to be billeted in public houses and inns. If these accommodations were insufficient, the governor and council were to hire vacant buildings. Quartering in private homes was scrupulously avoided. In this way, the Grenville ministry thought to quiet American complaints. But the law missed the most important point; namely, that Americans had insisted that only their own legislatures could enact such laws. This was the assumption underlying the opposition to the Quartering Act that developed in Massachusetts, New York, New Jersey, South Carolina, and Georgia. About a decade later the First Continental Congress reiterated this same position when it listed the Quartering Act as one of those arbitrary laws "which demonstrate a system formed to enslave America." In short, as a direct result of one part of their experience during the French and Indian War, Americans had come to believe that an assertive English imperialism presented a real danger to American liberty.[17]

The controversey between the British army and colonial governments over quartering helped to create a lasting resentment and a hardening of political attitudes which contributed to the alienation of the colonies from Great Britain. Colonial political leaders would not quickly forget that military power had been used to force them to comply with what they considered an unconstitutional procedure, a practice which posed a grave danger to political liberty in America. Indeed, those who observed how British generals settled the quartering problem by threatening to use the King's soldiers against recalcitrant colonials could scarcely avoid the conclusion that in the event of future serious differences with the Crown the colonies would either have to submit to royal force or devise a resistance in kind.

REFERENCES

1. See, for example, Lawrence Henry Gipson, *The Coming of the Revolution* (New York, 1959), p. 128, and the more sympathetic but similar treatment of the colonists' arguments in Stanley M. Pargellis, *Lord Loudoun in North America* (New Haven, 1933), p. 210; Theodore Thayer, *Pennsylvania Politics and the Growth of Democracy, 1740-1776* (Philadelphia, 1948), p. 60; John Zimmerman, "Governor Denny and the Quartering Act of 1756," *Pennsylvania Magazine of History and Biography*, XCI (1967), 280-381; Nicholas B. Wainwright, "Governor William Denny in Pennsylvania," *ibid.*, LXXXI (1957), 178-79; John Shy, *Toward Lexington: The Role of the British Army in the Coming of the American Revolution* (Princeton, 1965), p. 143; John Schutz, *Thomas Pownall, British Defender of American Liberty* (Glendale, Calif., 1951), pp. 109, 115; Ralph L. Ketcham, "Conscience, War and Politics in Pennsylvania, 1755-1757," *William and Mary Quarterly*, 3rd ser., XX (1963), 419; Bernard Bailyn, *Ideological Origins of the American Revolution* (Cambridge, Mass., 1967), pp. 61-64, brilliantly demonstrates how much the political culture of America was shaped by the ideas and fears of England's radical Whigs. In particular, they pointed out the dangers of arbitrary military power.

2. Edward Shippen to Joseph Shippen, 19 Mar. 1755, "Military Letters of Captain Joseph Shippen of the Provincial Service, 1756-1758," *Pennsylvania Magazine of History and Biography*, XXXVI (1912), 35.

3. Loudoun to Col. John Stanwix, 23 Sept. 1756, Loudoun Papers (Henry E. Huntington Library, LO 1885 [hereafter cited as LO]). Loudoun had already received reports from John Rutherford that made it clear there was going to be trouble between the army and the Pennsylvania government; see Rutherford to Loudoun, 12, 14, 16 Aug. 1756, LO 1473, 1485, 1499.

4. Attorney General William Murray told the Privy Council that Pennsylvania's 1755 quartering law should be disallowed because "the application of such propositions to a Colony in time of War, in the case of Troops raised for their Protection by Authority of the Parliament of Great Britain made the first time by an Assembly, many of whom plead what they call Conscience, for not making or assisting Military operations to resist the Enemy; should not be allowed to stand as Law." *Acts of the Privy Council*, IV, 337-39. Samuel Hazard, et al., eds., *Pennsylvania Archives*, 9 ser., 138 vols. (Philadelphia and Harrisburg, 1852-1949), 8th ser., VI, 4440, 4442, 4447, 4450.

5. 15 Dec. 1756, *Minutes of the Provincial Council of Pennsylvania*, 10 vols. (Philadelphia, 1851-1853), VII, 358-59 [hereafter cited as *Pennsylvania Colonial Records*]. Doctor James Stevenson had asked Col. Bouquet to see to it that a hospital was provided for those soldiers suffering from small pox.

6. *Ibid.*, 18 Dec. 1756, VII, 361-62.

7. Assembly to Denny, 20 Dec. 1756, *ibid.*, VII, 364-69.

8. *Ibid.*, pp. 371, 373-74; Richard Peters to Thomas and Richard Penn, 26 Dec. 1756, Penn Papers (Historical Society of Pennsylvania); Bailyn, *Ideological Origins*, pp. 63-64n.

9. Richard Peters to Provincial Commissioners, 26 Dec. 1756, *ibid.*, VII, 380.

10. Not all of Pennsylvania's political leaders were willing to press their claim to the rights of Englishmen, if it meant damaging the war effort. Joseph Shippen, for example, seemed to support the Assembly's position on quartering, but he was anxious that the quarrel should not persist. It was this concern for the wellbeing of the Empire, rather than any basic disagreement over the quartering issue that was one of the key factors separating Pennsylvania's politicians. Joseph Shippen to Edward Shippen, 19 Jan. 1757, Shippen Family Papers (Historical Society of Pennsylvania), II, 99.

11. Governor Hardy to Assembly, 6 July 1756; Assembly to Hardy, 8 July *Votes and Proceedings of the General Assembly of the Colony of New York*, Public Record Office/Colonial Office, 5/1216; Loudoun to the Duke of Cumberland, 29 Aug. 1756, LO 1626.

12. The Assembly's bill may be found in *Votes and Proceedings of the General Assembly of the Colony of New York*, Public Record Office/Colonial Office, 5/1216, 9 Oct. 1756; Hardy's initial reaction to the bill is contained in his letter to the Lords of Trade, 13 Oct. 1756, in E. B. O'Callaghan, ed., *Documents Relative to the Colonial History of the State of New York*, 15 vols. (Albany, 1856), VII, 163; Hardy's letter to Loudoun on 11 Nov. 1756 reveals his change, LO 2199; Loudoun to Hardy, 21 Nov. 1756, LO 2250.

13. Loudoun to the Duke of Cumberland, 22 Nov. 1756, LO 2262; according to a survey Loudoun ordered made, there were 329 households in Albany. He calculated that it would be possible in a pinch to quarter 190 officers and 2,082

soldiers in Albany's 329 homes. This meant there would be approximately five soldiers to each home, LO 3515.

14. Loudoun, Diary, II (26 Jan. 1757).

15. Pownall to Loudoun, 4 Nov. 1757, LO 4757.

16. Pownall was in complete agreement with the Assembly's position. See, for example, Pownall to the General Court, March 1758, LO 5941; Abercromby to Amherst, 19 Oct. 1758, Abercromby Papers (Henry E. Huntington Library), AB 778. General Jeffery Amherst expressed his views on quartering in a letter to Governor Denny, 7 insisted that the question was not whether the Quartering Act was constitutional, but whether "People . . . had rather part with their Money, tho' rather unconstitutionally, than to have a parcel of Military Masters put by Act of Parliament a bed to their Wives and Daughters" (Watts to James Napier, 1 June 1765, New York Historical Society, Collections [1928], p. 355); the New Jersey legislature contended that the act was "as much an Act for laying Taxes on the Inhabitants as the Stamp Act," (William A. Whitehead, ed., *Archives of the State of New Jersey*, 33 vols. [Newark, 1880-1928], IX, 577); William W. Abbot, *The Royal Governors of Georgia, 1754-1775* (Chapel Hill, N.C., 1959), pp. 126-44; Merrill Jensen, ed., *English Historical Documents* (London and New York, 1955), IX, 805-808.

Mar. 1759, *Minutes of the Provincial Council of Pennsylvania from the Organization to the Termination of the Proprietary Government*, 10 vols. (Philadelphia, 1851-1853), VIII, 285; for the Pennsylvania Assembly's reply, *ibid.*, 330-31. Other lower houses opposed forced quartering in the late 1750's: Captain Anthony Wheelock to Abercromby, 2 May 1758, Abercromby Papers, AB 227, for New Jersey's quartering law; Ensign Richard Nickleson to Col. John Forbes, 9 Dec. 1757, LO 4976, for New Hampshire's law; and the South Carolina Assembly to Governor Lyttleton, 18 Mar. 1758, LO 5763.

17. New York's flat refusal to make any military appropriation is well known (O'Callaghan, *Doucments Relative to the State of New York*, VII, 845-46, 867-68); New York merchant John Watts

The Current Value of English Exports, 1697 to 1800

John J. McCusker[*]

EVER since Charles Whitworth first published his volume on the *State of the Trade of Great Britain* in 1776, scholars have used his figures to evaluate England's balance of trade with the rest of the world.[1] Perhaps the most interested in this endeavor have been historians of colonial America who have related Whitworth's numbers to the changing fortunes of the colonies, to their currency problems, and, naturally, to the American Revolution. They have not been alone, for England traded with the world, and others have used his data in discussions of the trade of Scandinavia, southern Europe, Africa, and the East Indies. Yet many historians remain unaware that this annual series of English trade figures does not record the actual value of trade with other countries of the world. We have in Whitworth's book not the current value of English imports and exports but rather a series of figures which express the volume of trade in money terms of constant value. As they stand, the data bear only an incidental relationship to the English balance of trade—with the thirteen North American colonies or anywhere else. The purpose of this discussion is to offer a systematic conversion of the constant value series of exports from England, Wales, and Scotland into a current value series through the mechanism of a commodity price index. The result is a closer approximation of the real annual value of British exports during the eighteenth century.

To determine the character of the series which Whitworth printed and to understand the uses to which we may put it, we must first consider

[*] Mr. McCusker is a Fellow of the Institute of Early American History and Culture. He wishes to express his appreciation for financial assistance received from the Council on Research in Economic History, the Smithsonian Institution, and the American Philosophical Society.

[1] Charles Whitworth, *State of the Trade of Great Britain in Its Imports and Exports . . . 1697 [to 1773]* (London, 1776), records data for England and Wales only. Two copies of the book exist with manuscript additions to 1801, one in the Rare Book Room, Library of Congress, and the other in the Board of Trade Papers, Class 6, Volume 185, foll. 1-167, Public Record Office. Hereafter cited as B. T. 6/185:1-167.

what it was that the compilers of these figures were attempting to measure and then assess the methods which they employed. Twentieth-century economists recognize the balance of trade as only one aspect of a nation's international balance of payments, which overall includes three main sectors: the balance on current account, the bullion account, and the capital account. The capital account deals with the long- and short-term overseas investments by residents of one area in the enterprises of another. English money used to underwrite an ironworks in Massachusetts or a sugar plantation in Barbados represents such a movement of capital as does colonial investment in securities of the East India Company or the Bank of England. The bullion account measures the flow of hard currency between one area and another. Here we would enter the value of gold and silver coin which individual merchants shipped from the colonies to Great Britain in payment of debts. The balance on current account concerns the value of goods imported and exported as well as of "invisibles" such as the cost of shipping services. The balance of trade, which deals solely with merchandise, thus constitutes only part of the last of these three categories. Yet its calculation provides an important starting point in the accounting of international indebtedness. We do well to examine it, as long as we remember that there is much more besides.

180

Regular records of the English balance of trade began only in the last decade of the seventeenth century. Divers national and international pressures after the Glorious Revolution of 1688 hurried Englishmen into a greater awareness of the necessity for an accurate record of their trade with the rest of the world. English mercantilism cried out for such an accounting, and abortive and fragmentary attempts to strike the balance of trade littered the seventeenth century.[2] The law had required a record

[2] G. N. Clark, *Guide to English Commercial Statistics 1696-1782*, Royal Historical Society Guides and Handbooks No. 1 (London, 1938), xi-xvi. See also A. M. Millard, The Import Trade of London, 1600-1640 (unpubl. Ph.D. diss., University of London, 1956). Similar pressures had an impact upon other European nations and led to the compilation of comparable balance of trade statistics in Ireland (beginning in 1681), France (1716), Sweden (1738), and Scotland (1755). Irish records for 1698 to 1829 survive as Board of Customs and Excise Records, Class 15, Volumes 1 to 140, Public Record Office. Hereafter cited as Customs 15/1-140. Four earlier ledgers for 1682 to 1686 are in Additional Manuscript 4759, British Museum, London. Arthur Dobbs in *An Essay on the Trade and Improvement of Ireland*, 2 vols. (Dublin, 1729-1731), reprinted in *A Collection of Tracts and Treatises Illustrative of the Natural History, Antiquities, and the Political and Social State of Ireland at Various Periods Prior to the Present Century* (Dublin, 1861), II, 334, gave evidence of having seen ledgers for 1681, 1695, 1696, 1697, and 1698, of which only the last is extant. For the French statistics see Ambroise Marie Arnould, *De la balance du commerce et des relations commerciales extérieures de la France dans toutes les parties du globe, par-*

of duties paid upon the importation and exportation of goods at each English port from as early as the fifteenth century, and these "port books" provided the basis for a more orderly check on London's trade by the 1660s.[3] But not until the late 1690s did the government begin to compile national trade statistics on a regular annual basis.

The office of inspector general of imports and exports came into being in 1696 as a division of the Customs House.[4] The first occupant, William Culliford, set his clerks to work immediately. Over a year later they completed the first of the eighty-three great annual folio ledgers of

---

ticulièrement à la fin du règne de Louis XIV et au moment de la Révolution (Paris, 1791), I, viii; II, 121-133; Friedrich Lohman, "Die amtliche Handelstatistik Englands und Frankreichs im XVIII. Jahrhundert," Sitzungsberichte der Königlich Preussischen Akademie des Wissenschaften zu Berlin, II (1898), 859-892; and Bertrand Gille, Les Sources statistiques de l'histoire de France. Des enquêtes du XVII' siècle à 1870 (Paris, 1964), 96-97. For the Swedish series see Bertil Boëthius and Eli F. Heckscher, Svensk handelsstatistik, 1637-1717 (Stockholm, 1938), xlvi. For Scotland, see n. 5.

[3] Clark, English Commercial Statistics, 52-56. Most of the extant port books are in Records of the Exchequer, Class 190, Public Record Office. Hereafter cited as E. 190. For further information about them see the introduction in Neville J. Williams, comp., Descriptive List of Exchequer, Queen's Remembrancer, Port Books (London, 1960-), I, v-ix; Williams, "The London Port Books," Transactions of the London and Middlesex Archaeological Society, XVIII (1955), 13-26; and D. M. Woodward, "Port Books," History: The Journal of the Historical Association, LV (1970), 207-210. See also Sven-Erik Åström, "The Reliability of the English Port Books," Scandinavian Economic History Review, XVI (1968), 125-136. By the 1690s some enterprising London editor had begun to print a daily record of the goods which paid Customs duty, either as imports or exports; he "sent [them] about the City to any merchant or other, that will pay for them forty shillings the year." These constituted, in effect if not in fact, extracts from the London port books. John Houghton described the service in A Collection for Improvement of Husbandry and Trade (London), Apr. 27, 1692. In the inventory of the books and papers which the outgoing secretary of the Board of Trade, John Povey, transferred to his successor, William Popple, in 1696 were listed 11 volumes of "bills of entry." Index 8301:188, Public Record Office. It is tempting to think that the Board of Trade had been among the subscribers to this service and that they had preserved and bound the daily reports. They do not appear to have survived, however. See C. S. S. Higham, The Colonial Entry-Books: A Brief Guide to the Colonial Records in the Public Record Office before 1696 (London, 1921), 43.

[4] Clark, English Commercial Statistics, 1-44, treats in detail the antecedents of the office, its establishment, and its subsequent history down to the end of the 18th century. Very useful also is E. B. Firuski (Schumpeter), Trade Statistics and Cycles in England, 1697-1825 (unpubl. Ph.D. diss., Radcliffe College, 1934). For the context of these developments turn to Elizabeth Evelynola Hoon, The Organization of the English Customs System 1696-1786 (New York, 1938); and Dora Mae Clark, The Rise of the British Treasury: Colonial Administration in the Eighteenth Century (New Haven, Conn., 1960).

181

imports and exports which make up the set known today as "Customs 3" in the Public Record Office in London.[5] Each volume contained six major

182

[5] Customs 3/1-80. Customs 2/1-10 duplicate Customs 3 up to 1702 and add an earlier volume for 1697. Ledgers for 1705, 1712, and 1727 no longer survive in the Public Record Office. Fortunately a copy of the 1727 ledger is among many duplicates in the Departmental Archives of H. M. Customs and Excise, King's Beam House, London. The Customs 3 ledgers were for a time complemented by, and later supplanted by, another series, the States of Navigation, Commerce and Revenue, 1772 to 1808, Customs 17/1-30. The "year" used in the Customs 3 ledgers changed twice between 1697 and 1780. The volumes for 1697 and 1698 were based on the 12 months from Michaelmas to Michaelmas, Sept. 29 through Sept. 28. (Customs 2/1-4 and 3/1.) The next volume (Customs 2/5 and 3/2) included only the 3 months from Michaelmas to Christmas 1698; figures from this ledger have been ignored in the present discussion because of the statistical difficulties in dealing with a quarter year. All later volumes incorporated data for a full 12 months. The year ran from Christmas to Christmas, Dec. 25 to Dec. 24, until 1752 when, as a result of the calendar reform, Treasury accounts for that year were extended to include 11 additional days through Jan. 5, 1753, to compensate for the loss of 11 days in Sept. (the 3rd through the 13th). After that the Treasury year ran from Jan. 6 through Jan. 5. See, for instance, E. 351/1265 and Treasury Papers, Class 38, Volume 340, Public Record Office. Hereafter cited as T. 38/340. Since the Ledgers of Imports and Exports were compiled under the jurisdiction of the Treasury, they must surely have followed suit even though the annual volumes continued to state that they included data only from Christmas to Christmas. A comparison of the same data from a volume of the Customs 3 ledgers and the volume for the same year from the Customs 17 ledgers, which were explicitly based on the new accounting year, shows them to be the same. See similar conclusions by Rupert C. Jarvis, "Official Trade and Revenue Statistics," *Economic History Review*, 2d Ser., XVII (1964-1965), 45, 47; and Phyllis Deane and W. A. Cole, *British Economic Growth 1688-1959: Trends and Structure* (Cambridge, Eng., 1962), 321, n. 4. See also Clark, *English Commercial Statistics*, 11-12, 37. Besides Whitworth, David Macpherson, *Annals of Commerce, Manufactures, Fisheries and Navigation, with Brief Notices of the Arts and Sciences Connected with Them* (London, 1805), III-IV, printed the annual summaries of English trade from 1760 through 1800. The Customs 3 ledgers and Customs 17 accounts also provided the source for Elizabeth Boody Schumpeter, *English Overseas Trade Statistics 1697-1808* (Oxford, 1960). Ledgers of Imports and Exports for Scotland, 1755 to 1827, are in Customs 14/1-39. The accounts for the years 1763 and 1769 have not survived. The Scottish ledgers used the Jan. 6 through Jan. 5 Treasury year, thus adding weight to the supposition that the English ledgers did also. No Scottish Customs returns were deposited with the English Customs House before 1761. An Account of the British Produce and Manufactures Exported from England to France between January 5, 1714, and January 5, 1761 (1787), Great Britain, Parliament, House of Commons, Sessional Papers to 1801, XIX (Accounts and Papers), No. 426. Hereafter cited as H. of C., Sessional Papers. Compare accounts Nos. 425 and 427 in *ibid.;* Customs Tariffs of the United Kingdom from 1800 to 1897, with Some Notes upon the History of the More Important Branches of Receipts from 1660, p. 24, H. of C., Sessional Papers, 1898, LXXXV (Accounts and Papers), No. 34 [Command Paper 8706]; and T. 64/274:131. Earlier

sections: imports, reexports, and exports for both London and "the Outports" (i.e., the remainder of England and Wales). Within each section trade was further broken down by the areas to or from which goods were shipped: the foreign nations of the world listed alphabetically, then the three Channel Islands, Alderney, Guernsey, and Jersey, and finally, again alphabetically, the English colonies. Under a separate heading for each area the clerk wrote across the page the name of the item traded, the quantity traded that year, the value per unit, and the total value. Item followed item down the page in an arrangement which was again basically alphabetical, but which grouped some commodities under headings such as "grocery" or "drugs." At the end of each area the clerk summed up the total for that area in that particular section. The grand totals from each of the six sections provided an annual summary of England's "balance of trade" on the final folio of the ledger.[6] Whitworth simply printed the summary table from each of the Customs 3 ledgers through the year 1773.[7]

183

---

records survive in Scotland. See the 17th-century port books, similar to those of England, and the Customs accounts dating from 1742 in the Scottish Record Office, Edinburgh, as well as the various records in the several major 18th-century ports. B. R. Crick *et al.*, eds., *A Guide to Manuscripts Relating to America in Great Britain and Ireland* (London, 1961); and Crick, "First List of Addenda to a Guide to Manuscripts Relating to America in Great Britain and Ireland," *Bulletin of the British Association for American Studies*, N. S., V (Dec. 1962), 47 63. Summaries of the annual Scottish Customs 14 figures can be found in B. T. 6/185:168-197 and were printed in Macpherson, *Annals of Commerce*, II-IV.

[6] Clark, *English Commercial Statistics*, 8-10, describes the internal arrangement of the ledgers. See also Schumpeter, *English Overseas Trade Statistics*, 1-2.

[7] An indication of their value for colonial historians is the repeated instances in which the series for the thirteen North American colonies has been extracted and printed separately. See Isaac Smith Homans, Jr., *An Historical and Statistical Account of the Foreign Commerce of the United States* (New York, 1857), 7-8; Charles H. Evans, comp., *Exports, Domestic and Foreign, from the American Colonies to Great Britain, from 1697 to 1789, Inclusive. Exports, Domestic, from the United States to All Countries, from 1789 to 1883, Inclusive* [United States Congress, House of Representatives], House Miscellaneous Documents, 49th Congress, 1st Session, No. 49, part 2, Serial No. 2236 (Washington, 1884); and Emory R. Johnson *et al.*, eds., *History of Domestic and Foreign Commerce of the United States*, Carnegie Institution of Washington, Publication No. 215A (Washington, 1915), I, 120-121. The earliest published colonial series had been sent to Lewis Evans, engineer and geographer of Philadelphia, at his request by a friend in London. Evans presented a copy of the data to the visiting Swedish botanist Pehr Kalm in 1748, and Kalm later printed it in his account of his journey: *En resa till Norra America pa Kong[igt] Svenska Vetenskaps Academiens befallning och publici kostnad* (Stockholm, 1753-1761), III, 187-188, 526. (Compare the English translation by Adolph B. Benson, *Peter Kalm's Travels in North America: The English Version of 1770* [New York, 1937], I, 28-29.) Kalm contributed part of the series to the dis-

Although there is little doubt about what Culliford and his successors were attempting to produce with the Customs 3 ledgers, we may legitimately question how successful they were. Moreover, we must do so before we as historians set out to use their figures. To begin with, as in any project of such scope, the room for simple clerical errors was abundant. Some we can find by checking calculations, but there are certainly others which we have yet to detect (or cannot). The presumption must be that they are not statistically important. Random errors have a tendency to balance out.[8]

Systematic distortions affecting both the quantities of goods recorded and the unit values used, on the other hand, pose more serious difficulties. Imports were taxed in England, sometimes at very high rates, and this created an impetus to smuggle. Official figures for certain imports, therefore, understate the actual volume, although some work has been done to repair this defect.[9] Figures for exports suffer much less from the problem

---

sertation of one of his students: Daniel Lithander, *Oförgripeliga Tanckar om Nödwändigheten of Skogarnas Bettre Wård och Ans i Finland* [Certain considerations about the necessity of better maintaining and improving the forests in Finland] (Åbo, Finland, 1753). What might well be Evans's original series still survives. See An Accot. of the Value of Exports from England to Pennsylvania, 1723-1747, dated Custom House, London, Apr. 4, 1749, in the Penn Manuscripts, 1629-1834, VII, Philadelphia Land Grants, 1684-1772, fol. 67, Historical Society of Pennsylvania, Philadelphia. See also Lawrence Henry Gipson, *Lewis Evans* (Philadelphia, 1939), 7. The most authoritative version is that prepared by Lawrence A. Harper for United States, Department of Commerce, Bureau of the Census, *Historical Statistics of the United States, Colonial Times to 1957* (Washington, 1960), 759 (Series Z 21-34). Hereafter cited as *Historical Statistics of the U. S.* Fairfield Publishers, Stamford, Conn., published this volume in 1965 under the title *The Statistical History of the United States from Colonial Times to the Present.*

[8] The figures used as the basis for Table III below differ in several instances from other published versions of the same data. Harper's *Historical Statistics of the U. S.*, 759, makes two minor mistakes in transcription from Whitworth and the original ledgers. Series Z 28 for 1715 should be £16,182 (not £17,182), and Series Z 27 for 1763 should be £53,989 (not £53,998). Both of these mistakes were carried through to the totals which have also been corrected. Harper himself silently corrected an error of Whitworth's for New York in 1767. The original ledgers contain much more significant mistakes. The sum of London's exports of English goods to Virginia and Maryland for 1773 was incorrectly cast; the total should be £428,904 (not £328,904). See Customs 3/73:87-89. Ralph Davis detected the error. See his "English Foreign Trade, 1700-1774," *Econ. Hist. Rev.,* 2d Ser., XV (1962-1963), 285, n. 2, where he points out other similar problems. Tables II and III below take cognizance of these alterations.

[9] See W. A. Cole, "Trends in Eighteenth-Century Smuggling," *Econ. Hist. Rev.,* 2d Ser., X (1957-1958), 395-409; and Deane and Cole, *British Economic Growth,* 44-45. Compare Hoh-Cheung Mui and Lorna H. Mui, "Smuggling and the

of smuggling, but according to contemporaries, contain a regular upward bias due to the practice among merchants of overstating the quantities of merchandise shipped abroad in the hope of discouraging competition. Recent discussions have played down the significance of such overentries to the point that they are no longer considered a serious threat to analyses built upon these statistics.[10] Far more important is the problem created by the unchanging unit values, to the resolution of which this study is devoted.

The English ledgers of imports and exports failed in their purpose of "ascertaining the real values of trade,"[11] because the values the inspectors general placed upon goods were not current market prices but formalized official values derived at the beginning of the eighteenth century. (Even if the ledgers did serve their intended function for England, they cannot be used to establish a colonial balance of trade, because they show a colony's trade only with England and Wales.) Culliford and his clerks, in establishing unit values for their calculations, sought out the actual market price in England of goods exported and reexported; for imported goods, they used estimates of the "first cost," the price in the place from which they were shipped to England.[12] During the earliest years the

185

British Tea Trade before 1784," *American Historical Review*, LXXIV (1968-1969), 44-73.

[10] Schumpeter, *English Overseas Trade Statistics*, 5-6, felt there was considerably less effect on trade returns "than might be inferred from the attention given to it in public debates and treatises on overseas trade." John Houghton, writing in 1692, agreed: "I presume, such doings, if any, are very trivial to the bulk of things." *Coll. for Improvement of Husbandry and Trade* (London), Apr. 27, 1692. See also Firuski (Schumpeter), Trade Statistics, 130-144. Compare John J. McCusker, The Rum Trade and the Balance of Payments of the Thirteen Continental Colonies, 1650-1775 (unpubl. Ph.D. diss., University of Pittsburgh, 1970), 881-882, 986-987, 11n-12n, where I advance conclusions similar to Firuski (Schumpeter)'s after examining the statistics for selected trades. It is significant that the complaints of 18th-century authors ascribing such a defect to the Customs 3 figures simply copy earlier writers' complaints about figures derived from London port books. Compare Josiah Child, *A New Discourse of Trade, . . .* (London, 1693), 137, with Joshua Gee, *The Trade and Navigation of Great-Britain Considered: . . .* (London, 1729), 17-18. See also Copies of all Entries of Goods and Merchandise Outwards for North America . . . from 22d. December 1775, to the 13th May 1776 . . . and also the several quantities of goods actually shipped . . . in consequence of such Entries . . . , dated Custom House, London, Nov. 8, 1776, North Manuscripts, Papers of Frederick, Baron North, afterward 2nd earl of Guilford, b. 69, Bodleian Library, University of Oxford.

[11] Clark, *English Commercial Statistics*, 39.

[12] *Ibid.*, 10, 59; Schumpeter, *English Overseas Trade Statistics*, 8, based upon William Irving, An Account of the Official and likewise of the Real or Current Value, at which Each Article of the Imports and Exports of Great Britain to and

search was renewed annually. The official values fluctuated with the market and consequently reflect the approximate value of England's trade with the world. But after about 1702, when the values were finally fixed, the Customs 3 ledgers, whatever their accuracy in the amount of goods imported and exported, are not an accurate record of England's balance of trade.

These statements are no revelation. Eighteenth-century writers were aware from the beginning of the unchanging nature of the official values and the effect upon the annual summaries, and nineteenth- and twentieth-century scholars have shared this knowledge.[13] The reactions have varied but can be classified broadly into two kinds: some writers have appreciated the potential of the ledgers as a constant value series of trade figures and used them as such; others have seen them only as a distorted

186

from Ireland during the Three Years Ending the 5th January 1803, Has Been Estimated, H. of C., Sessional Papers, 1803-1804, VIII (Accounts and Papers), No. 190. This means that the figures for the continental colonies' imports from and exports to England included no freight or insurance costs; each was valued FOB at the point of export.

[13] The earliest authors to expound upon this subject were naturally the inspectors general of imports and exports. See the comments of Charles Davenant, the second inspector general, in *The Political and Commercial Works of That Celebrated Writer Charles D'Avenant, L.L.D.,* . . . ed. Sir Charles Whitworth (London, 1771), V, 350; of Henry Martin, the third inspector general, in Colonial Office Papers, Volume 12, foll. 9-10, Public Record Office. Hereafter cited as C. O. 390/12:9-10. Also, of Thomas Irving, the twelfth inspector general, in Customs 17/12:3-4. Martin's observations have been printed by Clark, *English Commercial Statistics,* 62-69, but with some significant though inadvertent omissions (compare C. O. 390/12:10 with p. 63, and fol. 17 with p. 66). Irving's conclusions can be reprinted in part by John Ehrman, *The British Government and Commercial Negotiations with Europe 1783-1793* (Cambridge, Eng., 1962), 212-214. See also the letter from John Oxenford to Board of Trade, London, Aug. 31, 1720, C. O. 388/22:75; George Chalmers, *An Estimate of the Comparative Strength of Great-Britain, During the Present and Four Preceding Reigns; and of the Losses of Her Trade from Every War Since the Revolution* (London, 1782), 35-36; and Macpherson, *Annals of Commerce,* III, 340; IV, 464. Warnings in the 19th century were sounded by, among others, J. Marshall, *A Digest of All the Accounts, Relating to the Population, Productions, Revenues, Financial Operations, Manufactures, Shipping, Colonies, Commerce, etc. etc., of the United Kingdom of Great Britain and Ireland* . . . (London, 1833), Pt. ii, 120a; Stephen Bourne, "The Official Trade and Navigation Statistics," *Journal of the Statistical Society of London,* XXXV (1872), 207; and Customs Tariffs 1800 to 1897, p. 16, H. of C., Sessional Papers, 1898, LXXXV (Accounts and Papers), No. 34. In the 20th century the most authoritative voices have been E. Lipson, *The Economic History of England.* Vol. III: *The Age of Mercantilism* (London, 1931), 93-94; Clark, *English Commercial Statistics,* 33-39; and T. S. Ashton, who followed Clark, in his introduction to Schumpeter, *English Overseas Trade Statistics,* 2-4. Compare *Historical Statistics of the U. S.,* 744.

4

approximation of the balance of trade to be repaired if possible or, if not, ignored.

As a constant value series, Customs 3 ledgers can be used both in national income accounting and in measuring the changing volume of trade. Analysis of changes in national growth through a study of alterations in the levels of consumer living or in the size of the gross national product requires a constant value series. Long-term trends in the volume of trade can be best traced by removing from consideration the changes due solely to varying price levels. "Thus it is simpler to describe the fluctuations of woollen exports in money than to give the number of short cloths and Spanish cloths, double bays, Colchester bays, perpetuanas, says, serges, worsted stuffs."[14] A constant value index, by removing the potentially distorting factor of changing prices, stands other key elements in relief.[15] So profitable is it to have a constant value series that, had the Customs 3 ledgers been prepared in current value terms, it is safe to say that some economic historian would by now have reduced them to constant value terms.[16]

187

[14] Clark, *English Commercial Statistics*, 37.

[15] Almost every writer cited in n. 13 not only warned that the Customs 3 figures were not a current value series but also pointed out their potential as a constant value series. Henry Martin was among the first to realize the significance of the changes that had taken place in the series and argued in 1718 that it was particularly well adapted "to discover at one view the increase or decrease of the quantitys of goods, imported or exported." C. O. 390/12:9-10. Deane and Cole, *British Economic Growth*, 40-97, employ the evidence of the Customs 3 ledgers as an index to the volume of trade in discussing the 18th century; similarly Lawrence A. Harper in *The English Navigation Laws: A Seventeenth-Century Experiment in Social Engineering* (New York, 1939). Schumpeter, *English Overseas Trade Statistics*, sought to make the Customs 3 series more useable by revaluing all the major commodities to the official value for one year. But Deane and Cole discovered that the series was a perfectly satisfactory volume index just as it stood. *British Economic Growth*, 43-44. See W. E. Minchinton, comp., *The Growth of English Overseas Trade in the Seventeenth and Eighteenth Centuries* (London, 1969), 54-55, n. 5.

[16] A current value series is converted to a constant value series by dividing the former through with a commodity price index (CPI). This division has the effect of reducing the value factor in a series to a common unvarying unit. Obviously the process can also be reversed and a constant value series converted to a current value series by introducing (or reintroducing) the changes in value through multiplication by a CPI. The interrelated character of these three elements is emphasized when we appreciate that one CPI, the Paasche index (after its inventor), is defined as the quotient of a division of the current value of a series by its value in constant prices. It has the formula:

$$\text{Paasche price index} = \frac{\Sigma p_1 q_1}{\Sigma p_0 q_1}.$$

This is a current weight CPI as opposed to a Laspeyres or fixed weight CPI. For a basic discussion of these considerations, see any manual of economic statistics

Yet anyone who sought the real value of English trade could not use the series as it existed. The necessity of converting to current value was recognized by many in the past, not the least of whom was Benjamin Franklin, who endeavored to bring the official values for the 1760s into accord with current market prices.[17] Others, contemporary with Franklin and later, have sought similar solutions.[18] Some recent economic historians,

---

(e.g., Daniel B. Suits, *Statistics: An Introduction to Quantitative Economic Research* [Chicago, 1963], 230-238). Compare Walter R. Crowe, *Index Numbers: Theory and Applications* (London, 1969), 56-65. The classic treatise on price indices is Irving Fisher, *The Making of Index-Numbers: A Study of Their Varieties, Tests, and Reliability* (Boston, 1922). Also important is Wesley C. Mitchell, *The Making and Using of Index Numbers*, United States, Department of Labor, Bureau of Labor Statistics, Bulletin No. 656, Part I (Washington, 1938).

[17] See the two letters, signed "F. B.," which appeared in the *London Chronicle*, Nov. 3 and Dec. 8, 1768, and which were reprinted in the *Pennsylvania Journal; and the Weekly Advertiser* (Philadelphia), Jan. 26, 1769, the *Pennsylvania Chronicle and Universal Advertiser* (Philadelphia), Mar. 6, 1769, and elsewhere. Franklin suggested an increase of one-third over the official values. His data, and perhaps his correction factor, came from John Huske, an American-born merchant and M.P. See Verner W. Crane, ed., *Benjamin Franklin's Letters to the Press 1758-1775* (Chapel Hill, N. C., 1950), 141-151. Compare Franklin's attempt with that of Bryan Edwards, *The History, Civil and Commercial, of the British Colonies in the West Indies* (London, 1793), I, 236, n. 1; II, 383-384.

[18] An early 19th-century economic writer attempted a revaluation of the official figures for several selected sets of years but on what basis does not appear. César Moreau, *Chronological Records of the British Royal and Commercial Navy, from the Earliest Period (A.D. 827) to the Present Time (1827)* (London, 1827), 13, 15, 17, 18, 23, 30 (note his "Observations," 17). Since World War II several economic historians have used various means to try to reach the same goal. Albert H. Imlah, "Real Values in British Foreign Trade, 1798-1853," *Journal of Economic History*, VIII (1948), 133-152, broke new ground when he corrected 19th-century figures using a rather involved process made necessary by the great length of time between the choice of the official values and the date of his series. See also Imlah, *Economic Elements in the Pax Britannia: Studies in British Foreign Trade in the Nineteenth Century* (Cambridge, Mass., 1958). Gordon Carl Bjork, Stagnation and Growth in the American Economy, 1784-1792 (unpubl. Ph.D. diss., University of Washington, 1963), 115-118, converted the official value of British imports from the United States in the years 1770 to 1775 and 1784 to 1792 into dollars using a weighted price index. Robert Paul Thomas, "A Quantitative Approach to the Study of the Effects of British Imperial Policy upon Colonial Welfare: Some Preliminary Findings," *Journal Econ. Hist.*, XXV (1965), 616 and n. 5, "adjusted" the prices of colonial imports "by the Schumpeter-Gilboy index" in order "to make them more accurate." James Floyd Shepherd, Jr., A Balance of Payments for the Thirteen Colonies, 1768-1772 (unpubl. Ph.D. diss., University of Washington, 1966), 80, concluded that the official values during his period were "95 per cent of the actual value" and corrected for this deficiency. Many others either have been ignorant of or have ignored the injunctions against using these figures as if they were a current value series and, blithely accepting the ledgers at face value, have proceeded to write about an

however, have doubted that it could be done. Sir G. N. Clark, Chichele Professor of Economic History in the University of Oxford, wrote that "it appears to be impossible to invent a formula of any practicable use for converting them, from year to year, to approximate real value."[19] With all deference to Professor Clark, I should like to try just that. Much work done during the first third of this century in both the history of prices and in the theory of index numbers supplies the elements for a solution of the problem. The key, of course, is the nature of the series as a constant value index.

By its very nature, a constant value series can be converted to a current value series through the use of a commodity price index. The CPI expresses the percentage variation over time in the level of prices relative to a base period. One merely multiplies each annual Customs 3 total by the appropriate figure from the CPI. The method assumes that the percentage variations of the CPI equal the percentage variations experienced by the net current value of the Customs 3 series over time compared with the same base period. The essential nature of the construct is the best support for the correctness of this procedure, but there are also objective tests of the results.

189

Obviously much depends on the choice of the CPI and base period. There are two very useful indices for England in the eighteenth century. The E. H. P. Brown and S. V. Hopkins series, which spans about three-quarters of the present milennium (1264 to 1954), has the advantage of reflecting long-term trends quite adequately.[20] On the other hand, to section out a century from their figures risks incurring distortions induced a hundred years earlier or later. Fortunately we need not debate the issue but can, instead, turn to a CPI constructed for precisely the period of interest to us here, 1697 to 1800. Prepared in the 1930s by E. B. Schumpeter and E. W. Gilboy, this unweighted CPI of English wholesale prices has two series, one for producers' goods and another for consumers'

---

apocryphal balance of trade. Most notably they have been historians of colonial America.

[19] Clark, *English Commercial Statistics,* 39. It should be noted that Clark considered his "criticism of the British trade statistics of the seventeenth and eighteenth centuries . . . [as] merely directives for effective work, not warnings against expecting useful results." *Ibid.,* 41.

[20] E. H. Phelps Brown and Shelia V. Hopkins, "Seven Centuries of the Prices of Consumables, compared with Builders' Wage-rates," *Economica,* N. S., XXIII (1956), 296-314. Much of the material used to compile the Brown-Hopkins series came from Sir William Beveridge, *Prices and Wages in England from the Twelfth to the Nineteenth Century* (London, 1939).

goods.[21] The average of the two series, recomputed to the required base period (1700-1702 = 100), appears in Table I.[22]

During the base period the official values for the Customs 3 ledgers were established at the levels they were to maintain well into the nineteenth century. Although some historians have thought that the values were all chosen in 1696, the year in which the first volume was begun, we now know that during the earliest years the inspector general and his clerks attempted to keep pace with changing prices.[23] In fact, for those commodities whose prices we can check in contemporary printed price currents, the success of the endeavor is most impressive.[24] Each new ledger brought fewer and fewer changes, however, with the period 1700-1702, Culliford's last years in office, marking the end of the effort to keep prices current. A few variations continued to be introduced, particularly during the next decade in the value of exported woollens,[25] and in 1724 a change in the collection of the customs duties reduced the number of items in the ad valorem category and substituted official values for some minor imported goods.[26] Even so, since the vast majority of the official values were set in the years 1700 to 1702, this period must be the base.

The reinflation of annual totals from Customs 3 ledgers upon which

[21] Elizabeth Boody Schumpeter, "English Prices and Public Finance, 1660-1822," *Review of Economic Statistics*, XX (1938), 21-37; Elizabeth W. Gilboy., "The Cost of Living and Real Wages in Eighteenth Century England," *ibid.*, XVIII (1936), 134-143. The series is reprinted in B. R. Mitchell and Phyllis Deane, *Abstract of British Historical Statistics* (Cambridge, Eng., 1962), 468-469. Note that the use of the harvest year by Schumpeter and Gilboy and its application here to trade data based on the calendar year creates potential statistical difficulties. Another index of English prices (for 1729 to 1800) appeared as Chart I in Earl J. Hamilton, "Prices, Wages, and the Industrial Revolution," in Wesley C. Mitchell *et al.*, eds., *Studies in Economics and Industrial Relations* (Philadelphia, 1941), 101. Compare as well the work of François Simiand, *Recherches anciennes et nouvelles sur le mouvement général des prix du XVI᷎ au XIX᷎ siècle* (Paris, 1932).

[22] This same averaging of the two Schumpeter-Gilboy series provided the CPI used by Deane and Cole, *British Economic Growth*, Fig. 7. See also p. 14.

[23] Clark, *English Commercial Statistics*, 10-11, traced the mistake back to Macpherson, *Annals of Commerce*, III, 340. See also Schumpeter, *English Overseas Trade Statistics*, Tables XLVI and XLVII.

[24] Based on a comparison of the Customs 3 valuations for the years 1697 through 1702 with prices from extant price currents. The former, from the ledgers themselves, are summarized in Schumpeter, *English Overseas Trade Statistics*, 70-71. Copies of price currents survive in several places. For their locations, see J. M. Price, "Notes on Some London Price-Currents, 1667-1715," *Econ. Hist. Rev.*, 2d Ser., VII (1954-1955), 240-250; and L. W. Hanson, *Contemporary Printed Sources for British and Irish Economic History 1701-1750* (Cambridge, Eng., 1963).

[25] Clark, *English Commercial Statistics*, 10-23, discussed the evidence thoroughly.

[26] See Customs 3/26-27A. Rum is an example of such a commodity. See McCusker, *Rum Trade*, 1071-1072.

TABLE I

ENGLISH WHOLESALE COMMODITY PRICE INDEX, 1697 TO 1800
(BASE: 1700-1702 = 100)

Year	CPI	Year	CPI	Year	CPI
1697	112.3	1732	87.0	1768	100.2
1698	111.3	1733	83.1	1769	92.9
1699	113.8	1734	84.6		
		1735	83.6	1770	94.3
1700	104.0	1736	82.2	1771	97.7
1701	97.2	1737	84.6	1772	104.5
1702	98.7	1738	83.6	1773	106.0
1703	96.3	1739	81.2	1774	104.0
1704	97.2			1775	102.6
1705	92.9	1740	91.9	1776	104.5
1706	96.8	1741	99.7	1777	102.1
1707	89.0	1742	95.3	1778	107.5
1708	91.9	1743	90.0	1779	107.5
1709	100.6	1744	88.5		
		1745	80.7	1780	108.4
1710	110.9	1746	89.5	1781	109.4
1711	118.6	1747	85.6	1782	114.8
1712	96.8	1748	89.0	1783	119.6
1713	94.8	1749	90.9	1784	113.8
1714	94.3			1785	110.4
1715	92.4	1750	89.0	1786	112.8
1716	91.4	1751	85.1	1787	110.9
1717	90.0	1752	84.6	1788	113.8
1718	89.5	1753	84.1	1789	108.9
1719	91.9	1754	87.0		
		1755	89.0	1790	112.3
1720	93.8	1756	90.0	1791	110.9
1721	91.9	1757	98.7	1792	113.3
1722	89.0	1758	100.6	1793	123.0
1723	85.1	1759	97.7	1794	124.0
1724	88.0			1795	130.8
1725	89.5	1760	97.2	1796	142.0
1726	94.3	1761	94.8	1797	140.5
1727	93.8	1762	95.3	1798	134.7
1728	94.3	1763	98.2	1799	144.9
1729	96.8	1764	98.7		
		1765	99.7	1800	177.5
1730	93 8	1766	100.2		
1731	89.0	1767	101.1		

191

Tables II and III are based is an aggregate procedure. (See Figure I.) The CPI from Table I becomes the percentage through which the constant values of the ledger are converted into the current values of these tables. As an aggregate procedure, two considerations restrict the correction to export values alone. Such a process obviously assumes that the CPI represents the value of all the commodities entered into the ledgers. A CPI need not be based on prices for all commodities but only be broadly enough grounded to reflect changes in the price levels of all commodities; one constructed on selected key commodities can quite adequately trace the variations of an entire market. But the Schumpeter-Gilboy index includes prices for only a few imported goods and, with reference to the Customs ledgers, is more representative of the price levels internal to England and, therefore, of exports.[27] For this reason, Table II corrects only the values of goods exported from England.

192

TABLE II

OFFICIAL[a] AND CURRENT[b] VALUE OF ALL GOODS EXPORTED FROM
ENGLAND, WALES, AND SCOTLAND[c]
(IN THOUSANDS OF POUNDS)
A. From England and Wales, 1697 to 1754

Year	Official Value (1)	Current Value (2)	Year	Official Value (1)	Current Value (2)	Year	Official Value (1)	Current Value (2)
1697[d]	3,453	3,453	1716	7,050	6,444	1735	9,329	7,799
1698[d]	6,464	6,464	1717	7,997	7,197	1736	9,702	7,975
1699[d]	5,871	5,871	1718	6,361	5,603	1737	10,082	8,529
			1719	6,835	6,281	1738	10,196	8,524
1700[d]	6,384	6,384				1739	8,844	7,181
1701[d]	6,813	6,813	1720	6,911	6,482			
1702[d]	4,739	4,739	1721	7,201	6,618	1740	8,198	7,534
1703	6,133	5,887	1722	8,265	7,356	1741	9,570	9,541
1704	6,099	5,929	1723	7,396	6,294	1742	9,574	9,124
1705	5,259	4,886	1724	7,601	6,689	1743	11,310	10,179
1706	6,191	5,993	1725	8,482	7,591	1744	9,190	8,134
1707	6,392	5,689	1726	7,693	7,254	1745	9,072	7,321
1708	6,564	6,033	1727	7,275	6,824	1746	10,767	9,636
1709	5,913	5,949	1728	8,707	8,211	1747	9,775	8,368
			1729	8,240	7,976	1748	11,141	9,916
1710	6,295	6,981				1749	12,679	11,525
1711	5,693	7,072	1730	8,549	8,019			
1712	6,869	6,644	1731	7,862	6,998	1750	12,699	11,302
1713	6,892	6,533	1732	8,870	7,718	1751	12,420	10,569
1714	8,004	7,545	1733	8,838	7,344	1752	11,595	9,809
1715	6,922	6,396	1734	8,299	7,021	1753	12,244	10,297
						1754	11,788	10,255

[27] For a discussion of these considerations, see Mitchell, *Making and Using Index Numbers*, 33-59.

TABLE II (Continued)

B. From England, Wales, and Scotland, 1755 to 1800

Year	From England and Wales		From Scotland		Total Current Value[a]
	Official Value	Current Value	Official Value	Current Value	
	(1)	(2)	(3)	(4)	(5)
1755	11,065	9,848	536	477	10,325
1756	11,721	10,549	626	563	11,112
1757	12,339	12,178	829	819	12,996
1758	12,618	12,694	831	836	13,530
1759	12,948	13,627	940	919	14,546
1760	14,695	14,284	1,086	1,056	15,339
1761	14,873	14,100	1,166	1,105	15,205
1762	13,545	12,909	998	951	11,860
1763	14,488	14,227	1,091	1,072	15,299
1764	16,202	15,992	1,244	1,228	17,220
1765	14,550	14,507	1,181	1,177	15,684
1766	14,025	14,053	1,164	1,166	15,219
1767	13,844	13,997	1,246	1,259	15,256
1768	15,118	15,148	1,502	1,505	16,653
1769	13,438	12,484	1,563	1,452	13,936
1770	14,267	13,454	1,728	1,629	15,083
1771	17,161	16,766	1,857	1,815	18,518
1772	16,159	16,887	1,561	1,631	18,518
1773	14,863	15,775	1,612	1,709	17,464
1774	15,916	16,553	1,372	1,427	17,980
1775	15,202	15,598	1,124	1,153	16,751
1776	13,730	14,348	1,026	1,072	15,420
1777	12,653	12,919	838	855	13,774
1778	11,551	12,417	703	756	13,173
1779	12,693	13,645	837	900	14,546
1780	12,552	13,606	1,002	1,086	14,693
1781	10,569	11,563	763	835	12,398
1782	12,356	14,184	654	750	14,935
1783	13,852	16,567	830	992	17,559
1784	14,171	16,127	930	1,058	17,185
1785	15,673	17,402	1,008	1,112	18,514
1786	15,386	17,355	915	1,032	18,387
1787	17,181	19,054	1,115	1,237	20,290
1788	16,935	19,272	1,189	1,353	20,625
1789	18,843	20,520	1,170	1,274	21,794
1790	18,885	21,208	1,235	1,387	22,595
1791	21,436	23,772	1,294	1,436	25,207
1792	23,674	26,823	1,231	1,395	28,218
1793	19,364	23,820	1,025	1,260	25,080
1794	25,663	31,822	1,085	1,345	33,168
1795	26,146	34,199	977	1,278	35,477
1796	29,196	41,459	1,323	1,878	43,337

193

TABLE II B (Continued)

Year	From England and Wales		From Scotland		Total Current Value[e]
	Official Value (1)	Current Value (2)	Official Value (3)	Current Value (4)	(5)
1797	27,700	38,918	1,217	1,710	40,628
1798	31,923	43,000	1,669	2,248	45,248
1799	31,724	45,968	1,917	2,777	48,745
1800	35,774	63,500	2,346	4,165	67,664

Notes: [a] Included are exports, reexports, and prize goods shipped from England and Wales to all markets except Scotland, and from Scotland to all markets except England and Wales. Omitted are English and Welsh exports to Scotland before the Act of Union of 1707 and all exports of gold and silver bullion. Schumpeter, *English Overseas Trade Statistics*, 7-9.

[b] Annual total values of all goods exported as recorded in Customs 2, 3, 14, and 17 ledgers multiplied by the revised Schumpeter-Gilboy CPI from Table I expressed as a percentage. For 1705 and 1712 the total values are as found in Whitworth, *State of the Trade of Great Britain*, Pt. i, 9, 16; for 1763 and 1769 the Scottish values are as found in B. T. 6/185: 168-197.

[c] Scottish official values for each commodity differed from the English. Nevertheless, Scottish annual export figures have been made to vary with the English CPI on the assumption that (1) the unit values were roughly the same in the base period (1700-1702) and (2) the annual fluctuations in the Scottish market paralleled those of English prices. Any error induced in the totals by these assumptions is thought to be insignificant if only because the Scottish portion of the whole was so small.

[d] For the year 1702 and earlier, when the official value was still being computed using actual market prices, no correction is required. Schumpeter, *English Overseas Trade Statistics*, 4.

[e] Totals may not equal sum of component parts because of rounding.

When this aggregate procedure is applied to the Customs 3 values for the American colonies, the potential for distortion depends directly on the breadth of the range of the products which entered into the trade. Little or no problem arises with English exports to the thirteen colonies since the records reveal that England and Wales sent a reasonably representative sampling of their goods westward across the Atlantic. On the other hand, imports into England from the colonies, dependent as they were on a rather narrow range of products saleable in the mother country, offer just the opposite case. A large margin of error would result should we attempt to ascertain the current value of imports into Britain from Maryland and Virginia by adjusting to constant value according to the English CPI since the price of one commodity, tobacco, was of overriding importance. The same would be true with regard to the sugar colonies. For this reason Table III corrects only the values of exports to the thirteen colonies. The current value of British imports must be computed on a different basis using wholesale market price series for the separate commodities involved or, perhaps, a colonial CPI.[28]

Although the statistical interrelationships between a current value series, a CPI, and a constant value series demonstrate sufficiently the

TABLE III

CURRENT OR REAL VALUE OF GOODS EXPORTED TO THE THIRTEEN COLONIES
(IN THOUSANDS OF POUNDS)
A. From England and Wales, 1697 to 1775

Year	To New England	To New York	To Pennsyl-vania	To Maryland and Virginia	To North and South Carolina	To Georgia	Total to All Colonies[a]
	(1)	(2)	(3)	(4)	(5)	(6)	(7)
1697[b]	68	5	3	59	5		140
1698[b]	94	25	11	311	18		458
1699[b]	127	43	17	205	11		404
1700[b]	92	49	18	174	11		344
1701[b]	86	32	12	200	14		344
1702[b]	65	30	9	72	10		187
1703	57	17	10	189	12		285
1704	73	22	12	59	6		171
1705	58	26	7	162	18		270
1706	55	31	11	56	4		156
1707	107	27	13	212	9		368
1708	106	25	6	73	11		221
1709	121	35	6	81	29		271
1710	118	35	10	142	22		326
1711	163	34	23	109	24		353
1712	124	18	8	130	19		300
1713	114	44	16	72	23		270
1714	114	42	14	120	22		313
1715	152	50	15	184	15		417
1716	111	48	20	164	25		368
1717	119	40	20	194	23		396
1718	118	56	20	172	14		381
1719	115	52	25	151	18		361
1720	121	35	23	104	17		300
1721	105	47	20	117	16		305
1722	119	51	24	154	31		378

[28] Series of prices for the continental colonies have been prepared in sufficient detail for the compilation of a CPI only back to 1720. U. S. Congress, Joint Economic Committee, *Employment, Growth, and Price Levels: Hearing on S. Con. Res. 13. Part Two: Historical and Comparative Rates of Production, Productivity, and Prices*, 86th Cong., 1st Sess., Apr. 7-10, 1959, 379-384, 394 (and two charts). The findings of several studies were summarized in Arthur Harrison Cole, *Wholesale Commodity Prices in the United States 1700-1861*, 2 vols. (Cambridge, Mass., 1938).

TABLE III A (Continued)

Year	To New England	To New York	To Pennsylvania	To Maryland and Virginia	To North and South Carolina	To Georgia	Total to All Colonies*
	(1)	(2)	(3)	(4)	(5)	(6)	(7)
1723	150	45	14	105	36		350
1724	148	56	27	142	33		406
1725	181	63	38	175	35		492
1726	189	80	36	175	41		522
1727	176	63	30	181	22		472
1728	184	77	35	161	31		488
1729	156	63	29	105	56		409
1730	195	60	46	142	61		504
1731	163	59	39	152	63		477
1732	188	57	36	129	51	1	462
1733	153	54	34	155	58	1	456
1734	124	69	46	146	84	2	471
1735	158	67	41	184	98	10	559
1736	183	71	51	168	83	2	557
1737	189	106	48	179	50	5	577
1738	170	112	51	216	73	5	628
1739	179	86	44	176	77	3	545
1740	157	109	52	259	167	3	748
1741	198	140	91	248	240	3	883
1742	142	160	72	252	121	16	762
1743	155	122	71	295	100	2	746
1744	127	106	55	208	70	1	567
1745	113	44	44	160	70	1	432
1746	187	78	66	253	92	1	677
1747	180	118	70	171	82	*	622
1748	176	128	67	225	143	1	739
1749	217	242	217	294	149	*	1,118
1750	305	238	194	311	118	2	1,169
1751	260	212	162	295	118	2	1,049
1752	231	164	171	275	128	3	971
1753	291	234	207	300	179	12	1,222
1754	287	110	213	282	130	2	1,023
1755	304	143	129	254	167	2	991
1756	346	225	180	301	164	*	1,217
1757	359	349	265	421	211	3	1,607
1758	468	359	262	441	182	10	1,723
1759	515	616	487	448	210	15	2,292
1760	583	467	688	589	212	0	2,539
1761	317	274	194	517	241	23	1,566
1762	236	274	196	398	185	23	1,312
1763	254	234	279	545	246	44	1,602
1764	454	509	430	508	302	18	2,220
1765	450	381	362	382	334	29	1,938
1766	410	332	328	373	297	67	1,808

TABLE III A (Continued)

Year	To New England	To New York	To Pennsyl- vania	To Maryland and Virginia	To North and South Carolina	To Georgia	Total to All Colonies[a]
	(1)	(2)	(3)	(4)	(5)	(6)	(7)
1767	411	423	376	442	247	24	1,922
1768	421	484	433	477	290	57	2,162
1769	193	70	186	454	285	54	1,241
1770	372	449	127	677	138	53	1,816
1771	1,388	639	712	899	400	69	4,106
1772	862	359	531	830	470	97	3,148
1773	559	307	452	455	366	68	2,204
1774	585	456	651	550	393	60	2,694
1775	74	1	1	2	6	117	201

197

B. From Scotland, 1762 to 1775[d]

Year	To New England	To New York	To Pennsyl- vania	To Maryland	To Virginia	To North Carolina	To South Carolina	To Georgia	Total to All Colonies
	(1)	(2)	(3)	(4)	(5)	(6)	(7)	(8)	(9)
1762	14	22		19	100	2	6		162
1763	20	17	12	21	172	5	10		256
1764	28	9	3	18	153	4	6		222
1765	17	5	6	27	108	7	5		175
1766	10	2	7	38	110	7	5		178
1767	10	6	11	31	186	15	10		270
1768	11	8	10	41	153	6	5		234
1769	15	1	5	48	163	11	9		250
1770	21	4	4	51	212	17	4	3	317
1771	15	2	13	52	245	14	10	1	356
1772	20	6	19	53	179	19	12	3	312
1773	17	7	1C	17	153	21	17	4	247
1774	15	23	21	25	142	25	6	2	259
1775	14							10	25

C. Total from Great Britain, 1762 to 1775

Year	To New England	To New York	To Pennsyl- vania	To Maryland and Virginia	To North and South Carolina	To Georgia	Total to All Colonies
	(1)	(2)	(3)	(4)	(5)	(6)	(7)
1762	249	296	196	517	193	23	1,474
1763	274	252	291	738	260	44	1,859
1764	482	518	433	680	312	18	2,442
1765	467	386	368	517	346	29	2,114
1766	420	334	335	521	309	67	1,986

TABLE III C (Continued)

Year	To New England	To New York	To Pennsyl-vania	To Maryland and Virginia	To North and South Carolina ·	To Georgia	Total to All Colonies
	(1)	(2)	(3)	(4)	(5)	(6)	(7)
1767	421	429	387	660	272	24	2,192
1768	432	492	443	671	302	57	2,395
1769	208	70	190	664	304	54	1,491
1770	393	453	132	940	159	56	2,133
1771	1,403	640	730	1,196	423	70	4,462
1772	882	365	550	1,061	501	100	3,460
1773	576	314	462	625	404	71	2,451
1774	600	478	671	718	425	61	2,953
1775	87	2	1	2	7	127	226

Notes: a Totals may not equal sum of component parts because of rounding.
b See Table II, note d.
c Less than £550.
d See Table II, note c. Scottish ledgers did not distinguish between exports to the thirteen colonies and the rest of "America" until 1762. A crude estimate of the annual current value in thousands of pounds of exports to the thirteen colonies between 1755 and 1761 is possible if we assume that they formed the same proportion (74.8%) of the total export to America in these years as they did in the next five (1762-1766):

Year	Value	Year	Value
1755	91	1759	235
1756	116	1760	248
1757	207	1761	216
1758	221		

validity of the procedures adopted here, two tests of the computed current value series offer further support of the results achieved. The first test compares the corrected series with the most authoritative eighteenth-century revaluation of England's balance of trade. The second test compares the corrected series with the best modern attempt to calculate the balance of trade of the thirteen colonies. In neither instance does the difference exceed two-tenths of one per cent.

At the end of the 1790s Thomas Irving, inspector general of imports and exports, sought to demonstrate the great divergence which had grown up between the official and real value of British trade by replacing the official unit values of the ledgers with current market prices. According to his figures, the annual real value of all goods exported from Great Britain during the years 1796 to 1798 averaged £43,138,000.[29] The

[29] Commercial Accounts of Great Britain, in Accounts and Papers Relative to the Commerce, Revenue, and Expenditure of the Kingdom of Great Britain and

FIGURE I

Current Value of Exports from England and Wales (Later Great Britain), 1697 to 1800

Upper Chart: To All Overseas Markets

Lower Chart: To the Thirteen North American Colonies

(In hundreds of thousands of pounds)

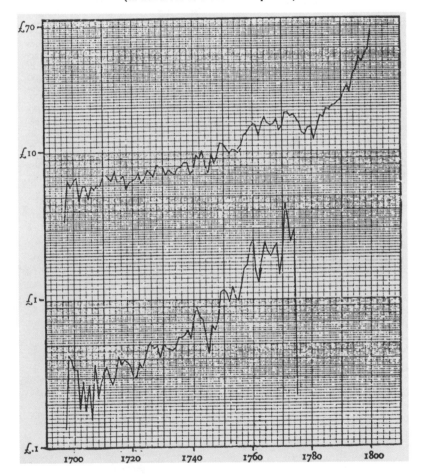

199

average current value for 1796 to 1798 from Table II-B, Column (5) comes to £43,071,000. The difference, roughly £67,000, falls shy of Irving's figures by 0.16 per cent.

Very recently, J. F. Shepherd reconstructed the balance of payments of the thirteen colonies on the eve of the American Revolution. He estimated that British exports averaged £2,790,000 per year during the period 1768 to 1772.[30] The comparable figure calculated from Table III-C, Column (7) is £2,788,000. The difference, less than £2,000, is 0.06 per cent of Shepherd's estimate.

Ireland, H. of C., Sessional Papers to 1801, CVII (Accounts and Papers), No. 981, 5, 9-11. Deane and Cole, *British Economic Growth,* 43, 315, compared the values which Irving used with current market prices and found them "remarkably accurate." See Thomas Tooke, *Thoughts and Details on the High and Low Prices of the Last Thirty Years* (London, 1823), IV, Appendix, 1-69; and Thomas Tooke and William Newmarch, *A History of Prices, and of the State of the Circulation, from 1793 to [1856],* 6 vols. (London, 1838-1857).

[30] Shepherd, Balance of Payments, 90 (Table III-14). The figure given in the text is the result of subtracting from Shepherd's total the 10% he added as an approximation of shipping costs in order to estimate the value as landed (CIF) in North America. *Ibid.,* 80-83, 87. See also Shepherd, "A Balance of Payments for the Thirteen Colonies, 1768-1772: A Summary," *Journal Econ. Hist.,* XXV (1965), 691-695; Shepherd and Gary M. Walton, "Estimates of 'Invisible' Earnings in the Balance of Payments of the British North American Colonies, 1768-1772," *ibid.,* XXIX (1969), 230-263.

Brothers in Arms?—Anglo-American
Friction at Louisbourg, 1745-1746

DOUGLAS EDWARD LEACH*

W HEN in 1768 a Boston mob rioted against British authority,
the Crown dispatched a man-of-war and subsequently several regiments of regular troops to uphold that authority
in the turbulent seaport. After about two years of unpleasant friction
between the local populace and the uniformed personnel there came
a sudden, shocking volley of musketry in a Boston square, and blood
on the snow. Five years later the church bells of the adjacent countryside summoned the Minutemen to Lexington Green, and the American Revolution was under way.

Casual observers of this rapid sequence of events between 1768 and
1775 might be surprised at the intensity of New England's hostility
toward royal naval and military personnel during that crucial period,
but anyone familiar with the experience of New Englanders during
the preceding two or three decades should not be. Indeed, ever since
the time of the late unlamented governor, Sir Edmund Andros, in
the 1680s the people of Massachusetts had tended to view the professional forces with suspicion and distaste, and were themselves
viewed by the professionals in much the same light. It was not a relationship that could be described as warm. Prof. John Shy has ex-
plored the depths of this mutual antipathy during the 1760s, and
Prof. Alan Rogers has pushed the investigation farther back into the
hard years of the last great French and Indian war.[1] Of course it
would be an exaggeration to insist that Bostonians invariably had an
unfavorable view of the King's men—when the victorious royal regiments of Gen. Jeffery Amherst passed through Boston in September
1758 after reconquering Louisbourg, the townspeople greeted them
as heroes—but momentary gratitude does not erase a long-formed
and deeply habitual attitude, not when old memories and new provo-

---

* This paper was read at the May 1977 meeting.

1. John Shy, *Toward Lexington: The Role of the British Army in the Coming of the
American Revolution* (Princeton, 1965); Alan Rogers, *Empire and Liberty: American
Resistance to British Authority, 1755-1763* (Berkeley, 1974).

cations combine as they did a few years later.[2] Many Bostonians in the 1760s had keener recollections of Louisbourg in 1745 and 1746 than of Louisbourg in 1758, and other unpleasant impressions as well. To these I wish to draw your attention this afternoon, as I ask you to consider how New England colonists and British professional military-naval personnel perceived each other in the decades prior to 1760.

On March 24, 1745 a fleet of 52 vessels carrying some 2,800 Massachusetts volunteer soldiers set sail at Nantasket Road for Canso and ultimately Cape Breton Island. Other units coming from New Hampshire and Connecticut would raise this home-grown New England army to a strength of well over 3,000 men, destined to undertake the capture of the heavily fortified French town and base of Louisbourg. The plan for this audacious operation (which Francis Parkman with some degree of dramatic exaggeration labeled "a mad scheme") had been hatched in New England without benefit of professional advice or assistance from the British government in London, and although the aid of the Royal Navy, seemingly essential for such an amphibious assault, had been sought, the senior naval commander in the West Indies had declined the invitation, pleading lack of orders from home. The New Englanders were determined to get on with it anyway. What gave them such zeal? There is only one realistic answer—the expectation of material gain, including plunder, houses, and land.

Past experience might have given pause to those men of New England in that fateful spring of 1745. Only five years earlier hundreds of volunteer soldiers from New England had sailed for Port Royal on the island of Jamaica to participate with a very powerful British expedition in an attack upon rich Spanish holdings along the shores of the Caribbean. Those New Englanders, along with men from other colonies, had been lured to the Caribbean by the prospect of Spanish gold and other booty.[3] What they found between them and such alluring gains, as everyone who is familiar with the story of the ill-fated Cartagena expedition well knows, was a mountain of hardship and suffering, and widespread mortality.

2. *The Journal of Jeffery Amherst, Recording the Military Career of General Amherst in America from 1758 to 1763*, ed. J. Clarence Webster (Chicago, 1931), pp. 85–86.

3. *Documents Relative to the Colonial History of the State of New-York*, ed. E. B. O'Callaghan and B. Fernow, 15 vols. (Albany, 1856–1887), VI, 164, 167, 171.

In Jamaica during long weeks of waiting they had to undergo not only the inevitable and wasting maladies always associated with un- sanitary camps and contaminated drinking water, but also serious shortages of pay and other essentials resulting from the inefficiency and cupidity of the British military administration. Also corrosive to American morale may have been the ill-concealed disapproval of regular British officers, who viewed with professional disdain the ragged ranks of half-trained, half-disciplined provincial soldiers.[4] When the expedition finally did make its attack upon Cartagena in March 1741, units of the American regiment were employed either as laborers or support troops, not being considered sufficiently trust- worthy for more honorable service. And perhaps rightly so, if some reports are worthy of belief, for it was said that the Americans, when they came under Spanish fire, behaved like cowards. With the failure to take Cartagena, all troops were recalled to the ships. There they encountered the next horror—tropical fever. Hundreds of the Ameri- cans sickened and died along with the lads from England, Scotland, and Ireland. Others were called upon to help fill vacant billets in the ships of the Royal Navy, where they doubtless suffered all the mis- eries of that unpopular service. Many unhappy months later, when the surviving Americans were released to return home, there was only a pitiful remnant to carry back to the North American colonies dismal tales of hardship and degradation while serving under the King's colors.[5]

203

Among the grievances nursed by New Englanders at the time of the Cartagena expedition and afterwards was the hated use of im- pressment by the Royal Navy. Because of low pay and highly un- attractive conditions aboard ship, the Navy always seemed to be short of deckhands, and impressment of civilian mariners was the solution

4. William Blakeney to the Duke of Newcastle, Kingston, Dec. 14, 1740, Colonial Office 5:41 (Public Record Office); William Gooch to [the Duke of Newcastle], Jamaica, Jan. 7, 1740/41, C.O. 5:41; [Charles Knowles], Expedition to Carthagena in the Year 1741, C.O. 5:41 (see also Knowles' *Account of the Expedition to Carthagena, with Ex- planatory Notes and Observations* [Edinburgh, 1743]); John Colebrooke to Charles Han- bury Williams, Kingston, April 21, 1741, Admiralty 96:512 (Public Record Office); Boston *Weekly News-Letter*, March 12–19, 1740/41; *The Vernon Papers*, Navy Records Society, *Publications*, XCIX, ed. B. McL. Ranft ([London], 1958), 154.

5. C.O. 5:41, 42, *passim*; Holles Newcastle to Edward Vernon, Whitehall, Aug. 28, 1741, Additional MSS 32697 (British National Library); Boston *Weekly News-Letter*, July 30–Aug. 6, 1741; Robert Beatson, *Naval and Military Memoirs of Great Britain, from 1727 to 1783*, 6 vols. (Boston, 1972), I, 103, 105–106, 108–109.

commonly employed. The practice was perfectly legal, within certain stipulated bounds, but was deeply feared and resented in seafaring circles including maritime New England. Captains of the Royal Navy felt fully justified in pressing New Englanders because they believed, not without cause, that many of their seamen who deserted ship in New England ports had been deliberately enticed away by local ship owners and merchant captains who needed them on board their own vessels and could offer wages considerably higher than the King's pay. Desertion really was a constant, serious problem for the Navy, infuriating to a captain who was expected to run his ship efficiently. Compensating for lost men by impressing others from the very region that had lured them seemed fair enough. The usual method was to patrol just off the coast or lie at anchor near the entrance to a harbor, stop any incoming merchant vessel, and impress one or more members of the crew, according to need. Sometimes, too, an armed press gang would be sent into a waterfront town such as Boston to search for alleged deserters. In the process they often managed to seize a few unwilling but able hands. Local merchants deplored the practice, not because they felt any great sympathy for seamen, but because it interfered with the normal operation of mercantile shipping.[6]

The decade of the 1740s, with Britain engaged in a widespread naval war first against Spain and later against both Spain and France, proved to be a time when the Navy resorted to impressment with avidity. This naturally fed the flames of resentment, producing constant evasion and occasional violent resistance including riots. In the spring of 1741 Boston served as the stage for an angry mob of several hundred men armed with clubs, cutlasses, and even axes, seeking an interview with one Capt. James Scott, commander of H.M.S. *Astrea*, who was lodging in the town after having been involved in some impressment activity. The captain prudently saved himself an unfathomed depth of unpleasantness by having his host repeatedly assure the mob that the person they sought was elsewhere.[7] Further dif-

6. C.O. 5:42, *passim*; William Shirley to the Lords of the Admiralty, Boston, Oct. 19, 1742, Admiralty 1:3817; *Journals of the House of Representatives of Massachusetts* (Boston, 1919–   ), XX, 84, 98–99; Jesse Lemisch, "Jack Tar in the Streets: Merchant Seamen in the Politics of Revolutionary America," *William and Mary Quarterly*, 3d Ser., XXV (1968), 387.

7. Deposition of Thomas Hutchinson, March 18, 1741/42, Massachusetts Archives, VIII, 170–271 (see also *ibid.*, LXIV, 93–94, 96–98, 163, 166–176); William Shirley to Isaac Townsend, Boston, Sept. 12, 1746, Admiralty 1:480; *Journals of the House of Rep-*

ficulties over the impressment activity of Capt. Edward Hawke of H.M.S. *Portland,* also at Boston, arose later that same year.[*] As a result of these and similar episodes, by the time of the great operation against Louisbourg in 1745 a sizable portion of New England's farmers, artisans, shopkeepers, seamen, and merchants were inclined to be antagonistic toward Britain's professional military and naval personnel. Recollections of deeply resented abuse, real or fancied, at the hands of press gangs, and of unpleasant experiences with the royal forces at Jamaica and Cartagena, had become embedded in the New England mind. In similar fashion, British officers had become accustomed to assuming that the colonists not only made slovenly, unreliable soldiers but were totally averse to any form of cooperation with the legitimate claims of British national defense. It was not a very flattering perception on either side.

205

Louisbourg was a heavily fortified town situated on a spacious harbor where French warships, as well as commercial vessels of several nations, found ample anchorage. In addition to the many private dwellings within the great walls there were a number of small scattered settlements in the adjacent countryside, making the opportunities for plunder and other gain all the more attractive. That plus the promise that volunteer soldiers would serve only in a New England army under their own officers, which had not been the case at Cartagena, was what had lured so many colonists to the colors.

The man selected to be their general was a son of Maine, a prominent and well-respected businessman named William Pepperrell. Essential authorization and backing for the expedition had been provided by the royal governor of Massachusetts, the shrewdly ambitious lawyer-politician William Shirley, who had been a resident of Massachusetts since 1731 and was by this time quite closely identified with the colony and its interests. After the army had sailed from Nantasket Road, Governor Shirley learned that the Navy had decided to join the party after all. This introduced the third of the principal actors on the Anglo-American side—Commodore Peter Warren, who led a

resentatives of Massachusetts, xix, 32, 195–199; Boston *Weekly News-Letter,* April 24–30, May 28–June 4, June 4–11, June 25–July 2, 1741; Boston *Evening-Post,* June 8, 15, July 6, 1741; *New England Weekly Journal,* June 16, 23, 1741.

8. Boston *Weekly News-Letter,* Aug. 6–13, Oct. 8–15, Oct. 29–Nov. 5, 1741; *A Report of the Record Commissioners of the City of Boston, Containing the Records of Boston Selectmen, 1736 to 1742* (Boston, 1886), p. 315.

squadron up from the West Indies. For reasons which by now must be obvious, I suspect that if the New England troops cheered when Warren's ships arrived at Canso, the advance base for the operation, they did so with reservations and only because the presence of the Navy increased the chances for victory.

Technically, Warren's royal commission gave him the right to supreme command at Louisbourg, for Pepperrell's commission was derived only from Governor Shirley. Recognizing the delicacy of the situation, Shirley wrote urging Pepperrell to avoid any quarrel with his naval counterpart.[9] Warren, too, trod lightly, and throughout a long and difficult siege Pepperrell's men understood that their general was in charge of all the activity on land, while Warren commanded the blockading ships at sea, including the armed vessels contributed by several of the New England colonies. Any attempt by the commodore to exercise direct command over the provincial army would have aroused fury among the troops and deep resentment in Massachusetts. Tensions did develop between Pepperrell and Warren, as the latter became impatient with the slow progress being made by the army, but always the anger of both men was kept within manageable bounds, and in the end they sealed their professional acquaintance with harmony and mutual respect.[10] Warren's wife, I might add parenthetically, was an American.

My principal concern here is not with any high-level tension, important as that may have been, but rather with the relationships between the inferior officers and enlisted men of the New England army on the one hand and the inferior officers and seamen of the Royal Navy on the other. Here is where old scores would arise in a particularly significant way. The evidence is scattered through official correspondence deposited in the Public Record Office in London, numerous private journals kept by persons engaged in the operation, the Peter Warren Papers and a collection of Louisbourg letters in the William L. Clements Library, contemporary newspapers, and of course the Pepperrell Papers and the Louisbourg Papers in the library of this Society. Although the evidence is widely dispersed and some-

206

9. *Correspondence of William Shirley*, ed. Charles Henry Lincoln, 2 vols. (New York, 1912), I, 205; John A. Schutz, *William Shirley: King's Governor of Massachusetts* (Chapel Hill, 1961), pp. 96–97.

10. G. A. Rawlyk, *Yankees at Louisbourg*, University of Maine, *Studies*, Ser. II, No. 85 (Orono, 1967), *passim.*

what sparse, when assembled it does enable us to form a reasonably clear picture of Anglo-American tensions at Louisbourg in 1745 and 1746.

British officers who observed the New England troops on an untidy battleground were not favorably impressed either with their discipline or their efficiency. One Capt. James McDonald of the Royal Marines made himself quite unwelcome in the American camp by declaring that "our encampment was not regular, or that the soldiers did not march as hansome as old regular troops, their toes were not turned enough out, &c." This kind of gratuitous criticism annoyed no less a New Englander than Pepperrell himself, who later remarked with some petulance, "I thought we encampt as regular as the hills and valeys would admit of."[11] When sailors from the fleet came ashore with hard cash in hand, they found that the New Englanders had ample supplies of rum for sale. And because a siege was in progress, the sailors also had come armed with weapons for personal defense. Now the result was not exactly what you might expect—a new war breaking out. But there did erupt some confusion and trouble whose nature is not clearly depicted in the surviving records. What seems clear is that at some time during the sailors' visit ashore, some of the New Englanders, by trickery or otherwise, got their greedy hands on a considerable number of the jack-tars' weapons, which were King's arms, and as a consequence the rum-full and rueful seamen returned to their ships barehanded and shamefaced to confront the wrath of their commanding officers. Their weapons had disappeared ashore. The commodore suspected, no doubt correctly, that if the missing arms were to be found anywhere it would be in the American camp.[12] Then came a further surprise. Some American weapons were found on board the English ships, which suggests that the sailors were able to take as well as give. Warren dutifully returned the stolen property with an explanatory note to Pepperrell saying, "I send you some arms belonging to your troops that my rascals brought of, and have lost a great many of ours."[13] The records do not reveal whether any of the Navy's missing weapons were ever discovered; the chances are

207

11. Massachusetts Historical Society, *Collections* (Boston, 1792–   ), 6th Ser., X, 330. See also *ibid.*, 1st Ser., I, 29.

12. *Ibid.*, 6th Ser., X, 162, 164.

13. *Ibid.*, 6th Ser., X, 169, 172. See also William Pepperrell to Peter Warren, Louisbourg, May 13 and 16, 1745, Louisbourg Papers (Massachusetts Historical Society).

that they eventually were sold for profit and perhaps taken to Boston.

Victory at Louisbourg was envisioned as the result of a massive combined assault by land and sea. A day or two before that decisive assault was to take place, Pepperrell actually sent out to the ships about 600 of his men to assist the Navy in its part of the attack, a purely temporary assignment but one that surely resurrected unpleasant stories of the Caribbean in 1741 and impressment in general. At about the same time, Warren made a visit to the army, addressed the assembled troops drawn up for the occasion, told them his ships were going to force the harbor, and urged them to fight their way into the fortress on the land side. The New Englanders, possibly excited by the commodore's oratory, responded with three cheers, which proved to be very nearly the last true echo of goodwill he was to hear from that source.[14] As it happened, the grand assault by land and by sea never was made, for only a short time before it was to begin the French capitulated.

Preceding the actual surrender were certain negotiations, the full details of which may never be known. It does appear that Warren sent a personal emissary into Louisbourg with advice that the French had better surrender to the Royal Navy in order to avoid the uncontrolled pillaging that would be the consequence, it was said, of a surrender to the New Englanders.[15] If such a suggestion was officially made by the Navy, it was premature, and when the French did come to the point of terms, they addressed themselves to both commanders. Then began a strange race between the army and the Navy to be first into the fortress. Pepperrell proposed to the French commander a time when the first units of the army would enter, but before that time arrived, Warren, it seems, had himself conveyed to the town by boat and conferred with the French commander, who apprised him of Pepperrell's proposal. Thereupon the commodore addressed to his

14. James Douglas Journal, DOU/1, June 4 and 16, 1745 (National Maritime Museum) (similar to the log kept aboard H.M.S. *Vigilant* by Thomas Shortland, Admiral Douglas Papers, Slipcase C, William L. Clements Library); William Pepperrell to Peter Warren, Louisbourg, June 19, 1745, Louisbourg Papers; Connecticut Historical Society, *Collections* (Hartford, 1860–1932), I, 135; American Antiquarian Society, *Proceedings* (Worcester, 1843–), XX, 164; Massachusetts Historical Society, *Collections*, 1st Ser., I, 44, 6th Ser., X, 301.

15. *The Anonymous Lettre d'un Habitant de Louisbourg*, University of Toronto, *Studies*, History, 2d Ser., I, ed. George M. Wrong (Toronto, 1897), 57–58; George A. Rawlyk, New England and Louisbourg, 1744–1745 (Ph.D. diss., Rochester, 1966), p. 295.

New England colleague yet another letter. "It is not regular, you will please to observe," lectured Warren, "to do it till the articles are ratifyed on both sides, which I will hasten to get done."[16] He continued, "*I am sorry to find by your letter a kind of jealousy, which I thought you would never conceive of me* . . . and give me leave to tell you, I do not want at this time to acquire reputation, as I flatter myself mine has long before I came here been pretty well established." A French inhabitant of Louisbourg who was in a position to view these peculiar maneuvers on the part of the English and the Americans later remarked that "one could never have told that these troops belonged to the same nation and obeyed the same prince."[17] It hardly seems necessary to point out that 31 years later, they did not.

209

So long as the siege had continued, Anglo-American friction was kept to a moderate level, but once the articles of capitulation had been signed, the tensions began to increase. In fact, the 12 months following the surrender, when Warren's ships rode at anchor in the littered harbor and Pepperrell's men garrisoned the battered town, constitute a most instructive period for the student of Anglo-American relations. During that period the officers and men of both services walked the streets of Louisbourg and doubtless sometimes found themselves sheltering under the same roofs. Inevitably there were inter-service arguments as to whether the army or the Navy contributed more to the victory, which must have afforded the rueful French inhabitants a modicum of amusement. Capt. Philip Durell of the Royal Navy was quick to advance the claim of his own service. The French, he said, "delivered the Keys of the Town to Mr. *Warren,* agreeable to Articles specified in the Capitulation, saying, That if it had not been for the Ships, the Land Forces would never have been in Possession of the Place." Furthermore, according to this same officer, the governor of Louisbourg had "insisted that our Forces [the Navy] should enter the Town, and not the *Americans,* whom they do not like."[18] Just as vehemently the Americans insisted that the French

16. Massachusetts Historical Society, *Collections,* 1st Ser., I, 46.

17. *Anonymous Lettre,* p. 58.

18. Philip Durell, *A Particular Account Of the Taking Cape Breton From the French, by Admiral Warren, and Sir William Pepperrell, The 17th of June, 1745* (London, 1745), pp. 3–5. Another correspondent on board one of Warren's ships testified that Louisbourg "Surenderd to the Fleet Upon Condittions, and We took Poss[ess]ion of the town and all their fortifications." Joseph Clement to James West, [Virginia, 1745], Additional MSS 34728. The question of which commander formally received the keys of Louisbourg be-

had capitulated not out of fear of a naval attack but because of the immense destruction wrought by the army's artillery.[19] Wrote one New Englander, "There is No Harmony between the Marine officers and N E ones. I take it to be because one stands on what they have Done and the others on what they are men with the Kings Commision. One of them Has been Pleas'd to tell the French Officers that He was the first man that went into the Grand Battrey which was absolutely false for not one man was ashore from the ships till 4 days after. Another of them told them that He had Lay'd 17 Nights in the trenches which was as false for he never was there but twice and both times staid not above ½ an hour in the Whole."[20]

Bickering such as this, not at all good-natured in tone, must have gone on for days in the damp and fog-shrouded town whenever New Englanders and Navy men found themselves together. At worst this was annoying, but there was a much more serious aspect. New England officers, and colonial leaders back in Massachusetts as well, suspected an even deeper thrust on the part of the Navy, a thrust that might well deprive Pepperrell, his army, and all New England of the ultimate advantages they believed they merited by their victory. Shortly after the capitulation Warren had dispatched a personal emissary to carry the good news to the British Ministry. Pepperrell apparently had not thought it necessary to match this move with an emissary of his own, and this gave rise to fears that the Navy's version, spoken first, would give all the glory to Warren and the Navy, with the probable result that the royal gratitude would fall in that direction.[21]

210

came a matter of concern in Boston, as did the equally trivial but nonetheless sensitive question of why Warren's name preceded Pepperrell's in the articles of capitulation. Massachusetts Historical Society, *Collections*, 1st Ser., I, 50–51, 6th Ser., X, 330.

19. W. Clarke's letter, Louisbourg, Dec. 13, 1745, Davis Papers, II (Massachusetts Historical Society).

20. Thomas Waldron to [Richard Waldron], Louisbourg, July 9, 1745, Louisbourg Letters (Clements Library).

21. Massachusetts Historical Society, *Collections*, 1st Ser., I, 50–51, 52–54, 6th Ser., X, 341–342. On paper, at least, both Pepperrell and Warren were generous with praise. Warren's letter to the Duke of Newcastle, dated the day after the surrender, included the interesting observation that the American colonists "have the highest notions of the Rights, and Libertys, of Englishmen, and indeed are almost Levellers, they must know when, where, how, and what service they are going upon, and be Treated in a manner that few Military Bred Gentlemen wou'd condecend to, but if they do the work in which they are Engag'd, every other Ceremony shou'd in my opinion be wink'd at." C.O. 5:44. A day later Pepperrell informed the Duke that "Nothing could have contributed more to the

The army's extreme sensitivity regarding all special claims by the Navy was to no small degree owing to one of the terms included in the articles of capitulation. All portable private property belonging to the French inhabitants was to remain in their possession and, insofar as practicable, go with them when they were evacuated. As Pepperrell must have known of this provision and accepted it, he should not have been surprised at his soldiers' reaction. During the siege the New England troops had found opportunity to scrape the environs fairly clean but without gaining any great wealth, and so they had looked forward all the more to getting their hands upon the French goods within Louisbourg itself. Now, after the surrender, they found this booty strictly denied them, with sentries stationed throughout the town to prevent unauthorized plundering. The New Englanders saw their dreams of personal gain rapidly dissolving, much as similar dreams had gone glimmering at Cartagena, and they were furious. When Pepperrell wrote to the Duke of Newcastle that his men had "generously acquiesced in the loss of the plunder they expected from the riches of the city," he was ignoring the truth in order to plaster over a very ugly situation.[22] Closer to the mark was an anonymous diarist at Louisbourg who had heard "hot Talk about a mobbs Risin and they Say that they Did Rise So as to git what they wanted."[23] One is not surprised to discover that some of the bitterly disappointed troops began stealing and concealing.[24] Under these circumstances, legitimate gains proved slender indeed. The army did lay claim to a number of French craft found sunk in the harbor or stranded along its edges, and some vendible material was salvaged, but it made a poor show beside the lands, houses, and goods for which the soldiers had thirsted so avidly all during the siege. One Massachusetts soldier wrote in his journal what may be taken to represent the common experience: "Received part of plunder, 9 small tooth combs."[25]

211

Success of his Majesty's Arms, than the Command of the Squadron being given to a Gentleman of Commodore Warren's distinguished Character: he is of such a Disposition as makes him greatly beloved by the people in New England, and in the Colonies, in General." C.O. 5:44.

22. Massachusetts Historical Society, *Collections*, 6th Ser., X, 300.

23. *Louisbourg Journals, 1745*, ed. Louis Effingham De Forest (New York, 1932), p. 94.

24. Connecticut Historical Society, *Collections*, I, 149, 153–154; Massachusetts Historical Society, *Collections*, 6th Ser., X, 32.

25. Essex Institute, *Historical Collections* (Salem, 1849–   ), VI, 194. See also "Benjamin Stearns's Diary, 11 March–2 August, 1745," ed. J. C. L. Clark, *Acadiensis*, VIII

All this was especially devastating to morale because of what the Navy was managing to accomplish at the same time. Here let it be said that Commodore Warren was not the man to neglect his own fortune. While stationed in the West Indies prior to becoming involved in the Louisbourg operation, he had profited greatly by the system in which the proceeds from the sale of enemy prizes taken by the Navy were distributed to all participating personnel, with a very large chunk reserved for the successful commander. At Louisbourg, after the capitulation, Warren saw to it that the French flag was left gaily flying over the town. As a result, during the course of the summer several French merchantmen returning from the South Seas and the East Indies, richly laden, dropped in unaware and were handily seized by Warren's alert and eager men-of-war. It was a perfect trap. Warren stood to gain immensely, his subordinates in the naval service would get their share, but the troops ashore, whether officers or enlisted men, had no access to any part of the prize money.[26] Stories of the Navy's great good fortune soon reached Boston, where they simply intensified the current unrest over the apparent slighting of the army. The *Evening-Post* for September 23, 1745 carried a report that Warren had pulled in nearly £500,000 sterling, adding gloomily that "what Share the poor Men in the Garrison are to have of this mighty Treasure (which seem'd all to be intended for *them*, as a Reward for their signal Service) is not yet certainly know[n]." The answer, of course, was nothing, and that really rankled.

Toward the end of July the New Englanders' resentment at being denied the anticipated fruits of victory while watching the men of the Royal Navy systematically building up large credits approached the

(1908), 325–326; Massachusetts Historical Society, *Proceedings* (Boston, 1859–), 2d Ser., XI, 437–438; Massachusetts Historical Society, *Collections*, 6th Ser., X, 33, 36–37, 40–41.

26. "The Success which has attended mee in this Conquest has been a great Addition to my fortune," stated Warren frankly on Aug. 28, 1745. George Clinton Papers, II (New-York Historical Society). See also Warren's letter of Aug. 21 in the same collection. Julian Gwyn, *The Enterprising Admiral: The Personal Fortune of Admiral Sir Peter Warren* (Montreal, 1974), explores this subject in detail. See also Philip Judd's Journal, July 29 and Aug. 2, 1745 (Connecticut Historical Society); "Extracts From Letters Written by Capt. Geo. Curwen of Salem, Mass., to His Wife, While on the Expedition Against Louisbourgh," Essex Institute, *Historical Collections*, III, 188; Thomas Waldron to Richard Waldron, Louisbourg, July 24–26, 1745, Louisbourg Letters; Joseph Clement to James West, [Virginia, 1745], Additional MSS 34728; [William Shirley], *Memoirs of the Principal Transactions of the Last War Between the English and French in North America* (London, 1757), pp. 60–61; Boston *Weekly News-Letter*, Aug. 15, 1745; Boston *Gazette*, Aug. 20, 1745; Massachusetts Historical Society, *Collections*, 6th Ser., X, 375.

boiling point. By that time the provincial troops had had more than five weeks of contact with Navy personnel in and around Louisbourg, involving considerable guying back and forth, boasts and threats, envy and contempt, and somewhere just below the surface, recollections of Cartagena and impressment, all of which helped inflate the ugly mood. On the warm and pleasant morning of July 29 the army, including some replacements arrived since the surrender, was drawn up for a speech by the general and another by the commodore. All armies which have had to endure difficult circumstances are acquainted with such addresses from on high, which may be called "incentive-raisers" or "morale-boosters." If the dispirited New Englanders cheered Warren at the end of his oration, as they had done on a previous occasion during the siege, it may have been because he took this opportunity to present them with three butts of wine, enough for every man to enjoy a pint. That very same day H.M.S. *Chester* and H.M.S. *Mermaid* proudly escorted into the harbor the crestfallen French merchantman *Heron*, bulging with a valuable cargo.[27] Sometime between the last speech and the arrival of the *Heron*, or possibly even later in the day, some New England troops and some sailors of the Royal Navy got into a free-swinging brawl. Unfortunately, the records at this juncture are anything but full, but I myself find it almost impossible not to believe that the affray was intimately linked with the two events just mentioned—the sudden availability of wine and the arrival of the Navy's latest prize.

213

Easy to imagine is some heavy drinking by groups of New England soldiers who were feeling very much victimized and therefore prone to self-pity and helpless anger, their roistering about Louisbourg loaded with emotional dynamite ready stacked and fused, their encountering similar groups of seamen who doubtless pointed with high glee to their new prize anchored under the guns of the Royal Navy and, without so much as being asked, freely offered estimates of the vast bounty to be distributed among the men of the ships involved in her capture. There must have been a crescendo of shouting, then shoving, and finally blows. Other men of the army and Navy, attracted by the uproar, would come running, and the brawl would intensify and spread. My description, of course, is imaginary, and I cannot be certain even of what triggered the trouble, but the account I have con-

27. American Antiquarian Society, *Proceedings*, XX, 172-173; Philip Judd's Journal, July 29, 1745; Essex Institute, *Historical Collections*, VI, 190.

structed seems highly plausible. We do not know how long it took the officers of army and Navy to restore peace among these infuriated brothers-in-arms. What is virtually certain, it seems to me, is that New England fists had found a way to vent a vast accumulation of resentment against the attitude and the ways of Britain's professional armed forces.[28]

Pepperrell's men were fed up and eager to go home. Weary from a hard campaign, sick of their foul quarters and disintegrating apparel, disappointed in the material gains of victory, and galled by the attitude and behavior of Warren's men, the New Englanders now reminded their commanders that they had enlisted only for the duration of the campaign against Louisbourg. In their view that campaign was over, and all troops who had been present during the siege were entitled to a quick discharge and a free voyage back to Boston. Pepperrell and Warren, in spite of any personal differences they might have, were united in recognizing that Louisbourg had to be garrisoned by New England troops until regular units could be brought from distant bases. Could the increasingly restive men of the siege army be kept under control while temporary replacements were being assembled and transported from New England to relieve them? Letters from Louisbourg brought home the problem to Governor Shirley, who was becoming more and more uneasy over the whole situation, including the sensitive issue of command and the disposal of the rich French prizes.

Well before the outbreak of inter-service violence, Shirley had decided that the situation was grave enough to require his presence at Louisbourg, and began making arrangements for an official visit. He arrived in mid-August, saluted by booming New England cannon, an honor that he himself had taken pains to arrange well in advance. Pepperrell and Warren greeted him warmly, eager to reassure him about their personal relations and hoping, as the commodore put it, that Shirley would be able to "keep The Troops easy with regard to their Construction of his Proclamation, which assures them they shou'd be only kept here till the Expedition was over, which they

28. So far as I am aware, the brawl is mentioned in only two of the many Louisbourg journals, which seems rather strange. Benjamin Stearns called it "Sumtheing of a Crumuge [scrimmage] Between Sum of the Land: armey and the Seafarreing men." *Acadiensis*, VIII, 329. Dudley Bradstreet of Groton, an officer in the same regiment as Stearns, wrote of "a Great Disturbance betweene the men of wars men and our men which was Exceeding hot." Massachusetts Historical Society, *Proceedings*, 2d Ser., XI, 440.

think is now."²⁹ The governor's visit stretched on for three months, as he sought to mollify the discontented New Englanders and deal decisively with incipient mutiny, promising the men that they would be released no later than the end of May. Finally, on November 27 Shirley and his entourage sailed for home, leaving behind Pepperrell, Warren, and an army not at all pleased with the prospect of spending the winter on windswept Cape Breton Island.³⁰

In the meantime, important decisions had been made in England which would affect the New Englanders remaining at Louisbourg. Warren, promoted to the rank of rear admiral, was appointed governor of Cape Breton. Two regiments of regular troops were ordered transferred from Gibraltar to Louisbourg for garrison duty. They were to be supplemented with two new regiments formed by enlisting troops from among Pepperrell's army and other colonists, one to be commanded by Pepperrell and the other by Shirley.³¹ The raising of these two regiments proceeded slowly, as might have been predicted.

Because the provincial garrison had hoped to be relieved before winter, the New Englanders had not been very thorough in preparing good, weathertight quarters for themselves, and when the severe weather did come they suffered greatly. Inadequate diet together with constant exposure to the damp and cold opened the way for debilitating disease which spread through the huddled companies like a plague. Conditions were made even worse by a shortage of fuel, forcing the men to scour the ruins for loose boards and other pieces of burnable wood, and even to tear down portions of their living quarters in order to keep the fires going. Men sickened and died by the dozens, and were committed to shallow graves laboriously scraped out of the frozen earth. A total of at least 900, or approximately one of every three New Englanders in the garrison, perished.³²

215

29. Warren to Clinton, Louisbourg, Aug. 21, 1745, Clinton Papers, II. See also *Boston Gazette*, July 30, 1745; Massachusetts Historical Society, *Collections*, 6th Ser., X, 322-324, 335-336, 341-342.

30. [Shirley], *Memoirs*, pp. 66-71; Peter Warren to Thomas Corbett, Louisbourg, Nov. 23, 1745, Admiralty 1:480; Boston *Gazette*, Sept. 10, 1745; Boston *Weekly News-Letter*, Sept. 12, 1745; Philip Judd's Journal, Oct. 19 and Nov. 27, 1745.

31. Duke of Newcastle to William Shirley, Whitehall, Sept. 11, 1745, Additional MSS 32705; Massachusetts Historical Society, *Collections*, 6th Ser., X, 419-420.

32. Peter Warren to Thomas Corbett, Louisbourg, [Jan. or Feb. 1745/46], Admiralty 1:480; William Shirley to the Duke of Newcastle, Boston, May 10, 1746, C.O. 5:901; Charles Knowles to the Admiralty, Louisbourg, July 5, 1746, Admiralty 1:2007; Charles Knowles to [the Duke of Newcastle], Louisbourg, July 9, 1746, C.O. 5:44; Massachusetts

The appalling conditions at Louisbourg from December to April may have put a temporary damper on Anglo-American strife. On December 30 a joint declaration by Pepperrell and Warren urged upon all personnel the "maintaining and promoting an universal good agreement and friendly correspondence, without any distinction in respect of the different parts of his Majesty's dominions to which they belong, or to their being in the land or sea service, but all treating each other as loyal and brave subjects." The two commanders went on to warn that their displeasure would fall upon anyone who should "cast any national reflections on any of his Majesty's subjects here, or use any other reproachful or abusive language tending to stir up disputes or quarrells."[32] Probably, as it turned out, the men simply were too miserable to bother others in similar circumstances.

By April the moderating weather and the decline of disease had begun to raise the men's spirits. On the 21st of that month arrived the bulk of the two regiments from Gibraltar, lending substance to a memory that had never long been out of the minds of the New England troops—Shirley's promise that they would be on their way home by the end of May. Nine days later was the first anniversary of the army's successful assault landing. While the impatient New Englanders were awaiting the next development, and possibly sizing up the redcoats at a distance, Commodore Charles Knowles, Warren's successor as governor of Cape Breton, arrived at Louisbourg. Knowles had had previous experience of American troops at Cartagena, and his opinion of them was anything but flattering. Their officers, he once wrote, were "Blacksmiths, Taylors, Barbers, Shoemakers, and all the Bandity them Colonies affords," which perhaps says more about the commodore than about the Americans.[34] Upon viewing the unkempt New Englanders he found in and around Louisbourg, Knowles had no desire to delay their departure. Commenting that the town was "the most miserable Ruinous place I ever beheld," he proceeded to lay most of the blame for the difficulties of the past months upon the provincial troops.[35] To the Duke of Newcastle he wrote that:

216

Historical Society, *Collections*, 6th Ser., X, 84, 437–445. Pepperrell estimated in May that the sickness of the past winter had caused about 1,200 deaths. Letter to the Duke of Newcastle, Louisbourg, May 21, 1746, C.O. 5:44.

33. Massachusetts Historical Society, *Collections*, 6th Ser., X, 79.

34. Expedition to Carthagena in the Year 1741, C.O. 5:41.

35. Charles Knowles to the Admiralty, Louisbourg, July 5, 1746, Admiralty 1:2007.

The confused, dirty, beastly Condition I found this Place in is not to be expressed, and I almost Suspect being credited when I tell your Grace, that these New England Folks were so lazy, that they not only pulled one End of the House down to burn which they lived in, but even buried their dead under the Floors and did their Filth in the Other corners of the House rather than go out of Doors in the Cold: They were of so Obstinate and licentious a disposition that not being properly under Military Discipline there was no keeping them in any Order, and as much as I rejoyce at getting rid of them, so do I pitty Mr. Warren who was Obliged to be so long amongst them."

Obviously, Warren had been pouring all his frustrations into his successor's receptive ears.

In particular, Knowles was appalled at the quantities of rum being brought into Louisbourg by New England vessels and traded among the troops there. He was positive in his assertion that profligate ingestion of this fiery beverage during the past winter had been the principal cause of the bad health and heavy mortality in Pepperrell's army. Acting decisively, the new governor revoked the licenses of all the sutlers and ordered all rum to be deposited under guard in the casemates of the citadel, with the result that many thousands of gallons were secured. Even with that, according to the commodore's observation, great quantities of liquor remained concealed among the troops, as evidenced by the prevalence of drunkenness for some time thereafter." Knowles, however, proved to be one of those great men not prone to worship the idol of consistency. His own subsequent experience of a Louisbourg winter, in 1746–1747, helped give him a somewhat different perspective on the merits of New England rum. In January we find him informing the Duke of Newcastle that allowing the men rum and spruce beer "I have found so necessary (and indeed it has proved so beneficial to them) that I am convinc'd the greatest part would have been dead without it."" By then, I am pleased to report, all the New England troops except those who had enlisted in the King's forces were far away from Louisbourg, probably at their own firesides in Boston or Groton or Worcester.

Presumably the story could be said to end here, but we know well enough that it did not. Adverse feelings about British professional

217

36. Charles Knowles to [the Duke of Newcastle], Louisbourg, July 9, 1746, C.O. 5:44.
37. Charles Knowles to the Duke of Newcastle, Louisbourg, July 8, 1746, C.O. 5:44.
38. Charles Knowles to the Duke of Newcastle, Louisbourg, Jan. 20, 1746/47, C.O. 5:44. See also Knowles' letter of Nov. 8, 1746 in the same volume.

forces did not subside quickly, for memories persisted and new grievances developed. Even in 1745 and 1746, when Americans were
garrisoning and supplying Louisbourg, the old game of impressment
had been continuing along the New England coast. Navy captains
based at Louisbourg charged that their men were being enticed and
concealed on board the very New England ships that plied to and
from the conquered French base. The more this occurred, the more
determined were the captains of the King's ships to recoup their losses
in New England.³⁹ After two men were fatally injured by a press
gang in Boston, local people complained emphatically about "the
Behaviour of the Officers, who with their lawless Rabble like Ruffians
entred the Houses of the Inhabitants in the Night, have committed
Murders, particularly upon two brave Men who had been in constant
Service in the late Expedition against *Cape-Breton*."⁴⁰

218

Impressment invariably aroused very strong emotion in Massachusetts. The captain of H.M.S. *Shirley*, it was said, "dar'd not set his
foot on shore for four Months for fear of being prosecuted . . . , or
murther'd by the mob for pressing."⁴¹ When in 1747 none other
than Commodore Knowles arrived in Boston with a squadron which
pressed 40 or more men, the elements of the populace most directly
threatened took matters into their own hands and began what quickly
developed into a dangerous series of riots. The angry mob made un-
mistakably clear its opinion of impressment by seizing several of
Knowles' officers who happened to be ashore, cracking open the head
of Boston's high sheriff and setting his terrified assistant in the stocks,
breaking windows in the Province House, where the General Court
was sitting, and causing Governor Shirley himself to take refuge in
Castle William.⁴² It all sounds much like a rehearsal for 1768.

39. Admiralty Office to the Earl of Granville, Feb. 11, 1745/46, State Papers 42:30
(Public Record Office); Isaac Townsend to William Shirley, Louisbourg, Aug. 17, 1746,
Admiralty 1:480; Boston *Weekly News-Letter*, Nov. 21, 28, Dec. 12, 1745; Boston
Evening-Post, Nov. 25 (Supplement), Dec. 9 and (Supplement), 1745; Boston *Gazette*,
Nov. 26, 1745.

40. *Journals of the House of Representatives of Massachusetts*, XXII, 205.

41. Peter Warren to Thomas Corbett, Louisbourg, June 2, 1746, Admiralty 1:480.

42. American Antiquarian Society, *Proceedings*, LXXIII, 113; [Samuel P. Savage's]
letter of Nov. 21, 1747, Samuel P. Savage Papers, II (Massachusetts Historical Society);
Journals of the House of Representatives of Massachusetts, XXIV, 212–216; Hopson to [the
Duke of Newcastle], Louisbourg, Nov. 30, 1747, C.O. 5:44; Shirley, *Correspondence*, I,
406–423; Charles Knowles to [the Admiralty], St. Kitts, Jan. 18, 1747/48, Admiralty

Let me close by summarizing briefly. Long before 1745 New Englanders had been having experiences with the British regular forces, as at Cartagena, which aroused mutual antipathy. The Louisbourg experience in 1745 and 1746 helped reinforce these unfavorable perceptions. Shirley, Pepperrell, and Warren all placed a high value upon harmonious relations at Louisbourg, but each was ambitious for promotion and personal gain, and correspondingly sensitive to slights and denigration. Pepperrell's officers came hoping to increase their fortunes by the acquisition of French real estate and plunder, his men expected at least good booty, but their dreams went largely unrealized, while the Navy swept up valuable ships and cargoes. In every respect, the long period of garrison duty after the conquest proved disillusioning for all involved. British regular officers came to perceive the provincials as undisciplined, unreliable, and sometimes cowardly. As soldiers the New Englanders seemed to reflect traits in colonial society as a whole which the disciplined professionals later would condemn as irresponsible or even disloyal. Provincial troops, for their part, tended to consider the professionals unsympathetic, disdainful, and downright arrogant. The practice of impressment, continuing all through this period and with especial intensity at Boston and certain other major seaports, was a constant reinforcement for these mutually antipathetic perceptions.

During the great international war of the 1750s the large-scale use of British regular forces in North America, far beyond anything previously known, increased the effect on both sides. This, in turn, undoubtedly contributed to the intensifying Anglo-American tensions of the 1760s and 1770s, which culminated, as we all know, in a major event that occurred precisely 200 years before the recent Bicentennial. Anglo-American tensions at Louisbourg are an important part of that story.

219

1:234; Boston *Evening-Post*, Nov. 30, Dec. 7, 1747; Boston *Weekly News-Letter*, Dec. 17, 1747; John Lax and William Pencak, "The Knowles Riot and the Crisis of the 1740's in Massachusetts," *Perspectives in American History*, X (1976), 161–214.

Warfare and Political Change in Mid-Eighteenth-Century Massachusetts

by

William Pencak[1]

'Join or Die.' So Benjamin Franklin warned his fellow American colonists shortly after the French and Indian War began in 1754. Beneath a diagram of a snake severed in thirteen pieces depicting the fragmented provinces of British North America, he lamented 'the extreme difficulty of bringing so many different governments and assemblies to agree in any speedy and effectual measures for our common defense and security, while our enemies have the very great advantage of being under one direction, with one council and one purse'.[2] Franklin's argument applied not only to the need for combination at this juncture among the mainland provinces. It articulated the particular case of a general truth: states hampered by internal bickering fail to mobilise their military resources effectively and rapidly find their domestic weaknesses compounded by impotence in foreign affairs.

Franklin need only have turned to eighteenth-century Europe for proof of his statement. Successful states developed efficient means of collecting taxes, conscripting soldiers, and neutralising resistance to political centralisation. Only such techniques could forge the principal tool of national survival—a competitive military establishment. The sorry decline of Poland, Sweden, and the Ottoman Empire from their seventeenth-century glory can be attributed to the monarch's inability to check the autonomy of the nobility. On the other hand, Prussia and England overcame the handicap of relatively small populations by developing brutal but effective means of recruiting respectively the most powerful army and navy in Europe, and succeeded in integrating the landowning class into civil and military administration. France, Austria, and Russia represented the intermediate case of large nations which eliminated local privileges and opposition intermittently and imperfectly, but maintained major power status through sheer size and periodically strong rulers. Nations able to neutralise the institution eighteenth-century Americans associated with liberty—the legislative assembly—survived and increased in strength; states too tender of the corporate privileges of their subjects deteriorated or expired.[3]

Yet the American colonies neither joined nor died during the great mid-century wars which finally eliminated the French menace. True, every mainland province furnished troops and supplies for the common cause, However. this voluntary cooperation proved so ineffectual that in addition to provincial levies, Britain had to furnish regular regiments greater in number than the French-Canadian forces in order to bring the war to an end. Even after Wolfe defeated Montcalm on the Plains of Abraham, British troops had to be summoned to deal with pockets of Indian resistance in Pennsylvania and South Carolina. Throughout the French and Indian War, British officers and administrators complained of soldiers who deserted or refused to fight outside their home colonies, merchants who traded with the enemy, and assemblies which incomprehensibly did not vote adequate supplies and quarters for the very troops which guaranteed their existence. Such resistance to a more centralised administration, understandable in terms of the eighteenth-century Whig ideology by which the colonists measured their freedom, appeared suicidal in the context of modern world history which has required nations to stand united or fall divided. Only the knowledge that eighty thousand French Canadians could never destroy them, coupled with the fact of assistance from the mother country, permitted the Americans the luxury of adhering to liberties rendered obsolete by the realities of European international politics.[4]

221

However, even if the North American colonies were united only minimally among themselves, it can be demonstrated convincingly that at least one province underwent, with respect to its *internal* government and administration, a transformation remarkably similar to the state-building process of the great European powers. Between the outbreak of King George's War in1740 and the signing of the Peace of Paris in 1763, the Massachusetts General Court roused itself from a quarter-century of lethargy and achieved feats of taxation and mobilisation which Frederick the Great might have envied. Under the tutelage of William Shirley, governor from 1741 to 1756, the Bay Colony changed from one of the most truculent provinces in the empire to the most cooperative. However, the province's mobilisation contained the seeds of its organisers' destruction: the suffering engendered convinced the people that both imperial and local leaders posed serious threats to their liberties and well-being.

To effect this about-face, the very nature of Massachusetts' political system had to change. A legislature primarily concerned with obstructing Britain's plans to strengthen royal authority and with resolving disputes presented by towns and individuals became an active body which designed and implemented vast military campaigns. A potent faction devoted to the royal prerogative developed virtually *ex nihilo* supplanting the influence of the previously dominant country faction which had convinced the assembly that any increase in the governor's power destroyed popular liberty. New systems of finance and public administration, and a new sense of mission emerged. For a quarter century, Massachusetts waged total war.

Massachusetts' pre-eminence among the American colonies in fighting King George's (1740–1748) and the French and Indian (1754–63) wars is indisputable. In the latter conflict, the Bay Colony outspent Virginia, the second most zealous province, £818,000 sterling to £385,000 collectively, or £20 to £14 per adult male. Annual levies from 1755 to 1759 numbered approximately 7000 soldiers; 5000 men were mustered in 1760 and 3000 per year until 1763. Such an army for a province with approximately 50,000 adult males meant that war was being waged on a scale comparable to the great wars of modern times.[5] And in King George's War, Massachusetts had the field almost to itself. Aside from grudging and minimal support from New York, the other New England colonies, and even Britain, the expedition which conquered Louisbourg in 1745 and the abortive Canada and Crown Point campaign of the following year were projected, manned, and supplied almost entirely by the Bay Colony.[6]

During King William's and Queen Anne's Wars, in 1690, 1706, 1709, and 1711, Massachusetts had prepared massive but unsuccessful expeditions to eliminate French power in Canada. Following the Peace of Utrecht in 1713, however, Massachusetts' government lost much of its energy. The province devoted itself to settling the recently won frontier, trying to solve the perplexing problem of a rapidly depreciating currency, and foiling the efforts of royal governors to increase their power at the expense of the lower house. Localism, ideological wrangling, stalemate, and stagnation best describe the politics of the interwar period. At this time 'the legislative agenda,' as Michael Zuckerman has noted, 'was substantially set by petitions from the towns and their inhabitants'.[7] The General Court functioned, as its name implies, primarily as a court, settling disputes that became too hot to handle on the town level, determining the ownership of frontier lands, granting licenses to sell liquor, and voting an annual budget of approximately £10,000 sterling. Most of the money went to pay the salaries of the legislators, judges, and the handful of soldiers who garrisoned Boston's Castle William and a few outposts in Maine. During the legislative session of 1743–1744, for instance, the last year before the Louisbourg campaign, 307 resolves passed. General provincial business accounted for only 98, and most of these consisted of routine matters such as voting salaries for all provincial officials from the governor to the door-keeper, approving the accounts of the county treasurers, and passing on bills to entertain various dignitaries. Over two-thirds of the business consisted of ajudicating items of interest to particular towns and individuals.[8]

In addition to settling local problems, the three branches of the Court devoted much of their energy to defining the limits of their respective powers. Beginning in 1720, Governor Samuel Shute (1716–1723) insisted that he had a right to veto the assembly's choice of its speaker, especially when it selected the obnoxious Elisha Cooke, who had repeatedly referred to Shute as a 'great blockhead' and once accosted him, while intoxicated and semi-dressed, late at night on a Boston street. The matter was only resolved in 1726 when the Privy Council forced the deputies to accept an Explanatory Charter which decided the case in Shute's favour.[9]

A similar dispute occurred when the home government saddled Shute's successor, Lieutenant-Governor William Dummer (1723–1728), with an instruction requiring the annual redemption of Massachusetts' paper currency—which derived its value by being redeemable for taxes in specified years—to forestall the inflation which had begun to affect British creditors. The house responded by refusing to vote any appropriations at all in 1727 until Dummer caved in and violated his orders. Massachusetts managed to circumvent instructions reducing its money supply until 1741, when parliamentary intransigence led to the abortive Land and Silver Bank schemes which nearly tore the province apart.[10]

The remaining two governors during the interwar years fared no better.

William Burnet (1728–1729) spent his entire year and three months in Massachusetts insisting that the assembly should permanently guarantee the executive a salary of at least £1000 sterling per year. Such an act would prevent the governor from pleasing his constituents at the expense of his superiors. This controversy dragged on until 1735. Burnet's successor Jonathan Belcher (1730–1741) finally worked out a compromise whereby the governor obtained an annually voted grant, but the house in turn promised that it would equal £1000 sterling and be voted at the beginning of each year's session, instead of at the end after the governor had approved all of the assembly's votes.[11] The last of these jurisdictional disputes occurred when Belcher had to persuade the house that all money appropriated for the treasury by the deputies be spent merely with the approval of the governor and council for each specific disbursement. The lower house refused to yield this right from 1730 to 1733, and responded to Belcher's demands by voting no money at all for nearly two years. As in the case of the Explanatory Charter, a sharp warning from the crown changed the deputies' minds.[12]

223

The nature of political conflict in peacetime Massachusetts must be defined if the changes produced by war are to be fully appreciated. As noted, the principal controversy centred on the division of powers within the General Court. When not handling local business, the assembly spent its time arguing with the governor and council. *House Journals* for the 1720s and 30s contain hundreds of pages of messages in which both sides based their arguments primarily on the province charter and English precedents, with the assembly claiming the powers of the House of Commons, derived from the charter clause guaranteeing all the rights of Englishmen. The 'Old Whig' appeal to the natural rights of man and the 'New Whig' attack on executive corruption were conspicuous by their absence. Ideological debate, while intense, utilised a common language and did not delve deeply into the relationship of society and government. Both sides confined themselves largely to technical points of law.

The composition of factions between Queen Anne's and King George's wars also contrasted markedly with future patterns. No effective prerogative party existed in the legislature, since on every disputed point the interests of Massachusetts and Britain clashed rather than coincided. For example, many of the house's denials of the governor's power over the speaker passed unanimously. The most favourable vote Burnet ever obtained on the permanent salary was a 54 to 18 rejection. Even this vote occurred on a watered-down proposition which guaranteed payment only for one particular executive's administration, and angered Burnet as much as the deputies.[13] In 1732, the assembly refused by 56 to 1 to supply the treasury unless it could control specific appropriations. True, the house reversed itself on this issue by 55–25 in 1733 under threat of the king's displeasure, just as it 'submitted to' (rather than 'accepted of') the Explanatory Charter by 48–32.[14] But such compliance clearly occurred under duress. Only Governor Belcher began to form a party loyal to himself and thereby successfully stifled the opposition from 1735 to 1739.[15] This faction can hardly be considered a court party, however, since Belcher spent much of his energy persuading Britain not to insist on the question of the permanent salary and to postpone redemption of the paper money supply. The governor had rather assumed leadership of the country faction.

The popular faction's one-sided dominance during the interwar period is explained by the fact that leadership in the assembly was concentrated in a few powerful hands. If service on fifteen committees—which examination of the *House Journals* suggests is a plausible dividing line between political leaders and the rank-and-file—be taken to indicate prominence, only 27 of 104 towns represented supplied any leader at all. If a deputy is counted once for every year he attained this position, seven towns provided 61 per cent of this select group. Boston headed the list with 32 per cent; with rare exceptions, all four of the capital's assemblymen appeared as leaders. Only Charlestown, Braintree, Ipswich, Salem, Northampton, and Roxbury supplied more than four per cent. Certain individuals (such as Speakers Edmund Quincy of Braintree and William Dudley of Roxbury) who served repeatedly account for the importance of these towns.[16]

Most of the leading political figures between 1713 and 1740 belonged to an extended kinship network, centred on Boston, which embraced the first families of Massachusetts. Even the few men who adhered to the unpopular governors' standards were related to their opponents. The famous Elisha Cooke, who founded the Boston Caucus in 1719 and led the popular party until his death in 1737, counted three of his brothers-in-law, Oliver Noyes, John Clarke, and William Paine, among his principal supporters in the house. But Clarke was also the brother-in-law of Cotton Mather, who consistently favoured the royal governor. Elizabeth Clarke, John's sister, was married to Elisha Hutchinson, that family's patriarch in the early eighteenth century. All the Hutchinsons except William, a Caucus supporter, favoured the prerogative. One of Cooke's uncles was Nathaniel Byfield, a brother-in-law of Governor Joseph Dudley (1702–1715) who turned against his kinsman's administration during its final years. If we go one step further, two of Dudley's three daughters had married sons of councillors Samuel Sewall and Wait Winthrop while their fathers were feuding violently with the governor.[17] However violent the rhetoric of peacetime political conflict, it was tempered by the fact that all the participants belonged to an elite which both the populace and representatives entrusted with the government.

Peacetime politics thus were plagued with superficial contention, but the system was essentially stable because administration was not expensive, government was stabilised through elite family participation and did not impinge on the lives of people except through request or mild taxation, and political issues rarely went beyond discussion of legislative prerogatives. But around 1740, two events shattered this political framework almost simultaneously: the currency crisis and the Great Awakening. Compelled by Britain to withdraw all except £30,000 of its £390,000 in circulation by 1741, two groups in Massachusetts tried to sidestep the order by creating private currencies—a Land Bank with province-wide support and a Silver Bank, favoured primarily by wealthy Boston merchants. The province overwhelmingly supported the Land Bank. Only 11 of the 43 deputies who opposed the measure in 1740 were re-elected in 1741, whereas 33 of the 63 who supported it retained their seats. Opposed by Governor Belcher and both

British and Massachusetts merchants, the Bank was ultimately declared illegal by Parliament, which provoked its supporters to threaten violent revolution. The situation was defused because Belcher was removed at the height of the crisis (ironically enough, because the ministry had been misinformed by his political opponents that he actually favoured the Land Bank) and was replaced by Advocate General William Shirley, who managed to liquidate the Bank to the satisfaction of most parties.[18]

The Awakening revived popular interest in religion at the same time that the Bank stirred up general political concern. Towns and families throughout Massachusetts split between 'Old Lights' who defended the traditional religious establishment and 'New Lights' who favoured more emotional preaching, which was to be judged by popular appeal rather than mere competence. Other differences set off the New Lights as potential threats to social order: salvation came all at once to an utterly depraved soul rather than as the culmination of 'good works' and socially acceptable 'preparation'. Itinerant ministers and preachers of different denominations were welcomed by the New Lights. These innovations clearly undermined the absolute position of each community's own established cleric. Young people, women, and the less well-to-do tended to support the Awakening. Also, three generations of high birth rates and low death rates had led to a substantial decline in economic opportunity in the province's older communities. The Awakening provided those who were worth less in worldly terms with the means to assert their superiority over those more elevated than them in the traditional socio-economic structure. For instance, the Second Church of Boston, the Mathers' congregation, split in two: the wealthier and older members followed 'Old Light' Samuel Mather when he was ousted by the younger, less affluent majority. The coincidence of overcrowding, economic distress, and a religious revival with a demonstrable social basis suggests that Massachusetts was sitting on dynamite by the early 1740s.[19]

That these social problems did not produce an explosion, it may be tentatively postulated, can be attributed to the outbreak of war between England and Spain in 1739 and England and France in 1744. The pressure of a common enemy redirected religious enthusiasm into another crusade, provided an outlet for young men with limited prospects, and brought ideological sparring within the General Court to an end for approximately two decades. Yet it can be argued that war did not so much solve these problems as mask them, since they re-emerged with even greater intensity in the 1760s. Furthermore, Anglo-American disagreement over the conduct of the war led to increasing popular discontent with Britain.

Massachusetts' limited involvement in the war with Spain from 1739 set several patterns for the greater conflicts which followed. In 1740 Governor Belcher issued a call for volunteers to serve as support troops for a British fleet destined to attack Cartagena in the West Indies. The response, thanks to promises of liberal pay, bounties, and plunder, was overwhelming despite the almost total decimation of a similar New England expeditionary force in 1703. Belcher raised one thousand men instead of the six hundred requested; this produced some embarrassment when Britain only supplied arms for

225

the number originally planned. Surviving muster rolls indicate that young men from the long-settled towns of eastern Massachusetts supplied most of the enlistments. The campaign was a total fiasco and few of the men returned, but it set a precedent which held throughout the mid-century wars: Massachusetts raised most of its forces through bounties and the inducement of receiving military pay, room, and board.[20]

Warfare also helped to relieve the monetary crisis. As early as October 1741, Governor Shirley had managed to persuade the ministry to revoke its instructions that all issues of paper money in excess of £30,000 must be approved by the Privy Council. When war with France broke out in 1744, all restrictions were waived for the duration of the conflict. Despite 'the extreme heavy burden' of which the General Court complained in 1748, Massachusetts financed the bulk of King George's War simply by rolling the presses: in 1749, £1.9 million were extant and the currency's value had depreciated to one-tenth of sterling.[21]

Finally, the war fever caused New Lights and Old Lights to bury the hatchet between themselves. Beginning with the Louisbourg expedition of 1745, Puritan millennial confidence revived for the first time since the 1630s and 40s. Conquest of the French and Indians was viewed as a prelude to the final triumph over the Anti-Christ (Popery), the universal spread of true religion, and the second coming of Christ. The millennium would come about as a capstone on the efforts of God's chosen people, rather than as a punishment for their declension and depravity as millenarians in the intervening century, such as Cotton and Increase Mather, had feared.[22]

The imperatives of war resolved political tensions between the governor and the legislature in addition to defusing potential social conflict. Throughout the 1740s and 1750s, a powerful prerogative faction headed by Thomas Hutchinson and Andrew Oliver of Boston obtained nearly all the troops requested by Britain, successfully implemented a currency backed by specie in 1749, and prevented inflation throughout the French and Indian War by imposing heavy taxes to finance current expenditures. This faction first appeared in Bostonian politics in the late 1730s: following the death of Elisha Cooke in 1737, the town began to elect supporters as well as opponents of the governor to office for the first time in a quarter-century. Even though Hutchinson and Oliver sought to alter Boston's town meeting government to a self-selecting corporation, the town recognised their administrative competence as the only alternative to the politics of the Caucus, which had wasted its energies quarrelling with governors while the town's economy and quality of life drastically declined. Composed of relatively young men, born mostly around 1710, the prerogative faction dominated provincial politics until it was dethroned during the revolutionary crisis.[23]

The rise of the prerogative faction coincided with a drastic change in the activities of the legislature. Attention shifted from resolving local problems to matters of defence. In 1745, 224 of the 324 resolves passed by the house involved provincial interests, an almost exact reversal of the ratio of general to local business of two years before. In 1757, at the height of the French and Indian War, the proportion was 202 bills to 94. Furthermore, the number of representatives involved in the house's committee work grew dramatically.

In the absence of a paid bureaucracy, and given the fact that many of the Massachusetts local justices and militia officers sat in the house, the activity of the so-called back-benchers had to increase as the legislature changed from an ideological forum and court of appeals to an organ of policy formation and public administration. Between 1740 and 1764, 70 per cent of all represented towns (86 out of 123) supplied deputies who sat on more than fifteen committees per year, as opposed to 26 per cent in peacetime. Boston's share declined to 15 per cent, and no other town had more than three per cent. The responsibility of power diffused itself throughout the province as effectively as government imposed itself on the general population. No longer could most political figures be cousins, uncles, and brothers-in-law; even within Boston itself, apart from the Hutchinson-Oliver connection, few leading legislators of either faction were related.[24]

227

The prerogative's success in the provincial sphere can in part be explained by the reason that it dominated Boston. Governor Belcher's willingness to meet the old country faction more than half-way caused its members to dissipate their energy in a dispute between Belcher and Cooke which disenchanted many of the back-benchers in the assembly. Furthermore, as with solving Boston's economic problems, the task of running a war required the patience and attention to detail which the free-wheeling Cooke and his followers had never possessed. Negotiations with Indians and other colonies, preparation of endless accounts and muster-rolls, and supervision of supply shipments transformed leading politicians into full-time civil servants as well. Massachusetts willingly overlooked the prerogative's mistrust of popular government and conspicuous consumption in the face of local hardship in the light of the overwhelming necessity required by the great 'crusade'.

Prerogative rule possessed even less savoury elements. Over three-quarters of the deputies held commissions either as justices of the peace, militia officers, or both. In addition to their pay, officers had the privilege of selling supplies to their troops. Especially recalcitrant opponents of the war could be removed from their posts by the governor with the council's consent. Governor Shirley and his supporters also used dubious parliamentary manoeuvres—warning that British displeasure and punitive measures would follow if the war were not fought with all possible vigour, holding the legislature in session until their opponents went home, and even expelling the country faction's most effective remaining leader—to get their way. Prerogative strength must be explained by a combination of consensus and coercion: to stress either unduly converts men like Hutchinson and Shirley into either villains or heroes, and leads to excessively partisan interpretations of provincial politics as either stable or conflict-ridden.

The manner in which Britain's promised financial compensation for Massachusetts' Louisbourg expenditures became a prerogative tool to obtain additional troops and funds provides an excellent example of how the lower house could be persuaded to act in spite of its own best judgment. Having launched the expedition and plunged themselves £50,000 into debt, the deputies begged 'His Majesty's favor and compassion . . . in relieving them from such part of the expenses and burden as to His wisdom should seem reasonable.' Once the representatives put themselves in this position, Shirley could extort further grants of troops and money by threatening that if the war effort proceeded with insufficient vigour, Britain might think twice about paying for Louisbourg. When he proposed the reduction of Canada on 31 May 1746 Shirley warned that 'a wrong step in the affair will endanger our being disappointed in our expectations'. The following July the governor impressed men who had enlisted for frontier garrison duty into the expedition contrary to the vote of the house. When the representatives refused to pay them, he obtained a reversal of this decision by promising to explain to his superiors that he was obliged to pay them from drafts on the British treasury. The house again acquiesced rather than lose all chance of receiving the Louisbourg grant.[25]

228   Tension between Shirley and the assembly also arose over the posting of soldiers and the duration of their service. Troops who had volunteered or been impressed for one theatre of war were sometimes transferred to a less attractive post, or else enlisted to obtain a more favourable one. These practices necessitated additional impressments to fill the vacated commands. The house protested in vain that 'we have always looked upon the impressing of men even for the defence of their own inhabitants as a method to be made use of in cases of great necessity only'. A second difficulty occurred when the governor held provincial soldiers on garrison duty long after their enlistments had expired. Some men were kept at Annapolis in Nova Scotia from mid-1744 until January 1746, and the entire 3000-men Louisbourg contingent (of whom more than 900 died from exposure and disease) remained at Cape Breton from June 1745 until a long-awaited British garrison arrived in April 1746. The assembly complained that such extended service reduced 'due confidence in the promises of government'.[26]

Discouragement with Shirley's conduct of the war brought it to a halt sooner than he would have preferred. He failed to obtain a second expedition to Canada in 1747. When Louisbourg was returned to France by the Peace of 1748, the assembly commented 'it affords us a very melancholy reflection when we consider the extreme heavy burden brought upon the people of this province, and the small prospect there is of any good effect from it . . . we have been the means of effectually bringing distress, if not ruin, upon ourselves'.[27]

In addition to side-stepping the legislature's wishes in mobilising forces, Shirley dealt harshly with opponents of his policies. Dr. William Douglass, the province's only European-trained physician, attacked the governor for permitting the impressment of sailors into the British navy, allowing sanitary conditions to deteriorate at Louisbourg, and authorising the issue of more paper money in eight years to finance his schemes than all his predecessors combined over the previous fifty. In a monumental *Summary, Historical and Political . . . of North America,* which he published serially in the *Boston Gazette* beginning in 1747, Douglass roundly attacked Shirley's military strategy and 'governors in general, who may be romantic (but in perquisites profitable) expeditions, depopulate the country'. Shirley instituted a libel suit for £10,000 on behalf of the British Admiral Charles Knowles, another target of Douglass' venom; Douglass answered with a

counter-suit and ultimately won £750 in damages against the absent admiral.
Shirley also sued Samuel Waldo, the Boston merchant and land speculator
to whom he owed his job, for £12,000. The governor blamed Waldo,
commander of the aborted Canada expedition, for failing to keep adequate
accounts and thereby denying Massachusetts compensation for its efforts
from the British treasury.[28] Although Waldo too was ultimately acquitted,
the governor's leading opponents could count on the threat of enormous
and potentially ruinous lawsuits for their pains.

After the war ended, Shirley and his supporters continued to use unsavoury
tactics to persuade the assembly to adopt and maintain a specie currency.
The Speaker of the House, Thomas Hutchinson, took the first step in this
direction by convincing the assembly that compensation for Louisbourg
would never be forthcoming unless the province pledged to use the money to
sink its paper currency. However, once the money arrived, a specific plan
for redeeming the outstanding bills only passed on 20 January 1749 by a vote
of 40–37 after five weeks of debate. To effect this vote, Hutchinson waited
until about one-quarter of the assembly had drifted away and ensured that
James Allen, Shirley's principal antagonist who had accused him of trading
with the enemy, would be expelled.[29]

Reaction to the new currency was overwhelmingly negative. Hutchinson
lost the next Boston election to Samuel Waldo by a margin of almost three
to one. His house burned down, mysteriously, and the fire companies
refused to put out the blaze.[30] Allen published a list of the supporters of the
currency plan: the next year, on 5 April 1750, the assembly responded by
voting 46 to 33 to issue a new form of paper money. But once again, the
hard money advocates had greater staying power. After the backcountry
opponents of silver melted away, seven deputies were persuaded to change
their minds and the new bills were rejected 31–28 on 20 April. In 1751 the
house again voted an inflationary supply bill by 36–26. That year only the
council's adamant refusal to concur ensured the survival of a stable
currency.[31]

The ability of the prerogative faction to outlast and intimidate the majority
of the representatives caused opposition spokesmen to adopt, for the first
time, the Old and New Whig ideology with which the leaders of the Revolution ultimately justified their cause. Shirley's administration presented the
novel phenomenon of a House of Representatives conducting an unpopular
and costly war against the wishes not only of individuals but—as some of
its messages and reversed votes made perfectly clear—against its own better
judgment. It therefore became necessary for the country faction, for the
first time, to detach itself from the assembly and go beyond the mere defence
of the deputies' right to make their own laws. Once the assembly itself was
conceived to be an instrument of oppression, an appeal to a higher standard
was required which explained how the people's own representatives could
betray their constituents.

Whig ideology suited the Massachusetts situation perfectly. The *Independent Advertiser*, America's first anti-war and protest newspaper was founded
one month after the great anti-impressment riot of 17–20 November 1747
by the twenty-five-year-old Samuel Adams, among others.[32] These opposition

229

writers cited John Locke to argue that a government which failed to protect the inhabitants' 'lives, liberties, and estates' by forcing them to fight against their wishes, impressing them into the navy, and taxing them oppressively could be opposed legitimately—even violently. Similarly, the New Whig ideas of William Trenchard and John Gordon were adapted to explain how only a morally and fiscally corrupted government would so betray its people, and that only an equally corrupted people would tolerate such oppression. The *Advertiser* blamed the war on representatives who had been corrupted by Sir Plume (Governor Shirley) and his 'prime minister' Alexander Windmill (Thomas Hutchinson) by being given military commissions, which paid officially from about £50 sterling per year for a captain to about £80 for a colonel. These, however, also entitled them to supply and pay their men and thereby opened the door for padded accounts and illegal profits.[33] Most of the complaints of corruption were directed against Shirley personally, who was alleged to have made an enormous sum of money by being granted the right to raise a royal regiment of colonials to garrison Louisbourg. New Whig ideology made sense in wartime because, unlike peacetime, real opportunities for making large sums of money in government service existed.[34]

230

There is little hint in The *Independent Advertiser* that the French and Indians were a real threat to Massachusetts: the 'Popish' refurbishing of King's Chapel by Shirley and the Boston Anglican community was a far greater menace. Colonists constantly denouced England as a den of iniquity and corruption instead. After the mother country gave Cape Breton back to France,[35] the most extreme critique of the war and its engineers occurred:

> Why is the security of the brave and virtuous . . . given up to purchase some short-lived and precarious advantages for lazy—f[oo]ls and idle All[ie]s? The security was purchased with the blood of the former and sacrificed to the indolence of the latter. The first won it by bravery; the latter forfeited it by Tr[e]ach[e]ry and Cow[ar]dice. As if our Min[i]stry . . . had determined to counteract the essential laws of equity, as much as possible, as they have done the rules of policy and prudence.

Reaction to British and prerogative policies not only took verbal form: wartime crowds began to focus on political issues. Between the Glorious Revolution and the 1740s, political violence in Massachusetts was committed by individuals against individuals—a bomb thrown through Cotton Mather's window, a pot shot taken at Samuel Shute, an assault against Elisha Cooke —whereas crowds restricted themselves to remedying local emergencies which could not conveniently be handled in courts of law. For example, mobs tore down bawdyhouses and market stalls under construction in the 1730s, and stopped ships trying to export food during shortages from sailing. A corrupt and brutal jailor found himself the target of a prison riot. Beginning in the 1740s, however, mobs for the first time directed themselves against imperial power and clashed with British rather than local authorities. The occasion was naval impressment: despite an Act of Parliament of 1707 forbidding impressment in American waters without the consent of local authorities, and in spite of Massachusetts' willingness to authorise the impressment of non-native seamen who happened to be in the province, British captains provoked hostility by their disregard for such points of law. Angered that their sailors deserted with local connivance, they sometimes simply impressed people indiscriminately and then sailed for the West Indies. In 1741, Captain James Scott seized over forty men and narrowly escaped with his life. A press gang killed two veterans of the Louisbourg campaign in 1745 for resisting efforts to seize them; in 1747 virtually the entire populace of Boston held many of the officers in Commodore Knowles' British fleet hostage pending the release of forty-six impressed men. Instead of negotiating Knowles threated to bombard Boston while a mob of several thousand people surrounded the governor's mansion and General Court to press their demands. The *Independent Advertiser* justified such violence as the legitimate response to lawless acts of nominally lawful authorities. Where the government could not protect its inhabitants, 'they have an undoubted right to use the powers [of self-defence] belonging to that state [of nature]'. Just before the paper closed down, it responded to critics of the Knowles Riot, 'that the sober sort, who dared to express a due sense of their injuries, were invidiously represented as a rude, low-lived mob'.[36]

231

The French and Indian War revived the same tendencies manifested in King George's War. The province was even more cooperative and self-sacrificing, but the prerogative faction's efforts to coordinate provincial and imperial policy again provoked resentment against British officials. Taxes, which the province had considered heavy at under £10,000 sterling in the 1740s, rose to £60,000 sterling or more from 1756 to 1760 and remained at over £30,000 for the rest of the provincial period.[37] Protesting against the fact that most of this money was raised from land taxes, the rural majority in the assembly struck back at the Boston-based prerogative faction by passing the infamous Excise Tax of 1754 and a Stamp Tax in 1755 (remarkably similar to the one Britain would later impose on the colonies) to shift the tax burden towards the urban communities. The new excise differed from the province's long-standing tax on liquor by taxing the consumption of spirits by individuals rather than the amount sold by retailers. To discover the quantity, the government appointed excise farmers who could then hire deputies to demand an account 'of all and every persons whomsoever in this government, of all the wine, rum, and brandy, and other distilled spirits expended by them (on oath if required)'; a penalty of £10 was established for false swearing. The prerogative faction and the Boston community joined forces (Boston was already paying 20 per cent of the taxes even though it had under 10 per cent of the population) to protest against this 'Total Eclipse of Liberty' and 'Monster of Monsters', as two pamphlets attacking the bill were entitled. Governor Shirley, who signed the bill under protest, himself took up the natural rights argument that had previously been used by his opponents, criticising the tax as 'altogether unprecedented in the English governments' and 'inconsistent with the natural rights of every person in the community'. The country's revenge on the court faction was short-lived: the people of the province were so angered by the excise that only 19 of the 52 deputies who approved it were re-elected, whereas 10 of the 17 who opposed it (they came from the Boston area, Salem, Marblehead, Plymouth, Maine) retained their seats.[38]

Taxes and economic difficulties during the French and Indian War rose to unprecedented heights. The legislature placed embargoes on exports of food which compelled farmers to sell provisions to British and American military commissaries at lower than usual prices; British commanders-in-chief also prohibited colonial overseas shipping intermittently when they considered trading with the enemy to be excessive. These restrictions continued until 1763: Massachusetts' new governor Francis Bernard (1760–1769) joined the legislature and protested to General Jeffrey Amherst that 'this public spirited province can ill afford to lose the small trade remaining to it' and that in any event illegal trading simply did not exist in Massachusetts. Things became so bad in 1758 that sixteen leading Bostonian merchants, all of whom paid taxes of between £95 and £540 per year, threatened to leave the province and take their business elsewhere. Bernard later argued that British taxation was unjust because Massachusetts itself had spent 'an immense sum for such a small state, the burden of which has been grievously felt by all orders of men.'[39] Economic hardship drove a large number of people into bankruptcy. To combat this problem, in 1757 the legislature passed the first major bill reforming the treatment of bankrupts in Massachusetts history. Instead of being forced to forfeit their entire estates and possibly go to debtors' prison, all persons who advertised bankruptcy in the Boston newspapers, did not try to hide any of their wealth, and permitted their affairs to be investigated by commissioners could begin life with a clean slate. Insolvents able to pay at least half their debts could retain five per cent of their wealth up to £200; those able to pay two-thirds could keep $7\frac{1}{2}$ per cent up to £250; anyone who could satisfy three-fourths of the claims against him was allowed ten per cent of his estate under £300. The reform was timely: joyous news of British victories were always tempered by lists of the financially distressed in the same issues of the province's journals. For instance, twenty-eight persons filed for bankruptcy the week Louisbourg was recaptured in 1758. As late as February 1765 the default of Nathaniel Appleton on £189,000 set off a chain reaction because his creditors in turn could not pay their debts.[40]

In addition to shouldering these burdens, Massachusetts had to bear with the arrogance of British commanders-in-chief who seemed determined to infringe provincial rights and sensibilities to the maximum while winning the war. Naval impressment continued, and Massachusetts again protested against this grievance in vain.[41] Britain and Massachusetts disagreed over the number, disposition, and ability of the provincial soldiers. Each year, the prerogative faction struggled long and hard to obtain the deputies' endorsement of the full number of troops requested by Britain. Even then, the assembly confined the troops to particular posts and enlisted them for limited periods of time which coincided poorly with military necessity. As Lord Loudoun, commander-in-chief during 1757 and 1758, complained at an intercolonial conference: 'The confining of your men to any particular service appears to me a preposterous measure. Our affairs are not in such a situation as to make it reasonable for any colony to be guided by its own

232

particular interest'. Other problems included soldiers sent to the frontier without arms; men enlisting and deserting several times to collect bounties; and officers and sutlers profiteering from the right to supply men with provisions. The province's insistence that impressment should only be used as a last resort ensured that each year's supply of men took several months to be mustered. Recruiting parties met with resistance in Boston and Marblehead. Loudoun also wanted colonial troops to be led by British officers and subjected to regular army discipline. His insistence that no provincial officer should rank higher than a British captain threatened local autonomy and insulted the province's military capability.[42]

When in camp, British officers frequently assigned colonials only the most onerous and demeaning work instead of committing them effectively to battle. General James Wolfe expressed the general British attitude: 'The Americans are in general the dirtiest, the most contemptible, cowardly dogs that you can conceive. There is no depending upon them in action. They fall down in their own dirt and desert by battalions, officers and all'.[43]

233

The most spectacular instance of Anglo-American animosity was the quartering dispute of December 1757 and January 1758. Massachusetts gladly offered to billet the troops for the winter, but Loudoun insisted that any legislative action was unnecessary because the British Quartering Act of 1694, which gave commanders such authority in England, applied to the colonies. The assembly could not see the reason for his indignation: 'We are really at a loss what steps to take to terminate this affair since His Lordship does not seem dissatisfied so much from the insufficiency of what we have done, as from the matter of its being done by a law of the province.' Loudoun, on the other hand, argued that if quartering were discretionary rather than automatic, 'my acquiescence under it would throw the whole continent into a turmoil, from South Carolina to Boston, and turn three-quarters of the troops at once into the streets to perish'. At stake was whether the commander-in-chief could conduct the war independently of local interference. Loudoun complained that 'even if the town of Boston was attacked, it would not by their rule be in my power to march the troops to its relief'. He then threatened that if things were not settled he would 'instantly order into Boston the three battalions from New York, Long Island, and Connecticut, and, if more are wanted, I have two in the Jerseys at hand besides those in Pennsylvania'. Loudoun also hinted that Britain would not think it reasonable to pay the colonies for their 'very extravagant' war expenses if they did not even provide lodging for the troops sent to protect them.[44]

While it lasted, the French and Indian War provoked less discontent than King George's: the country faction did not oppose any expeditions or the war itself this time, only the proportion to be shouldered by Massachusetts rather than by Britain. However, the peculiar manner in which the war ended led to increased political strife, both within Massachusetts and between Massachusetts and Britain, after hostilites were concluded. With respect to the New England colonies, the French menace ended forever when British forces raised the Union Jack over Quebec in 1759. But the war dragged on four more years, both in the West Indies and on the frontier of the middle and southern colonies. Britain expected all the mainland colonies to contribute soldiers for frontier duty so that the more valuable redcoats could be sent to Europe or the islands. Thanks largely to persuasive speeches by Massachusetts' popular new governor Francis Bernard, the Bay Colony complied and supplied 3000 soldiers per year until 1763 and also sent 700 men to the Ohio Valley in the wake of Pontiac's rebellion as late as 1764.[45] Because the war ended in 1759 in the Northeast while elsewhere it continued until 1764, Massachusetts felt little urgency or need for further sacrifices, and yet she was still required to maintain embargoes, levy taxes, and raise troops.

These difficulties were exacerbated by Britain's plans for imperial reorganisation which were implemented before the war's end. Despite the embargoes and taxes suffered by the Boston merchant community, British customs officials in Boston could not leave well enough alone and provoked the famous challenge to their general search warrants, the Writs of Assistance Case in 1761. The Sugar Act and Proclamation of 1763 were promulgated while Massachusetts still had several thousand men in service.

The manner in which Parliament's promised reimbursement finally arrived did not help matters. Massachusetts always insisted that its exertions went far beyond those of the other colonies. As a result the province was entitled to special treatment. This was not forthcoming: Jasper Mauduit, the province agent in the early 1760s, did little to force the issue. He urged acquiescence with British policy: since the other colonies were content with requesting compensation for about half their wartime expenditures, Massachusetts would appear 'in a very disadvantageous light to present a petition to Parliament setting forth that we are content with nothing less than the whole of ours'. Massachusetts ultimately received only £390,000 out of some £818,000 spent.[46]

Internal strife also broke out while the war was ending. Religious controversy between the province's Congregational establishment and a small but influential community of wealthy Anglicans began in 1761. The latter belonged mostly to wealthy Boston area families which had strongly supported and profited from the war. Charles Apthorp, a young Anglican cleric, established a 'mission' at Cambridge, causing many of the clergy to think that the long-feared Anglican bishopric was finally upon them.[47] In Maine, two land companies, the Kennibeck and the Waldo heirs, the former composed largely of future patriots, the latter of future loyalists, squabbled for control of vast tracts of land.[48] Western Massachusetts, which staunchly supported a maximum war effort, began to develop a sense of regional consciousness and in 1762 tried unsuccessfully to obtain its own college.[49] These disputes tended to coincide with divisions between the prerogative faction and its opponents: once war ended, regional, religious, and economic differences between the two factions began to take political form.

The conclusion of war also brought the problem of underemployment and overcrowding to the fore again. Massachusetts had developed something approaching a European standing army. Youths from overcrowded towns and lower class men enlisted year after year under the command of an officer

class consisting of the province's leading men.[50] Battle deaths had also
helped to alleviate population pressure. But beginning in 1765, the first
year since 1754 Massachusetts and its fellow colonies did not muster forces
for battle, the situation drastically changed. A postwar decline in overseas
trade and the catastrophic drought of 1763-4 let loose an unprecedented
wave of rootless persons throughout the province.[51] Boston's Warning
Out records (which do not indicate who was forced to leave town, but only
listed entering migrants who would then not be eligible for public relief if
they became destitute) show that migration increased astronomically at
precisely this time. Beginning in 1745, the first year systematic records were
kept, and for the following two decades of war, migration to Boston was
primarily female and mostly from Massachusetts. But in 1765, not only did
the number expand greatly, but the migrants were mostly male, many men
with families, and came from both Massachusetts and overseas. Eighty per
cent of all male migrants to Boston from 1745–1773 arrived between 1765
and 1773. Total migration rose each decade: 458 households (1745–1755);
925 (1755–1765); 2479 (1765–1773).[52] The presence of so many additional
single men in Boston undoubtedly swelled the size and added to the vigour
of the Boston mob. Once again, during the revolution itself, in eastern
Massachusetts long term military service was largely confined to young
men who did not have sufficient wealth to pay taxes or were still dependent
on their fathers.[53] But during the decade of 1765–1775, many men had
nowhere to go except into the revolutionary movement.

235

The most notable political effect of the ending of the war was the swift
demise of the prerogative faction. By 1766, its leading members were purged
from the council seats some of them had held for decades. Its strength
dwindled quickly from approximately half the house in 1765 to almost zero
by 1768. Massachusetts would tolerate the leadership of a Thomas Hutchinson during wartime when administrative skills and capacity for hard work
were of the utmost importance. Sacrifices in the interest of the common
cause were tolerable, and even Hutchinson and his cohorts protested against
such enormities as naval impressment and the quartering act. Once war
ended, however, restrictions on Massachusetts' trade, tighter and possibly
corrupt enforcement of customs regulations, and taxation by Britain rather
than the province itself all appeared to undermine the prerogative's
contention that Anglo-American interests were compatible.

The faction which had dominated Massachusetts for a quarter-century
was swept away with remarkable ease between 1761 and 1768 largely because
it had a distorted conception both of itself and of Massachusetts politics.
Although most of its leaders were initially Bostonians, they disliked townmeeting politics and preferred to spend as little time in town as possible,
moving to their suburban imitations of English country houses and socialising
among themselves, instead of staying in contact with the common folk.[54] In
consequence, they deluded themselves into thinking that they were entitled
to hold office through *noblesse oblige;* they did not perceive it as a reward
bestowed on them for their competent administration of the war in spite of
their profiteering and aloofness. Once the war ended the sole basis of their
support vanished.

The inability of the prerogative to put up a better fight can also be traced to the roots of its power. Believing that the correct role of the populace in government was passively to sanction the decisions of an administrative elite, they could not effectively use newspapers, harangue crowds, or cater to popular support through organisations such as the Boston Caucus. They had little experience in such matters, considered 'politics' as opposed to administration both a social evil and beneath their dignity, and were simply too set in their ways to adjust to a new world of politics as they approached in most cases the age of sixty.[55]

The prerogative's wartime strength was also translated into post-war weakness in another way. The opposition had been hampered throughout the war by weak or self-serving leaders; in the early 1760s, for example, Benjamin Pratt and John Tyng were respectively bought off with the Chief Justiceship of New York and an inferior court post in Middlesex County.[56] As a result of the default or death of the old popular party's leaders, a new one arose to express general indignation. Composed primarily of much younger men without previous personal or familial ties to provincial politics, the new country faction drew its strength from journalistic skills, Boston machine politics, and the 'Boston mob'. It used extreme rhetoric which equated its enemies with the anti-Christ and predicted the total suppression of American liberty if the corrupt opposition were not totally destroyed. Coming from outside the legislature, the new politics had to employ more extreme means to resist British policy in Massachusetts than in other colonies simply because in no other province did the people have to be persuaded to purge the legislature of such a strong pro-British faction.

One of the most potent arguments the revolutionaries advanced to resist British policy in Massachusetts was that it was both unfair and unnecessary because the province had indeed borne more than its share of the war. In Massachusetts requisitions had most certainly worked. For instance, when James Otis protested against the Stamp Act with his 'Rights of the British Colonies Asserted and Proved', he not only appealed to natural rights, but also to past experience:[57]

> We have spent all we could raise, and more; for notwithstanding the parliamentary reimbursements of part, we still remain much in debt. The province of the Massachusetts I believe, has expended more men and money in war since the year 1620, when a few families first landed at Plymouth, in proportion to their ability, than the three Kingdoms together. The same, I believe, may be truly affirmed of many of the other colonies, though the Massachusetts has undoubtedly had the heaviest burden.

Otis's argument was taken up by other colonials. In 1764 the New York assembly protested against British taxation because 'in many wars we have suffered an immense loss of both blood and treasure, to repel the foe, and maintain a valuable dependency on the British crown'. And when Benjamin Franklin appeared before the House of Commons in February 1766 to make his famous false distinction between the colonies' objection to internal taxes and their willingness to acquiesce in external, he was right on the mark when

236

he argued that 'the colonies raised, clothed, and paid, during the last war, near 25,000 men, and spent many millions'.[58]

Even leading Massachusetts Tories agreed with this analysis although not with the deduction that resistance and revolution were the only correct responses. Thomas Hutchinson argued forcefully though privately that the Stamp Act was unjust because the colonies had contributed more men to the 'Great War for Empire' in proportion to their population than the mother country. Secondly, the colonies had defended themselves for the century before 1754 without much British assistance, and through their own exertions had increased the strength and prosperity of the empire. Third, whatever contribution the colonies had made as a whole, Massachusetts' efforts deserved special mention: 'No other government has been at any expense to set against this', with the result that during the war 'the public debt increased annually thirty or forty thousand pounds lawful money.' Finally, Canada was of no economic value to the colonies and would greatly depreciate existing colonial land values.[59] Loyalist Isaac Royall, a wealthy West India planter who had lived in Charlestown and Medford since 1737, similarly remonstrated with Lord Dartmouth in 1774 that 'this province Sir has always been foremost even beyond its ability and notwithstanding the present unhappy disputes would perhaps be so again if there should be the like occasion for it in promoting the Honour of their King and Nation. Witness their twice saving Nova Scotia from falling into French hands, the reduction of Louisbourg . . . and many other expensive and heroic expeditions against the common enemy'.[60]

237

Yet the loyalists also insisted that whatever the colonists' own exertions, British aid had still been necessary. Even if taxation were unfair or onerous, the indisputable fact remained that without Britain Canada could not have been taken. In his *History of Massachusetts,* Hutchinson argued the opposite position to that which he adopted in his letter on the Stamp Act. Without help, the colonies 'would have been extirpated by the French', and even at Louisbourg in 1745, the deciding factor was 'the superior naval power of Great Britain'. Hutchinson agreed with the patriots that the mother country had no altruistic motives for aiding the colonies—'fear of losing that advantageous trade' rather than 'paternal affections' was the true cause of intervention. But Britain had undeniably 'expended a far greater sum' rescuing the colonies during the final war 'than the whole property, real and personal, in all the colonies would amount to'. Therefore, 'in a moral view, a separation of the colonies which must still further enfeeble and distress the other parts of the empire, already enfeebled by exertions to save the colonies', was reprehensible.[61] Of course, the revolutionaries argued that Hutchinson and his fellow loyalists' real motive for defending British policy was that their own careers and pocketbooks had benefited greatly through their participation in the war, whereas many of their countrymen had lost sizeable portions of their estates or even their lives.

A persuasive case can be made that serious popular resentment against British imperial policy—which had been loosely enforced during the age of 'Salutary Neglect' between Queen Anne's and King George's Wars—occurred because in two decades Massachusetts had launched a war effort which to be effective required a major transformation of its political system. War greatly increased the role of government in Massachusetts society and transformed the nature of the General Court. Increased taxation, regulation of the economy in the form of food embargoes and requistion of needed supplies, and the drafting of perhaps a fifth of the male population into the army and navy characterised military policy in mid-eighteenth century Massachusetts. To manage King George's and the French and Indian Wars, the house's committee work involved a large majority rather than a small minority of representatives. War proved a centralising experience in that the legislature no longer spent most of its time reacting to petitions from the towns and inhabitants and then settling disputes. Beginning in the 1740s and 1750s, deputies from throughout the province, not just a few leading men from Boston and some of the larger towns, initiated and shaped government policy instead of merely voting on issues laid before them by the leadership.

238

Perhaps even more importantly, as Lawrence Henry Gipson has noted, the American Revolution was an aftermath of the 'Great War for Empire'. Gipson stresses that Britain's effort to regulate the colonies originated in unsolved problems of the Anglo-American connection (frontier defence, trading with the enemy, effective inter-colonial coordination of forces) which seriously hampered the war effort. Had not Canada fallen to the British, the Americans would still have depended on the mother country for defence and could not have rebelled.[62]

But the revolution was also an aftermath of Massachusetts' war for empire. Since the 1740s, the dominant faction in the province, led by men such as Hutchinson and Oliver, had staked its fortunes on whole-hearted American cooperation with British war measures. Functioning as full-time civil servants for years on end, they continued to support submission to post-war impositions even when the military necessity which had compelled such docility in the past had vanished. Convinced that the population as a whole lacked the knowledge and competence to govern itself, the future loyalists lacked any understanding that the successful careers and cordial relationships they had enjoyed with British officials during the war were not typical. They were not insensitive; they sought to alleviate impressment and imperial taxation. But if Britain proved adamant, they always counselled forbearance rather than resistance. Estranged from their suffering countrymen, they emerged in the revolutionary decade as a government without a country.

NOTES

1. William Pencak is Andrew W. Mellon Fellow in the Humanities, Duke University, Durham, North Carolina. Much of the article is adapted from his dissertation, 'Massachusetts Politics in War and Peace, 1676–1776' (Columbia University, 1978). A revised version will be published by Northeastern University Press. He wishes to thank Ralph Crandall, Jack P. Greene, Alden T. Vaughan, and Chilton Williamson for their assistance.
2. *Boston Gazette*, 21 May, 1754.
3. See generally Charles Tilly, ed., *The Formation of the Nation State in Western Europe* (Princeton, 1975), esp. 5–83.

4. Good accounts of Anglo-American relations during the French and Indian War are
    Lawrence Henry Gipson, *The British Empire Before the American Revolution* 15 vols.
    (New York, 1948–1974); Stanley Pargellis, *Lord Loudoun in North America* (New
    Haven, 1933); and Alan Rogers, *Empire and Liberty: American Resistance to British
    Authority, 1755–1763* (Berkeley, 1974).
5. *Journals of the House of Representatives of Massachusetts Bay* (Boston, 1919),
    XXII, 17, 84, 99, 110, 116, 153; XXIII, 26, 45, 110 (hereafter cited as *House Journals*);
    Gipson, *British Empire*, VII, 159–163; 316–24; IX, ch. iii; Jack P. Greene, 'Social
    Context and the Causal Pattern of the American Revolution: A Preliminary Con-
    sideration of New York, Virginia, and Massachusetts', (unpublished paper delivered
    at the Colloque Internationale du Centre National de la Recherche Scientifique: La
    Révolution Americaine et l'Europe, February 1977), 6.
6. Accounts of the Louisbourg campaign may be found in John A. Schutz, 'Imperialism
    in Massachusetts During the Governorship of William Shirley, 1741–1746', *Huntington
    Library Quarterly*, XXII (1960), 217–36; and Douglas Leach, 'Brothers in Arms?
    —Anglo-American Friction at Louisbourg, 1745–1746', *Massachusetts Historical
    Society Proceedings*, LXXXIX (1977), 36–54.
7. Michael Zuckerman, *Peaceable Kingdoms: The New England Towns in the Eighteenth
    Century* (New York, 1970), 35.
8. Abner C. Goodell and Ellis Ames, eds., *The Acts and Resolves of the Province of
    Massachusetts Bay* (Boston, 1869–1922), III 1107–51; IV, 1079–1116 for index of
    taxation and fiscal acts; for resolves for 1743, see XIII (Hereafter cited as *Acts*).
    Conversion of pounds Massachusetts to pounds sterling follows William Douglass,
    A Summary . . . Historical and Political . . . of North America (London, 1755), I, 493,
    and *Historical Statistics of the United States* (Washington, 1960), 771. After 1750
    four pounds Massachusetts equalled three pounds sterling.
9. *House Journals*, II, 228–33; VII, 450 ff; various letters for 1724–1726 in the Belknap,
    Pepperrell, Cushing, Colman, and Saltonstall Papers, Massachusetts Historical
    Society; Albert C. Matthews, 'The Acceptance of the Explanatory Charter', *Colonial
    Society of Massachusetts Publications*, XVII (1913), 389–400.
10. *House Journals*, VII, 229; VIII, *passim*, esp. 140, 163.
11. *Ibid.*, VIII, 251–435; IX, 1–81, *passim*; various letters for William Burnet and Jonathan
    Belcher to Lords of Trade and the Duke of Newcastle in W. Noel Sainsbury *et. al.*,
    eds., *Calendar of State Papers, Colonial Series* (London, 1869), XXXVI–XLII
    (hereafter cited as *CSP*); Lords of Trade to Privy Council, 26 Aug. 1735, *ibid.*, XLII,
    no. 82.
12. *House Journals*, X, 104, 123, 256, 415; XI, 67, 73, 93, 228, 309; Belcher to Newcastle,
    26 Dec. 1732 and 19 May 1733, *CSP*, XXXIX, no. 285; XL, no. 170.
13. William Dummer to Duke of Newcastle, *CSP*, 15 Sep. 1729, XXXVI, no. 904;
    Benjamin Prescott to John Chandler, 23 June 1729, MsC. 2041, New England Historic
    Genealogical Society, Boston, Mass.
14. *House Journals*, VI, 73, 93, 278, 309; Massachusetts Archives, Office of the Secretary
    of the Commonwealth, State House, Boston, XX, 248–9.
15. John A. Schutz, 'Succession Politics in Massachusetts, 1730–1741', *William and Mary
    Quarterly*, 3rd ser. XV (1958), 508–20.
16. Pencak, 'Massachusetts Politics', 445–53 for names of house leaders and statistical
    tables.
17. Information on kinship connections among the elite are most conveniently found
    in the appropriate biographies in Oliver O. Roberts, *The History of the Ancient and
    Honorable Artillery Company* (Boston, 1854–8), I, II; and John L. Sibley and Clifford
    K. Shipton, *Biographical Sketches of Those Who Attended Harvard College* (Cambridge,
    1873), III–VIII.
18. Good descriptions of the crisis are found in Andrew M. Davis, *Currency and Banking
    in Massachusetts Bay* (New York, 1901), I, 111–51; II, 102–218; 'Boston Banks and
    those who were Interested in Them', *New England Historic Genealogical Register*,
    LVII (1903), 279–81; and 'Provincial Banks, Land and Silver', *Colonial Society of
    Massachusetts Publications*, III, (1905–07) 2–41; George A. Billias, *Massachusetts
    Land Bankers of 1740* (Orono, Me., 1954); For specific information see *House Journals*,
    XVIII, 42–8, 185–6; Thomas Hutchinson to Benjamin Lynde, 12 Aug. 1741, in

239

Fitch E. Oliver, ed., *Diaries of Benjamin Lynde and Benjamin Lynde, Jr.* (Boston, 1880), 222–3.

19. J. M. Bumsted, 'Revivalism and Separatism in New England: The First Society of Norwich, Connecticut, as a Case Study', *William and Mary Quarterly*, 3rd. ser., XXIV (1967), 588–612; Philip Greven, 'Youth, Maturity, and Religious Conversion: A Note on the Ages of Converts in Andover, Massachusetts, 1718–1744', *Essex Institute Historical Collections*, CVIII (1972), 119–34; John C. Miller, 'Religion, Finance, and Democracy in Massachusetts', *New England Quarterly*, VI (1933), 29–58. I am indebted to Frank Granato, in a seminar paper written at Tufts University, 1979, for the information on the Second Church of Boston. For overpopulation, see Philip Greven, *Four Generations: Land, Population, and Family in Colonial Andover, Massachusetts* (Ithaca, 1970); Kenneth Lockridge, 'Social Change and the Meaning of the American Revolution', *Journal of Social History*, VI (1973), 403–39.

20. *House Journals*, XVIII, 103; Jonathan Belcher to William Shirley, 12 July 1740, Belcher Papers II, *Massachusetts Historical Society Collections*, 6th. ser. VII, 360; William Shirley to Duke of Newcastle, 4 Aug. 1740, in C. H. Lincoln, ed. *Correspondence of William Shirley* (New York, 1912), I, 24–6. For a profile of the soldiers, see Myron Stachiw's excellent introduction to the forthcoming *Massachusetts Officers and Soldiers During French and Indian Wars, 1722–1743*, to be published by the New England Historic Genealogical Society.

21. Shirley to Newcastle, 17 Oct. 1741, 23 Jan. 1742, and to Lords of Trade, 10 Aug. 1744, *Shirley Correspondence*, I, 76, 80, 140; Lords of Trade to Shirley, 9 Sep. 1744, *ibid.*, 144.

22. See, among other sources, Nathan O. Hatch, 'The Origins of Civil Millennialism in America: New England Clergymen, War with France, and the Revolution', *William and Mary Quarterly*, 3rd. ser., XXXI (1974), 417–22; Alan Heimert, *Religion, and the American Mind from the Great Awakening to the American Revolution* (Cambridge, 1966), 82–4; George A. Wood, *William Shirley: Governor of Massachusetts, 1741–1756* (New York, 1920), 169–70; 275–6.

23. G. B. Warden, *Boston, 1689–1776* (Boston, 1970), ch. vii; William Pencak and Ralph Crandall, 'Metropolitan Boston Before the American Revolution: An Urban Interpretation of the Imperial Crisis', (unpublished paper delivered at the Colonial Society of Massachusetts, February 1979).

24. See n. 8, 16, 17 above. Many leading supporters of the prerogative who had withdrawn from politics—especially those who became Anglicans—were related. But they exercised no influence in the legislature.

25. *House Journals*, XXI, 198; XXII, 162, 182; XXIII, 42.

26. *Ibid.*, XXII, 207, 246, 252.

27. *Ibid.*, XXV, 37, 52, 66; XXVI, 307–8.

28. John Noble, 'The Libel Suit of Knowles v. Douglass, 1748, 1749', *Colonial Society of Massachusetts Publications*, I (1895–7), 213–40; quotation from *The Independent Advertiser*, 4 July 1748; William Shirley to Samuel Waldo, 28 June 1748 and 7 July 1748; Waldo to Shirley, 28 June 1748; The Case of Waldo vs. Shirley, 22 April 1749; and Waldo to Christopher Kilby, 24 April 1749; all in Henry Know Papers, L, Massachusetts Historical Society.

29. *House Journals*, XXV, 116, 148, 150, 157; James Allen, *Letter to the Freeholders and Other Inhabitants of Massachusetts Bay* (Boston, 1749).

30. Thomas Hutchinson, 'Hutchinson in America', 58, 59, Egremont Mss. no. 2664, British Museum, Microfilm at Massachusetts Historical Society; Hutchinson to Israel Williams, 17 May 1749, Israel Williams Papers, Masachusetts Historical Society.

31. Allen, *Letter to Freeholders; House Journals*, XXVII, 35, 47, 56, 62, 97, 198, 234; XXVIII, 42, 52, 56, 69.

32. For a general discussion of the riot and its aftermath, see John Lax and William Pencak, 'The Knowles Riot and the Crisis of the 1740s in Massachusetts', *Perspectives in American History*, X (1976), 153–214.

33. For these nicknames, see *The Independent Advertiser*, 27 March, 1 April and 21 Nov. 1748. For salaries, see, for example, *Acts*, IV, 218; for government contracts, William T. Baxter, *The House of Hancock: Business in Boston, 1724–1775* (Cambridge, 1950),

240

92–110; 118–23; 129–41; 150–6; 253–5. Soldiers in out-of-province military expeditions were not liable to be sued for debt, a further inducement to enlist.

34. For a similar interpretation of why an ideology stressing government corruption appeared at this time, see Jack P. Greene, 'Political Mimesis; A Consideration of the Historical and Cultural Roots of Legislative Behavior in the British Colonies in the Eighteenth Century', *American Historical Review*, LXXV (1969), 337–67.

35. *The Independent Advertiser*, 4 Jan., 10 Oct. and 14 Nov. 1748; 17 July, and 17 Aug. 1749.

36. See Lax and Pencak, 'The Knowles Riot', for discussions of these mobs and bibliographical footnotes. Quotations from *The Independent Advertiser*, 8 Feb. 1748 and 5 Dec. 1749.

37. See n. 8 above.

38. *House Journals*, XXX, 43; XXXI, 38, 63–72; 202–3, 283–8; XXXII, 10, 56–9, 340–53; XXXIII, 294, 304, 307. For a discussion of the pamphlet literature see Paul Boyer, 'Borrowed Rhetoric: The Massachusetts Excise Controversy of 1754', *William and Mary Quarterly*, 3rd, ser., XXXI (1964), 328–51. For Boston's tax problems, see Warden, *Boston*, ch. vii., and William Pencak, 'The Social Structure of Revolutionary Boston: The Evidence From the Great Fire of 1760 Manuscripts', forthcoming in *The Journal of Interdisciplinary History*.

39. For embargoes, see, for example, *House Journals*, XXXII, 87, 93, 249, 305, 404; Francis Bernard to Jeffrey Amherst, 30 May, 2 June, 29 Aug. and 5 Sep. 1762, Bernard Papers, II, 155, 157, 280, 282, Sparks Manuscripts, Houghton Library, Harvard University; Bernard to Lords of Trade, 1 Aug. 1763, Bernard Papers, III, 162; Massachusetts Archives, LV, 301.

40. *Acts*, IV, 29–38; Francis Bernard to Lords of Trade, 18 April 1765, Bernard Papers, III, 203; Carl Bridenbaugh, *Cities in Revolt* (New York, 1955), 252–3.

41. Impressment during the French and Indian War is discussed in William Pencak, 'Thomas Hutchinson's Fight Against Naval Impressment', *New England Historic and Genealogical Register*, CXXXII (1978), 25–36.

42. Lord Loudoun to [Massachusetts House of Representatives], 29 Jan. 1757, Israel Williams Papers; *House Journals*, XXXV, 351f; Thomas Hutchinson to Loudoun, 21 Feb. 1757, Loudoun Papers, Huntington Library, San Marino, California, photostat at the Massachusetts Historical Society; various letters in Massachusetts Archives, LVI, Pargellis, *Lord Loudoun*, 175–6; 185–6; 214–5; 269–78; John A. Schutz, *Thomas Pownall: Defender of American Liberty* (Glendale, California, 1951), 125, 130.

43. Quoted in Rogers, *Empire and Liberty*, 63.

44. Lord Loudoun to Governor Thomas Pownall (1757–1760), 8 and 15 Nov., 8 Dec. 1757, Massachusetts Archives, LVI, 256–66; Pownall to Loudoun, 26 Dec. 1757, *ibid.*, 278, 286; *House Journals*, XXXIV, 208, 256.

45. *House Journals*, XXXVII, 250; XXXVIII, 302; Francis Bernard to Lords of Trade, 17 April 1762, Bernard Papers, II, 180.

46. Jasper Mauduit to Massachusetts House of Representatives, 8 Feb. 1763, Mauduit Papers, *Massachusetts Historical Society Collections*, LXXIV (1918), 100; Gipson, *British Empire*, IX, ch. ii.

47. Carl Bridenbaugh, *Mitre and Sceptre: Transatlantic Faiths, Ideas, Personalities, and Politics, 1689–1775* (New York, 1962), ch. vii; Mauduit Papers, *passim*, esp. 30, 76, 104–19; Francis Bernard to Richard Jackson, 23 Jan. 1763, Bernard Papers, II, 249–50; for families which profited from the war, see Gary Nash, 'Social Change and the Growth of Pre-Revolutionary Urban Radicalism', in Alfred E. Young, ed., *The American Revolution*, (DeKalb, Ill., 1976), 21–3.

48. Warden, *Boston*, 356–57; Gordon E. Kershaw, *'Gentlemen of Large Property and Judicious Men': The Kennebeck Proprietors, 1749–1775* (Somersworth, N. H., 1975); also see various documents in Henry Knox Papers, L–LI, Massachusetts Historical Society.

49. Henri Lefavour, 'The Proposed College in Hampshire County in 1762', *Massachusetts Historical Society Proceedings*, LXVI (1936–41), 53–80; Mauduit Papers, 70–3; Oxenbridge Thacher to Benjamin Pratt [1762], Thacher Papers, Massachusetts Historical Society.

50. John Shy, *A People Numerous and Armed* (New York, 1976), 30–1, 173.

241

51. Joseph Ernst and Marc Egnal, 'An Economic Interpretation of the American Revolution', *William and Mary Quarterly*, 3rd. ser., XXIX (1972), 3–32; Anne Cunningham, ed., *Diary and Letters of John Rowe*, (Boston, 1903), 61, 67–70; Warden, *Boston*, ch. viii.
52. Warning Out Records in Overseers of the Poor Mss., Massachusetts Historical Society. These themes are developed further in William Pencak, 'The Revolt Against Gerontocracy: Genealogy and the Massachusetts Revolution', *National Genealogical Society Quarterly*, LXVI (1978), 291–304.
53. David Ader, Arthur Landry, and David Peete, in course papers written at Tufts University, 1979, have studied the Medford and Roxbury contingents in the continental army during the Revolution. In gerneal, young men who did not pay taxes comprised the rank-and-file of those who enlisted for more than a few days when the British were in the neighbourhood. See also B. Michael Zuckerman, 'Neighbours Divided: The Social Impact of the Continental Army—Massachusetts, 1774–1786', (Wesleyan University, A. B. honors thesis, 1971).
54. For a detailed discussion of the residences and migration pattern of the prerogative faction, see Pencak and Crandall, 'Metropolitan Boston'.
55. John A. Schutz, 'Those Who Became Tories: Town Loyalty and the Revolution in New England', *New England Historic Genealogical Register*, CXXIX (1975), 94–105. For age of loyalists, see Pencak, 'Revolt Against Gerontocracy'.
56. Waldo died in 1759, Allen in 1754; for Pratt and Tyng see Shipton, *Harvard Graduates*, VI, 540–49; VII, 595–600.
57. James Otis, *The Rights of the British Colonies Asserted and Proved* (Boston, 1764), 72.
58. Quoted in Jack P. Greene, *Colonies to Nation, 1763–1789* (New York, 1967), 34, 72.
59. Edmund S. Morgan, 'Thomas Hutchinson and the Stamp Act', *New England Quarterly* XXI (1948), 488, 489; Hutchinson to William Bollan, 14 July 1760, Massachusetts Archives XXV, 14–17, pagination to typescript copy at the Massachusetts Historical Society prepared by Catherine Barton Mayo.
60. Isaac Royall to Lord Dartmouth, 18 Jan. 1774, Ms. L., Massachusetts Historical Society.
61. Thomas Hutchinson, *History of the Colony and Province of Massachusetts Bay* (Cambridge, 1936), III, 253.
62. Lawrence Henry Gipson, 'The American Revolution as an Aftermath of the Great War for Empire, 1754–1763', *Political Science Quarterly*, LXV (1950), 86–104.

242

"Under the Banner of King Death": The Social World of Anglo-American Pirates, 1716 to 1726

Marcus Rediker

WRITING to the Board of Trade in 1724, Governor Alexander Spotswood of Virginia lamented his lack of "some safe opportunity to get home" to London. He insisted that he would travel only in a well-armed man-of-war.

> Your Lordships will easily conceive my Meaning when you reflect on the Vigorous part I've acted to suppress Pirates: and if those barbarous Wretches can be moved to cut off the Nose & Ears of a Master for but correcting his own Sailors, what inhuman treatment must I expect, should I fall within their power, who have been markt as the principle object of their vengeance, for cutting off their arch Pirate Thatch [Teach, also known as Blackbeard], with all his grand Designs, & making so many of their Fraternity to swing in the open air of Virginia.[1]

Spotswood knew these pirates well. He had authorized the expedition that returned to Virginia boasting Blackbeard's head as a trophy. He had done his share to see that many pirates swung on Virginia gallows. He knew that pirates had a fondness for revenge, that they often punished ship captains for "correcting" their crews, and that a kind of "fraternity" prevailed among them. He had good reason to fear them.

The Anglo-American pirates active between 1716 and 1726 occupied a grand position in the long history of a robbery at sea. Their numbers, near five thousand, were extraordinary, and their plunderings were exceptional in both volume and value. Spotswood and other officials and merchants produced a plentiful body of written testimony on pirates and their ways, but historians, though long fascinated by sea-rovers, have not used this

Mr. Rediker is a graduate student in the Department of History at the University of Pennsylvania. He wishes to thank Alan V. Briceland, Richard S. Dunn, Roma Heaney, Dan Schiller, Steven Zdatny and, especially, Nancy Hewitt and Michael Zuckerman for their critical discussion and encouragement of this essay. He expresses special gratitude to Kent Willis for drawing the chart.

[1] Alexander Spotswood to the Board of Trade, June 16, 1724, C.O. 5/1319, Public Record Office.

material to full advantage.[2] This essay explores the social and cultural dimensions of piracy, focusing on pirates' experience, the organization of their ships, and their social relations and consciousness, with observations on the social and economic context of the crime and its culture. Piracy represented crime on a massive scale—crime as a way of life voluntarily chosen, for the most part, by large numbers of men and directly challenging the ways of the society from which the pirates excepted themselves. The main intent of this essay is to see how piracy looked from the inside and to examine the kinds of social order that pirates forged beyond the reach of traditional authority. Beneath the Jolly Roger, "the banner of King Death," a new social world took shape once pirates had, as one of them put it, "the choice in themselves."[3]

244

[2] Studies of piracy include general surveys, descriptive chronicles of exploits, and specific, often monographic examinations of certain features of pirate life. Daniel Defoe was the first historian of these pirates. Under the name Charles Johnson, he published an invaluable collection of mostly accurate information, *A General History of the Pyrates,* ed. Manuel Schonhorn (Columbia, S.C., 1972 [orig. publ. in 2 vols., London, 1724, 1728]), hereafter cited as *History of Pyrates.* George Roberts (believed to have been Defoe), *The Four Years Voyages . . .* (London, 1726), contains believable accounts of pirates. The best recent study is Hugh F. Rankin, *The Golden Age of Piracy* (New York, 1969). More ambitious are Philip Gosse, *The History of Piracy* (New York, 1932); Neville Williams, *Captains Outrageous: Seven Centuries of Piracy* (London, 1961); and P. K. Kemp and Christopher Lloyd, *Brethren of the Coast: Buccaneers of the South Seas* (New York, 1960). Patrick Pringle's *Jolly Roger* (New York, 1953), a piece of popular history, has some fine insights. Charles Grey, *Pirates of the Eastern Seas, 1618-1723: A Lurid Page of History,* ed. George MacMunn (Port Washington, N.Y., 1971 [orig. publ. London, 1933]); George Francis Dow and John Henry Edmonds, *The Pirates of the New England Coast, 1630-1730* (Salem, Mass., 1923); and John Biddulph, *The Pirates of Malabar; and, An Englishwoman . . . in India . . .* (London, 1907) are somewhat descriptive but present important data. Stanley Richards, *Black Bart* (Llandybie, Wales, 1966), is a biography of Bartholomew Roberts. See also Shirley Carter Hughson, *The Carolina Pirates and Colonial Commerce, 1670-1740,* Johns Hopkins University Studies in Historical and Political Science, XII (Baltimore, 1894); B. R. Burg, "Legitimacy and Authority: A Case Study of Pirate Commanders in the Seventeenth and Eighteenth Centuries," *American Neptune.* XXXVII (1977), 40-49; James G. Lydon, *Pirates, Privateers, and Profits* (Upper Saddle River, N.J., 1970); and Richard B. Morris, "The Ghost of Captain Kidd," *New York History,* XIX (1938), 280-297. The literature on piracy is vast. For the newcomer, these works provide a solid beginning.
[3] S. Charles Hill, "Episodes of Piracy in Eastern Waters," *Indian Antiquary,* XLIX (1920), 37; Arthur L. Hayward, ed., *Lives of the Most Remarkable Criminals . . .* (London, 1735), 37. Following E. P. Thompson, *Whigs and Hunters: The Origin of the Black Act* (New York, 1975), and Douglas Hay *et al., Albion's Fatal Tree: Crime and Society in Eighteenth-Century England* (New York, 1975), this study uses the social history of crime as access to lower-class life in the early eighteenth century. I define a pirate as one who willingly participates in robbery on the sea, not discriminating among nationalities in his choice of victims. Part of the empirical base of this study was accumulated in piecemeal fashion from documents of all

Contemporary estimates of the pirate population during the period under consideration placed the number between one and two thousand at any one time. This range seems generally accurate. From records that describe the activities of pirate ships and from reports or projections of crew sizes, it appears that eighteen to twenty-four hundred Anglo-American pirates were active between 1716 and 1718, fifteen hundred to two thousand between 1719 and 1722, and one thousand to fifteen hundred declining to fewer than two hundred between 1723 and 1726. In the only estimate we have from the other side of the law, a band of pirates in 1716 claimed that there were "30 Company of them," or roughly twenty-four hundred men, around the world. In all, some forty-five to fifty-five hundred men went, as they called it, "upon the account."[4]

These sea-robbers followed lucrative trade and, like their predecessors, sought bases for their depredations in the Caribbean Sea and the Indian Ocean. The Bahama Islands, no longer defended or governed by the crown, began in 1716 to attract pirates by the hundreds. By 1718 a torrent of complaints moved George I to commission Woodes Rogers to lead an expedition to bring the islands under control. Rogers's efforts largely succeeded, and pirates scattered to the unpeopled inlets of the Carolinas and to Africa. They had frequented African shores as early as 1691; by 1718, Madagascar served as both an entrepôt for booty and as a spot for temporary settlement. At the mouth of the Sierra Leone River on Africa's western coast pirates stopped off for "whoring and drinking" and to unload goods. Theaters of operation among pirates shifted, however, according to the policing designs of the Royal Navy. Pirates favored the Caribbean

245

varieties: individual pirates were recorded by name and dates of activity. Information on age, labor, class, and family background, and miscellaneous detail were noted. This file (519 men, 2 women) can be replicated only by consulting all the sources that follow in the notes. Since I have found mention of only 2 female pirates, and since the maritime world was predominantly male, the latter gender is used in references.

[4] James Logan, 1717, estimated 1,500, in Hughson, *Carolina Pirates*, 59; Gov. of Bermuda, 1717, "at least 1,000," in Pringle, *Jolly Roger*, 181, and in H.C.A. 1/54, f. 113, P.R.O.; Woodes Rogers, 1718, "near a thousand," in *History of Pyrates*, 615; Daniel Defoe, 1720, 1,500, *ibid.*, 132; Gov. of S.C., 1718, "near 2,000," in W. Noel Sainsbury *et al.*, eds., *Calendar of State Papers, Colonial Series, America and the West Indies* (London, 1860-), XXXI, 10, hereafter cited as *Cal. St. Papers;* [Anonymous], 1721, 1,500, in Abel Boyer, ed., *The Political State of Great Britain . . .* (London, 1711-1740), XXI, 659. Quotation from Representation from Several Merchants Trading to Virginia to Board of Trade, Apr. 15, 1717, C.O. 5/1318, P.R.O. Estimates of the sizes of crews are available for 37 pirate ships: the mean is 79.5. I have found references to 79 crews through mentions of ship or captain. Totals were obtained by arranging ships according to periods of activity and multiplying by the mean crew size. If this mean holds, the total population would have been 6,281. Yet this figure counts some pirates more than once. For example, many who sailed with both Howell Davis and Bartholomew Roberts are counted twice. The range 4,500-5,500 expresses the uncertainty of the calculations. It seems that, in all, some 5,000 men were involved.

because of its shallow waters and numerous unsettled cays, but generally, as one pirate noted, these rovers were "dispers't into several parts of the World." Sea-robbers sought and usually found bases near major trade routes, as distant as possible from the powers of the state.[5]

Almost all pirates had labored as merchant seamen, Royal Navy sailors, or privateersmen.[6] The vast majority came from captured merchantmen as volunteers, for reasons suggested by Dr. Samuel Johnson's observation that "no man will be a sailor who has contrivance enough to get himself into a jail; for being in a ship is being in jail with the chance of being drowned. . . . A man in jail has more room, better food, and commonly better company."[7] Merchant seamen got a hard, close look at death: disease and accidents were commonplace in their occupation, rations were often meager, and discipline was brutal. Each ship was "a little kingdom" whose captain held a near-absolute power which he often abused. Peacetime wages for sailors were consistently low between 1643 and 1797; fraud and irregularities in the distribution of pay were general. A prime purpose of eighteenth-century maritime laws was "to assure a ready supply of cheap, docile labor."[8] Merchant seamen also had to contend with impressment as practiced by the Royal Navy.

246

[5] Deposition of John Vickers, 1716, C.O. 5/1317, P.R.O.; Spotswood to Council of Trade and Plantations, May 31, 1717, C.O. 5/1364; History of Pyrates, 31-34; Leo Francis Stock, ed., Proceedings and Debates of the British Parliaments respecting North America, III (Washington, D.C., 1930), 399; deposition of Adam Baldridge, in John Franklin Jameson, ed., Privateering and Piracy in the Colonial Period: Illustrative Documents (New York, 1923), 180-187; R. A. Brock, ed., The Official Letters of Alexander Spotswood . . . (Virginia Historical Society, Collections, N.S., II [Richmond, 1882]), 168, 351, hereafter cited as Brock, ed., Letters of Spotswood; William Snelgrave, A New Account of Some Parts of Guinea and the Slave-Trade (London, 1734), 197; Abbé Rochon, "A Voyage to Madagascar and the East Indies," in John Pinkerton, ed., A General Collection of the Best and Most Interesting Voyages and Travels . . . , XVI (London, 1814), 767-771; William Smith, A New Voyage to Guinea . . . (London, 1744), 12, 42. On Defoe's credibility see Schonhorn's introduction to History of Pyrates, xxvii-xl; Gosse, History of Piracy, 182; and Rankin, Golden Age, 161.

[6] Biographical data indicate that 155 of the 157 for whom labor background is known came from one of these employments; 144 had been in the merchant service. Probably fewer than 5% of pirates originated as mutineers. See History of Pyrates, 116, 196, 215-216; Snelgrave, Account of the Slave-Trade, 203; deposition of Richard Symes, Cal. St. Papers, XXXII, 319; and ibid., XXXIII, 365 on volunteers.

[7] James Boswell, The Life of Samuel Johnson . . . (London, 1791), 86.

[8] Jesse Lemisch, "Jack Tar in the Streets: Merchant Seamen in the Politics of Revolutionary America," William and Mary Quarterly, 3d Ser., XXV (1968), 379, 375-376, 406; Richard B. Morris, Government and Labor in Early America (New York, 1946), 246-247, 257, 262-268; History of Pyrates, 244, 359; A. G. Course, The Merchant Navy: A Social History (London, 1963), 61; Samuel Cox to Council of Trade, Cal. St. Papers, XXXII, 393; Ralph Davis, The Rise of the English Shipping

Some pirates had served in the navy where conditions aboard ship were no less harsh. Food supplies often ran short, wages were low, mortality was high, discipline severe, and desertion consequently chronic. As one officer reported, the navy had trouble fighting pirates because the king's ships were "so much disabled by sickness, death, and desertion of their seamen."[9] In 1722 the crown sent the *Weymouth* and the *Swallow* in search of a pirate convoy. Royal surgeon John Atkins, noting that merchant seamen were frequently pressed, underlined precisely what these sailors had to fear when he recorded that the "*Weymouth,* who brought out of *England* a Compliment [*sic*] of 240 Men," had "at the end of the Voyage 280 dead upon her Books."[10] Epidemics, consumption, and scurvy raged on royal ships, and the men were "caught in a machine from which there was no escape, bar desertion, incapacitation, or death."[11]

Pirates who had served on privateering vessels knew well that this employment was far less onerous than on merchant or naval ships: food was usually more plentiful, the pay considerably higher, and the work shifts generally shorter.[12] Even so, owing to rigid discipline and to other grievances, mutinies were not uncommon. On Woodes Rogers's spectacularly successful privateering expedition of 1708-1711, Peter Clark was thrown

247

Industry in the Seventeenth and Eighteenth Centuries (London, 1962), 144, 154-155; Nathaniel Uring, *The Voyages and Travels of Captain Nathaniel Uring,* ed. Alfred Dewar (London, 1726), xxviii, 176-178; Arthur Pierce Middleton, *Tobacco Coast: A Maritime History of Chesapeake Bay in the Colonial Era* (Newport News, Va., 1953), 8, 13, 15, 18, 271, 281; Christopher Lloyd, *The British Seaman, 1200-1860: A Social Survey* (Rutherford, N.J., 1970), 249, 264; John Atkins, *A Voyage to Guinea, Brasil, and the West-Indies* ... (London, 1735), 261; G. T. Crook, ed., *The Complete Newgate Calendar* ..., III (London, 1926), 57-58; S. Charles Hill, "Notes on Piracy in Eastern Waters," *Indian Antiq.,* LVI (1927), 130; Hayward, ed., *Remarkable Criminals,* 126.

[9] Gov. Lowther to Council of Trade, *Cal. St. Papers,* XXIX, 350; Morris, *Government,* 247; Lemisch, "Jack Tar," *WMQ,* 3d Ser., XXV (1968), 379; Davis, *English Shipping,* 133-137; R. D. Merriman, ed., *Queen Anne's Navy: Documents Concerning the Administration of the Navy of Queen Anne, 1702-1714* (London, 1961), 170-172, 174, 221-222, 250; Lloyd, *British Seaman,* 44-46, 124-149; Peter Kemp, *The British Sailor: A Social History of the Lower Deck* (London, 1970), chaps. 4, 5; Arthur N. Gilbert, "Buggery and the British Navy, 1700-1861," *Journal of Social History,* X (1976-1977), 72-98.

[10] Atkins, *Voyage to Guinea,* 139, 187; *The Historical Register, Containing an Impartial Relation of All Transactions* ..., VII (London, 1722), 344.

[11] Merriman, *Queen Anne's Navy,* 171. Lloyd, *British Seaman,* 44, estimates that $^1/_2$ of all men pressed between 1600 and 1800 died at sea.

[12] Course, *Merchant Navy,* 84; Lloyd, *British Seaman,* 57; Edward Cooke, *A Voyage to the South Sea, and Round the World* ..., I (London, 1712), v-vi, 14-16; Woodes Rogers, *A Cruising Voyage Round the World,* ed. G. E. Manwaring (New York, 1928 [orig. publ. London, 1712]), xiv, xxv; George Shelvocke, *A Voyage Round the World* ... (London, 1726), 34-36, 38, 46, 157, 214, 217; William Betagh, *A Voyage Round the World* ... (London, 1728), 4.

into irons for wishing himself "aboard a Pirate" and saying that "he should be glad that an Enemy, who could over-power us, was a-long-side of us."[13]

Whether from the merchant service, the navy, or the privateering enterprise, pirates necessarily came from seafaring employments. Piracy emphatically was not an option open to landlubbers since sea-robbers "entertain'd so contemptible a Notion of Landmen."[14] Men who became pirates were grimly familiar with the rigors of life at sea and with a single-sex community of work.

Ages are known for 117 pirates active between 1716 and 1726. The range was seventeen to fifty years, the mean 27.4, and the median 27; the twenty-to-twenty-four and the twenty-five-to-twenty-nine age categories had the highest concentrations, with 39 and 37 men respectively. Significantly, 59.3 percent were aged twenty-five or older. Given the high mortality rates within the occupations from which pirates came, these ages were advanced.[15] Though evidence is sketchy, most pirates seem not to have been bound to land and home by familial ties or obligations. Wives and children are rarely mentioned in the records of trials of pirates, and pirate vessels, to forestall desertion, often would "take no Married Man."[16] Almost without exception, pirates came from the lowest social classes. They were, as a royal official condescendingly observed, "desperate Rogues" who could have little hope in life ashore.[17] These traits served as bases of unity when men of the sea decided, in search of something better, to become pirates.

These characteristics had a vital bearing on the ways pirates organized their daily activities. Contemporaries who claimed that pirates had "no regular command among them" mistook a different social order—different from the ordering of merchant, naval, and privateering vessels—for disorder.[18] This social order, articulated in the organization of the pirate ship, was conceived and deliberately constructed by the pirates them-

[13] Rogers, *Cruising Voyage*, 205. See also Shelvocke, *Voyage*, 43, 221-225.

[14] *History of Pyrates*, 228.

[15] See above, n. 3. Ages were taken at time of first known piracy.

[16] Only 23 in the sample of 521 are known to have been married. In pirate confessions, regrets were often expressed to parents, seldom to wives or children. See Cotton Mather, *Useful Remarks: An Essay upon Remarkables in the Way of Wicked Men: A Sermon on the Tragical End, unto which the Way of Twenty-Six Pirates Brought Them; At New Port on Rhode-Island, July 19, 1723* . . . (New London, Conn., 1723), 38-42; and *Trials of Eight Persons Indited for Piracy* . . . (Boston, 1718), 24, 25. Quotation from John Barnard, *Ashton's Memorial: An History of the Strange Adventures, and Signal Deliverances of Mr. Philip Ashton* . . . (Boston, 1725), 3.

[17] Peter Haywood to Council of Trade, Dec. 3, 1716, C.O. 137/12, P.R.O.; Lemisch, "Jack Tar," *WMQ*, 3d Ser., XXV (1968), 377; Davis, *English Shipping*, 114. Biographical data show that 71 of 75 class backgrounds were of low status.

[18] Betagh, *Voyage*, 148.

selves. Its hallmark was a rough, improvised, but effective egalitarianism
that placed authority in the collective hands of the crew.

A striking uniformity of rules and customs prevailed aboard pirate
ships, each of which functioned under the terms of written articles, a compact drawn up at the beginning of a voyage or upon election of a new
captain, and agreed to by the crew. By these articles crews allocated authority, distributed plunder, and enforced discipline.[19] These arrangements made the captain the creature of his crew. Demanding someone
both bold of temper and skilled in navigation, the men elected their captain. They gave him few privileges: he "or any other Officer is allowed no
more [food] than another man, nay, the Captain cannot keep his Cabbin to
himself."[20] A merchant captain held captive by pirates noted with displeasure that crew members slept on the ship wherever they pleased, "the
Captain himself not being allowed a Bed."[21] The crew granted the captain
unquestioned authority "in fighting, chasing, or being chased," but "in all
other Matters whatsoever" he was "governed by a Majority."[22] As the
majority elected, so it could depose. Captains were snatched from their
positions for cowardice, cruelty, or refusing "to take and plunder English
Vessels."[23] One captain incurred the class-conscious wrath of his crew for
being too "Gentleman-like."[24] Occasionally, a despotic captain was summarily executed. As pirate Francis Kennedy explained, most sea-robbers,
"having suffered formerly from the ill-treatment of their officers, provided
carefully against any such evil" once they arranged their own command.[25]

To prevent the misuse of authority, countervailing powers were desig-
nated for the quartermaster, who was elected to protect "the Interest of

249

[19] *History of Pyrates*, 167, 211-213, 298, 307-308, 321; Hayward, ed., *Remarkable Criminals*, 37; H.C.A. 1/55, f. 23, P.R.O.; Snelgrave, *Account of the Slave-
Trade*, 220; Jameson, ed., *Privateering and Piracy*, 337; Rankin, *Golden Age*, 31.
The vast differences between pirate and privateer articles can be seen by comparing the above to Rogers, *Cruising Voyage*, xiv, xxv, 22-23; Shelvocke, *Voyage*,
34-36, 159, 218, 223; Cooke, *Voyage*, iv-vi; and Betagh, *Voyage*, 205-206.

[20] Clement Downing, *A Compendious History of the Indian Wars* . . . (London,
1924 [orig. publ. London, 1737]), 99; *History of Pyrates*, 121, 139, 167-168, 195,
208, 214, 340, 352; Snelgrave, *Account of the Slave-Trade*, 199; *Trials of Eight
Persons*, 24; Boyer, ed., *Political State*, XXVIII, 152; Roberts, *Four Years Voyages*,
39.

[21] Snelgrave, *Account of the Slave-Trade*, 217; *History of Pyrates*, 213-214.

[22] *History of Pyrates*, 139; Hayward, ed., *Remarkable Criminals*, 37; Boyer, ed.,
Political State, XXVIII, 153; Burg, "Legitimacy and Authority," *Am. Neptune*,
XXXVII (1977), 40-49.

[23] Jameson, ed., *Privateering and Piracy*, 294; *History of Pyrates*, 139, 67; Dow
and Edmonds, *Pirates of New England*, 217; *Trials of Eight Persons*, 23; Morris,
"Ghost of Kidd," *N.Y. Hist.*, XIX (1938), 282.

[24] Snelgrave, *Account of the Slave-Trade*, 199; Burg, "Legitimacy and Authority,"
Am. Neptune, XXXVII (1977), 44-48.

[25] Hayward, ed., *Remarkable Criminals*, 37; *History of Pyrates*, 42, 296, 337.

the Crew."[26] His tasks were to adjudicate minor disputes, distribute food and money, and in some instances to lead attacks on prize vessels. He served as a "civil Magistrate" and dispensed necessaries "with an Equality to them all."[27] The quartermaster often became the captain of a captured ship when the captor was overcrowded or divided by discord. This containment of authority within a dual executive was a distinctive feature of social organization among pirates.[28]

The decisions that had the greatest bearing on the welfare of the crew were generally reserved to the council, a body usually including every man on the ship. The council determined such matters as where the best prizes could be taken and how disruptive dissension was to be resolved. Some crews continually used the council, "carrying every thing by a majority of votes"; others set up the council as a court. The decisions made by this body constituted the highest authority on a pirate ship: even the boldest captain dared not challenge a council's mandate.[29]

The distribution of plunder was regulated explicitly by the ship's articles, which allocated booty according to skills and duties. Captain and quartermaster received between one and one-half and two shares; gunners, boatswains, mates, carpenters, and doctors, one and one-quarter or one and one-half; all others got one share each.[30] This pay system represented a radical departure from practices in the merchant service, Royal Navy, or privateering. It leveled an elaborate hierarchy of pay ranks and decisively reduced the disparity between the top and bottom of the scale. Indeed, this must have been one of the most egalitarian plans for the disposition of resources to be found anywhere in the early eighteenth century. The scheme indicates that pirates did not consider themselves wage laborers but rather risk-sharing partners. If, as a noted historian of piracy,

[26] *History of Pyrates*, 423; Lloyd Haynes Williams, *Pirates of Colonial Virginia* (Richmond, 1937), 19.
[27] Roberts, *Four Years Voyages*, 37, 80; *The Tryals of Major Stede Bonnet and Other Pirates* ... (London, 1719), 37; Snelgrave, *Account of the Slave-Trade*, 199-200, 238-239; Boyer, ed., *Political State*, XXVIII, 153; *History of Pyrates*, 213-225; *Trials of Eight Persons*, 24, 25; *Tryals of Thirty-Six Persons for Piracy* ... (Boston, 1723), 9; *Boston News-Letter*, July 15-22, 1717. Quotations from *History of Pyrates*, 213; Downing, *Indian Wars*, 99.
[28] Boyer, ed., *Political State*, XXVIII, 151; Snelgrave, *Account of the Slave-Trade*, 272; *History of Pyrates*, 138-139, 312. Davis, *English Shipping*, 113, discusses the quite different role of the quartermaster in the merchant service.
[29] *History of Pyrates*, 88-89, 117, 145, 167, 222-225, 292, 595; *Trials of Eight Persons*, 24; Downing, *Indian Wars*, 44, 103; H.C.A. 24/132, P.R.O.; Hill, "Episodes of Piracy," *Indian Antiq.*, XLIX (1920), 41-42, 59; Roberts, *Four Years Voyages*, 55, 86; Boyer, ed., *Political State*, XXVIII, 153. Quotation from Betagh, *Voyage*, 148.
[30] *History of Pyrates*, 211-212, 307-308, 342-343; Dow and Edmonds, *Pirates of New England*, 146-147; Hayward, ed., *Remarkable Criminals*, 37; *Tryals of Bonnet*, 22; Morris, "Ghost of Kidd," *N.Y. Hist.*, XIX (1938), 283.

Philip Gosse, has suggested, "the pick of all seamen were pirates,"[31] the equitable distribution of plunder and the conception of the partnership may be understood as the work of men who valued and respected the skills of their comrades. But not all booty was dispensed this way. A portion went into a "common fund" to provide for the men who sustained injury of lasting effect.[32] The loss of eyesight or any appendage merited compensation. By this welfare system pirates attempted to guard against debilities caused by accidents, to protect skills, and to promote loyalty within the group.

The articles also regulated discipline aboard ship, though "discipline" is perhaps a misnomer for a rule system that left large ranges of behavior uncontrolled. Less arbitrary than that of the merchant service and less codified than that of the navy, discipline among pirates always depended on a collective sense of transgression. Many misdeeds were accorded "what Punishment the Captain and Majority of the Company shall think fit," and it is noteworthy that pirates did not often resort to the whip. Their discipline, if no less severe in certain cases, was generally tolerant of behavior that provoked punishment in other maritime occupations. Three major methods of discipline were employed, all conditioned by the fact that pirate ships were crowded: an average crew numbered near eighty on a 250-ton vessel. The articles of Bartholomew Roberts's ship revealed one tactic for maintaining order: "No striking one another on board, but every Man's Quarrels to be ended on Shore at Sword and Pistol." Antagonists were to fight a duel with pistols, but if both their first shots missed, then with swords, and the first to draw blood was declared the victor. By taking such conflicts off the ship (and symbolically off the sea), this practice promoted harmony in the crowded quarters below decks.[33] The ideal of harmony was also reflected when, in an often-used disciplinary action, pirates made a crew member the "Governor of an Island." Men who were incorrigibly disruptive or who transgressed important rules were marooned. For defrauding his mates by taking more than a proper share of plunder,

251

---

[31] See above, n. 20; Gosse, *History of Piracy,* 103; Biddulph, *Pirates of Malabar,* x, 155; and [John Fillmore], "A Narrative of the Singular Sufferings of John Fillmore and Others on Board the Noted Pirate Vessel Commanded by Captain Phillips," Buffalo Historical Society, *Publications,* X (1907), 32.

[32] *History of Pyrates,* 212, 308, 343; Dow and Edmonds, *Pirates of New England,* 147; pirate Jeremiah Huggins, quoted in Morris, "Ghost of Kidd," *N.Y. Hist.,* XIX (1938), 292; Hill, "Episodes of Piracy," *Indian Antiq.,* XLIX (1920), 57.

[33] *History of Pyrates,* 307, 212, 157-158, 339; see above, n. 4. James F. Shepherd and Gary M. Walton, *Shipping, Maritime Trade, and the Economic Development of Colonial North America* (Cambridge, 1972), 201-203, show that for the ports of Jamaica (1729-1731), Barbados (1696-1698), and Charleston (1735-1739) respectively, merchant seamen in vessels over 150 tons handled 8.6, 10.7, and 12.0 tons per man. Pirates, by more general calculations, handled only 3.1 tons per man; the difference reveals how much more crowded their ships were.

for deserting or malingering during battle, for keeping secrets from the crew, or for stealing, a pirate risked being deposited "where he was sure to encounter Hardships."[34] The ultimate method of maintaining order was execution. This penalty was exacted for bringing on board "a Boy or a Woman" or for meddling with a "prudent Woman" on a prize ship, but was most commonly invoked to punish a captain who abused his authority.[35]

Some crews attempted to circumvent disciplinary problems by taking "no Body against their Wills."[36] By the same logic, they would keep no unwilling person. The confession of pirate Edward Davis in 1718 indicates that oaths of honor were used to cement the loyalty of new members: "at first the old Pirates were a little shy of the new ones, . . . yet in a short time the *New Men* being sworn to be faithful, and not to cheat the Company to the Value of a *Piece of Eight*, they all consulted and acted together with great unanimity, and no distinction was made between *Old* and *New*."[37] Yet for all their efforts to blunt the cutting edge of authority and to maintain harmony and cohesion, conflict could not always be contained. Occasionally, upon election of a new captain, men who favored other leadership drew up new articles and sailed away from their former mates.[38] The social organization constructed by pirates, although flexible, was unable to accommodate severe, sustained conflict. The egalitarian and collective exercise of authority by pirates had both negative and positive effects. Although it produced a chronic instability, it also guaranteed continuity: the very process by which new crews were established helped to ensure a social uniformity and, as we shall see, a consciousness of kind among pirates.[39]

One important mechanism in this continuity can be seen by charting the connections among pirate crews. The accompanying diagram, arranged according to vessel captaincy, demonstrates that by splintering, by sailing in

---

[34] *Tryals of Bonnet*, 30; *History of Pyrates*, 211, 212, 342; Biddulph, *Pirates of Malabar*, 163-164; Rankin, *Golden Age*, 37.

[35] *History of Pyrates*, 212, 343; Snelgrave, *Account of the Slave-Trade*, 256; *American Weekly Mercury* (Philadelphia), May 30-June 6, 1723. This discussion of discipline takes into account not only the articles themselves but also observations on actual punishments from other sources.

[36] Jameson, ed., *Privateering and Piracy*, 304; *Trials of Eight Persons*, 19, 21; Brock, ed.; *Letters of Spotswood*, 249; *History of Pyrates*, 260. Some men, usually those with skills, were occasionally pressed: see *Cal. St. Papers*, XXXIII, 365.

[37] *Trials of Eight Persons*, 21; deposition of Samuel Cooper, 1718, C.O. 37/10, f. 35, P.R.O.; *History of Pyrates*, 116, 196, 216, 228; Boyer, ed., *Political State*, XXVIII, 148; Gov. of Bermuda quoted in Pringle, *Jolly Roger*, 181; deposition of Richard Symes, 1721, C.O. 152/14, f. 33, P.R.O.; *Am. Wkly Mercury*, Mar. 17, 1720; *New-England Courant* (Boston), June 25-July 2, 1722.

[38] Dow and Edmonds, *Pirates of New England*, 278; *History of Pyrates*, 225, 313; Lt. Gov. Bennett to Mr. Popple, Mar. 31, 1720, *Cal. St. Papers*, XXXII, 19.

[39] Hayward, ed., *Remarkable Criminals*, 37; *History of Pyrates*, 226, 342.

CONNECTIONS AMONG ANGLO-AMERICAN
PIRATE CREWS, 1714 TO 1726

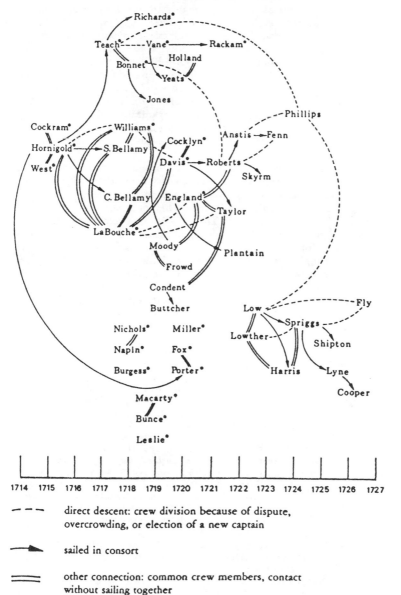

253

--- direct descent: crew division because of dispute,
overcrowding, or election of a new captain

→ sailed in consort

= other connection: common crew members, contact
without sailing together

o used the Bahama Islands as rendezvous

consorts, or by other associations, roughly thirty-six hundred pirates—
more than 70 percent of all those active between 1716 and 1726—fit into
two main lines of genealogical descent. Captain Benjamin Hornigold and
the pirate rendezvous in the Bahamas stood at the origin of an intricate
lineage that ended with the hanging of John Phillips's crew in June 1724.
The second line, spawned in the chance meeting of the lately mutinous
crews of George Lowther and Edward Low in 1722, culminated in the
executions of William Fly and his men in July 1726. It was primarily within
and through this network that the social organization of the pirate ship
took on its significance, transmitting and preserving customs and meanings, and helping to structure and perpetuate the pirates' social world.[40]

254

Pirates constructed that world in defiant contradistinction to the ways of
the world they left behind, in particular to its salient figures of power, the
merchant captain and the royal official, and to the system of authority
those figures represented and enforced. When eight pirates were tried in
Boston in 1718, merchant captain Thomas Checkley told of the capture of
his ship by pirates who "pretended," he said, "to be Robbin Hoods
Men."[41] Eric Hobsbawm has defined social banditry as a "universal and
virtually unchanging phenomenon," an "endemic peasant protest against
oppression and poverty: a cry for vengeance on the rich and the oppres-
sors." Its goal is "a traditional world in which men are justly dealt with, not
a new and perfect world"; Hobsbawm calls its advocates "revolutionary
traditionalists."[42] Pirates, of course, were not peasants, but they fit Hobs-

---

[40] The total of 3,600 is reached by multiplying the number of ship captains
shown in the figure by the average crew size of 79.5. *History of Pyrates*, 41-42, 72,
121, 137, 138, 174, 210, 225, 277, 281, 296, 312, 352, 355, 671; *N.-Eng. Courant*, June 11-18, 1722; *Am. Wkly Mercury*, July 6-13, 1721, Jan. 5-12 and Sept.
16-23, 1725; Pringle, *Jolly Roger*, 181, 190, 244; Biddulph, *Pirates of Malabar*, 135,
187; Snelgrave, *Account of the Slave-Trade*, 196-197, 199, 272, 280; Hughson, *Carolina Pirates*, 70; *Boston News-Letter*, Aug. 12-19, 1717, Oct. 13-20 and Nov. 10-
17, 1718, Feb. 4-11, 1725, June 30-July 7, 1726; Downing, *Indian Wars*, 51, 101;
Morris, "Ghost of Kidd," *N.Y. Hist.*, XIX (1938), 282, 283, 296; *Tryals of Bonnet*,
iii, 44-45; Dow and Edmonds, *Pirates of New England*, 117, 135, 201, 283, 287;
Trials of Eight Persons, 23; Jameson, ed., *Privateering and Piracy*, 304, 341; Boyer,
ed., *Political State*, XXV, 198-199; Hill, "Notes on Piracy," *Indian Antiq.*, LVI
(1927), 148, 150; Capt. Matthew Musson to Council of Trade, *Cal. St. Papers*,
XXIX, 338; *ibid.*, XXXI, 21, 118; *ibid.*, XXXIII, 274; John F. Watson, *Annals of
Philadelphia and Pennsylvania ...*, II (Philadelphia, 1844), 227; *Boston Gazette*,
Apr. 27-May 4, 1724; C.O. 152/12, P.R.O.; C.O. 5/1319, P.R.O.; Additional
Manuscripts 40806, 40812, 40813, Manuscripts Division, British Library.
[41] Testimony of Thomas Checkley, 1717, in Jameson, ed., *Privateering and Piracy*, 304; *Trials of Eight Persons*, 11.
[42] E. J. Hobsbawm, *Primitive Rebels: Studies in Archaic Forms of Social Movement
in the 19th and 20th Centuries* (New York, 1959), 5, 17, 18, 27, 28; see also his
Bandits (New York, 1969), 24-29.

bawm's formulation in every other respect. Of special importance was their "cry for vengeance."

Spotswood told no more than the simple truth when he expressed his fear of pirate vengeance, for the very names of pirate ships made the same threat. Edward Teach, whom Spotswood's men cut off, called his vessel *Queen Anne's Revenge;* other notorious craft were Stede Bonnet's *Revenge* and John Cole's *New York Revenge's Revenge.*[43] The foremost target of vengeance was the merchant captain. Frequently, "in a far distant latitude," as one seaman put it, "unlimited power, bad views, ill nature and ill principles all concur[red]" in a ship's commander. This was a man "past all restraint," who often made life miserable for his crew.[44] Spotswood also noted how pirates avenged the captain's "correcting" of his sailors. In 1722, merchant captains Isham Randolph, Constantine Cane, and William Halladay petitioned Spotswood "in behalf of themselves and other Masters of Ships" for "some certain method . . . for punishing mutinous & disobedient Seamen." They explained that captains faced great danger "in case of meeting with Pyrates, where we are sure to suffer all the tortures w[hi]ch such an abandoned crew can invent, upon the least intimation of our Striking any of our men."[45]

Upon seizing a merchantman, pirates often administered the "Distribution of Justice," "enquiring into the Manner of the Commander's Behaviour to their Men, and those, against whom Complaint was made" were "whipp'd and pickled."[46] In 1724, merchant captain Richard Hawkins described another form of retribution, a torture known as the "Sweat": "Between decks they stick Candles round the Mizen-Mast, and about twenty-five men surround it with Points of Swords, Penknives, Compasses, Forks &c in each of their hands: *Culprit* enters the Circle; the Violin plays a merry Jig; and he must run for about ten Minutes, while each man runs his

255

[43] *The Tryals of Sixteen Persons for Piracy* . . . (Boston, 1726), 5; *Tryals of Bonnet,* iii, iv; Crook, *Newgate Calendar,* 61; Hughson, *Carolina Pirates,* 121; Rankin, *Golden Age,* 28; *History of Pyrates,* 116, 342; Downing, *Indian Wars,* 98. An analysis of the names of 44 pirate ships reveals the following patterns: 8 (18.2%) made reference to revenge; 7 (15.9%) were named *Ranger* or *Rover,* suggesting mobility and perhaps, as discussed below, a watchfulness over the treatment of sailors by their captains; 5 (11.4%) referred to royalty. It is noteworthy that only two names referred to wealth. Other names indicated that places (*Lancaster*), unidentifiable people (*Mary Anne*), and animals (*Black Robin*) constituted less significant themes. Two names, *Batchelor's Delight* and *Batchelor's Adventure,* tend to support the probability (p. 208, n. 16 above) the most pirates were unmarried. See *History of Pyrates,* 220, 313; William P. Palmer, ed., *Calendar of Virginia State Papers* . . . , I (Richmond, 1875), 194; and *Cal. St. Papers,* XXX, 263.

[44] Betagh, *Voyage,* 41.

[45] Petition of Randolph, Cane, and Halladay, 1722, in Palmer, ed., *Virginia State Papers,* 202.

[46] *History of Pyrates,* 338, 582; Snelgrave, *Account of the Slave-Trade,* 212, 225; Dow and Edmonds, *Pirates of New England,* 301; Uring, *Voyage,* ed. Dewar, xxviii. To pickle is to place in a salty solution; in this case, to put salt on the wounds.

Instrument into his Posteriors."[47] Many captured captains were "barbarously used," and some were summarily executed. Pirate Philip Lyne carried this vengeance to its bloodiest extremity, confessing when apprehended in 1726 that "during the time of his Piracy" he "had killed 37 Masters of Vessels."[48]

Still, the punishment of captains was not indiscriminate, for a captain who had been "an honest Fellow that never abused any Sailors" was often rewarded by pirates.[49] The best description of pirates' notions of justice comes from merchant captain William Snelgrave's account of his capture in 1719. On April 1, Snelgrave's ship was seized by Thomas Cocklyn's crew of rovers at the mouth of the Sierra Leone River. Cocklyn was soon joined by men captained by Oliver LaBouche and Howell Davis, and Snelgrave spent the next thirty days among two hundred forty pirates.[50]

The capture was effected when twelve pirates in a small boat came alongside Snelgrave's ship, which was manned by forty-five sailors. Snelgrave ordered his crew to arms; though they refused, the pirate quartermaster, infuriated by the command, drew a pistol. He then, Snelgrave testified, "with the but-end endeavoured to beat out my Brains," until "some of my People . . . cried out aloud 'For God sake don't kill our Captain, for we never were with a better Man.' " The quartermaster, Snelgrave noted, "told me, 'my Life was safe provided none of my People complained against me.' I replied, 'I was sure none of them could.' "[51]

Snelgrave was taken to Cocklyn, who told him, "I am sorry you have met with bad usage after Quarter given, but 'tis the Fortune of War sometimes. . . . [I]f you tell the truth, and your Men make no Complaints against you, you shall be kindly used." Howell Davis, commander of the

---

[47] Hawkins in Boyer, ed., *Political State*, XXVIII, 149-150; *History of Pyrates*, 352-353; Dow and Edmonds, *Pirates of New England*, 278; Betagh, *Voyage*, 26. This torture may have exploited that meaning of the verb "to sweat" which was to drive hard, to overwork. The construction of a literally vicious circle here seems hardly coincidental. See *Oxford English Dictionary*, s.v. "sweat"; *Tryals of Sixteen Persons*, 14. Knowledge of this ritualized violence was evidently widespread. In 1722, Bristol merchants informed Parliament that pirates "study how to torture": see Stock, ed., *Proceedings and Debates of Parliaments*, 453. Torture was also applied to captains who refused to reveal the whereabouts of their loot. It seems that Spanish captains received especially harsh treatment.

[48] Crook, *Newgate Calendar*, 59; Boyer, ed., *Political State*, XXXII, 272; *Boston Gaz.*, Oct. 24-31, 1720; Rankin, *Golden Age*, 35, 135, 148; [Cotton Mather], *The Vial Poured Out upon the Sea: A Remarkable Relation of Certain Pirates* . . . (Boston, 1726), 21; Watson, *Annals of Philadelphia*, 227. Quotation from *Boston Gaz.*, Mar. 21-28, 1726. It should be stressed that Lyne's bloodletting was exceptional.

[49] *Boston News-Letter*, Nov. 14-21, 1720.

[50] Snelgrave, *Account of the Slave-Trade*, 196, 199. This is a marvellous source written by an intelligent and perceptive man of long experience at sea. The book mainly concerns the slave trade, was addressed to the merchants of London, and apparently was not intended as popular reading.

[51] *Ibid.*, 202-208.

largest of the pirate ships, reprimanded Cocklyn's men for their roughness and, by Snelgrave's account, expressed himself "ashamed to hear how I had been used by them. That they should remember their reasons for going a pirating were to revenge themselves on base Merchants and cruel commanders of Ships. . . . [N]o one of my People, even those that had entered with them gave me the least ill-character. . . . [I]t was plain they loved me."[52]

Snelgrave's character proved so respectable that the pirates proposed to give him a captured ship with full cargo and to sell the goods for him. Then they would capture a Portuguese slaver, sell the slaves, and give the proceeds to Snelgrave so that he could "return with a large sum of Money to London, and bid the Merchants defiance."[53] The proposal was "unanimously approved" by the pirates, but fearing a charge of complicity, Snelgrave hesitated to accept it. Davis then interceded, saying that he favored "allowing every Body to go to the Devil in their own way" and that he knew that Snelgrave feared for "his Reputation." The refusal was graciously accepted, Snelgrave claiming that "the Tide being turned, they were as kind to me, as they had been at first severe."[54]

Snelgrave related another revealing episode. While he remained in pirate hands, a decrepit schooner belonging to the Royal African Company sailed into the Sierra Leone and was taken by his captors. Simon Jones, a member of Cocklyn's crew, urged his mates to burn the ship since he had been poorly treated while in the company's employ. The pirates were about to do so when another of them, James Stubbs, protested that such

257

[52] Ibid., 212, 225. Piracy was perceived by many as an activity akin to war. See also History of Pyrates, 168, 319. Francis R. Stark, The Abolition of Privateering and the Declaration of Paris (New York, 1897), 14, 13, 22, claims that war in the 17th and early 18th centuries was understood in terms of "individual enmity" more than national struggle. Victors had "absolute right over (1) hostile persons and (2) hostile property." This might partially explain pirates' violence and destructiveness. Rankin, Golden Age, 146, correctly observes that "as more pirates were captured and hanged, the greater cruelty was practiced by those who were still alive."
[53] Snelgrave, Account of the Slave-Trade, 241. For other examples of giving cargo to ship captains and treating them "civilly" see deposition of Robert Dunn, 1720, C.O. 152/13, f. 26, P.R.O.; deposition of Richard Symes, 1721, C.O. 152/14, f. 33; Biddulph, Pirates of Malabar, 139; Brock, ed., Letters of Spotswood, 339-343; Boston Gaz., Aug. 21, 1721; Hill, "Episodes of Piracy," Indian Antiq., XLIX (1920), 57; Morris, "Ghost of Kidd," N.Y. Hist., XIX (1938), 283; Elizabeth Donnan, ed., Documents Illustrative of the History of the Slave Trade to America, IV (Washington, D.C., 1935), 96; Tryals of Bonnet, 13; Boyer, ed., Political State, XXVII, 616; deposition of Henry Bostock, Cal. St. Papers, XXX, 150-151; Boston News-Letter, Nov. 14-21, 1720; and Spotswood to Craggs, May 20, 1720: ". . . it is a common practice with those Rovers upon the pillageing of a Ship to make presents of other Commodity's to such Masters as they take a fancy to in Lieu of that they have plundered them of." C.O. 5/1319, P.R.O.
[54] Snelgrave, Account of the Slave-Trade, 241, 242, 243.

action would only "serve the Company's interests" since the ship was worth but little. He also pointed out that "the poor People that now belong to her, and have been on so long a voyage, will lose their Wages, which I am sure is Three times the Value of the Vessel." The pirates concurred and returned the ship to its crew, who "came safe home to England in it." Captain Snelgrave also returned to England soon after this incident, but eleven of his seamen remained behind as pirates.[55]

Snelgrave seems to have been an exceptionally decent captain. Pirates like Howell Davis claimed that abusive treatment by masters of merchantmen contributed mightily to their willingness to become sea-robbers. John Archer, whose career as a pirate dated from 1718 when he sailed with Edward Teach, uttered a final protest before his execution in 1724: "I could wish that Masters of Vessels would not use their Men with so much Severity, as many of them do, which exposes us to great Temptations."[56] William Fly, facing the gallows for murder and piracy in 1726, angrily said, "I can't charge myself,—I shan't own myself Guilty of any Murder,—Our Captain and his Mate used us Barbarously. We poor Men can't have Justice done us. There is nothing said to our Commanders, let them never so much abuse us, and use us like Dogs."[57] To pirates revenge was justice; punishment was meted out to barbarous captains, as befitted the captains' crimes.

Sea-robbers who fell into the hands of the state received the full force of penalties for crimes against property. The official view of piracy as crime was outlined in 1718 by Vice-Admiralty Judge Nicholas Trott in his charge to the jury in the trial of Stede Bonnet and thirty-three members of his crew at Charleston, South Carolina. Declaring that "the Sea was given by God for the use of Men, and is subject to Dominion and Property, as well as the Land," Trott observed of the accused that "the Law of Nations never granted to them a Power to change the Right of Property." Pirates on trial were denied benefit of clergy, were "called *Hostis Humani Generis*, with whom neither Faith nor Oath" were to be kept, and were regarded as "*Brutes,* and *Beasts of Prey.*" Turning from the jury to the accused, Trott circumspectly surmised that "no further Good or Benefit can be expected from you but by the Example of your Deaths."[58]

The insistence on obtaining this final benefit locked royal officials and pirates into a system of reciprocal terrorism. As royal authorities offered bounties for captured pirates, so too did pirates "offer any price" for cer-

[55] *Ibid.,* 275, 276, 284.

[56] *History of Pyrates,* 351; Jameson, ed., *Privateering and Piracy,* 341.

[57] [Mather], *Vial Poured Out,* 21, 48; Boyer, ed., *Political State,* XXXII, 272; Benjamin Colman, *It is a Fearful Thing to Fall into the Hands of the Living God . . .* (Boston, 1726), 39.

[58] *Tryals of Bonnet,* 2, 4, 3, 34. See also Hughson, *Carolina Pirates,* 5; *History of Pyrates,* 264, 377-379; Dow and Edmonds, *Pirates of New England,* 297; and Brock, ed., *Letters of Spotswood,* 339.

tain officials.[59] In Virginia in 1720 one of six pirates facing the gallows "called for a Bottle of Wine, and taking a Glass of it, he Drank Damnation to the Governour and Confusion to the Colony, which the rest pledged." Not to be outdone, Governor Spotswood thought it "necessary for the greater Terrour to hang up four of them in Chains."[60] Pirates demonstrated disdain for state authority when George I extended general pardons for piracy in 1717 and 1718. Some accepted the grace but refused to reform; others "seem'd to slight it," and the most defiant "used the King's Proclamation with great contempt, and tore it into pieces."[61] One pirate crew downed its punch proclaiming, "Curse the King and all the Higher Powers."[62] The social relations of piracy were marked by vigorous, often violent, antipathy toward traditional authority.

259

At the Charleston trial over which Trott presided, Richard Allen, attorney general of South Carolina, told the jury that "pirates prey upon all Mankind, their own Species and Fellow-Creatures without Distinction of Nations or Religions."[63] Allen was mistaken in one significant point: pirates did not prey on one another. Rather, they consistently expressed in numerous and subtle ways a highly developed consciousness of kind. Here we turn from the external social relations of piracy to the internal, in order to examine this consciousness of kind—in a sense, a strategy for survival—and the collectivistic ethos it expressed.

Pirates showed recurrent willingness to join forces at sea and in port. In April 1719, when Howell Davis and crew sailed into the Sierra Leone River, the pirates captained by Thomas Cocklyn were wary until they saw on the approaching ship "her Black Flag," then "immediately they were easy in their minds, and a little time after" the crews "saluted one another with their Cannon." Others crews exchanged similar greetings and, like Davis and Cocklyn who combined their powers, frequently invoked an unwritten code of hospitality to forge spontaneous alliances.[64]

[59] Boyer, ed., *Political State*, XIV, 295; XXI, 662; XXIV, 194; *History of Pyrates*, 79; *Cal. St. Papers*, XXXII, 168; Hill, "Episodes of Piracy," *Indian Antiq.*, XLIX (1920), 39; *Am. Wkly Mercury*, July 13-20, 1721.

[60] *Am. Wkly Mercury*, Mar. 17, 1720; Brock, ed., *Letters of Spotswood*, 338. For other cases of hanging in chains see *ibid.*, 342; Jameson, ed., *Privateering and Piracy*, 344; *Tryals of Sixteen Persons*, 19; *History of Pyrates*, 151; *Boston Gaz.*, Aug. 27-Sept. 3, 1722; Boyer, ed., *Political State*, XXIV, 201; and Gov. Hart to Council of Trade, *Cal. St. Papers*, XXXIII, 275. For a brilliant analysis of this type of terror see Michel Foucault, *Discipline and Punish: The Birth of the Prison*, trans. Alan Sheridan (New York, 1977), chap. 2.

[61] Deposition of Henry Bostock, 1717, C.O. 152/12, P.R.O.; Snelgrave, *Account of the Slave-Trade*, 253; *History of Pyrates*, 217; Spotswood to Board of Trade, May 31, 1717, C.O. 5/1318, P.R.O.; Jameson, ed., *Privateering and Piracy*, 315.

[62] Deposition of Edward North, 1718, C.O. 37/10, P.R.O.

[63] *Tryals of Bonnet*, 8.

[64] Snelgrave, *Account of the Slave-Trade*, 199; *History of Pyrates*, 138, 174; Morris, "Ghost of Kidd," *N.Y. Hist.*, XIX (1938), 282.

This communitarian urge was perhaps most evident in the pirate strong-
holds of Madagascar and Sierra Leone. Sea-robbers occasionally chose
more sedentary lifeways on various thinly populated islands, and they contributed a notorious number of men to the community of logwood cutters
at the Bay of Campeachy in the Gulf of Mexico. In 1718 a royal official
complained of a "nest of pirates" in the Bahamas "who already esteem
themselves a community, and to have one common interest."[65]

To perpetuate such community it was necessary to minimize conflict not
only on each ship but also among separate bands of pirates. Indeed, one of
the strongest indicators of consciousness of kind lies in the manifest absence of discord between different pirate crews. To some extent this was
even a transnational matter: French and Anglo-American pirates usually
cooperated peaceably, only occasionally exchanging cannon fire. Anglo-
American crews consistently refused to attack one another.[66]

In no way was the pirate sense of fraternity, which Spotswood and others noted, more forcefully expressed than in the threats and acts of re-
venge taken by pirates. Theirs was truly a case of hanging together or
being hanged separately. In April 1717, the pirate ship *Whidah* was
wrecked near Boston. Most of its crew perished; the survivors were jailed.
In July, Thomas Fox, a Boston ship captain, was taken by pirates who
"Questioned him whether anything was done to the Pyrates in Boston
Goall," promising "that if the Prisoners Suffered they would Kill every
Body they took belonging to New England."[67] Shortly after this incident,
Teach's sea-rovers captured a merchant vessel and, "because she belonged
to Boston, [Teach] alledging the People of Boston had hanged some of the
Pirates, so burnt her." Teach declared that all Boston ships deserved a
similar fate.[68] Charles Vane, reputedly a most fearsome pirate, "would
give no quarter to the Bermudians" and punished them and "cut away
their masts upon account of one Thomas Brown who was (some time)
detain'd in these Islands upon suspicion of piracy." Brown apparently had
plans to sail as Vane's consort until foiled by his capture.[69]

[65] James Craggs to Council of Trade, *Cal. St. Papers*, XXXI, 10; Board of Trade
to J. Methuen, Sept. 3, 1716, C.O. 23/12, P.R.O.; *History of Pyrates*, 315, 582;
Downing, *Indian Wars*, 98, 104-105; Uring, *Voyages*, ed. Dewar, 241; Shelvocke,
Voyage, 242; H. R. McIlwaine, ed., *Executive Journals of the Council of Colonial Virginia*, III (Richmond, 1928), 612; Dow and Edmonds, *Pirates of New England*, 341;
deposition of R. Lazenby in Hill, "Episodes of Piracy," *Indian Antiq.*, XLIX
(1920), 60; [Anonymous], "Voyage to Guinea, Antego, Bay of Campeachy, Cuba,
Barbadoes, &c, 1714-1723," Add. MS, 39946, British Library.
[66] *Boston News-Letter*, Aug. 15-22, 1720; *Am. Wkly Mercury*, Sept. 6-13, 1722.
[67] Trial of Thomas Davis, 1717, in Jameson, ed., *Privateering and Piracy*, 308;
Boston News-Letter, Nov. 4-11, 1717.
[68] *Tryals of Bonnet*, 45.
[69] Lt. Gov. Benjamin Bennet to Council of Trade, *Cal. St. Papers*, XXX, 263;
Tryals of Bonnet, 29, 50; *History of Pyrates*, 195.

In September 1720, pirates captained by Bartholomew Roberts "openly and in the daytime burnt and destroyed . . . vessels in the Road of Basse-terre [St. Kitts] and had the audaciousness to insult H. M. Fort," avenging the execution of "their comrades at Nevis." Roberts then sent word to the governor that "they would Come and Burn the Town [Sandy Point] about his Ears for hanging the Pyrates there."[70] In 1721, Spotswood relayed information to the Council of Trade and Plantations that Roberts "said he expected to be joined by another ship and would then visit Virginia, and avenge the pirates who have been executed here."[71] The credibility of the threat was confirmed by the unanimous resolution of the Virginia Execu-tive Council that "the Country be put into an immediate posture of Defense." Lookouts and beacons were quickly provided, and communica-tions with neighboring colonies effected. "Near 60 Cannon," Spotswood later reported, were "mounted on sundry Substantial Batteries."[72]

In 1723 pirate captain Francis Spriggs vowed to find a Captain Moore "and put him to death for being the cause of the death of [pirate] Low-ther," and, shortly after, similarly pledged to go "in quest of Captain Sol-gard," who had overpowered a pirate ship commanded by Charles Harris.[73] In January 1724, Lieutenant Governor Charles Hope of Bermu-da wrote to the Board of Trade that he found it difficult to procure trial evidence against pirates because residents "feared that this very execution wou'd make our vessels fare the worse for it, when they happen'd to fall into pirate hands."[74]

Pirates also affirmed their unity symbolically. Some evidence indicates that sea-robbers may have had a sense of belonging to a separate, in some manner exclusive, speech community. Philip Ashton, who spent sixteen months among pirates in 1722, noted that "according to the Pirates usual Custom, and *in their proper Dialect*, asked me, If I would sign their Arti-cles."[75] Many sources suggest that cursing, swearing, and blaspheming

[70] Gov. Walter Hamilton to Council of Trade, *Cal. St. Papers*, XXXII, 165; *Am. Wkly Mercury*, Oct. 27, 1720; *Boston Gaz.*, Oct. 24-31, 1720.

[71] Spotswood to Council of Trade, *Cal. St. Papers*, XXXII, 328.

[72] Council Meeting of May 3, 1721, in McIlwaine, *Council of Colonial Virginia*, 542; abstract of Spotswood to Board of Trade, June 11, 1722, C.O. 5/1370, P.R.O.; Spotswood to Board of Trade, May 31, 1721, C.O. 5/1319.

[73] Dow and Edmonds, *Pirates of New England*, 281-282; *History of Pyrates*, 355; *Am. Wkly Mercury*, May 21-28, 1724.

[74] Hope to Council of Trade, Jan. 14, 1724, C.O. 37/11, f. 37, P.R.O. See also Treasury Warrant to Capt. Knott, Aug. 10, 1722, T52/32, P.R.O. Capt. Luke Knott, after turning over eight pirates to authorities, prayed relief for "his being obliged to quit the Merchant Service, the Pirates threatning to Torture him to death if ever he should fall into their hands." Robert Walpole awarded Knott £230 for the loss of his career.

[75] Barnard, *Ashton's Memorial*, 2, 4; emphasis added. Perhaps this was what M.A.K. Halliday has called an anti-language. This is "the acting out of a distinct social structure [in speech]; and this social structure is, in turn, the bearer of an

may have been defining traits of this style of speech. For example, near the Sierra Leone River a British official named Plunkett pretended to cooperate with, but then attacked, the pirates with Bartholomew Roberts. Plunkett was captured, and Roberts

> upon the first sight of Plunkett swore at him like any Devil, for his Irish Impudence in daring to resist him. Old Plunkett, finding he had got into bad Company, fell a swearing and cursing as fast or faster than Roberts; which made the rest of the Pirates laugh heartily, desiring Roberts to sit down and hold his Peace, for he had no Share in the Pallaver with Plunkett at all. So that by meer Dint of Cursing and Damning, Old Plunkett . . . sav'd his life.[76]

Admittedly we can see only outlines here, but it appears that the symbolic connectedness, the consciousness of kind, extended into the domain of language.

Certainly the best known symbol of piracy is the flag, the Jolly Roger. Less known and appreciated is the fact that the flag was very widely used: no fewer, and probably a great many more, than two thousand five hundred men sailed under it.[77] So general an adoption indicates an advanced state of group identification. The Jolly Roger was described as a "black

---

alternative social reality." An anti-language exists in "the context of *resocialization.*" See his "Anti-Languages," *American Anthropologist,* LXXVIII (1976), 572, 575.

[76] Smith, *New Voyage,* 42-43. See also Morris, "Ghost of Kidd," *N.Y. Hist.,* XIX (1938), 286.

[77] Anthropologist Raymond Firth argues that flags function as instruments of both power and sentiment, creating solidarity and symbolizing unity. See his *Symbols: Public and Private* (Ithaca, N.Y., 1973), 328, 339; Hill, "Notes on Piracy," *Indian Antiq.,* LVI (1927), 147. For particular pirate crews known to have sailed under the Jolly Roger, see *Boston Gaz.,* Nov. 29-Dec. 6, 1725 (Lyne); *Boston News-Letter,* Sept. 10-17, 1716 (Jennings? Leslie?); *ibid.,* Aug. 12-19, 1717 (Napin, Nichols); *ibid.,* Mar. 2-9, 1719 (Thompson); *ibid.,* May 28-June 4, 1724 (Phillips); *ibid.,* June 5-8, 1721 (Rackham?); Jameson, ed., *Privateering and Piracy,* 317 (Roberts); *Tryals of Sixteen Persons,* 5 (Fly); Snelgrave, *Account of the Slave-Trade,* 199 (Cocklyn, LaBouche, Davis); *Trials of Eight Persons,* 24 (Bellamy); Hughson, *Carolina Pirates,* 113 (Moody); *Tryals of Bonnet,* 44-45 (Bonnet, Teach, Richards); Dow and Edmonds, *Pirates of New England,* 208 (Harris), 213 (Low); Boyer, ed., *Political State,* XXVIII, 152 (Spriggs); Biddulph, *Pirates of Malabar,* 135 (Taylor); Donnan, ed., *Documents of the Slave Trade,* 96 (England); and *History of Pyrates,* 240-241 (Skyrm), 67-68 (Martel), 144 (Vane), 371 (captain unknown), 628 (Macarty, Bunce), 299 (Worley). Royal officials affirmed and attempted to reroute the power of this symbolism by raising the Jolly Roger on the gallows when hanging pirates. See *History of Pyrates,* 658; *N.-Eng. Courant,* July 22, 1723; and *Boston News-Letter,* May 28-June 4, 1724. The symbols were commonly used in the gravestone art of this period and did not originate with piracy. The argument here is that new meanings, derived from maritime experience, were attached to them.

Ensign, in the Middle of which is a large white Skeleton with a Dart in one hand striking a bleeding Heart, and in the other an Hour Glass."[78] Although there was considerable variation in particulars among these flags, there was also a general uniformity of chosen images. The flag background was black, adorned with white representational figures. The most common symbol was the human skull, or "death's head," sometimes isolated but more frequently the most prominent feature of an entire skeleton. Other recurring items were a weapon—cutlass, sword, or dart—and an hour glass.[79]

The flag was intended to terrify the pirates' prey, but its triad of interlocking symbols—death, violence, limited time—simultaneously pointed to meaningful parts of the seaman's experience, and eloquently bespoke the pirates' own consciousness of themselves as preyed upon in turn. Pirates seized the symbol of mortality from ship captains who used the skull "as a marginal sign in their logs to indicate the record of a death."[80] Seamen who became pirates escaped from one closed system only to find themselves encased in another. But as pirates—and only as pirates—these men were able to fight back beneath the somber colors of "King Death" against those captains, merchants, and officials who waved banners of authority.[81] Moreover, pirates self-righteously perceived their situation and the excesses of these powerful figures through a collectivistic ethos that had been forged in the struggles for survival.

The self-righteousness of pirates was strongly linked to the "traditional world in which men are justly dealt with," as described by Hobsbawm.[82] It found expression in their social rules, their egalitarian social organization, and their notions of revenge and justice. By walking "to the Gallows without a Tear," by calling themselves "Honest Men" and "Gentlemen," and by speaking self-servingly but proudly of their "Conscience" and "Honor," pirates flaunted their certitude.[83] When, in 1720, ruling groups concluded that "nothing but force will subdue them," many pirates responded by intensifying their commitment.[84] It was observed of Edward Low's crew in 1724 that they "swear, with the most direful Imprecations, that if ever they should find themselves overpower'd they would immediately

263

---

[78] Boyer, ed., *Political State*, XXVIII, 152. Pirates also occasionally used red or "bloody" flags.

[79] *Ibid.*

[80] Hill, "Episodes of Piracy," *Indian Antiq.*, XLIX (1920), 37.

[81] *Ibid.*; Snelgrave, *Account of the Slave-Trade*, 236.

[82] See above, n. 42.

[83] *History of Pyrates*, 286, 43, 244, 159, 285, 628, 656, 660; Hayward, ed., *Remarkable Criminals*, 39; Rankin, *Golden Age*, 155; [Mather], *Vial Poured Out*, 47; Jameson, ed., *Privateering and Piracy*, 341; Lt. Gen. Mathew to Gov. Hamilton, *Cal. St. Papers*, XXXII, 167; Bartholomew Roberts, the pirate, to Lt. Gen. Mathew, *ibid.*, 169.

[84] Gov. Hamilton to Council of Trade, *Cal. St. Papers*, XXXII, 165.

blow their ship up rather than suffer themselves to be hang'd like Dogs."
These sea-robbers would not "do Jolly Roger the Disgrace to be struck."[85]
    This consciousness of kind among pirates manifested itself in an elabo-
rate social code. Through rule, custom, and symbol the code prescribed
specific behavioral standards intended to preserve the social world that
pirates built for themselves. As the examples of revenge reveal, royal officials recognized the threat of the pirates' alternative order. Some authorities feared that pirates might "set up a sort of Commonwealth"[86]—a
correct designation—in uninhabited regions, since "no Power in those
Parts of the World could have been able to dispute it with them."[87] But
the consciousness of kind never took national shape, and piracy was soon
suppressed. We now turn to the general social and economic context of
the crime and its culture.

    Contemporary observers seem to have attributed the rise of piracy to
the demobilizing of the Royal Navy at the end of the War of the Spanish
Succession. A group of Virginia merchants, for instance, wrote to the Admiralty in 1713, setting forth "the apprehensions they have of Pyrates
molesting their trade in the time of Peace."[88] The navy plunged from
49,860 men at the end of the war to 13,475 just two years later, and only
by 1740 did it increase to as many as 30,000 again.[89] At the same time, the
expiration of privateering licenses—bills of marque—added to the number of seamen loose and looking for work in the port cities of the empire.
Such underemployment contributed significantly to the rise of piracy,[90]
but it is not a sufficient explanation since, as already noted, the vast majority of those who became pirates were working in the merchant service at

[85] Boyer, ed., *Political State*, XXVIII, 153. For similar vows and actual attempts
see *Tryals of Bonnet*, 18; *History of Pyrates*, 143, 241, 245, 298, 317; *Cal. St. Papers*,
XXXII, 168; Dow and Edmonds, *Pirates of New England*, 239, 292; Watson, *An-
nals of Philadelphia*, 227; Hayward, ed., *Remarkable Criminals*, 296-297; Atkins,
Voyage, 12; Jameson, ed., *Privateering and Piracy*, 315; Arthur L. Cooke, "British
Newspaper Accounts of Blackbeard's Death," *Virginia Magazine of History and
Biography*, LXI (1953), 305-306; *Am. Wkly Mercury*, June 16-23, 1720; *Tryals of
Thirty-Six*, 9; and Spotswood to Board of Trade, Dec. 22, 1718, C.O. 5/1318,
P.R.O.
[86] Cotton Mather, *Instructions to the Living, From the Condition of the Dead: A
Brief Relation of Remarkables in the Shipwreck of above One Hundred Pirates . . .* (Bos-
ton, 1717), 4; meeting of Apr. 1, 1717, in H. C. Maxwell Lyte, ed., *Journal of the
Commissioners for Trade and Plantations . . .*, III (London, 1924), 359.
[87] *History of Pyrates*, 7.
[88] Virginia Merchants to Admiralty, 1713, C.O. 389/42, P.R.O.
[89] Lloyd, *British Seaman*, 287, Table 3.
[90] Jameson, ed., *Privateering and Piracy*, 291; Pringle, *Jolly Roger*, 95; Lydon,
Pirates, Privateers, and Profits, 17-20; Rankin, *Golden Age*, 23; Nellis M. Crouse,
The French Struggle for the West Indies (New York, 1943), 310.

the moment of their joining. The surplus of labor at the end of the war had jarring social effects. It produced an immediate contraction of wages; merchant seamen who made 45-50s. per month in 1708 made only half that amount in 1713. It provoked greater competition for seafaring jobs, favorable to the hiring of older, more experienced seamen. And it would, over time, affect the social conditions and relations of life at sea, cutting back material benefits and hardening discipline.[91] War years, despite their dangers, provided seafarers with tangible benefits. The Anglo-American seamen of 1713 had performed wartime labor for twenty of the previous twenty-five years, and for eleven years consecutively. But conditions did not worsen immediately after the war. As Ralph Davis explains, "the years 1713-1715 saw—as did immediate post-war years throughout the eighteenth century—the shifting of heaped-up surpluses of colonial goods, the movement of great quantities of English goods to colonial and other markets, and a general filling in of stocks of imported goods which had been allowed to run down."[92] This small-scale boom gave employment to some of the seamen who had been dropped from naval rolls. But by late 1715, a slump in trade began, to last into the 1730s. All of these difficulties were exacerbated by the century-long trend in which "life on board [a merchant] ship was carried on amid a discipline which grew harsher with the passage of time."[93] Many seamen knew that things had once been different and, for many, decisively better.

By 1726, the menace of piracy had been effectively suppressed by governmental action. Circumstantial factors do not account for its demise. The number of men in the Royal Navy did increase from 6,298 in 1725 to 16,872 in 1726, and again to 20,697 in 1727. This increase probably had some bearing on the declining numbers of sea-robbers. Yet some 20,000 sailors had been in the navy in 1719 and 1720, years when pirates were numerous.[94] In addition, seafaring wages only twice rose above 24-25s. per month between 1713 and the mid-1730s: there were temporary increases to 30s. in 1718 and 1727.[95] Conditions of life at sea probably did not change appreciably until war broke out in 1739.

The pardons offered to pirates in 1717 and 1718 largely failed to rid the sea of robbers. Since the graces specified that only crimes committed at certain times and in particular regions would be forgiven, many pirates saw enormous latitude for official trickery and refused to surrender. Moreover, accepting and abiding by the rules of the pardon would have meant for most men a return to the dismal conditions they had escaped. Their tactic failing, royal officials intensified the naval campaign against piracy—

---

[91] Davis, *English Shipping*, 136-137.
[92] *Ibid.*, 27.
[93] *Ibid.*, 154.
[94] Lloyd, *British Seaman*, 287, Table 3; Davis, *English Shipping*, 27, 31.
[95] Davis, *English Shipping*, 136-137.

with great and gruesome effect. Corpses dangled in chains in British ports around the world "as a Spectacle for the Warning of others."[96] No fewer than four hundred, and probably five to six hundred, Anglo-American pirates were executed between 1716 and 1726.[97] The campaign to cleanse the seas was supported by clergymen, royal officials, and publicists who sought through sermons, proclamations, pamphlets and the newspaper press to create an image of the pirate that would legitimate his extermination. Piracy had always depended in some measure on the rumors and tales of its successes, especially among seamen and dealers in stolen cargo. In 1722 and 1723, after a spate of hangings and verbal chastisements, the pirate population began to decline. By 1726, only a handful of the fraternity remained.

266

Finally, pirates themselves unwittingly took a hand in their own destruction. From the outset, theirs had been a fragile social group. They produced nothing and were economically parasitic on the mercantile system. And they were widely dispersed, virtually without geographic boundaries. Try as they might, they were unable to create reliable mechanisms through which they could either replenish their ranks or mobilize their collective strength. These deficiencies of social organization made them, in the long run, easy prey.

We see in the end that the pirate was, perhaps above all else, an unremarkable man caught in harsh, often deadly circumstances. Wealth he surely desired, but a strong social logic informed both his motivation and his behavior. Emerging from lower-class backgrounds and maritime employments, and loosed from familial bonds, pirates developed common symbols and standards of conduct. They forged spontaneous alliances, refused to fight each other, swore to avenge injury to their own kind, and even retired to pirate communities. They erected their own ideal of justice, insisted upon an egalitarian, if unstable, form of social organization, and defined themselves against other social groups and types. So, too, did they perceive many of their activities as ethical and justified, not unlike the eighteenth-century crowds described by Edward Thompson.[98] But pi-

[96] Pringle, *Jolly Roger*, 266-267; Violet Barbour, "Privateers and Pirates of the West Indies," *American Historical Review*, XVI (1910-1911), 566; Boyer, ed., *Political State*, XXVIII, 152; Hayward, ed., *Remarkable Criminals*, 37; [Anonymous], "A Scheme for Stationing Men of War in the West Indies for better Securing the Trade there from Pirates," 1723, C.O. 323/8, P.R.O.; *Boston News-Letter*, July 7-14, 1726. Gary M. Walton, "Sources of Productivity Change in American Colonial Shipping, 1675-1775," *Economic History Review*, 2d Ser., XX (1967), 77, notes that the economic uncertainty occasioned by piracy declined after 1725.

[97] If the population range discussed above is accurate, about 1 pirate in 13 died on the gallows.

[98] E. P. Thompson, "The Moral Economy of the English Crowd in the Eighteenth Century," *Past and Present*, No. 50 (1971), 76-136.

rates, experienced as cooperative seafaring laborers and no longer disciplined by law, were both familiar with the workings of an international market economy and little affected by the uncertainties of economic change. Perhaps their dual relationship to the mode of production as free wage laborers and members of a criminal subculture gave pirates the perspective and resources to fight back against brutal and unjust authority, and to construct a new social order where King Death would not reign supreme. This was probably a contradictory pursuit: for many, piracy, as strategy of survival, was ill-fated.

Piracy, in the end, offers us an extraordinary opportunity. Here we can see how a sizeable group of Anglo-Americans—poor men in canvas jackets and tarred breeches—constructed a social world where they had "the choice in themselves."[99] Theirs was truly a culture of masterless men: Pirates were as far removed from traditional authority as any men could be in the early eighteenth century. Beyond the church, beyond the family, beyond disciplinary labor, and using the sea to distance themselves from the powers of the state, they carried out a strange experiment. The social constellation of piracy, in particular the complex consciousness and egalitarian impulses that developed once the shackles were off, might provide valuable clarification of more general social and cultural patterns among the laboring poor. Here we can see aspirations and achievements that under normal circumstances would have been heavily muted, if not rendered imperceptible, by the power relationships of everyday life.

[99] Hayward, ed., *Remarkable Criminals*, 37. See also Christopher Hill, *The World Turned Upside Down: Radical Ideas during the English Revolution* (London, 1972).

267

The Fur Trade and
Eighteenth-Century Imperialism

W. J. Eccles

T HE North American fur trade of the seventeenth and eighteenth centuries has usually been viewed, until recently, as merely another commercial enterprise governed by the premise "buy cheap, sell dear" in order to reap the maximum profit. Of late, the Canadian end of the trade has come to be regarded as having been more a means to a noncommercial end than a pursuit conducted solely for economic gain. As European penetration and dominance of the continent progressed, the trade, which had begun as an adjunct of the Atlantic shore fishery, became a commercial pursuit in its own right. After 1600, when the first Roman Catholic missionaries were sent to New France, it became a means to finance and further that tragic drive to convert the Indian nations to Christianity. This attempt continued until mid-century, when the Jesuit mission in Huronia was destroyed, along with the Hurons as a nation, by the Iroquois Confederacy.[1] For the rest of the century the fur trade of New France went through vexed and troubled times.[2]

Stability was temporarily restored to the trade in 1663, when the crown took over the colony from the Company of One Hundred Associates. Near the end of the century a huge glut of beaver fur completely disrupted the market in Europe and caused Louis Phélypeaux de Pontchartrain, the minister of marine responsible for the colonies, to try to force the Canadian fur traders to withdraw from the west completely. For political reasons this could not be done. Despite its economic unviability,

Mr. Eccles is Professor of History Emeritus at the University of Toronto and currently James Pinckney Harrison Professor of History at the College of William and Mary. A preliminary version of this article was read at and subsequently published in the *Transactions* of the Quarto Convegno Internazionale dell' Associazione Italiana de Studi Canadesi, held at the University of Messina in 1981. The present version was discussed at a colloquium of the Newberry Library Center for the History of the American Indian.

[1] On the Huron-Iroquois conflict see Bruce G. Trigger, *The Children of Aataentsic: A History of the Huron People to 1660*, 2 vols. (Montreal, 1976), and John A. Dickinson, "Annaotaha et Dollard vus de l'autre côté de la palissade," *Revue d'histoire de l'Amérique française*, XXXV (1981), 163-178.

[2] The best study of this early period is Marcel Trudel, *The Beginnings of New France, 1524-1663*, trans. Patricia Claxton (Toronto, 1973). The period 1663-1701 is covered in W. J. Eccles, *Canada under Louis XIV, 1663-1701* (Toronto, 1964). The latter work is now somewhat dated.

the French, in order to maintain good relations with the Indian nations, were forced to continue the trade in furs. Then, in 1700, on the eve of a new war in Europe, Louis XIV embarked on an expansionist policy in North America to hem in the English colonies on the Atlantic seaboard. From that point forward, the fur trade was used mainly as a political instrument to further the imperial aims of France.

In the 1650s, after the Iroquois had virtually destroyed the Huron nation and scattered the Algonkian nations allied with it far to the west, French traders began to push into the interior of the continent, where they established direct trade relations with the hunting nations that had previously supplied furs to the Huron middlemen. These traders, a mere handful at first, voyaged through the Great Lakes and beyond, then down into the Mississippi Valley. This French thrust into the west occurred just as the Five Nations Iroquois Confederacy, having subdued the tribes surrounding them and being well supplied with firearms by the Dutch and English merchants of Albany, embarked on an imperialistic drive to conquer and control the Ohio Valley, a region almost as vast as the kingdom of France.[3] Their first incursion into the region in 1678 was repelled by the Illinois nation. The following year Robert Cavelier de La Salle began establishing fur trade posts on the Illinois River and thereby claimed suzerainty for the French crown over the lands of both the Illinois and the Miami nations.[4]

In 1680 the inevitable clash came between these rival imperial powers. La Salle's lieutenant, Henri de Tonty, attempted to mediate when an Iroquois army invaded the Illinois country. He received a nasty wound for his pains but managed to escape to Michilimackinac with his men.[5] The French presence in the west was now seriously threatened. An attempt to cow the Iroquois by military force failed miserably. Instead, the Iroquois dictated humiliating peace terms to the governor general of New France, Le Febvre de La Barre, and stated their determination to destroy the Illinois, whom the French claimed to be under the protection of Louis XIV. When La Barre protested this arrogant Iroquois declaration, the great Onondaga chief and orator, Hotreouati, brusquely retorted, "They deserve to die, they have shed our blood."[6] To that La Barre could make no response. He was, when Louis XIV was informed of what had

269

---

[3] In order of conquest or dispersal these tribes were the Mahicans, 1628; Hurons, 1649; Neutrals, 1651; Eries, 1653-1657; and Susquehannocs, 1676.

[4] Mémoire de Henri Tonty, Nouvelles Acquisitions, Vol. 7485, fol. 103, Bibliothèque Nationale, Paris; Duchesneau au ministre, Nov. 13, 1680, C11A, Vol. 5, fols. 39-40, Archives Nationales, Colonies, Paris.

[5] W. J. Eccles, *Frontenac: The Courtier Governor* (Toronto, 1959), 82-84, 107-110; François Vachon Belmont, *Histoire du Canada, D'après un manuscrit à la Bibliothèque du Roi à Paris* (Quebec, 1840), 14.

[6] Belmont, *Histoire du Canada*, 15-16; Eccles, *Frontenac*, 167-171; Presens des Onontaguez à Onontio à la Famine le Cinq Septembre 1684, Le febvre de la barre, C11A, Vol. 6, fols. 299-300.

transpired, summarily dismissed from his post and recalled to France in disgrace.[7]

The long-range aim of the Confederacy appears to have been to bring under subjection all the Indian nations south of the Great Lakes as far as the Mississippi, and at the same time to divert the western fur trade from Montreal to Albany with the Confederacy controlling it. Because the Iroquois failed to provide a written record of their aims, their motives cannot be determined with certainty, yet their actions and the policies they pursued during the ensuing decades indicate clearly enough that what they sought was power—dominance over this vast region—rather than mere commercial advantage.

270

A few years after this Franco-Iroquois struggle in the interior of North America was joined, events occurred in Europe that were to affect it profoundly. The Revolution of 1689 ousted James II and brought William of Orange, bitter enemy of Louis XIV, to the throne of England. This ushered in hostilities between England and France that were to occupy nineteen of the ensuing twenty-four years. The Iroquois, now confident of English military aid, pressed their attacks against the French in the west and at their settlements in the St. Lawrence Valley, inflicting heavy casualties. The settlers, aided by some 1,500 *Troupes de la Marine,* regular troops sent from France, managed to beat back these attacks and in the process became, of necessity, highly skilled at guerrilla warfare. The alliance with the Indian nations who had long feared the Iroquois was strengthened, and the war carried to the enemy. Iroquois casualties mounted, and the frontier settlements of their ineffectual English allies were ravaged by Canadian war parties. Both the Iroquois and the English colonials were relieved when, in 1697, the war ended in Europe. The Iroquois, now bereft of English logistical support, their fighting strength reduced by casualties and disease to half what it had been, were forced to sue for peace.[8]

This proud people had, however, not been brought so low that they would accept any terms that the French cared to impose. Consequently, the negotiations dragged on for four years. Moreover, the twenty-eight tribes allied with the French had to be party to the peace treaty that was eventually drawn up at Montreal in 1701. The principal factor that now made possible an enduring peace between the French and the Iroquois, thereby ending a war that had lasted for nearly a century, was that the French negotiators recognized the Iroquois presence to be an essential buffer between their Indian allies in the northwest and the English colonies. Moreover, the Iroquois had learned to their cost that they could not rely on the English for military support. Rather, they perceived that the English had always sought to make use of them merely to serve English ends. There was no longer any question of the French seeking to destroy the Iroquois; in fact, just the reverse had become the case. The Iroquois

---

[7] Le roy au Sr. de Meules, Mar. 10, 1685, B, Vol. 11, fol. 96, Archs. Nationales.
[8] Eccles, *Frontenac,* 157-197, 244-272.

had now to abandon all hope of ever driving the French out of Canada or from the posts in the west. The French presence had become essential to them to balance that of the English and to allow them to play one off against the other. Thus the French negotiators were able to insert a clause into the peace treaty declaring that in any future war between England and France the Iroquois would remain neutral. At one stroke the greatest military threat to New France and the main defense of New York had been eliminated; and this occurred just as England and France were preparing for a renewal of hostilities that were to last for more than a decade.[9]

On the French side, the preceding wars had been fought for a specific Canadian aim, control of the western fur trade, and France had provided the military aid needed to achieve that end. The ensuing wars were to be fought solely for French imperial aims. In 1701, with the War of the Spanish Succession about to erupt, Louis XIV declared that the English colonies must be hemmed in between the Atlantic and the Appalachians. On no account were the English to be allowed to flood over that mountain range to occupy the region between it and the Mississippi. Were they to do so, Louis feared, their numbers would swell immeasurably and England's wealth and power would increase proportionately. In all likelihood they would then push southwest to conquer Mexico with its silver mines. With Louis XIV's grandson now on the throne of Spain, France had to defend the Spanish colonies as though they were her own.[10] Louis XIV feared that English domination of North America would upset the balance of power in Europe. The French in America, with their Indian allies, were to be the means of containing the English colonies.[11] In the implementation of this imperial policy the fur trade had a vital role to play, of an importance far in excess of its economic value.

In 1701 Louis XIV gave orders for the creation of the new colony of Louisiana, in the Mississippi Valley, to forestall the English, who, it was reported, planned to establish a settlement at the mouth of that great river.[12] Another French settlement was ordered to be placed at the narrows between Lake Erie and Lake Huron. This new colony, to be named Detroit, was intended to bar English access to the northwest and maintain French control of the western Great Lakes.[13] It is not without significance that the Canadian merchants and the royal officials at Quebec were bitterly opposed to both these settlements, declaring that they would be the ruin of Canada—Detroit, because it would bring the Indian nations

271

[9] *Ibid.*, 328-333.
[10] *Ibid.*, 334-337; Marcel Giraud, *Histoire de la Louisiane française*, I: *Le règne de Louis XIV (1698-1715)* (Paris, 1953), 13-23.
[11] M. Tremblay à M. Glandelet, May 28, 1701, Lettres, Carton O, No. 34, Archives du Séminaire de Québec, Quebec, Canada.
[12] Giraud, *Histoire de la Louisiane*, I, 39-43.
[13] Yves F. Zoltvany, *Philippe de Rigaud de Vaudreuil: Governor of New France, 1703-1725* (Toronto, 1974), 39-41.

allied with the French into close proximity to the Iroquois, who might grant them access to the Albany traders; Louisiana, because the fur traders who obtained their trade goods on credit from the Montreal merchants would be tempted to defraud their creditors by shipping their furs to France from the port to be established on the Gulf of Mexico.[14]

French imperial policy now required that the Indian nations of the west and of Acadia be welded into a close commercial alliance and that all contact between them and the English colonists be prevented by one means or another. The main instruments of this policy, it was envisaged, would be missionaries and fur traders. The great age of French proselytization that had produced the Jesuit martyrs was, however, a thing of the past. The clergy were eager enough to serve, but some of them were ill suited for the task and too often their efforts were hampered by squabbling among rival groups, secular priests with Jesuits, Capuchins with both. For several years the bishop of New France was an absentee, unable to restore order and discipline from his residence in Paris.[15] Thus the implementation of this new policy was left to two groups, the Canadian fur traders and the officers and men of the colonial regulars, the *Troupes de la Marine*, who garrisoned the reestablished posts.

The fur trade was now definitely subordinated to a political end. It was required to pay a large share of the costs of maintaining a French presence in the interior to bar the English from it. The west was divided into regions, each with a central post commanded by an officer of the colonial regulars. For some years these officers were not permitted to engage in the trade, the sole right to which in each region was auctioned off to merchants on a three-year lease.[16] When it was found that this led to exploitation of the Indians by merchants whose only aim was to make as great a profit as possible during their lease, the trade was turned over to the commandants, who could, it was thought, be kept under tighter control by the senior officials at Quebec.[17] Complaints against them by the Indians could bring instant recall and might jeopardize promotion or the granting of commissions to sons.

[14] *Ibid.*, 40, 86-87; Champigny au ministre, Aug. 8, 1688, C11A, Vol. 10, fols. 123-124; Callières et Champigny au ministre, Oct. 5, 1701, *ibid.*, Vol. 19, fols. 6-7. That this fear was soon to be realized is made clear in d'Iberville's journal for 1702 where he mentions his accepting furs from Canadian *coureurs de bois* for shipment to France. See Richebourg Gaillard McWilliams, trans. and ed., *Iberville's Gulf Journals* (University, Ala., 1981), 165, 178.

[15] Charles Edwards O'Neill, *Church and State in French Colonial Louisiana: Policy and Politics to 1732* (New Haven, Conn., 1966), *passim*.

[16] Archives nationales du Québec, *Rapport de l'Archiviste de la Province de Québec* (Québec, 1921-   ), 1938-1939, 69, hereafter cited as *Rapport de l'Archiviste*.

[17] Beauharnois et d'Aigremont au ministre, Oct. 1, 1728, C11A, Vol. 50, fols. 31-33; minister to La Jonquière and Bigot, May 4, 1749, State Historical Society of Wisconsin, *Collections*, XVIII (1908), 25-26; Beauharnois to the minister, Oct. 18, 1737, Michigan Pioneer and Historical Society, *Historical Collections*, XXXIV (1905), 146-147.

The post commandants usually formed companies in partnership with Montreal merchants who provided the trade goods, hired the voyageurs, and marketed the furs, and professional traders who took charge of the actual trading with the Indians. The modus operandi was thus very simple; the companies usually comprised three men for a three-year term, at the end of which the merchant who had supplied the goods withdrew their cost, and whatever profit or loss remained was shared by the partners.[18] At the main bases of Michilimackinac and Detroit the trade was open to all who obtained a permit from the governor general and paid the base commandant his 500 *livre* fee. From these fees the commandants had to pay the costs of maintaining the posts, thereby sparing the crown the expense.[19]

Louis XIV, in order to end the war that was reducing his government to bankruptcy, agreed to make sweeping concessions on the Atlantic frontier of New France to avoid having to make them in Europe. He therefore agreed to cede Newfoundland and Acadia, the latter "within its ancient limits," to England. A joint commission was appointed to determine those limits, but, predictably, no agreement could be reached and France retained Cape Breton, where it proceeded to construct the fortress of Louisbourg as a naval base for the protection of French maritime interests in the North Atlantic. The British continued to claim title to all the land up to the St. Lawrence River, and it was upon the Indian nations of the region—the Abenakis, Micmacs, and Malecites—that the French relied to hold the English back from the vital St. Lawrence waterway.[20] The governor general at Quebec made sure that those nations were well supplied with all the European goods they needed and that a continual state of hostility existed between them and the expanding population of New England.[21]

273

[18] For a revealing commentary on the working of a typical fur trade company of the period see Meuvret au Lt. Joseph Marin de la Malgue [Commandant, la Baie des Puants], May 15, 1752, Fonds Verreau, Boite 5, no. 38 1/2, Archs. Sém. Québec. See also Acte de Société, May 23, 1726, Jean Le Mire Marsolet, de Lignery, Guillaume Cartier, Greffe J-B, Adhemar, No. 1854, Archives Nationales du Québec à Montréal.

[19] Pierre-Jacques Chavoy de Noyan to the minister, Oct. 18, 1738, Mich. Pioneer Hist. Soc., *Hist. Colls.*, XXXIV (1905), 158-159; Le Conseil de Marine à MM de Vaudreuil et Bégon, Oct. 20, 1717, CIIA, Vol. 37, fols. 378-379; Beauharnois et Hocquart au ministre, Oct. 5, 1736, *ibid.*, Vol. 65, fols. 57-58; Greffe J., David, Apr. 28, 1723, Archs. Québec (Mtl.), is but one of hundreds of permits that specify the obligations to the crown of those allowed to trade in the west. See also *ibid.*, Greffe J-B, Adhemar, No. 1257, May 23, 1724, and No. 1211, May 8, 1724; Beauharnois et d'Aigremont au ministre, Oct. 1, 1728, CIIA, Vol. 50, fols. 31-33; Wilbur R. Jacobs, *Dispossessing the American Indian: Indians and Whites on the Colonial Frontier* (New York, 1972), 194, n. 38; and Zoltvany, *Vaudreuil*, 174-175.

[20] Zoltvany, *Vaudreuil*, 166-168, 196-209.

[21] Canada. Conseil. MM de Vaudreuil et Bégon, Oct. 26, 1720, CIIA, Vol. 41, fols. 390-391.

In the implementation of this policy the French received unwitting aid from the New England settlers. What the latter coveted most was land for settlement, the very lands that the Indians required to maintain their hunting economy and that they believed had been granted them by God for that very purpose. The Indians denied that they were or ever had been subjects of either the French or the English crown. They asserted vehemently that the French could not have ceded their land by treaty as the Massachusetts authorities claimed, since no one could cede what had never been his.[22] Although the French, with their meager population, did not covet any of that land, they were determined to deny it to the English. In 1727 the king stated in a *memoire* to the governor general and intendant at Quebec that he had learned with pleasure that the Abenakis of Saint-François and Bécancourt intended to continue the war against the English and not to entertain any proposals for peace until the English had razed the forts they had built on Abenaki lands. "This is so important for Canada," the *memoire* went on, "that the Sieur de Beauharnois could not take measures more just than such as would foment that war and prevent any accommodation."[23]

To the north, where France had relinquished its claims to Hudson Bay, a dispute arose over the interpretation of the covering clause in the Treaty of Utrecht. The British claimed that they had thereby gained title to all the lands whose waters drained into Hudson Bay—almost a quarter of the continent. They themselves, however, negated their claim by insisting that the operative clause in the treaty state that France *restored* rather than *ceded* to Great Britain the lands claimed by the latter—this in order to establish that Britain had always had the prior claim. France agreed but riposted by declaring that only the lands that Britain had formerly occupied could be restored to her: by definition, restoration could not be made of lands that had never been conquered, purchased, or occupied.[24] In fact, merely an infinitesimal fraction of that vast territory had ever even been seen by a British subject. The argument was really an academic one since the

[22] Parole de toute la Nation Abenaquise et de toutes les autres nations sauvages ses alliés au gouverneur de Baston au sujet de la Terre des Abenaquise dont les Anglois s'Emparent depuis la Paix ... fait à KenasK8K au bas de la Rivière de Kenibeki Le 28 Juillet 1721, F3 Moreau de St. Méry, Vol 2, fols. 413-416, Archs. Nationales.

[23] Mémoire du Roy à MM de Beauharnois et Dupuy, Apr. 29, 1727, *Nouvelle-France. Documents historiques. Correspondance échangée entre les autorités française et les gouverneurs et intendants*, I (Québec, 1893), 64.

[24] E. E. Rich, *The History of the Hudson's Bay Company, 1670-1870*, I: *1670-1763* (London, 1958), 423-425, 482-486; "Memorial of the Governor and Company of Adventurers of England Trading into Hudson's Bay to the Council of Trade and Plantations," in W. Noel Sainsbury *et al.*, eds., *Calendar of State Papers, Colonial Series, America and the West Indies* (London, 1860-   ), XXXI, No. 360; Mr. Delafaye to the Council of Trade and Plantations, Nov. 4, 1719, *ibid.*, No. 443; Observations et réflexions servant de réponses aux propositions de Messieurs les Commissaires anglais au sujet des limites a régler pour la Baie d'Hudson, *Rapport de l'Archiviste*, 1922-1923, 95-96.

Hudson's Bay Company made no attempt to challenge French control of the interior. As long as enough furs reached its posts to produce a dividend for its shareholders, the company's servants were content to remain in a "sleep by the frozen sea."[25]

The French now established fur trade posts on the rivers that ran down to the bay and thereby controlled the flow of furs to the English. They kept the choicest furs for themselves and allowed the Indians to trade only their poorer quality pelts at the Bay Company's posts.[26] Had it not been that the Indians were astute enough to maintain trade relations with both the English and the Canadians in order to reap the advantages of competition, Britain's hold on Hudson Bay would early have been severed.[27]

From the signing of the Treaty of Utrecht in 1713 to the conquest of New France, the French maintained their presence among the nations of the west, penetrating steadily farther into the interior until they eventually reached the barrier of the Rocky Mountains.[28] Only at Detroit, Kaskaskia, and Cahokia in the Illinois country, and on the lower Mississippi, were they able to establish small agricultural settlements.[29] Elsewhere they merely maintained fur trade posts consisting of three or four log buildings surrounded by a palisade. Always these posts were placed in an area that no Indian nation claimed as its own—Detroit, for example—or were established with the express permission of the dominant nation of the region. Some of the posts had been maintained during the Iroquois war, ostensibly as bases and places of refuge for the nations allied with the French against the Iroquois Confederacy. Experience had proven that posts on the fringe of Iroquois-controlled territory were more prisons than forts. Their garrisons did not dare venture beyond musket range of the palisades, and too many of the men, deprived of fresh meat or fish, reduced to hard rations of stale salt pork and sea biscuit, succumbed to scurvy.[30]

275

[25] Rich, *Hudson's Bay Company*, I, 554, 434, 556, 575, and *The Fur Trade and the Northwest to 1857* (Toronto, 1967), 118.

[26] Lawrence J. Burpee, ed., "The Journal of Anthony Hendry, 1754-55," Royal Society of Canada, *Proceedings and Transactions*, 2d Ser., XIII, Pt. ii (1907), 352-353.

[27] Rich, *Hudson's Bay Company*, I, 482, 526, 529; Arthur J. Ray, "Indians as Consumers in the Eighteenth Century," in Carol M. Judd and Arthur J. Ray, eds., *Old Trails and New Directions: Papers of the Third North American Fur Trade Conference* (Toronto, 1980), 255-271; W. J. Eccles, "A Belated Review of Harold Adams Innis, *The Fur Trade in Canada*," *Canadian Historical Review*, LX (1979), 427-434.

[28] Memoire ou Extrait du Journal Sommaire du Voyage de Jacques Legardeur Ecuyer Sr de St. Pierre . . . chargé de la Descouverte de la Mer de l'Ouest, Fonds Verreau, Boite 5, No. 54, Archs. Sém. Québec.

[29] The population figures for these settlements are revealing: Detroit in 1750, 483; Illinois in 1752, 1,536; lower Louisiana in 1746, 4,100.

[30] Denonville et Champigny au ministre, Nov. 6, 1688, C11A, Vol. 10, fol. 8, and le ministre à Denonville, Jan. 8, 1688, B, Vol. 15, fol. 20, Archs. Nationales.

After the Iroquois wars of the seventeenth century, and with the proclamation of Louis XIV's containment policy in North America, fur trade posts had to be sustained among all the nations that could conceivably have contact, direct or indirect, with the English colonials or the Hudson's Bay Company. With the exception of the Sioux nation, who always kept the French at arm's length, most of the nations were glad to have these posts on their territory. Although the French maintained that the posts gave them title to the land, their claims were made to exclude the English, not to deny the Indians' title, something they did not dare do. The French were certainly not sovereign in the west, for sovereignty implies the right to impose and collect taxes, and to enforce laws—and they were never able to do either. The Indians never considered themselves to be French subjects, and the French were never able to treat them as such.[31] Moreover, the Canadian voyageurs who transported trade goods and supplies to the western posts and took the furs back to Montreal always had to travel in convoy for protection against the Indians through whose lands they passed. One or two canoes alone were an invitation to extortionate demands or outright pillage.[32] The Indians allowed the French only the right of passage to the posts, since this assured them a ready supply of European goods close at hand. The land on which the trading posts stood they considered still to be theirs, the French occupants being mere tenants during the Indians' pleasure.

Another significant factor in this imperial rivalry was the superiority of most French trade goods. In only one item, woolen cloth, did the English have an advantage, and even this is open to question. The factors at the Hudson's Bay Company's posts were continually pleading with their superiors in London to provide them with goods of the same quality as those traded by the French.[33] In one of the more important trade items, liquor, the French had a distinct advantage. Showing commendable good taste, the Indians greatly preferred French brandy to the rot-gut rum and gin supplied by the British and Americans. The Hudson's Bay Company produced imitation brandy made from cheap gin with alarming additives to give it the color and something resembling the taste of cognac, but it

[31] Similarly the Iroquois specifically rejected British claims that they were subjects of the British crown. See Acte authentique des six nations iroquoises sur leur indépendance (Nov. 2, 1748), *Rapport de l'Archiviste, 1921-1922*, unnum. plate following p. 108.

[32] d'Iberville au ministre, Feb. 26, 1700, C13A, Vol. 1, fol. 236, Archs. Nationales; Pièces détachées judiciares 1720, Archs. Québec (Mtl.); Vaudreuil à Beauharnois, Nov. 9, 1745, Loudon Collection, Henry E. Huntington Library, San Marino, Calif.; Ordonnance de Beauharnois, June 8, 1743, Fonds Verreau, Boite 8, No. 96, Archs. Sém. Québec; Duquesne à Contrecoeur, June 12, 1753, *ibid.*, Boite 1, No. 19; Duquesne à Contrecoeur, June 24, 1754, Fernand Grenier, ed., *Papiers Contrecoeur et autres documents concernant le conflit anglo-français sur l'Ohio de 1745 à 1756* (Québec, 1952), 193.

[33] On this controversial issue see Ray, "Indians as Consumers," in Judd and Ray, eds., *Old Trails and New Directions*, 255-271, and Eccles, "Belated Review of Innis," *Canadian Hist. Rev.*, LX (1979), 419-441.

never replaced the real thing in the Indians' opinion.[34] Alcohol was crucial in the fur trade for two reasons. First, the Indians craved it more than anything else; even though they knew that it could destroy them, they could not resist it, and they would go to any lengths to obtain all that was available.[35] Second, from the purely economic aspect of the trade, alcohol was the ideal exchange item. Of other goods—cloth, wearing apparel, pots, knives, axes, muskets—the Indians had a limited need. It is now coming to be recognized that they were by no means as dependent on European goods as has been claimed.[36] A musket would last many years, as would other metal goods. A few items of clothing each year per family did not result in large entries in the Montreal merchants' ledgers. An Indian hunter could garner enough pelts in a couple of months' good hunting to provide for his family's needs, but the appetite for *eau de vie* was virtually insatiable, driving the Indians to produce furs in ever larger quantities. In the 1790s a Nor'wester, Duncan McGillivray, remarked, "When a nation becomes addicted to drinking it affords a strong presumption that they will soon become excellent hunters."[37]

277

The French traders who lived among the Indians were only too well aware of the terrible effects that liquor had on their customers. Frequently they paid for it with their lives when Indians, in their cups, went berserk and set about them with knife or *casse tête.*[38] Some of the senior French officials who were involved in the fur trade for personal gain tried to make light of these dread effects. Gov. Gen. Louis de Buade, comte de Frontenac, for example, contended vociferously that the Indians did not get any more drunk, or behave any worse when in their cups, than did the average Englishman or Netherlander.[39] The French missionaries, in particular the Jesuits who resided in the Indian villages, knew better. They fought to have liquor barred completely from the trade and threatened excommunication for any traders who persisted in its use.[40] Gov. Gen. Philippe de Rigaud de Vaudreuil and his successor, Charles de la Boische, marquis de Beauharnois, both recognized the horrors caused by the liquor trade, but for political reasons they had to condone it, while at the same

---

[34] Rich, *Hudson's Bay Company,* I, 545.

[35] Calvin Martin, *Keepers of the Game: Indian-Animal Relationships and the Fur Trade* (Berkeley, Calif., 1978), 63-64; André Vachon, "L'eau de vie dans la société indienne," Canadian Historical Association, *Report* (1960), 22-32.

[36] Ray, "Indians as Consumers," in Judd and Ray, eds., *Old Trails and New Directions,* 255-271.

[37] Arthur S. Morton, ed., *The Journal of Duncan M'Gillivray of the North West Company at Fort George on the Saskatchewan, 1794-5* (Toronto, 1929), 47.

[38] Beauharnois et Hocquart au ministre, Oct. 12, 1736, C11A, Vol. 65, fols. 49-51; Observation de la Conseil de la Marine, June 1, 1718, *ibid.,* Vol. 39, fols. 242-246. See also Reuben Gold Thwaites, ed., *The Jesuit Relations and Allied Documents: Travels and Explorations of the Jesuit Missionaries in New France, 1610-1791* (Cleveland, Ohio, 1896-1901), *passim.*

[39] Eccles, *Frontenac,* 66.

[40] For a brief overview of this contentious issue see *ibid.,* 61-68.

time striving to restrict its use to prevent the worst abuses. As they and others pointed out to Jean-Fréderic Phélypeaux, comte de Maurepas, appointed minister of marine in 1723, were they to refuse to trade alcohol the Indians would go to the Anglo-American traders, who had no scruples whatsoever, despite frequent pleas from tribal chieftains to keep the rum pedlars out of their villages.[41] Thus in the imperial contest liquor was a powerful but pernicious weapon.

Throughout the eighteenth century the Montreal fur traders took the lion's share of the North American fur trade. The customs figures for fur imports at London, La Rochelle, and Rouen make this plain.[42] Moreover, the Albany merchants who dominated the Anglo-American fur trade admitted that they obtained the bulk of their furs clandestinely from the Canadians.[43] It could hardly have been otherwise since they did not have access to the northwest, which produced the fine quality furs. The minister of marine, Maurepas, and after 1749 his successor, Antoine-Louis Rouillé, comte de Jouy, continually demanded that the smuggling of Canadian furs to Albany be stopped, but to no avail.[44] They simplemindedly believed that if the English desired something, then France must strive to deny it them. The senior officials at Quebec well understood the complexity of the situation. They declared vociferously that they were doing everything possible to curb this clandestine trade, but the evidence indicates that their unenthusiastic efforts were less than efficacious. They tolerated the existence of an agent of the Albany traders at Montreal and frequent visits of the merchants themselves. Similarly, Montreal traders called at Albany from time to time, and credit arrangements between the merchants of the two centers were extensive.[45] One suspects that the

[41] Peter Schuyler to Gov. Dongan, Sept. 2, 1687, E. B. O'Callaghan *et al.*, eds., *Documents Relative to the Colonial History of the State of New-York* ... (Albany, N.Y., 1856-1887), III, 479, hereafter cited as *N.-Y. Col. Docs.*; Propositions made by four of the Chief Sachems of the 5 Nations to his Excell. Benjamin Fletcher ... in Albany, Feb. 26, 1692/3, *ibid.*, IV, 24; Dec. 27, 1698, Peter Wraxall, *An Abridgement of the Indian Affairs ... Transacted in the Colony of New York, from the Year 1678 to the Year 1751*, ed. Charles Howard McIlwain (Cambridge, Mass., 1915), 31; Relation de ce qui s'est passé de plus remarquable en Canada ... 1695, F3 Moreau de St. Méry, Vol. 7, fols. 370-372, Archs. Nationales; Vaudreuil au ministre, Oct. 25, 1710, *Rapport de l'Archiviste*, 1946-1947, 385; Vaudreuil et Bégon au ministre, Sept. 20, 1714, *ibid.*, 1947-1948, 275-276; Beauharnois et Hocquart au ministre, Oct. 12, 1736, C11A, Vol. 65, fols. 44-46.

[42] Eccles, "Belated Review of Innis," *Canadian Hist. Rev.*, LX (1979), 434.

[43] Thomas Elliot Norton, *The Fur Trade in Colonial New York, 1686-1776* (Madison, Wis., 1974), 100-103, 122, 124.

[44] Jean Lunn, "The Illegal Fur Trade out of New France, 1713-1760," Canadian Hist. Assn., *Report* (1939), 61-76; Wraxall, *New York Indian Records*, ed. McIlwain, *passim*.

[45] Le Ch[er] Dailleboust à Madame d'Argenteuil, Jan. 5, 1715, Collection Baby, g 1/12, Université de Montréal, Montréal, Que.; Ordonnance de Gilles Hocquart, Apr. 25, 1738, C11A, Vol. 69, fols. 180-183; Pierre-Georges Roy, ed., *Inventaire*

governor general and the intendant despaired of bringing first Maurepas, then Rouillé, ministers of marine, to grasp how closely intertwined were the economics and politics of the situation. Certainly, they did not make a determined attempt to explain the subtleties of the issue.

The main agents of this clandestine trade were the Christian Indians of Sault St. Louis and Lake of Two Mountains missions, both close by Montreal.[46] The Canadian officials claimed that they dared not forbid these Indians to trade at Albany whenever they pleased lest they become disaffected and remove from New France. Since their services were vital in time of war, and in peacetime as intelligence agents, they had to be indulged. Thus they quite openly transported Canadian furs to Albany, along with fine French cloth, wines, and spirits, for the accounts of Canadian merchants.[47] In fact, Governor General Beauharnois declared that the Mission Iroquois of Sault St. Louis constituted virtually an independent republic over which he had no authority.[48]

Although the Canadian fur traders undoubtedly reaped considerable benefits from this clandestine trade, a far more significant consequence was that it removed any incentive the Albany merchants might have had to contest the hold of the French over the western nations.[49] This issue was of great concern to the crown officials of New York, who took an imperial view of the situation, but the Albany merchants were interested only in preserving their well-established Canadian trade. When furs were shipped to their doors by the Canadians at prices that afforded them a good profit, they saw no reason to incur the great risks, capital outlay, and trouble that would be involved in trying to compete with the Canadians on their ground, the Indian country of the northwest. Moreover, they lacked the birchbark canoes, the voyageurs to man them, and the prime requisite, the willingness to accept the Indians on their own terms—in short, all the special skills needed for this particular trade.[50] In November 1765 Sir

279

---

des Ordonnances des Intendants de la Nouvelle-France, conservées aux Archives provinciales de Québec, I (Beauceville, Que., 1919), 160-161, 222; J. W. De Peyster à Jean Lidius, Sept. 23, 1729, NF 13-17, Procédures Judiciares, III, fols. 389-393, Archs. Québec (Mtl.); Myndert Schuyler à Jean Lidius, Oct. 15, 1729, *ibid.;* Extrait des Registres du Conseil Supérieur de Québec, Sept. 28, 1730, *ibid.,* fols. 385-388.

[46] Lunn, "Illegal Fur Trade," Canadian Hist. Assn., *Report* (1939), 61-76.

[47] Vaudreuil et Bégon au ministre, Nov. 12, 1712, *Rapport de l'Archiviste,* 1947-1948, 183-184; Mémoire du Roy pour servir d'instructions au Sieur marquis de Beauharnois, gouverneur et lieutenant-général de la Nouvelle-France, May 7, 1726, *Nouvelle-France. Documents historiques,* I, 57; Report of Messrs. Schuyler and Dellius' Negotiations in Canada, July 2, 1698, *N.-Y. Col. Docs.,* IV, 347; Bellomont to Council of Trade and Plantations, Aug. 24, 1699, Sainsbury *et al.,* eds., *Calendar of State Papers,* XVII, 406.

[48] Beauharnois to Maurepas, Sept. 21, 1741, *N.-Y. Col. Docs.,* IX, 1071.

[49] Arthur H. Buffinton, "The Policy of Albany and English Westward Expansion," *Mississippi Valley Historical Review,* VIII (1922), 327-366.

[50] For contemporary British comment on the superior skills of the Canadian traders see *American Gazetteer . . .* (London, 1762), II, s.v. "Montreal": "The

William Johnson commented sadly on this phenomenon to the Lords of Trade:

> I have frequently observed to Your Lordships, that His Majesty's subjects in this Country seem very ill calculated to Cultivate a good understanding with the Indians; and this is a notorious proof of it, for notwithstanding the Expence of transporting Goods from New Orleans to the Ilinois is greater than by the Lakes and Consequently French goods are in general Dearer than Ours, yet such is the Conduct of all persons under the Crown of France, whether Officers, Agents, Traders, that the Indians will go much farther to buy their Goods, and pay a much higher price for them. This all persons acquainted with the nature of the Commerce to the Westward can fully evidence.[51]

280

Nor was the trade all one way. The Iroquois made annual trips to Canada to confer with the French authorities. The crown officials of New York were deeply worried by the influence that the French gained over the Iroquois during these visits. The French entertained the Iroquois delegates lavishly, after a fashion that the British officials could not or would not match.[52] In October 1715 the Albany Indian commissioners stated: "Trade between Albany & Canada is of fatal Consequence to the Indian Interest of this Colony, that of our Indians who are employed in it many stay at Canada & others return so Attached to the French Interest & so Debauched from ours that it puzzels them how to preserve amongst them that Respect & Regard to this Gov't so necessary to the Public Good and Tranquillity."[53]

By 1720 the French had gained a secure hold on the Great Lakes basin by ringing it with garrisoned fur trade posts. Although the mercantile interests of New York were not perturbed by this development, the crown officials were, and they sought to counter it. In 1719 the governor general of New France, Vaudreuil, heard reports that New York intended to establish a fort at Niagara, which would have given the English access to the west, including the Mississippi Valley. Vaudreuil very adroitly forestalled them by obtaining the permission of the Senecas to establish a post on their land at the mouth of the Niagara River. Ostensibly, the post was

---

French have found some secret of conciliating the affections of the savages, which our traders seem stranger to, or at least take no care to put it in practice." See also Burpee, ed., "Journal of Anthony Hendry," Royal Soc. Canada, *Procs. and Trans.*, 2d Ser., XIII, Pt. ii (1907), 307.

[51] Johnson to the Lords of Trade, Nov. 16, 1765, C.O. 5/66, fol. 296, Public Record Office. I am indebted to Dr. Francis P. Jennings for providing me with this piece of evidence.

[52] For a specific instance of this see the entry for Teganissorens in David M. Hayne, ed., *Dictionary of Canadian Biography*, II (Toronto, 1969), 619-623.

[53] Wraxall, *New York Indian Records*, ed. McIlwain, 111.

to serve their needs; in reality, it barred the west to the English.[54] The following year another post was established at the Toronto portage, barring that route from Lake Ontario to Lake Huron.[55]

Although the Iroquois had given the French permission to establish the post at Niagara and bluntly told the protesting Albany authorities that they had "given the French liberty of free Passage thru Lake Ontario,"[56] they had no desire to see the French become overpowerful in the region. To balance their position they therefore granted New York permission to build a trading post at Oswego on the south shore of Lake Ontario across from Fort Frontenac. At the same time, deputies from the Iroquois Confederacy met with the Albany Indian commissioners, who reported that the Indians "exhort us to live in Peace and Quiet with the French and carry on our Trade without Molesting each other."[57] The Quebec authorities responded by claiming that the south shore of the Great Lakes belonged to France by right of prior discovery and conquest.[58] Governor General Beauharnois began making preparations for a campaign to take and destroy Oswego, but he was restrained by the government in France, which at the time enjoyed good relations with Great Britain, this being the era of the *entente cordiale* established by Cardinal André-Hercule de Fleury and Robert Walpole.[59] Nevertheless, the Canadian authorities replaced the trading post at Niagara with a solid stone edifice that would have required heavy cannon to demolish, greatly to the dismay of the Albany authorities.[60]

281

Events were to demonstrate that Oswego posed no serious threat to French control of the Great Lakes. The fear was that it would seduce the western nations out of the French alliance by undercutting the French prices for furs and, more particularly, by the unrestricted sale of liquor. But here again, as at Albany, the New York traders were their own worst enemies. They did indeed supply all the cheap liquor the Indians desired, but the latter, when under its influence, were unmercifully cheated and their womenfolk debauched.[61] This bred bitter resentment.

[54] Zoltvany, *Vaudreuil*, 168-169; Wraxall, *New York Indian Records*, ed. McIlwain, 132-135.

[55] Percy J. Robinson, *Toronto during the French Régime: A History of the Toronto Region from Brulé to Simcoe, 1615-1793,* 2d ed. (Toronto, 1965), 66.

[56] Wraxall, *New York Indian Records*, ed. McIlwain, 161.

[57] *Ibid.*

[58] Memoire touchant le droit françois sur les Nations Iroquoises, Nov. 12, 1712, CIIA, Vol. 33, fol. 284. The Iroquois admitted to the Albany commissioners that the French had five posts on the south side of Lake Ontario, from Niagara to Cayouhage, east of Oswego. See Sept. 10, 1720, Wraxall, *New York Indian Records,* ed. McIlwain, 130-131.

[59] On Anglo-French relations at this time see Paul Vaucher, *Robert Walpole et la politique de Fleury (1713-1742)* (Paris, 1924).

[60] Zoltvany, *Vaudreuil*, 199.

[61] Wraxall, *New York Indian Records*, ed. McIlwain, 111, 113; Charles Thomson, *An Enquiry into the Causes of the Alienation of the Delaware and Shawanese Indians*

Oswego posed an additional problem for the authorities at Quebec. Some of the less scrupulous Canadian traders found it convenient to obtain large supplies of cheap rum there, as well as English woolens, which they traded at the distant Indian villages.[62] In an attempt to keep both the allied Indians and the renegade Canadians away from the English post, the French government retained the trade at forts Frontenac, Niagara, and Toronto as crown monopolies so that prices could be kept competitive with those at Oswego by selling at a reduced profit or even a loss if necessary. The commandants at these posts had to see to it that nothing transpired that could upset the Indians and endanger their alliance with the French.[63]

282 The French thus managed to maintain a tenuous hold over the interior of North America west of the Appalachians and in the vast region north and west of the Great Lakes as far as the Rocky Mountains. This tremendous feat was, moreover, accomplished at very little cost to the French crown and by a mere handful of men. In 1754, when this military fur trade empire was nearing its greatest extent, the cost to the crown for maintaining the garrisoned posts was but 183,427 *livres*.[64] The number of officers and enlisted men in these garrisons in 1750 was only 261,[65] but in addition there were the men engaged directly in the trade with the Indians—the voyageurs, traders, clerks, and merchants—whose number cannot be calculated with any great degree of accuracy. All that can be offered here is an educated guess that the number directly employed in the western fur trade for the period 1719-1750 would range from about 200 for the earlier years to some 600 at most by mid-century.[66] This

---

from the British Interest ... (London, 1759), 56, 76, 114, 118-122; Wilbur R. Jacobs, ed., *The Appalachian Indian Frontier: The Edmond Atkin Report and Plan of 1755* (Columbia, S.C., 1954), *passim*.

[62] Duquesne à Contrecoeur, Apr. 30, 1753, Fonds Verreau, Boite 1, No. 13, Archs. Sém. Québec.

[63] Mar. 14, 1721, Apr. 25, 1726, Roy, ed., *Inventaire des Ordonnances des Intendants*, I, 196, 282; Hocquart au ministre, Oct. 25, 1729, C11A, Vol. 51, fol. 264; Vaudreuil, Beauharnois, et Raudot au ministre, Oct. 19, 1705, *Rapport de l'Archiviste*, 1938-1939, 87-88.

[64] Mémoire sur les postes de Canada ... en 1754 ..., *Rapport de l'Archiviste*, 1927-1928, 353.

[65] Extrait Général des Reveues des Compagnies Entretenues en la Nouvelle-France ... 1750, D2C, Vol. 48, fol. 130, Archs. Nationales.

[66] Many of the voyageurs hired to serve in the west had notarized contracts, a copy of which had to be preserved in an official register by the notary. Unfortunately, many voyageurs were instead hired *sous seing privé*, that is, with a written contract not drawn up by a notary. A few of the latter type of contract have survived by accident or because they were submitted as evidence in legal proceedings. Many men may well have been hired with a mere verbal understanding of the terms of service. Statistical studies based on the notarized contracts alone therefore cannot help but be misleading since there is no way of knowing what proportion of the total number of voyageurs employed in any given year the

means that with fewer than 1,000 men France maintained its claim to more than half the continent.

Had the French been content to confine their activities to the fur trade they might well have retained their control, in alliance with the Indian nations, over the northern half of the continent, that is, over the area that today forms the Dominion of Canada. However, the interests of the Canadian fur traders and French imperial policy began to diverge at mid-century, immediately after the War of the Austrian Succession. Fur traders from Pennsylvania and Virginia, serving as advance agents of land speculation companies, had begun to penetrate the Ohio Valley by way of the Cumberland Gap with pack-horse trains.[67] To win the allegiance of the Indian nations they flooded the region with cheap trade goods, liquor, and expensive presents for the chiefs. A Canadian officer later declared, "The presents that they receive are so considerable that one sees nothing but the most magnificent gold, silver, and scarlet braid."[68] The Canadian fur traders had no interest in the furs of that region, which were of poor quality.[69] They preferred to confine their activities to the northwest, where the furs were the best obtainable, river communications far easier than they were south of the Great Lakes, and the Cree tongue a *lingua franca* in the entire region.

Marquis Roland-Michel Barrin de la Gallissonière, governor general of New France, in opposition to the prevailing and strongly held Canadian sentiment, advocated that the Ohio Valley be occupied by the French and that forts be built and garrisoned, merely to deny the region to the English. He freely admitted that it would be of no economic benefit to France in the foreseeable future, but he feared that were the English to succeed in occupying and settling the valley they would become extremely powerful and dangerous. They would eventually sever communications along the Mississippi between Canada and Louisiana and then go on to conquer Mexico with its silver mines.[70]

The minister of marine, Rouillé, newly appointed to the post and

283

---

contracts represent. See Gratien Allaire, "Les engagements pour la traite des fourrures, évaluation de la documentation," *Revue d'histoire de l'Amérique française,* XXXIV (1980), 3-26.

[67] W. J. Eccles, *France in America* (New York, 1972), 178-179.

[68] La Chauvignery à [Contrecoeur], Feb. 10, 1754, Fonds Verreau, Boîte 1, No. 77, Archs. Sém. Québec.

[69] As early as 1708 François Clairambault d'Aigremont, sent to investigate conditions in the west, stated in a momentous report to the minister that the French could not take enough precautions to conserve the trade north of Lake Superior, since the furs at Detroit and those of the region to the south were not worth much. The reluctance of the Canadian fur traders to engage in trade in the Ohio country is made plain in Gov. Gen. Duquesne's correspondence with Claude-Pierre Pécaudy de Contrecoeur, commandant at Fort Duquesne. Le Sr Daigremont au Ministre Pontchartrain, Nov. 14, 1708, C11A, Vol. 29, fol. 175; Grenier, ed., *Papiers Contrecoeur,* 126, 128, 209, 224, 248-249, 253.

[70] Gallissonière au ministre, Sept. 1, 1748, C11A, Vol. 91, fols. 116-122.

without previous experience in colonial affairs, accepted this policy. Despite the strong opposition of the senior Canadian officials in the colonial administration,[71] and at immense cost in funds and Canadian lives,[72] the French drove the American traders out of the region. They established a chain of forts and supply depots from Lake Erie to the fork of the Ohio, thereby overawing the local tribes, who quickly abandoned their commercial alliance with the Anglo-Americans and pledged their support to the French.[73] This was accomplished by force majeure pure and simple, and the Indian nations remained in this uneasy alliance only as long as it appeared to them to suit their interests and, as events were to show, not a day longer.

Previously when the French had extended their fur trade empire into new territory, they had always done so at the invitation, or at least with the tacit consent, of the Indians. In the Ohio Valley, however, Gallissonière's successor, Ange de Menneville, marquis Duquesne, made it plain to the Iroquois, who claimed sovereignty over the region, that he would brook no interference, that he regarded the valley as belonging to the French crown, and that if they chose to oppose him he would crush them.[74] Some of his Canadian officers, long accustomed to dealing with the Iroquois, were more diplomatic. They pointed out that the French did not covet the land but merely wished to prevent the English from seizing it, and that the Indians could hunt right up to the walls of the French forts, whereas wherever the English went the forest was destroyed and the animals driven out, the Indians with them.[75]

Here also the Anglo-Americans were the agents of their own defeat.

[71] Donald H. Kent, *The French Invasion of Western Pennsylvania, 1753* (Harrisburg, Pa., 1954), 12; Sylvester K. Stevens and Donald H. Kent, eds., *Wilderness Chronicles of Northwestern Pennsylvania* . . . (Harrisburg, Pa., 1941), 56; Duquesne à Contrecoeur, Sept. 8, 1754, Grenier, ed., *Papiers Contrecoeur*, 250; Duquesne à Rouillé, Nov. 31(*sic*), 1753, C11A, Vol. 99, fols. 139-143; Duquesne à Rouillé, Sept. 29, 1754, *ibid.*, fols. 242-243; Duquesne à Rouillé, Nov. 7, 1754, *ibid.*, fol. 259.

[72] By Oct. 1753, of over 2,000 men who had left Montreal the previous spring and summer only 880 were fit for service. Duquesne à Marin, Nov. 16, 1753, Grenier, ed., *Papiers Contrecoeur*, 81; Ministre à Duquesne, May 31, 1754, B, Vol. 99, fol. 199, Archs. Nationales; Kent, *French Invasion*, 64.

[73] Duquesne à Contrecoeur, July 1, 1754, Grenier, ed., *Papiers Contrecoeur*, 207-208.

[74] In Apr. 1754 Capitaine de Contrecoeur warned the Indians who were trading with the English at their post on the Ohio that he intended to drive the English out. If the Indians chose to support the enemy, they too would be crushed; it was up to them to decide whether or not they wished to be destroyed. Paroles de Contrecoeur aux Sauvages, Grenier, ed., *Papiers Contrecoeur*, 116-117. See also Duquesne à Contrecoeur, Apr. 15, 1754, *ibid.*, 113-116.

[75] Duquesne à Contrecoeur, Aug. 14, 1754, *ibid.*, 248; Duquesne to the minister, Oct. 31, 1754, *N.Y. Col. Docs.*, X, 269; Thomas Pownall, cited in Louis De Vorsey, Jr., *The Indian Boundary in the Southern Colonies, 1763-1775* (Chapel Hill, N.C., 1961), 56-57.

They had treated two nations on the frontiers of Pennsylvania and
Virginia, the Shawnee and the Delaware, so ruthlessly, seizing their land
by dint of fraudulent title deeds, debauching them with liquor, murdering
them with impunity, that it did not require a great deal of persuasion by
the French to bring these Indians into a close military alliance once
hostilities broke out.[76] This rejection of the Anglo-Americans was immeasurably strengthened by the initial French victories, first over Maj. George
Washington's motley provincial force at Fort Necessity, where Washington accepted humiliating terms and fled back over the mountains; then, a
year later when Maj. Gen. Edward Braddock's army of 2,200 British
regulars and American provincials was destroyed near Fort Duquesne by
250-odd Canadian regulars and militia and some 600 Indians.[77]

The French were now able to arm and send out Indian war parties, 285
accompanied by a few Canadian regulars or militia, to ravage the frontiers
of the English colonies from New York to Georgia, thereby retaining the
initiative and tying down large British and provincial forces. Successful
though it was, this strategy posed massive problems in logistics that the
minister of marine, Jean-Baptiste de Machault d'Arnouville, and his staff
at Versailles were never able to comprehend. Appalled by the Canadian
accounts for 1753, he warned Governor General Duquesne that unless
the excessive costs of the western posts were reduced, the king would
abandon the colony.[78] He thereby blandly overlooked the fact that the
expenditures had been incurred in consequence of his ministry's policy
and direct orders. To implement this policy all the needs of the Indian
allies had to be supplied.[79] This required the transport of vast amounts of
goods from Montreal to forts Niagara and Duquesne by canoe, barque,
horse, and pirogue. The wastage at the Niagara portage alone was
appalling. In 1753 Duquesne complained to Capt. Paul Marin de la
Malgue, commander of the Ohio expedition, that he had learned that
forty-eight canoe loads of supplies had been stolen or spoiled by being left
uncovered in the rain. He voiced the suspicion that the Canadians, who
were bitterly opposed to the Ohio adventure, were destroying the
supplies deliberately to force its abandonment.[80]

For many years the western Iroquois had demanded and received the
right to carry all fur trade and military supplies over the portage, which
they regarded as their territory. This was a cost that the crown officials at
Quebec had been quite willing to see imposed on the fur traders in order

[76] Thomson, *Enquiry into the Causes, passim;* Journal de Chaussegros de Léry, *Rapport de l'Archiviste,* 1927-1928, 409-410.
[77] For French and British casualties see Grenier, ed., *Papiers Contrecoeur,* 390-391.
[78] Ministre à Duquesne, May 31, 1754, B, Vol. 99, fol. 199, Archs. Nationales.
[79] Vaudreuil au ministre, Oct. 13, 1756, C11A, Vol. 101, fols. 117-119.
[80] Duquesne à Marin, June 20, July 10, 1753, Fonds Verreau, Boîte 5, Nos. 62, 66:6, Archs. Sém. Québec; Duquesne à Contrecoeur, July 22, Aug. 6, 1753, *ibid.,* Boîte 1, Nos. 27, 28; Varin à Contrecoeur, Aug. 18, 1753, *ibid.,* Boîte 5, No. 311.

to maintain good relations with the Iroquois Confederacy. Governor General Duquesne, however, considered excessive the 40,000 *livres* a year that it was now costing the crown to have military supplies transported around Niagara Falls by the Senecas. At the grave risk of alienating them and the other Iroquois nations, he had horses shipped from Montreal and dispensed with the Senecas' services. Many of the horses then mysteriously vanished.[81]

For the Canadian officers charged with the implementation of these orders, the task at times seemed insuperable. A lack of rain meant low water in the shallow rivers that linked Lake Erie, with a fifteen-mile portage, to the Ohio. The supply boats and pirogues then had to be manhandled along the river beds, driving both officers and men to despair.[82] To make matters worse, the Indian allies were extremely demanding and wasteful. Their loyalty could be counted on only as long as their demands for goods and services were met, and frequently not even then. In 1756 Vaudreuil ruefully explained to the minister of marine:

286

I am not in the least surprised that expenses have risen so high, the Indians are the cause of immense expenditures, forming the largest part of those charged to the crown in the colony. One has to see to believe what they consume and how troublesome they are. I deny and reduce their demands as much as I can at Montreal, but despite it they succeed in having themselves equipped several times in the same campaign. They continually come and go between the army or the posts and Montreal, and one is forced to supply them with food for every trip which they justify by claiming that they have been refused things by the army, or that having been on a raid they must now return home, or they dreamt that they ought to do so. Every time that one wants to send them to support the army one cannot avoid supplying them. When they go on a war party they are given 10, 12, or 15 days rations . . . at the end of two days they return without food or equipment and say they have lost it all, so they have to be provided

[81] Memoire sur les sauvages du Canada jusqu'à la Rivière de mississippi . . . Donné par M. de Sabrevois en 1718, C11A, Vol. 39, fol. 354; Varin à Contrecoeur, May 17, June 1, July 26, 1753, Fonds Verreau, Boite 4, Nos. 501, 502, 307, Archs. Sém. Québec; Varin à de la Perrière, Oct. 21, 1754, *ibid.*, Boite 8, No. 78; Contrecoeur à Douville, Apr. 14, 1755, Grenier, ed., *Papiers Contrecoeur*, 310-311.
[82] Duplessis Faber à Lavalterie, Apr. 16, 1756, BABY, No. 137; Péan à Contrecoeur, June 15, 1754, Fonds Verreau, Boite 1, No. 80, Archs. Sém. Québec; Varin à Contrecoeur, Feb. 4, 1753, *ibid.*, No. 294; Varin à (?), May 10, 1753, *ibid.*, No. 300; Contrecoeur à Douville, Apr. 14, 1755, Grenier, ed., *Papiers Contrecoeur*, 310; La Perrière à Contrecoeur, Apr. 20, 1755, *ibid.*, 321; Benoist à Contrecoeur, June 30, 1755, *ibid.*, 370-373; Saint-Blin à Contrecoeur, au for [*sic*] de la riviere au beouf [*sic*] le 3 juilietts [*sic*] 1755, *ibid.*, 374-375; Journal de Joseph-Gaspard Chaussegros de Léry, 1754-1755, *Rapport de l'Archiviste, 1927-1928*, 385.

afresh. They consume an astonishing quantity of brandy and a Commandant would be in grave difficulties were he to refuse them, and so it is with all their requests.[83]

One important factor, all too often overlooked, was that these Indian nations fought alongside the French purely to serve their own ends. They were allies, not mercenaries. In fact, they regarded the French as little more than an auxiliary force aiding them in their struggle to preserve their hunting grounds from further encroachment by the Anglo-Americans and to oblige the latter to treat them with respect.[84] This was compellingly illustrated when, in May 1757, the American colonial authorities entered into negotiations with Iroquois, Shawnee, and Delaware tribes to end the fighting that had destroyed their frontier settlements to a depth of over a hundred miles. For once, the Indian negotiators refused to be put off with vague promises; in the past, they had been hoodwinked all too often. Eventually a Moravian missionary, Frederick Post, who sympathized deeply with the Indians, went to the villages of the Shawnee and Delaware. There, within sight of Fort Duquesne, with frustrated French officers in attendance the proposed terms of the Easton Treaty were promulgated.[85]

287

The Indian nations south of the Great Lakes then ceased to support the French. When Brig. Gen. John Forbes, marching on Fort Duquesne with an army of some 7,000 British regulars and American provincial troops, suffered heavy and humiliating losses at the hands of the Canadians and Indians in one brisk battle, he deliberately slowed his advance until he received word that the Indians had signed a separate peace, the Easton Treaty. That defection left the French no choice but to abandon Fort Duquesne and, with it, control of the Ohio Valley. Col. Henry Bouquet commented: "After God the success of this Expedition is intirely due to the General, who by bringing about the Treaty of Easton, has struck the blow which has knocked the French in the head . . . in securing all his posts, and giving nothing to chance."[86]

The following year, 1759, Quebec and Niagara fell. Despite a valiant last attempt by the French and Canadians under François de Lévis to retake Quebec in the spring of 1760, six months later they were compelled to surrender to the armies of Maj. Gen. Jeffery Amherst at Montreal. This spelled the end of French power on the mainland of North America.

The fate of that empire had been decided by the incompetence of its government at home and that of the headquarters staff—with the exception of the Chevalier de Lévis—of the army sent to defend Canada. During

[83] Vaudreuil au ministre, Oct. 13, 1756, C11A, Vol. 101, fols. 117-119.
[84] Thomson, *Enquiry into the Causes*, 108-114.
[85] *Ibid.*, 138-160.
[86] Niles Anderson, "The General Chooses a Road," *Western Pennsylvania Historical Magazine*, XLII (1959), 138, 249, quotation on p. 396.

the course of the war there had been four controllers general of finance, four of foreign affairs, four of war, and five of the marine.[87] In the fateful year, 1759, the minister of marine was Nicolas-René Berryer. Before his appointment to that post in November 1758 he had been *lieutenant de police* for Paris.[88] As for the army sent to Canada, its morale and efficiency steadily deteriorated under the command of the incompetent, defeatist Louis-Joseph, marquis de Montcalm. It was not a shortage of supplies or overwhelming enemy superiority or corruption that brought on the British conquest of Canada. The west was lost when the Indian allies defected. Louisbourg fell because it lacked a fleet to protect it. Canada fell after the loss of Quebec in a battle that should have been won crushingly by the French but was lost owing to the stupidity and panic of Montcalm.[89] Even then Quebec might well have been retaken by Lévis had the minister of marine dispatched in time the reinforcements that Lévis had requested.[90] Etienne-François, duc de Choiseul, who was given charge of the ministries of war, foreign affairs, and marine, then decided that it would serve the interests of France better were England to acquire Canada, since, with the menace of French power removed from mainland America, England's colonies could be counted on to strike for independence in the not-too-distant future. France's loss of Canada, Choiseul decided, would be as nothing compared to England's loss of her American colonies.[91]

If the Canadians had had control of French policy in North America, neither the decisive battle at Quebec nor, for that matter, the war itself would likely have taken place, for the Canadians had no real quarrel with the English colonies. In war the Anglo-Americans had demonstrated time and again that they were no match for the Canadians and their Indian allies. Their record in the Seven Years' War indicated clearly enough their lack of enthusiasm for the conflict.[92] The Canadians knew that they had

[87] Lee Kennett, *The French Armies in the Seven Years' War: A Study in Military Organization and Administration* (Durham, N.C., 1967), 3-13.

[88] H. Carré acidly remarked, in describing the chaos that reigned in the Ministry of Marine, "enfin le lieutenant de police Berryer, sous l'administration duquel s'effondra la marine. A la fin, il suspendit les travaux des ports et vendit à des particuliers le matériel des arsenaux. Choiseul, son successeur, relèvera la marine, mais trop tard pour le succés de la guerre engagée" (*La Règne de Louis XV (1715-1774),* in Ernest Lavisse, ed., *Histoire de France . . . ,* VIII, Pt. ii [Paris, 1909], 272).

[89] W. J. Eccles, "The Battle of Quebec: A Reappraisal," French Colonial Historical Society, *Proceedings of the Third Annual Meeting* (Athens, Ga., 1978), 70-81.

[90] Dec. 28, 1758, C11A, Vol. 103, fols. 453-455; Guy Frégault, *La guerre de la conquête* (Montréal, 1955), 365-372.

[91] Memoire du duc de Choiseul, Dec. 1759, Manuscrits français, Nouvelles Acquisitions, Vol. 1041, fols. 44-63, Bib. Nationale.

[92] One interesting aspect of this attitude, as manifested in New England, is discussed by F. W. Anderson, "Why Did Colonial New Englanders Make Bad Soldiers? Contractual Principles and Military Conduct during the Seven Years' War," *William and Mary Quarterly,* 3d Ser., XXXVIII (1981), 395-417.

little to fear from that quarter, nor did they have any illusions that they could conquer the English colonies. In commerce there was no real conflict between them. The fur trade was of vital economic importance to the Canadians but certainly not to France, and of little, and that declining, importance to the Anglo-Americans. Among the latter, a group of well-placed, rapacious land speculators and a barbarian horde of would-be settlers coveted the lands of the Indian nations on their frontier, a region that the Canadians had made plain was of no interest to them. The Albany merchants who dominated the Anglo-American fur trade chose not to compete with the Canadians; instead they entered into a cosy commercial partnership. They had not exhibited any eagerness to dispute the French hold on the west. As for the Hudson's Bay Company, its steadily declining returns indicated its inability to compete with the Canadians; moreover, it no longer had the same influence that it once had wielded in government circles. It was a monopoly, and all trade monopolies were then being looked at askance in Britain.[93] Only the shareholders would have wept had the Hudson's Bay Company been driven to the wall by the Canadians.

289

For over half a century the fur trade was used by France as an instrument of its foreign policy and, owing to the peculiar skills of the Canadians, with considerable success. By means of it, most of the Indian nations supported the French cause in the colonial wars, but they did so only as long as it appeared to them to serve their immediate interests. The French were acutely aware of the Indians' true feeling toward them. Governor General Beauharnois remarked that they had their policies just as had the French. "In general," he stated, "they greatly fear us, they have no affection for us whatsoever, and the attitudes they manifest are never sincere."[94] A certain Monsieur Le Maire put the French position very succinctly, explaining that there was no middle course: one had to have the Indians either as friends or as foes, and whoever desired them as friends had to furnish them with their necessities, on terms they could afford.[95] The policy of the Indian nations was always to play the French off against the English, using the fur trade as an instrument of their own foreign policy.[96] Their tragedy was not to have foreseen the consequences were the French to be eliminated from the equation.

[93] Rich, *Fur Trade and the Northwest*, 115, and *Hudson's Bay Company*, I, 554, 572, 575-586.

[94] Beauharnois au ministre, Oct. 17, 1736, C11A, Vol. 65, fol. 143.

[95] MG7, I, A-Z, Fonds français, MS 12105, Memoire de Le Maire 1717, fol. 83, Public Archives of Canada.

[96] Conférence avec les Onondagués et Onneiouts, July 28, 1756, and Conférence, Dec. 21, 1756, C11A, Vol. 101, fols. 55-61, 263.

Why Did Colonial New Englanders Make Bad Soldiers? Contractual Principles and Military Conduct during the Seven Years' War

F. W. Anderson

BRITISH army officers who served in North America during the
Seven Years' War never tired of reminding one another that the
American colonists made the world's worst soldiers. As they saw
matters, provincial troops were overpaid and underdisciplined, a sickly,
slack, faint-hearted rabble incapable of enduring even the mildest priva-
tions, officered by men unwilling to exercise authority for fear of losing
favor with the mob. The populace as a whole seemed as bad as its soldiery:
a greedy, small-minded people incapable of disinterested action in defense
of the Empire. Contacts between regulars and New England provincials
largely fostered this image of Americans, and the image in turn created the
dominant British impression of colonial military abilities at the outset of
the War for Independence.[1]

Although this was a profoundly mistaken impression, it was in no sense
a groundless one: provincials in the Seven Years' War often behaved
unprofessionally or in ways detrimental to the war effort. Yet their
behavior was not unreasoned, nor was it merely self-interested, as the
British too readily assumed. Instead, the unmilitary deportment of New

Mr. Anderson is a doctoral candidate in history at Harvard University. He
wishes to acknowledge with gratitude the comments and criticism, on earlier drafts
of this article, of Virginia DeJohn Anderson, Bernard Bailyn, Barbara DeWolfe,
Randy Fertel, David Jaffee, Christopher Jedrey, Jon Roberts, and Helena Wall.
The staffs of the Henry E. Huntington and the William L. Clements libraries
provided valuable assistance. Financial support was received from Harvard University's Charles Warren Center and from the Department of the Army Center of
Military History. Materials from the Huntington Library, San Marino, Calif., are
reprinted by permission.

[1] Examples abound: see, for instance, Peter Wraxall to Henry Fox, Sept. 27,
1755, in Stanley Pargellis, ed., *Military Affairs in North America, 1748-1765:
Selected Documents from the Cumberland Papers in Windsor Castle* (New York, 1936),
137-145, and John Campbell, earl of Loudoun, to William Augustus, duke of
Cumberland, Aug. 29, 1756, *ibid.*, 231-233.

Englanders, in every rank from general officer to private soldier, reflected an almost unfailing tendency to base arguments and actions upon contractual principles whenever they confronted what they regarded as the unwarranted pretension of superiors.

These principles were explicitly articulated in the course of a seemingly minor dispute between the provincial officers of Massachusetts, headed by Major General John Winslow, and the supreme commander of the British forces, John Campbell, fourth earl of Loudoun, in the summer of 1756. Contractual principles, like the ones Winslow and his officers invoked, were applied throughout the war by enlisted men to justify much of the unmilitary behavior—the mutinousness and desertion—that so appalled regular officers. Far from being merely bad soldiers, as the British assumed and subsequent historians have agreed,[2] colonial New Englanders were bad soldiers in a special way, and for reasons that help illuminate late colonial attitudes toward authority—especially the sovereign authority of the crown.

291

Seventeen fifty-six brought a French victory—the capture of Fort Oswego, Great Britain's main fur-trading post on Lake Ontario—and a change in the British command. In July, the earl of Loudoun, "a rough Scotch lord, hot and irascible," succeeded Major General William Shirley, governor of Massachusetts and an amateur soldier who had been commander in chief since the death of Edward Braddock.[3] The change

---

[2] For example, Stanley McCrory Pargellis maintained that provincial troops were essentially encumbrances on the British command in the Seven Years' War (*Lord Loudoun in North America* [New Haven, Conn., 1933], 354 and *passim*). Lawrence Henry Gipson's estimate of provincial performance was somewhat more favorable but mainly sought to palliate the conduct of troops who "undeniably acted badly" at Ticonderoga and elsewhere (*The Great War for the Empire: The Victorious Years, 1758-1760*, The British Empire before the American Revolution [New York, 1936-1954], VII, 233). Such discussions have usually taken place in the context of a venerable debate over the relative merits of regular troops versus militia, deriving from the post-Civil War writings of Emory Upton and John A. Logan. The emphasis has been on describing (or excusing) provincial misconduct, not on explaining it. A notable exception to this partisan tendency is John W. Shy's brief and influential essay, "A New Look at Colonial Militia," *William and Mary Quarterly*, 3d Ser., XX (1963), 175-185. Shy contended that 18th-century provincials were drawn increasingly from socially marginal groups and consequently fought with less commitment than men who believed that they were fighting for their homes and families. For reasons I hope are clear from this article, I disagree. Nonetheless, Shy's work marks an advance in the interpretation of colonial and Revolutionary military affairs without which this article would not have been possible; my debt is, I trust, evident in the very formulation of the question addressed here.

[3] Francis Parkman, *Montcalm and Wolfe*, I (Boston, 1899 [orig. publ. Toronto, n.d.]), 412. Historians who have addressed this campaign, in addition to Parkman, include Pargellis, *Loudoun*, chaps. 2, 3, 5; Gipson, *The Great War for the Empire:*

produced an intermission in offensive military activity that left plenty of time for quarrels between regular and provincial officers. The most significant dispute concerned the rank of colonial officers and the extent of the supreme commander's authority over provincial troops; and the course of this argument showed that Loudoun and the provincial officers of Massachusetts espoused fundamentally antagonistic conceptions of military service.

Lord Loudoun took command only after the campaign of 1756, as planned by Shirley, was well under way. The centerpiece of the effort was an action against the French forts at Crown Point and Ticonderoga on Lake Champlain; the expeditionary force was composed wholly of New England and New York provincial troops under the leadership of Major General John Winslow, one of Massachusetts's most able and distinguished commanders. In order to induce the New England assemblies to contribute men and money, Shirley had given assurances that the command would be independent, that the officers would be New England men, and that the troops would serve only within a strictly bounded area in New York. By these undertakings, Shirley in effect promised that he would not try to turn the provincial troops into regulars—the sine qua non for suspicious assemblymen who feared the consequences of unlimited military service (that is, service during the pleasure of the crown), and who regarded protection from such oppression as a part of their charter privileges.

If Shirley did not in fact exceed his authority in making such commitments, he was at least offering guarantees that only he was prepared to honor. For example, by promising an independent command to Winslow,

292

The Years of Defeat, 1754-1757, Brit. Empire before the Am. Rev., VI, chap. 7, hereafter cited as Gipson, Years of Defeat; Thomas Hutchinson, The History of the Colony and Province of Massachusetts-Bay, ed. Lawrence Shaw Mayo, III (Cambridge, Mass., 1936), 33-37; Herbert L. Osgood, The American Colonies in the Eighteenth Century, IV (New York, 1924), chaps. 15, 16; and Douglas Edward Leach, Arms for Empire: A Military History of the British Colonies in North America, 1607-1763 (New York, 1973), 379-391. The most recent commentator on the events of 1756, Alan Rogers, in Empire and Liberty: American Resistance to British Authority, 1755-1763 (Berkeley, Calif., 1974), adopts Gipson's "Great War" terminology but alters his emphasis; his sixth chapter is the most complete contemporary discussion of the disputes of 1756 and their larger context. In the officers' internecine feudings he discerns one of many early indications of the rift between colonies and mother country that widened into a "chasm" (p. 67) in the years before the Revolution. I differ from Rogers principally in regarding the links between the Seven Years' War and the Revolution as indirect, rather than straightforward, an argument I am elaborating in my doctoral thesis, "War and the Bay Colony."

This account of events follows Osgood, American Colonies, IV, 377-378, 382-388, the same structure of occurrences can be found in any of the general accounts cited above.

he effectively bound himself not to combine the provincial army with any regular force during the campaign, since to do so would make the provincials explicitly and unpleasantly subordinate to regular officers. The Rules and Articles of War stipulated that in cases of joint service between redcoats and provincials, colonial field officers—those holding the ranks of major and above—were to rank as "eldest captains" of the regular establishment. In practice, this meant that the admixture of so much as a battalion of regulars would reduce the whole command structure of the provincial army to a subordinate role; Winslow himself would be subject to orders from the most junior redcoat major in the field. Beyond this, the Mutiny Act of 1754 required that colonial troops serving jointly with regulars be subject to British military justice, not to the milder provisions of the colonies' mutiny acts. Applied together, the Rules and Articles of War and the Mutiny Act would virtually have achieved what the assemblies had sought guarantees against: the transformation of provincial troops into regulars.[4]

293

Lord Loudoun, of course, in no way felt bound to honor Shirley's highly irregular promises. Indeed, as Loudoun saw it, he had been sent to America to straighten out the horrible mess Shirley had made of the war. One of the new commander's first acts, therefore, was to summon Winslow with his chief subordinates to headquarters in Albany in order to inform them that he considered a junction between regulars and provincials both desirable and well within his authority.[5] The provincial major general and his officers maintained in response what they had announced even before Loudoun's arrival: that the conditions under which the provincials had been raised could not be altered without extreme prejudice to the colonial war effort.[6] To Loudoun, who had engineered the confrontation to force the balky colonials to submit to his authority, their refusal to be overawed amounted to insubordination, almost mutiny. He tried to raise the stakes by requiring Winslow to make a formal response to a heavily loaded query: "I desire to be informed by you, in writing, whether the Troops now raised by the several Provinces & Colonies of New England, and Armed with His Majesty's Arms, will in Obedience with His Majesty's Commands, . . . Act in Conjunction with His Majesty's Troops and under the Command of His Commander in Chief, in whose hands he has been pleased to place the Execution of all those Matters."[7]

[4] Gipson, *Years of Defeat*, 205; Pargellis, *Loudoun*, 85-87; Osgood, *American Colonies*, IV 387.

[5] Loudoun to Winslow, Aug. 5, 1756, Loudoun Papers, LO 1415, Henry E. Huntington Library, San Marino, Calif.; Gipson, *Years of Defeat*, 206-208.

[6] Winslow's earlier pronouncements can be found in Almon W. Lauber and Alexander C. Flick, eds., *The Papers of Sir William Johnson*, IX (Albany, N.Y., 1939), 484-485; Winslow to Shirley, Aug. 2, 1756, LO 1386; and "The Resolution of the Provincial Field Officers . . . ," July 25, 1756, LO 1352.

[7] Loudoun to Winslow, Aug. 9, 1756, LO 1450.

Winslow's reply was carefully weighed, respectful, and completely obdurate. He had consulted with his principal subordinates, he wrote, and they all agreed that the provincials would indeed consent to being joined with His Majesty's regular troops, provided, however, "that the Terms & Conditions Agreed upon & Established, by the Several Governments to whome they Belong and upon which they were rais'd be not altered."[8] He directed one of his colonels to write another letter to Loudoun "with the Termes, and Conditions, on which the Provincial Troops, now on their March towards Crown Point were raised." The specifications were that the commander of the expeditionary force should be an officer from Massachusetts; that the pay, bounties, and provisions of the men should be as set by the provincial assemblies; that the service would not extend south of Albany or west of Schenectady, and that its term should not exceed twelve months from the date of enlistment.[9] The provincials, in other words, gave no ground at all.

294

Loudoun, who was keenly aware that he could not defend the New York frontier without the aid of his stubborn auxiliaries, now realized that he could not bully them into acquiescence. Reluctantly, he compromised. On August 12 he extracted a declaration of the provincial officers' allegiance to the king; in return he promised to refrain from bringing about a junction of forces for the time being and to allow the expedition against Crown Point to proceed under Winslow's command.[10]

The supreme commander, of course, was hardly pleased with this modus vivendi. Once Winslow left Albany to return to his army at Lake George, Loudoun sent to Whitehall a long complaint about military affairs in America. The stubborn opposition of the provincials, he believed, came from the meddling of his predecessor, Shirley, who had raised a faction among the Massachusetts officers in the army and who even now was conspiring to thwart the whole war effort. Shirley and his accomplices had been profiting handsomely from the war, Loudoun wrote, and, fearful of being exposed, were doing their utmost to undermine the honest and efficient administration he was trying to establish.[11]

Just as Loudoun was finishing his report—on August 19—the post brought a long letter from Shirley, enclosing among other items a letter from John Winslow that explained provincial opposition to joint service.[12] Aware that Loudoun intended to blame him for the sorry state of the American war, Shirley had busily been gathering information, from

[8] Winslow to Loudoun, Aug. 10, 1756, LO 1462.

[9] Joseph Dwight to Loudoun, Aug. 11, 1756, LO 1471.

[10] Loudoun to Henry Fox, secretary of state, Aug. 19, 1756, LO 1522.

[11] Ibid.

[12] Shirley to Loudoun, Aug. 10, 1756, in Charles Henry Lincoln, ed., *Correspondence of William Shirley: Governor of Massachusetts and Military Commander in America, 1731-1760*, II (New York, 1912), 501-510, hereafter cited as *Corr. of Shirley*; Winslow to Shirley, Aug. 2, 1756, *ibid.*, 497-498.

Winslow and others, with which to defend himself. Now he was writing to
Loudoun in defense of his conduct, and attempting to explain the
Massachusetts officers' behavior as well. Shirley's letter and the one from
Winslow that Shirley had enclosed vexed Loudoun mightily; furious, he
annotated both to show the "fallacious Assertions" they contained and
sent them off to Whitehall with his report.[13] In Winslow's letter he
underlined the phrases that he found especially repugnant.

> The grand Debate with the Officers in regard to the Junction arises
> from the General and Field Officers losing their Rank and Command
> which they were Universally of Opinion they could not give up as the
> Army was a proper Organiz'd Body and that they by the Several
> Governments from whom these Troops were rais'd were Executors in
> Trust which was not in their power to resign, and, even should they
> do it, it would End in a DISSOLUTION OF THE ARMY as the Privates
> Universally hold it as one part of the Terms on-which they Enlisted
> that they were to be Commanded by their own Officers and this is a
> Principle so strongly Imbib'd that it is not in the Power of Man to
> remove it.[14]

295

As Loudoun angrily perceived, Winslow saw the provincial army as the
creature, not of the crown, but of the provincial governments. The army as
Winslow portrayed it was organized on the basis of contractual understandings. Officers understood when they received their commissions that
they would hold specific ranks and exercise the authority granted by law;
privates understood when they enlisted that they would serve under the
men who enlisted them. Such understandings made the army "proper"; if
the conditions of the contract were violated, the army would cease to
exist. Appropriately, Winslow used an everyday legal metaphor to describe his officers' position: they regarded themselves as "Executors in
Trust," like the executors of an estate, men named in a will or court
proceeding to settle an estate's just debts and distribute legacies. Once
made, the contract could not be altered by any human agency, although it
could be destroyed. Officers had it "not in their power to resign" their
"Trust"; even the privates had "so strongly Imbib'd" the principle of
service under "their own Officers . . . that it [was] not in the Power of Man
to remove it" without dissolving the army along with the agreement. This

---

[13] "Refutations of the Fallacious Assertions advanced by Maj. Gen. Shirley in his
letter to the Rt. Hon. the Earl of Loudoun . . . ," [Aug. 19, 1756], LO 1461; see
also the parallel-text version in tandem with Shirley to Loudoun, Aug. 10, 1756, in
Corr. of Shirley, 501-510.
[14] Winslow to Shirley, Aug. 2, 1756, in *Corr. of Shirley*, 497-498. Lincoln in an
editorial comment notes that the underlinings he reproduces in Winslow's letter to
Shirley were Loudoun's way of marking passages he found particularly offensive.
The Loudoun Papers contain a secretary's copy (LO 1386), which is identically
worded but lacks the underscorings.

was a homely argument, rooted in the officers' social experience; they were, after all, the sort of men who would be named the executors of estates, and all of them had surely seen such trustees at work. In vocabulary and conception, it suggests that Winslow and his comrades understood military relationships to be founded in principle upon contracts. Theirs was an argument especially resonant in New England, a society fairly steeped in covenants: marriage covenants binding husbands and wives, church covenants among members of congregations, the great covenant of salvation between God and his chosen people. It did not, however, particularly resonate for Lord Loudoun.

Loudoun fixed upon this passage in Winslow's letter because to him its reasoning seemed wholly, self-evidently specious. The order concerning the rank of provincial officers was the *king's* order; the provincial troops were royal subjects; the king or his representative might command them as he saw fit in defense of the realm. That they could characterize themselves as the "executors" of some "trust" other than the prompt execution of their superiors' commands was virtually seditious. When Loudoun thought of proper command relationships and soldierly qualities, he thought first of obedience, loyalty, and subordination. He unhesitatingly obeyed his own direct superiors, the duke of Cumberland and George II; it was quite incomprehensible to him that the bumpkins of New England could fail to understand so basic a relationship. The only reasonable conclusion, and the one Loudoun drew, was that the provincials were self-interested, perverse, and actively opposed to his (hence, the king's) authority.[15]

What the irascible Scot failed to understand was that the provincial field officers had had no first-hand experience with the two institutions that had fostered his ideas of proper social and military relationships: a professional army and a highly stratified social system. English society, with its elaborate clientage networks and its vast distances between the great and the humble, operated on far different assumptions and followed different rules from the much smaller-scale societies of colonial North America.

At about the time Loudoun was composing his report to Whitehall, he received a letter from Governor Thomas Fitch of Connecticut that made explicit some of the curious assumptions of the colonial world. Fitch had learned of the possibility of a junction between regular and provincial troops and was writing to register his concern. Loudoun doubtless found the letter meddlesome and offensive, full of the same egregious sophistry that Winslow and his officers had employed to justify their resistance to his authority. Fitch, the elected governor of a highly insular colony, was very much a product of the same small world as the provincial officers, and the principles he articulated were their principles, too. "Your Lordship will see," he wrote,

15 "Refutations of the Fallacious Assertions . . . ," [Aug. 19, 1756], LO 1461; Loudoun to Fox, Aug. 19, 1756, LO 1522.

that these [provincial] Troops were not raised to act in conjunction with the Kings Troops, as we were then [when the provincials were raised] altogether unacquainted with his Majesty's Intentions respecting the Operations that would be Directed for annoying the Enemy; Yet are nevertheless raised for the same Service and Sent forth under the command of Officers appointed and commissioned for that purpose; it therefore seems necessary that these Troops be continued under the same Command and Employed agreeable to the Design of their Enlistments, otherwise the Contract between them and their Constituants made for promoting his Majesty's service in this particular may be broken and their Rights violated; the Consequence of which may be greatly prejudicial not only to the King's Interest and the Safety of the Country at this Time but may prove a great Discouragement on future Occasions.[16]

297

None of the key ideas Fitch employed—the "Rights" of the soldiers, the "Contract between them and their Constituants"—had any compelling meaning for Loudoun; yet New Englanders thought in precisely these terms. The governor was explaining that the operative relationship, so far as the provincial soldier was concerned, was between himself and the province that he understood to be his employer. Although he surely assumed that he was fighting on the king's behalf, the soldier did not regard himself as an employee of the king; it was, after all, the colony that paid his wages and supplied him with food, according to the contract ("made for promoting his Majesty's service") to which he subscribed at enlistment. The idea of the king's intervening, by virtue of his sovereign authority, to alter the terms of an agreement to which he was not a party made no sense: no contract could be changed without the mutual consent of the parties involved. An enlistment contract was no exception: any unilateral attempt to change the agreement simply nullified it and voided the soldier's contractual responsibilities. Such thinking produced an army that was wholly alien to Loudoun's experience: an army made up of men who assumed that soldiers' rights and the conditions of their enlistment had a real bearing on day-to-day operations—men who behaved as if they were in fact the equals of their leaders.

To Lord Loudoun, the talk of contractual commitments and obligations was a smokescreen generated by a few provincial officers who were intent on keeping their rank and command; who were, moreover, intent on thwarting him and the war effort to promote their own fortunes and those of the master conspirator, William Shirley. Loudoun sincerely thought that the provincial privates were amenable to joint service with the regulars, and that whatever fears had grown up among them had been "industriously raised" by Shirley's henchmen.[17] Evidence exists, however,

[16] Gov. Thomas Fitch to Loudoun, Aug. 3, 1756, LO 1407.
[17] Loudoun to Cumberland, Aug. 20, 1756, in Pargellis, ed., *Military Affairs*, 223-230; Loudoun to Cumberland, Aug. 29, 1756, *ibid.*, 230-233; Loudoun to

to suggest that this was not the case. Numerous soldiers' diaries that
survive from the war demonstrate that the men in fact agreed with their
officers about the centrality of contract, although they frequently disagreed over the application of the principle. A survey of thirty journals,
mostly those of junior officers and enlisted men, reveals instances of
soldiers' actions that reflected motivating ideas of contract, from the
beginning to the end of the American phase of the war.

Virtually every private's diary begins with a formalized entry. For
example: "April 5 1758 I Lemuel Lyon of Woodstock Inlisted under
Captain David holms of Woodstock in newingLand For this present
Cannody Expordition—I Received of Captain Holms £2.0s.,0d."[18] Or this
one, by Jonathan French of Andover: "there Being Orders By the great
and Generall Court or Assembly to raise 1800 Men Under the Command
of His Excelency ye Right Honle the Earl of Loudoun; for the Defence of
His Majestys Colonies and for the anoyance of His Majties Enemies in
North:America and upon Consideration of Six dollars Bounty and Some
other articles I inlisted in Sd Service William Arbuthnot of Boston being
apointed Capt of a Company in the Rigmt Comanded by Coll Joseph
Fry."[19] Such entries record the undertaking of an agreement (enlistment),
its parties (the soldier and the enlisting officer), and the receipt of a
consideration by which the contract was confirmed. The province, of
course, kept muster lists and payrolls—official records of service that
conveyed the same information—so the diarists did not in fact need to
record the data they habitually placed in their initial entries. That they did
so with great consistency suggests that the soldiers were consciously
keeping track of the bargain between themselves and their province, as
well as its fulfillment—a written record to which they could refer in case

298

Cumberland, Oct. 3, 1756, *ibid.*, 239-243. Loudoun averred that the suspicions of
the privates had been "industriously raised" in his report to Fox, Aug. 19, 1756,
LO 1522.

[18] Lemuel Lyon, Apr. 5, 1758. This and subsequent references are to sources in
Appendix 1, cited by author's name and date of entry.

[19] Jonathan French, initial entry. See also Joseph Nichols, Mar. 27, 1758;
Obadiah Harris, Apr. 14, 1758; Samuel Morris, Apr. 4, 6, 1759; Gibson Clough,
Apr. 4, 1759; Enoch Poor, Apr. 6, 1759; James Hill, Apr. 18, 1755; David Holdin,
Feb. 20, 1760; and Constantine Hardy, Apr. 2, 1759. A variation on what is
otherwise an almost formulaic beginning, but one that nevertheless preserves the
same information, is found in Luke Gridley's diary:

> March 29 Ad 1757
> Luke Gridly His Book
> Aprel 8th this Day was musterd and took our oaths
> Mondy the 18th Day: this Day Receved Wages: Bounty furst month wages
> & Biliting: 3=18=9=0

Gridley apparently purchased the book on Mar. 29 but recorded nothing other
than the date and his name until he was mustered, sworn, and paid.

their employer reneged on any part of its obligation. Hence the frequent notations concerning the issue and quality of provisions take on additional significance, since the province agreed to supply the men with stated quantities of food and rum each week, as well as specified articles of bedding and clothing.[20]

The province sometimes failed to keep its soldiers supplied with the articles it had promised; conveying huge volumes of provisions and other necessaries across vast stretches of wilderness was always difficult and frequently impossible.[21] When the logistical system broke down, the diaries reveal that the troops often took concerted action in the form of mutiny or mass desertion to register their discontent with what from their perspective looked like an employer that was failing to live up to its end of the bargain. The fourteen instances of troop disorder mentioned in the diaries indicate that Winslow and his fellow officers were not in the least exaggerating their warnings to Loudoun.[22] Once they became convinced that the province had broken faith with them, provincial soldiers did not hesitate to show their dissatisfaction by refusing to work or by marching off. Furthermore, these instances of willful disobedience demonstrate remarkable consistencies in causation and in the actions undertaken by the protesting troops.

299

The causes the diarists ascribed to each of the mutinies and desertions (and they invariably gave each incident a cause) fall into three broad categories. In about a third of the cases, the soldiers were convinced that the army had failed to fulfill its obligations to provide food and rum; half of the instances reflect the soldiers' conviction that they were being forced to serve longer than they had agreed at the time of enlistment; in the remainder, the troops sought assurances that they would be additionally compensated for work not covered in their initial understanding.[23] In

---

[20] See, for example, David Holdin, May 16, 20, 26, 1760; John Frost, May 26, 27, June 17, 1760; John Burrell, Aug. 5, Oct. 1, 1759; Luke Gridley, May 5, June 2, Sept. 22, 1757; John Woods, Sept. 11, 28, 30, 1759; William Henshaw, June 19, July 10, 17, 1759; Obadiah Harris, Aug. 20-22, 1758; James Hill, Nov. 6, 9, 14, 1755; and Lemuel Lyon, June 16, 26, July 4, 1758.

[21] As John Shy has pointed out, the problem of supply was paramount in the Seven Years' War, in which even the small forces deployed in the wilderness were "huge in terms of logistical effort" (*Toward Lexington* [Princeton, N.J., 1965], 88).

[22] These 14 "disorders" were not, of course, all of the mutinies and desertions among provincials during the war but only the ones that happened to be recorded in the diaries. For a summary, by date of occurrence, see Appendix 2.

[23] In 4 of the 14 cases, the cause ascribed was a deficiency in supply. See Elisha Hawley, Sept. 1, 1755; James Hill, Nov. 14-17, 1755; Samuel Chandler, Nov. 22, 1755; Lemuel Lyon, July 22, 1758; and Caleb Rea, July 22, 1758.

In 7 cases, troops rebelled as a consequence of the expiration of their term of enlistment or the fear that they would be retained beyond the end of their term. See Nathaniel Dwight, Nov. 11, 20, 1755; Lyman to Loudoun, Oct. 6, 1756, LO 2855; John Woods, Oct. 27-Nov. 4, 1759; Samuel Morris, Nov. 1, 1759; William Henshaw, Oct. 29-31, 1759; and Gibson Clough, Sept. 30, Oct. 31-Nov. 3, Dec.

every case, the grievance was essentially a matter of contract, and each collective action bespoke the soldiers' concern for their compensation. This in turn suggests that provincial troops were motivated at least in part by the expectation of monetary gain.[24]

The intermingling of contractual and pecuniary concerns in the common soldiers' reactions to deficiencies in supply comes through clearly in Private Obadiah Harris's description of a near-mutiny among Massachusetts troops in Colonel Timothy Ruggles's regiment a few miles north of Albany in August 1758:

> the 20th Day The Saborth Nothing Remarcable but full of fatgue and our Provition Grows Short—
> *300* the 21 Day—We Eate up all Clean that was in our Tents and whare to get the Next Mouth full we Know not but hope that Providence will provide for us Now men are so Cross and tachey that they Cant Speak to one and other what Shall we do for Sumthing to Eate is the Crye The old Saing is a days Life is hunger and Ease and used to Compare it to a Solders Life but hunger and toyl is our Present State.

Such grousing is common enough in the soldiers' diaries; but Harris, uniquely, continued his complaint in fourteeners, New England's traditional ballad meter:

> And Now when times are Grown so bad
> and our Provition Dun
> Let Every one take up his Pack
> and Make a March for home
> for if we stay within the Camp
> and on our Wages Spend
> We Shall have Nothing for to take
> When our Campane will Eand

The next day, supplies arrived, grumbling ceased, and Harris commemorated the event with twelve more couplets.[25] That he had taken the time

---

22, 1759. (For a parallel incident among civilians employed by the military, see Nathaniel Knap, Mar. 19-20, June 17-18, and July 1-3, 1759.)

In the remaining 3 cases, troops protested by refusing to work unless paid additionally for extra duty. See Obadiah Harris, July 1, 1758, and Enoch Poor, June 14, Oct. 17, 1759.

[24] For wage rates see *The Acts and Resolves, Public and Private, of the Province of the Massachusetts Bay*, XV (Boston, 1908), 442, 454-455. These represented a rate about double that at which regulars were paid, even if the provincials' bounties were not included. See Pargellis, *Loudoun*, 281-285. A private's wages were almost the same as those a civilian agricultural laborer would receive, according to wages quoted in William B. Weeden, *Economic and Social History of New England, 1620-1789*, II (Boston, 1891), 896-898.

[25] Obadiah Harris, Aug. 20-22, 1758.

and effort necessary to turn his complaint into verse, however, and that he had not obviously been uneasy about seditiously advocating that "Every one take up his Pack / and Make a March for home," imply that he thought little of subordination and service to the cause once the provisions ran out. Similarly, the candor of diarists in recording their participation in mutinies and desertions,[26] and the very frequency and openness of such rebellions, indicate that ideas of duty and loyalty mattered less to provincial soldiers than equity, once they concluded that they were being abused. Such considerations justified resistance and protest of a sort that was, by military definition, irresponsible.

Beyond their consistency in cause, the mass desertions and mutinies show a strikingly consistent pattern of action—what might be characterized as a protocol of protest governing the behavior of the rebels and the responses of their commanders. Two cases from the diaries, one an account of a mutiny, the other of a desertion, exemplify provincial patterns of resistance.

301

Gibson Clough was a private soldier who served at Louisbourg in 1759 and 1760. A native of Salem and a mason by trade, Clough had lived at home until he enlisted at age twenty-one in Colonel Jonathan Bagley's regiment, one of the units that garrisoned the fortress. He and his fellows joined in April for what they thought would be the standard eight-month tour. A month before their enlistments expired, they began to worry that they would not be allowed to go home as promised.

> [30 September 1759] Cold weather—hear a great talk of things uncertain and thus time spends a way and so we spend our days. . . . [C]old weather is coming on apace which will make us look round about us and put [on] our Winter Clothing and we shall stand in need of good Liquors for to keep our Spirits on cold Winter's days, and we being here within Stone walls are not likely to get Liquors or Clothes at this time of the year and although we be Englishmen Born we are debarred Englishmens Liberty therefore we now see what it is to be under Martial Law and to be with the regulars who are but little better than slaves to their Officers; and when I get out of their [power] I shall take care how I get in again.

At the end of October, the provincials' worries were realized.

> 31 [October] And so now our time has come to an end according to enlistment, but we are not yet got home nor are like to.
> NOVEMBER
> 1 The Regiment was ordered out for to hear what the Coll. had to say to them as our time was out and we all swore that we would do no more duty here so it was a day of much Confusion with the Regiment.

[26] John Woods, Oct. 27-Nov. 4, 1759; Gibson Clough, Oct. 31-Nov. 3, 1759.

In effect, what happened on November 1 was that the soldiers of Bagley's regiment determined to go on strike. Since their term of service had expired, they felt no particular responsibility to perform their duties. They may indeed have reasoned that to serve without a new agreement might obligate them to service over which they could exercise no control at all. At any rate, the regiment struck as a unit, and as a unit accepted the consequences.

302

2nd [November] The Regiment was turned out for duty and we all stood to it that we would not do any duty at all, for which we was all sent to the Guard house prisoners, but myself and three men were released because we belonged to the Kings works [Clough had recently been detailed to the engineers who were at work refurbishing the fortifications], and there was a letter read to the regiment which came from the governor and Council [of Massachusetts] which informed us that we were to Stay here till the first of December or till we have news from Genl Amherst which I hope will be very soon for our Redemption from this Garrison.

There were obvious problems with imprisoning a whole regiment, amounting to a quarter of the complement of the fortress, and the command soon decided to compromise by releasing some of the men to return to Massachusetts. This, in combination with a carefully orchestrated show of force, was enough to break the strike:

3rd [November] The Regiment was turned out for to hear their doom for denying their duty and for sending a round robin [petition] to the Coll desiring him to get us sent home according to enlistment, which they say was mutiny but it was all forgave by the Genll [Brigadier General Edward Whitemore, military governor of Louisbourg] and a detachment of 140 embarked on board of the Ship Oliver, a transport bound to Boston and the three Regular regiments was drawn up on the grand parade, so was our regiment all but the prisoners and they were brought up by four files of men and place in the centre and the General made a speech to them ye articles of war was read to us and the letter that come from Boston, and then the Coll. made a speech to us and told us that we was to stay one month more at least and more if wanted.

On December 5, a brig and two schooners arrived from Boston, with word that the regiment would be required to remain all winter. Bagley thereupon promised the remaining troops that he would carry their cause to the General Court; three weeks later, he and another officer left for Boston. This plunged Clough into gloom: "and now the Major [Ezekiel

Goldthwait] takes command of the Reg't here according to orders and we are all like to be here all winter and God Help us."[27]

Clough's experiences in many ways typify mutinous resistance among provincial troops. A similar response was desertion, an option not readily available to the members of a garrison on the isolated northeastern tip of Cape Breton Island. The constraints of isolation, however, did not apply in the case of John Woods, a private from Worcester who in 1759 was serving in Colonel Abijah Willard's regiment at Fort Ticonderoga. Like Clough, he had enlisted at the beginning of April for an eight-month tour of duty. On October 27, Woods mentioned "a great Stir a Bout going home," but noted no further unrest until

Nov. 1 This morning a Pertition Carried in to the Coll Willard for a Discharge the Coll agreed to send to the General [Amherst] for one—So then went back to work & to our duty   *303*

2 Last night the Sargent Came back from the Gene'l with orders we should no go of. . . .

2 This morning Draw'd up to hear what the Gen. orders was when heard all agreed to go of all got there packs went on to the perade Leut French march't us off march't one mile made a halt, Came three officers and Said they were coming after us to bring us back But not minding Kept on our march a Bout Twelve miles Then Came Three more officers and would have us come back & that the Coll had sent to Coll Lyman & that he had sent 3 hundred men & one hundred highlanders Down the South Bay to Stop us But Refused to go back A good Day. . . .

3 This morning Cloudy but march't off Soon began to Rain & held all Day met with nothing worse than the mountains went about twelve then Campt

4 About three oClock Cle'd of Cold & look like A fair day about Sun Rise set out & made a fine march this day met with Nothing to scare us at all.

Several characteristics of the troops' activity in these cases were apparent in virtually every rebellion. In the first place, there was nothing secretive about the actions of the discontented soldiers, and they made no attempt to conceal their identities. Unlike the classic desertion—an individual soldier slipping away from an encampment under the cover of

---

[27] Gibson Clough, Dec. 22, 1759. Col. Bagley succeeded in obtaining an additional bounty for the men detained over the winter but did not himself manage to return until June 13, 1760, two weeks ahead of the replacement troops for his regiment. In the meantime, on Apr. 1, Clough and his remaining comrades had all, more or less unwillingly, reënlisted for the 1760 campaign. Clough finally returned to Salem on Jan. 1, 1761, overjoyed at the end of what he had come to regard as his captivity.

darkness or ducking out of the line of march—the provincial desertions occurred in broad daylight, and usually after some notice had been given, either informally or by a petition to the commanding officer.[28] Furthermore, they were always corporate, involving from a score or two of men to several hundred.[29] Provincial mutinies did not resemble the classic mutiny in regard to the participants' disposition toward authority; rather than seeking to overthrow or kill their commanders, the rebellious troops apparently either behaved with respect toward them or treated them with simple indifference. In this it would seem that the mutineers were in effect informing their commanding officer that they no longer acknowledged his authority, and that they would not do so until he had made a proposal that they as a group found acceptable. Their actions also bespoke a sharp limitation in their goals: rather than permanently rejecting the leadership of their officers, they did so only until the grievance had been rectified or until they were forced by superior strength to submit.[30] In line with these characteristics, it is noteworthy that the mutinies were nonviolent in every case; although the soldiers retained their arms, there is no mention of any use or threatened use of them.

304

Mutinies seem sometimes to have been led by junior officers, and the band of deserters to which John Woods belonged marched under the leadership of one "Leut French." This suggests, at the very least, a degree of identification between company officers and enlisted men that would simply have been incomprehensible in the British or any other European army.[31] In a larger sense, the actions of mutineers and deserters seem to reflect an achieved consensus not dissimilar to that of a small town meeting. Clough and his fellow mutineers "all swore" that they "would do no more duty," and "all stood to it that [they] would not do any duty at all" when threatened with the stockade; Woods's deserters "all agreed to go of[f]" together. Another diarist, Private Enoch Poor of Newbury, noted in June 1760 that everyone in the three provincial companies that garrisoned Fort Frederick, in Nova Scotia, "was of One Mind [and] That was Not To work with thout Pay" for extra duties not comprehended in the enlistment understanding.[32] Evidence that whole units, like Clough's regiment, submitted to imprisonment after being given the opportunity to reconsid-

---

[28] See also Elisha Hawley, Sept. 1, 1755; Seth Pomeroy, Sept. 1, 1755; Nathaniel Dwight, Nov. 11, 20, 1755; Lemuel Lyon, July 22, 1758; Caleb Rea, July 22, 1758; and William Henshaw, Oct. 30-Nov. 1, 1759.

[29] See also Elisha Hawley, Sept. 1, 1755; Seth Pomeroy, Sept. 1, 1755; Nathaniel Dwight, Nov. 11, 20, 1755; Lemuel Lyon, July 22, 1758; Caleb Rea, July 22, 1758; and William Henshaw, Oct. 30-Nov. 1, 1759.

[30] See also Elisha Hawley, Sept. 1, 1755; Seth Pomeroy, Sept. 1, 1755; Nathaniel Dwight, Nov. 11, 20, 1755; Caleb Rea, July 22, 1758; Samuel Morris, Nov. 1, 1759; and Enoch Poor, June 14, Oct. 17, 1759.

[31] See also Enoch Poor, Oct. 17, 1759.

[32] Enoch Poor, June 14, 1760; see also Samuel Morris, Nov. 1, 1759.

er their conduct suggests that the solidarity of the mutineers could be sustained under considerable stress.[33]

The discontented soldiers often acted in richly symbolic, even theatrical ways. Several diarists note that participants in mass desertions marched off with "clubbed arms": they carried the muskets over their shoulders, grasping the weapons at the muzzles, not by the buttstocks—a posture that, in contemporary drilling conventions, signalled the completion of duty.[34] Furthermore, the fact that the men marched off carrying arms that were for the most part crown property indicates an additional measure of defiance, a signal that the rebels intended to appropriate their own compensation.

The sequence of events in the mutiny and the desertion described above, and indeed in most of the other rebellions for which a good record of events exists, closely paralleled the sequence described by Nathaniel Knap of Newbury in his account of a refusal to work at Louisbourg in 1759. Significantly, Knap was not a soldier but a civilian artificer employed as a ship carpenter at the fortress. Although he worked directly for the military and was, to a degree, subject to military discipline, he was explicitly a contract worker, employed under a twelve-month agreement. The striking similarity between the dispute he described and the mutinies and desertions discussed above suggests the great extent to which New Englanders' military behavior derived from civilian patterns of response that were clearly governed by reasoning from contractual principles. When soldiers and civilian workers were confronted with the expiration of their contracts, their reactions were not merely parallel: they were

305

[33] See also Samuel Morris, Nov. 1, 1759. These collective actions by soldiers show obvious affinities to those of civilian crowds in the late colonial and Revolutionary periods, as described in a now-voluminous secondary literature. The deserters and mutineers do not seem, however, to have been acting to extend the authority of the community by extra-legal means, nor were they expressing explicit class (or proto-class) antagonisms. In their motivation by principle, they were behaving in much the same way as English crowds that sought to enforce their conceptions of "moral economy," but differed from the English case in that they appealed to a principle on which colonial New Englanders of every social station agreed.

[34] Seth Pomeroy, Sept. 1, 1755; Samuel Chandler, Nov. 22, 1755; Caleb Rea, July 22, 1758. Rea: "[July] 22nd . . . This Day the Regt of Royal Hunters [the nickname of Col. Oliver Partridge's regiment] Clubbed Muskets and were marching out of the Camp by reason the allowance of Provision (which at this time was very mean thro' the whole Camp) had been detain'd one Day or more, but Col. Preble [Jedediah Preble of Massachusetts] persuaded'm to stop (after they had march'd near a mile) and he wou'd see they had the allowance imediately, which they had and returned."

I am grateful to Gregory J. W. Urwin of the University of Notre Dame for pointing out the exact nature of the clubbed muskets' symbolism to me; see Humphrey Bland, A Treatise of Military Discipline . . . (London, 1746), 8-9, 16-17, 27-28, 160-161, for contemporary instructions on the practice.

identical, and reflected identical assumptions. Knap's account of the event begins:

> Monday the 19th [of March 1759] this Day fair Weather & it being Our Freedom Day we all kept a holiday & Gave the Day to the King the Govenor [Edward Whitemore] would not let but three men go home & we Draw'd Lots & I got a Blank
>
> teusday the 20th this Day fair Weather went to work on Mr Laslys Scooner Capt herriman Sail'd to Day & Isaac Ridgway & frances Holiday & Rd Lowell went home with him they got the Lot to go home & the Govenor Said that we Should all be Discharg'd in three Months if we would stay

306

Three months later, Knap and his fellow carpenters found that Whitemore still required their services.

> Sunday June the 17th 1759—this Day fair Weather . . . we went to the Govenor to Day for our Discharge but we Could not Get a Direct Answer he wanted us to tarry till we had Relief sent us from Boston. . . .
>
> Monday 18th this Day fair Weather We all Concluded not to Do any work and was still trying for a Discharge Coln Bagley is our Agent and he Came and told us that if we would stay one fortnight Longer that the Govenor would pay us our wages and pay our Passage home and allows us 14 Day Pay and 14 Day Provisions all this on the Govenors word and honour.

Once again, they returned to work. Two weeks later, Whitemore again proved unwilling to dismiss the homesick artisans. As before, they refused to work without an agreement.

> Monday July the 2 1759 this Day fair Weather none of us Did any work the Govenor said that there should be but 12 men Go home and that the Married Men Should go which is 8 that Desir'd to go and 4 young men then there was 4 of them that Came from Snt Johns allow'd to go
>
> teusday the 3 this Day foul Weather I am one that's to go home and I am a getting Ready
>
> Teusday the 3 this Day foul Weather the Govenor Rather than Come under a Bond he said that all the Compe mite go home & we ware a Geting Ready to go home.

No soldier, of course, could ever threaten to make his commander execute a bond for the fulfillment of an agreement, as the carpenters evidently threatened to make Whitemore do—the tactic by which they secured their release. Because the governor was compelled to deal with the carpenters as civilians, not soldiers, he was unable to coerce them by applying force, as a military commander might apply it to stubborn soldiers. The carpenters' repeated strikes and Whitemore's hapless attempts to renegotiate their work contract thus offer exceptionally clear examples of the process at work in the mutinies and desertions of provincial troops. In military cases, the commander's duty and legal right to suppress the rebellion by force of arms (if not his actual ability to do so), complicated the pattern; but the important fact is that the rebellious troops' behavior reflected assumptions identical to those of the carpenters. In case after case, the aggrieved soldiers notified their commander that they intended to take independent action if the commander did not remedy the grievance. Sometimes an officer responded as Governor Whitemore did, agreeing to the demands of the rebels or offering a compromise. More often, the leader responded by reminding the soldiers of his authority and threatening them with severe punishment should they carry through their threats. Despite such warnings, troops persisted: like the carpenters, they waited until the agreed deadline and then refused to work, or they proceeded to muster themselves without orders and march out of camp in a body. Here the soldiers acted out their defiance symbolically—openly disregarding orders, clubbing muskets, and so on— a dramatized version of the carpenters' repeated refusal to go to work. Commanders reacted to these challenges in several ways: by trying to reason with the mutinous men; by offering to represent their case to the next higher commander; by giving in; or by trying to suppress the disorder by force. This was the point at which the command generally performed its own symbolic counter-theater, to give point to its power—perhaps by surrounding the rebellious troops with regulars, bayonets fixed, and beating the prisoners' march; perhaps by seizing and summarily punishing a ringleader, if one could be identified and caught. Finally, the mutinous soldiers determined whether to accept the conditions offered or to continue to resist. The most frequent solution was to accept the commander's offer; the most frequent outcome was some form of accommodation. In only one instance was a troop rebellion crushed by force (and that without bloodshed); every other incident either ended peacefully, with some degree of success for the rebels, or circumstances changed in such a way as to eliminate the grievance.[36]

307

[36] Diarists other than Clough and Woods who give a complete account of this sequence are Nathaniel Dwight, Nov. 11, 20, 1755; James Hill, Nov. 14, 16, 1755; Samuel Merriman, Oct. 23, 1759, with Samuel Morris, Nov. 1, 1759 (an account that parallels that of Woods, above); William Henshaw, Oct. 29-Nov. 1, 1759; and Enoch Poor, June 14, Oct. 17, 1759.

The mutiny crushed by force was described by Samuel Morris, Nov. 1, 1759: "Novemr the 1 Thursday 1759 Att Crown Point this Day the Jersey Blews Stood Out and would Not go on the Workes because there time was out this day and the bay men and Hampshiers and Yorkers—and this Day the Newjerseys they all as one went Under Guard and This Day the Regulars Came and Surrounded their

New England provincial officers and enlisted men conceived of military service in terms that were worlds apart from those familiar to British professional officers. The New Englanders for the most part lacked a military ethos recognizable to officers like the earl of Loudoun, who identified loyalty, subordination, discipline, and regularity as the primary martial virtues. When defining their relationship to military and civil authority, provincials seemed instead to regard themselves as employees of their provinces, contracted workers whose work consisted of bearing arms against the French and Indians.[36] Accordingly, they conducted themselves exactly as civilians would when confronted with the expiration of a work contract or when faced with an unacceptable alteration in the terms of their employment.

308   To Loudoun and those like him, the provincials looked like incredibly bad soldiers and, given their professional perspective on the matter, the New Englanders *were* bad. On the other hand, the provincials believed they were adequate (if not perfect) soldiers, whose actions were above all consistent, sensible, and necessary. From their point of view, anyone who tried singlehandedly to alter previously agreed arrangements was behaving in a dangerously unacceptable way. The truth, of course, is that the regulars and provincials were operating from contradictory premises about society, warfare, and military service. Colonials and regulars, without realizing it or even having a name for it, were culturally different from each other; and because they did not recognize that the premises from which they reasoned differed so profoundly, each believed the worst about the other.

Camp With fixd Bayonets and they Beat the Prisoners [possibly Pioneers?] mar[ch] for to see who wold Work & who would not and they all concluded to go to Work but 5 they went Under the Provost Guard." The instance of seizure and summary punishment of ringleaders was recorded in the diary of William Henshaw, Nov. 1, 1759: "1st Novr. Thursday Fort Edward . . . This morng. the Officers in the Garrison up by Dawn of Day to stop the Men in Case they should attempt to Desert; at 8 oClock, 18 or 20 of the New Jersey Regt. March'd out of the Barracks with their Firelocks & Haversacks: 6 or 7 was stop'd before they got out of the Sally port, 3 or 4 Officers Headed the Rest & Drove them into the Fort One was whip'd Imediately: 3 or 4 more Confin'd but Soon after Releas'd—A party of our Men took about 20 of Colo. Willards Regt. that Deserted from the Lake Sent them back by a party of our men: Lt Stiles Comanded them as soon as they Ariv'd at the Lake they was Imediately sent over the Lake to go to the Genll."

[36] I wish to reiterate that they regarded themselves as such in legal or formal terms. There is also abundant evidence that New Englanders were motivated by a sense of millennial mission in opposing the French and Indians, whom they identified with Antichrist. See Nathan O. Hatch, *The Sacred Cause of Liberty: Republican Thought and the Millennium in Revolutionary New England* (New Haven, Conn., 1977), 21-55. Here I have meant to address the question of how they in practice defined their position with regard to military and civil authority, not the larger question of their motives in joining the army.

The behavior of the provincial officers in opposing Loudoun in 1756, and of provincial troops in their various mass desertions and mutinies throughout the war, demonstrates that contractual ideals were not only deeply held but broadly shared among men of all the social standings represented in the colonial forces. Contractual relations had been much more central to their social experience than either royal authority or highly deferential social relationships. The cultural context of a covenanted society and the demands of the provincial economy made contracts a part of everyday life and talk, while notions of royal sovereignty and of a naturally superior, titled elite remained for the vast majority of the colonists rather distant and abstract. The long-standing practice of fighting wars against the French without direct aid from the mother country had generated at all levels of New England society assumptions of autonomy that complemented this home-grown contractualism. New Englanders, accustomed to having their own governments raise, direct, supply, and pay the provincials, automatically identified the colonial assemblies as the agencies responsible for defense. For the soldier, the locus of authority was the annually negotiated contract of enlistment that tied him to his government, specifying the service he would render and the care and compensation he would receive in return.

309

The Seven Years' War transformed the scale of colonial military conflict and introduced the immediate participation and command of professional British soldiers. It also brought a sharp and unexpected confrontation with New England's tradition of a contract-based soldiery. No matter how hard they tried, however, British officers found that they could not prevent provincial soldiers from acting on ingrained notions about the contractual nature of military service. The result was twofold. On one hand, regular officers concluded that New Englanders (and by extension, all Americans) lacked the character to make good soldiers. Ultimately, their belittling of Americans' martial virtue would lead to one officer's famous boast in 1774 that he could take a thousand grenadiers to America "and geld all the Males, partly by force and partly by a little Coaxing."[37] On the other hand, the war eventually put under arms a third or more of all men in New England who were eligible to serve, and directly exposed them to imperial authority, even as it graphically illustrated the divergences betwen British and American thinking. Just as the regulars drew conclusions from the war about Americans, so New Englanders drew their own conclusions about the British. The war was an education for both sides, and the lessons each learned would inform the crucial decisions made in the years that followed the Peace of Paris.

[37] Benjamin Franklin to William Strahan, Aug. 19, 1784, quoted in Charles Royster, *A Revolutionary People at War: The Continental Army and American Character, 1775-1783* (Chapel Hill, N.C., 1979), 10. Royster surmises that the officer was probably Gen. Thomas Clarke, aide-de-camp to George III.

Appendix 1

The sources consulted, by year of composition, are as as follows.

1754

John Barber, clerk: "Journal of Capt. Eleazer Melvin's Company, Shirley's Expedition, 1754 . . . ," *New England Historical and Genealogical Register*, XXVII (1873), 281-286.

1755

Rev. Samuel Chandler: "Extracts from the Diary of Rev. Samuel Chandler . . . ," *ibid.*, XVII (1863), 346-354.

310

Capt. Nathaniel Dwight: "The Journal of Capt. Nathaniel Dwight of Belchertown, Mass. . . . ," *New York Genealogical and Biographical Record*, XXXIII (1902), 3-10, 65-70.

Capt. Elisha Hawley: James Russell Trumbull, *History of Northampton* . . . , II (Northampton, Mass., 1902), 254-259.

Pvt. James Hill: Edna V. Moffett, ed., "The Diary of a Private on the First Expedition to Crown Point," *New England Quarterly*, V (1932), 602-618.

Lt. Col. Seth Pomeroy: Louis Effingham de Forest, ed., *The Journal and Papers of Seth Pomeroy: Sometime General in the Colonial Service* (New Haven, Conn., 1926), 100-150.

1757

Pvt. Luke Gridley: F. M., ed., *Luke Gridley's Diary of 1757 While in Service during the French and Indian War* (Hartford, Conn., 1906).

Pvt. Jonathan French: "Journal of Jonathan French," MS #74, William L. Clements Library, University of Michigan, Ann Arbor.

1758

Rev. John Cleaveland: "Journal of Rev. John Cleaveland, June 14, 1758-October 25, 1758," *Bulletin of the Fort Ticonderoga Museum*, X (1959), 192-233.

Capt. Asa Foster: "Diary of Capt. Asa Foster of Andover . . . ," *NEHGR*, LIV (1900), 183-188.

Cornet Archelaus Fuller: "Journal of Col. Archelaus Fuller of Middletown . . . ," *Essex Institute Historical Collections*, XLVI (1910), 209-220.

Pvt. Obadiah Harris: "Obadiah Harris Journal," HM 591, Henry E. Huntington Library, San Marino, Calif.

Nathaniel Knap: "The Diary of Nathaniel Knap of Newbury . . . ," Colonial Society of Massachusetts, *Publications*, II (1895), 1-42.

Pvt. Lemuel Lyon: Abraham Tomlinson, ed., *The Military Journals of Two Private Soldiers, 1758-1775* . . . (Poughkeepsie, N.Y., 1855), 11-45.

Samuel Morris, clerk: "Samuel Morris Diary," MS #153, Clements Lib.

Joseph Nichols, clerk: "Joseph Nichols Journal," HM 89, Huntington Lib.

Pvt. John Noyes: "Journal of John Noyes of Newbury . . . ," *Essex Inst. Hist. Colls.*, XLV (1909), 73-77.

Dr. Caleb Rea: Fabius Maximus Ray, ed., *The Journal of Dr. Caleb Rea* . . . (Salem, Mass., 1881).

Rev. Daniel Shute: "The Journal of the Rev. Daniel Shute, D.D., Chaplain . . . ," *Essex Inst. Hist. Colls.*, XII (1874), 132-151.

1759

Sgt. John Burrell: "Diary of Sergeant John Burrell, 1759-1760," *NEHGR*. LIX (1905), 352-354.

Pvt. Gibson Clough: "Extracts from Gibson Clough's Journal," *Essex Inst. Hist. Colls.*, III (1861), 99-106, 195-201.

Pvt. Constantine Hardy: Charles A. Flagg, ed., "Extracts from the Journal of Constantine Hardy . . . ," *NEHGR*. XL (1906), 236-238.

Lt. William Henshaw: "William Henshaw's Orderly & Journal Book . . . ," American Antiquarian Society, *Transactions*. IX (1909), 183-254; Ellery Bicknell Crane, ed., "William Henshaw's Journal for the Campaign in the Year 1759," Worcester Society of Antiquity, *Proceedings*. XXV (1912), 43-64.

Sgt. Samuel Merriman: George Sheldon, *A History of Deerfield. Massachusetts: The Times When and the People by Whom It Was Settled* . . . . I (Deerfield, Mass., 1895), 661-665.

Corp. Josiah Peary: "The Orderly Book of Sergeant Josiah Perry [sic]." *NEHGR*. LIV (1900), 70-76, 164-167.

Pvt. Enoch Poor: "Enoch Poor Journal," HM 610, Huntington Lib.

Pvt. John Woods: Alice Lee Clark, ed., "John Woods, His Book," *Genealogical Magazine*. I (1906), 307-312, 339-342.

Lt. John Frost: *The Diary of John Frost. Jun'r. Eliot* . . . (Eliot, Me., 1899).

Sgt. David Holdin: "Journal of Sergeant Holden [sic]." Massachusetts Historical Society, *Proceedings*. XXIV (1889), 387-409.

1760

Capt. Samuel Jenks: "Samuel Jenks, His Journall of the Campaign in 1760," *ibid.*. XXV (1890), 352-391.

APPENDIX 2

In chronological order, the fourteen provincial "troop disorders"—mutinies and mass desertions—were as follows (sources in parentheses):

September 1, 1755: Thirty to fifty men attempted to desert from the Massachusetts provincial camp at Lake George because they were denied their overdue rum issue. They marched four or five miles from the camp with clubbed muskets before being overtaken and returned. (Elisha Hawley, Sept. 1, 1755; Seth Pomeroy, Sept. 1, 1755.)

November 10, 1755: Five hundred to seven hundred Connecticut provincials made known their intention of deserting from Lake George; they agreed to remain for a few days on the promise of prompt dismissal. On November 20 they attempted to desert; they were dissuaded with difficulty by the personal appeal of Phineas Lyman, their commander. (Nathaniel Dwight, Nov. 11, 20, 1755.)

November 11, 1755: Thirty New York troops deserted from the camp at Lake George with guns and packs; they were convinced that their enlistment term had expired. (Nathaniel Dwight, Nov. 11, 1755.)

November 16-17, 1755: A company of carpenters at work on fortifications at Fort William Henry ceased work in protest over short rations. An additional allowance was made and they returned to work. (James Hill, Nov. 14-17, 1755.)

November 22, 1755: An unspecified number of men clubbed arms and marched from Fort William Henry as a result of short rations; they returned, apparently in a body. (Samuel Chandler, Nov. 22, 1755.)

About September 26, 1756: A mixed body of about 150 provincials at Fort Edward deserted on the basis of a rumor that, having accepted an issue of rations from the king's stores, they were now liable for service during the king's pleasure; they were overtaken, reassured, and returned to service. (Phineas Lyman to Loudoun, Oct. 6, 1756, Loudoun Papers, LO 2855, Henry E. Huntington Library, San Marino, Calif.)

July 1, 1758: Soldiers detailed to work with civilian carpenters refused to obey orders unless they received additional pay; they required a written assurance from the commanding general before "part" of them returned to work. (Obadiah Harris, July 1, 1758.)

July 22, 1758: The Massachusetts provincial regiment commanded by Oliver Partridge deserted from Fort William Henry with clubbed muskets in protest over short rations; they returned after receiving their full allowance. (Lemuel Lyon, July 22, 1758; Caleb Rea, July 22, 1758. See n. 34, above, for a transcription of Rea's account.)

November 1, 1759: New Jersey's provincial regiment refused to work beyond the term of enlistment at Crown Point; they were surrounded by regular troops and acquiesced, except five men who persisted in refusal and were made prisoner. Similar disorders, which did not apparently need to be suppressed by force, occurred among the regiments from Massachusetts, New Hampshire, and New York. (Samuel Morris, Nov. 1, 1759; see transcription above, n. 35.)

November 1, 1759: A group of Massachusetts provincials, perhaps an entire regiment, deserted the command of Colonel Abijah Willard at Fort Ticonderoga when their enlistment term expired. (John Woods, Oct. 27-Nov. 1, 1759; see above, p. 408.)

November 1, 1759: A score of New Jersey troops attempted to desert from Fort Edward following the expiration of their enlistments; the men were captured and returned. (William Henshaw, Oct. 29-Nov. 1, 1759; see transcription above, n. 35.)

November 1-3, 1759: The Massachusetts provincial regiment of Colonel Jonathan Bagley, garrisoning the fortress of Louisbourg, refused to perform duty when their enlistment term expired. Accommodation was achieved by a combination of negotiation and coercion. (Gibson Clough, Sept. 30, Nov. 1-3, 1759; see above, pp. 406-408.)

June 14, 1759: Three provincial companies garrisoning Fort Frederick, Nova Scotia, refused to perform fatigue duty without additional pay; the provincial commander acquiesced in their demand and the troops returned to work on his promise of reimbursement. (Enoch Poor, June 14, 1759.)

October 17, 1759: A woodcutting party under two lieutenants at Fort Frederick (probably amounting to about fifty men) refused to work without additional pay; the colonel commanding the fort gave personal reassurances that they would be paid, and the party returned to woodcutting. (Enoch Poor, Oct. 17, 1759.)

312

The publisher and editor gratefully acknowledge the permission of the authors and the following journals and organizations to reprint the copyright material in this volume; any further reproduction is prohibited without permission:

The American Historical Association for material in *The American Historical Review*; *The English Historical Review*; The Colonial Society of Massachusetts for material in their *Publications*; *The William and Mary Quarterly*; *The Journal of American History* & Organization of American Historians for material in *The Mississippi Valley Historical Review*; *The Economic History Review*; The Economic History Association for material in *The Journal of Economic History*; *Military Affairs*; The Massachusetts Historical Society for material in their *Proceedings*; Frank Cass & Co., Ltd. for material in *The Journal of Imperial and Commonwealth History*.

CONTENTS OF THE SET

9.
AFRICANS BECOME AFRO-AMERICANS
Selected Articles on Slavery in the American Colonies

10.
COMMERCE AND COMMUNITY
Selected Articles on the Middle Atlantic Colonies

11.
COLONIAL WOMEN AND DOMESTICITY
Selected Articles on Gender in Early America

12.
AMERICAN PATTERNS OF LIFE
Selected Articles on the Provincial Period of American History

13.
THE MARROW OF AMERICAN DIVINITY
Selected Articles on Colonial Religion

14.
AN AMERICAN ENLIGHTENMENT
Selected Articles on Colonial Intellectual History

15.
THE STRESSES OF EMPIRE
Selected Articles on the British Empire in the Eighteenth Century

16.
THE PACE OF CHANGE
Selected Articles on Politics and Society in Pre-Revolutionary
America

17.
A NATION IN THE WOMB OF TIME
Selected Articles on the Long-term Causes of the
American Revolution

18.
A RAGE FOR LIBERTY
Selected Articles on the Immediate Causes of the
American Revolution